THE
FEDERAL REPUBLIC
IN SPAIN

Oxford University Press, Amen House, London E.C.4

GLASGOW NEW YORK TORONTO MELBOURNE WELLINGTON
BOMBAY CALCUTTA MADRAS KARACHI LAHORE DACCA
CAPE TOWN SALISBURY NAIROBI IBADAN ACCRA
KUALA LUMPUR HONG KONG

THE
FEDERAL REPUBLIC
IN SPAIN

Pi y Margall and the
Federal Republican Movement
1868–74

BY

C. A. M. HENNESSY

OXFORD
AT THE CLARENDON PRESS
1962

61962

FOR MELLOR

ACKNOWLEDGEMENTS

I SHOULD like to express my deep gratitude to the Warden and Fellows of St. Antony's College, Oxford (whose award of a Senior Scholarship provided the impetus for this work), and especially to Mr. F. W. Deakin and Mr. James Joll for all their personal interest and help.

To Mr. Raymond Carr of New College I am greatly indebted for his constructive criticism: his vast and authoritative knowledge has guided me through the labyrinth of nineteenth-century Spanish history, although he cannot, of course, be held responsible for any opinions expressed here. My old tutor, Mr. Felix Markham of Hertford College, has always been a source of strength and wisdom. I should also like to thank Professor Frank Barlow for his very real encouragement.

Libraries and librarians have been extraordinarily helpful in obtaining rare books and documents—particularly the Roborough Library of Exeter University, the British Museum, the Public Record Office, the Biblioteca Nacional and the Hemeroteca of Madrid, and Municipal Archives, large and small, throughout Spain.

CONTENTS

INTRODUCTION

THE nineteenth century in Spain has been ill-served by historians. Events of the last twenty-five years have not tended to encourage research on the period after 1808 except in terms of contemporary political issues. Abroad, lack of research on this period can be explained by its complexity and confusion, by the difficulties of finding and consulting archival material but perhaps also by a feeling that Spanish problems have little relevance for non-Spaniards. Whatever problems faced European powers in the nineteenth and early twentieth century they were scarcely those posed by a widening gap between the political and real life of the country, by the adjustment to loss of empire and the constant drain of a rebellious colony as in Cuba, by a militant clerical party aiming to re-create an idyllic Catholic past, by a spoils system which pervaded all branches of public life, and by an overstaffed bureaucratic army whose officers were promoted for political services rather than military efficiency—factors which, taken with the country's poverty and its small middle class, made the establishment of stable parliamentary government impossible.

What were once regarded as mainly indigenous problems are not now so unfamiliar to non-Hispanic experience. Countries 'underdeveloped' as Spain was in the nineteenth century face similar difficulties in trying to apply liberal and democratic principles in a social context where the validity of these concepts is often called into question. Instances of soldiers entering politics as the guardians of social order and the arbiters of political life, claiming to represent the real will of the people against the corrupt rule of politicians (the twin Hispanic phenomena of *caudillismo* and the *pronunciamiento* and virtually confined to Spain, Portugal, and Latin America in the nineteenth century), have increased rather than diminished. It would obviously be unwise to press parallels too far, but phenomena unfamiliar and unrelated to our experience a little over a generation ago have now become widespread.

In contrast to the complexities of parliamentary liberalism the main lines of Spanish republican history are comparatively clear. As with so many other Spanish political parties, the history of Federal Republicanism is the history of its dominant personality. The party was so closely associated with Pi y Margall and the group around him, which included Castelar and Salmerón, that a study of the leaders and the party overlap. The movement's active history lasted from the 1868 Revolution to the Bourbon Restoration of 1874—the six-year revolutionary period of political experiment —with origins in the 1850's and repercussions in the later years of the century. Although some common attitudes may be traced between the First and Second Spanish Republics there is no fundamental connexion; it is not possible to trace a continuous republican tradition as might be done in French history. This is not a study of the origins of twentieth-century Spanish Republicanism, but an analysis of a self-contained movement in relation to the nineteenth century.

As with many radical opposition parties, much of its inner history is locked away in police archives or must remain obscure through lack of conclusive evidence. We do not know exactly how it was financed or the precise nature of its relationship with the Cuban rebels or, to take a current topic of modern French historiography, the role and composition of urban mobs. This was particularly significant in Madrid during the First Republic but, as no work has been done or can be accomplished in the present state of historical knowledge, the real importance and nature of popular demonstrations in Spain cannot be estimated with any certainty. Nevertheless, since the Federal Republicans were to a great extent an ideological party, believing in the value of open discussion, their attitudes and policy changes can be followed comparatively easily in their daily and periodical press, although even here gaps and omissions in provincial newspapers sometimes present difficulties to the formation of a clear picture.

Federal Republicanism is interesting not only in terms of its originality in Spanish politics, which is the main concern of this study, but also in relation to a wider European framework. Republicans believed themselves part of an international movement, protagonists in an ideological struggle. In common with the

International, since its foundation in 1864, and the militant clerical parties after the Syllabus of Errors, they felt their main enemy was the aggressive national state. In the mid-1860's considerable efforts were made to revive the almost defunct European republican tradition. At the League of Peace and Freedom in 1867, 6,000 delegates meeting in Geneva under the presidency of Garibaldi declared their faith in a United States of Europe, believing that only a union of anti-dynastic and pacifist republics could provide an alternative to wars between aggressive nationalist powers. Europe could only be saved and regenerated by the redemptive force of republicanism and by the revival of the beliefs of utopian republicans such as Considérant and Cattaneo. Republicans believed that nationalism had been the great regenerating force of the 1848 era but that it had been perverted. The unification movements in Germany and Italy were creating 'false' nations because their unity was being achieved by wars, secret diplomacy, and power politics rather than through the efforts of the 'people'. So far from being the solution to Europe's problems, nationalism appeared potentially the most dangerous of them.

In 1868 the Spanish Revolution, which overthrew Isabella II, released the energies of a new vocal, militant party whose leaders regarded themselves as in the vanguard of this reviving European republicanism. It was obvious by 1868 that Spain was due for a political overhaul and, in an open letter to Castelar, Victor Hugo expressed the view of European republicanism that Spain's political regeneration could only come from the adoption of republican institutions. Although Spanish Republicanism must be interpreted in terms of national conditions and traditions, much of its significance lay in the eagerness with which its leaders tried to break down their country's intellectual isolation from the rest of Europe and to justify their own political beliefs by relating them to the general European scene. The originality in Spain of these beliefs lay in the conception of politics as a national regeneration movement within the context of a reviving international republicanism.

The singularity of the Spaniards was their equation of republicanism with federalism. They were able to appeal both to historical traditions of regional autonomy and to the political resentment of provinces chafing under misrule from Madrid, and as an illustration of successful federalism they quoted the War of Independence when, in Pi y Margall's words, 'Spain had been virtually a federal republic'. They argued that by restoring political sovereignty to 'natural groups' such as the towns, federalism would harmonize interests and create a balance of forces which would prevent the abuse of power by Madrid politicians. However, in common with a type of nineteenth-century radical, they were not content with an historical and political justification but maintained ideologically in Hegelian terms that federalism was the synthesis of the nineteenth-century historical process. Haunted by the failures of French republicanism, which they attributed to Jacobin centralization creating a state machinery which could be adapted for dictatorial ends, and bemused by the example of Switzerland and the United States, they adapted their theories to show that federalism was the form of government towards which European States were inevitably moving. It is true that federal and confederal solutions to nationality problems had been canvassed in the 1850's and early 1860's, but by the 1870's they had been abandoned in favour of unitarian or mock federal States. Pi y Margall, however, could even find confirmation for his federal theories in the constitution of the new German Empire. His party's doctrinaire mentality also made it impervious to the criticism that in formulating their views they had ignored the federalist failures in Latin America and the immense cost at which federalism had been confirmed in the United States.

The main theoretical justification for federal republicanism came from Proudhon and it was in Spain that his political views found their first practical expression outside France. Proudhon's acceptance by Pi y Margall contrasts forcibly with his reception by Mikhailovsky and the Russian populists, among whom his influence was also considerable. They were attracted to his subjective, moralistic critique of society and incorporated this moralism into their social philosophies. But in Spain, Proudhon's *De la Justice dans la Révolution et dans l'Église*, a key book for the comprehension of his social theories, was his only major work not to be translated into Spanish at this time. Much of the profundity of his thought therefore eluded the Spaniards, who merely used his concept of political federalism to justify their own tentatively formed views. Their reading was more superficial than the Russians', reflecting the reaction of radical intellectuals in differing political situations. Unlike the Russians, the Spaniards were not denied the possibility of active political involvement, and impelled by an urgency for drastic reform, and with the opportunity to fill a political vacuum after 1868, they used quite uncritically whatever theoretical justification was available. Moral regeneration would not come from Proudhon's Spanish admirers: the philosophical impetus leading to a deeper analysis of Spanish society came from the Krausists, who were not tied to a doctrinaire view of politics and whose criticisms were more profound and influential.

Spanish Republicans also shared the common belief of nineteenth-century radicals in the mystical regenerating force of the 'people' but there is little in Spain to correspond to Russian populists of the 1860's and 1870's. We find no Spanish examples of a conscience-stricken nobility; the radicals were town dwellers to whom *el pueblo* meant in practice the small minority who lived in the larger cities, swollen by immigration from a barren countryside, not the mass of the agrarian population who even in the south were barely touched by federal ideas and were already beginning to come under Bakuninist influence by the early 1870's.

The impelling need of Federal leaders to sanctify their politics in ideological terms was linked to a belief that a regenerating movement must have a philosophic justification: a truism perhaps, but one reflecting the way in which repressive and corrupt government had led to a flight to theory and a cult of great ideas in opposition to 'hypocritical and opportunist' Liberals. Their quasi-religious adherence to 'federal principles' brought into Spanish politics another ideological party like the Carlists, who couched their programme in the terms of a universal truth. But the Carlist leaders' language was that of their supporters, the Federals' was not and this gave them an air of unreality, talking in terms which few of their followers understood. There might have been some justification for this had they had a realistic grasp of foreign affairs, but, out of touch with supporters at home, they were not even in accord with sympathizers abroad. The main hope for European republicanism lay with the French, but the inspiration behind international republicanism was finally killed off by the Paris Commune. This effectively split European republicans over the social issue by destroying the myth of class harmony—a basic belief of utopian middle-class republicanism. After the collapse of French federalism the French centralized republic seemed to the Spaniards to be little better than a monarchy. When first Thiers and then Gambetta expressed their distrust of the radical implications of Spanish federalism, the Spaniards found themselves isolated.

The whole structure of Federal Republicanism was built on the two flimsy assumptions that the 'people' would be the new regenerating force and that European republicanism was still active in the 1870's. The Federals only learnt that both were false after they had come to power in 1873. By then it was too late to adapt their theories to changed conditions. Republican failure meant that Restoration politics after the collapse of the First Republic in 1874 reverted to a pre-revolutionary pattern, but with the difference that Cánovas pessimistically accepted parliamentary corruption as the prerequisite for the survival of parliament and, in his 'rotation' system, gave to politics during the Restoration a stability it had not had before.

The price was a continuing corruption of public life, but, in the self-questioning after the Spanish-American war, political action was no longer seen as a panacea. The Republicans had shed their illusions in 1873 and by 1898 they lacked the moral fibre as well as the power to propose a political alternative. The Anarchists now claimed to be the new regenerating force and by regarding Pi y Margall as one of their forerunners, they provided a tenuous link between working-class anarchism and the middle-class republicanism of the 1870's, but when Proudhonist ideas made their reappearance in Spain they were almost unrecognizable under the accretions of Bakuninism and the Sorelian myth of violence.

When a political atmosphere has been tainted by compromises and half-truths it may seem that its corruption must be purged by revolutionary violence. Spanish nineteenth-century history cannot be understood if the spell of the barricades and of the appeal to the redemptive force of 'the people' is forgotten. This is truer of the Federals than of any other political group before the Anarchists. Here were the believers in the 'messianism of chaos'— revolutionaries whose violence of language was in such contrast with the mildness and quiet reserve of their leader, whose rationale had its roots in the parliamentary liberalism they were trying to destroy. In Spain, where it has taken longest to lay Bakunin's ghost, a transitory phase of political development is crystallized in the career of Pi y Margall and his Federal Republican movement.

I

The Formative Years, 1833–66

(I) THE EMERGENCE OF THE DEMOCRATS

IN September 1868 Isabella II was driven from the Spanish throne
by a coalition of discontented generals and civilian politicians.
Although during her reign of twenty-five years Spain had become
a byword for endemic civil disturbance, racked by internal wars,
revolutions, and military risings, the ease with which the monarchy
fell brought excited comment from home and abroad:

> To-day [wrote the republican orator Castelar][1] we are the first of the
> great nations of Europe since the opening of this new period of contem-
> porary history in 1852 to start on its own a popular revolution as a
> substitute for the governmental and diplomatic revolutions realized in
> Piedmont and Prussia.

The Times immediately compared it to the French Revolution:[2]

> It is not difficult to foresee that it will stand out in future days as one
> of the most terrible judgements and warnings of history. . . . Since the
> first fall of the French Monarchy in 1792 there has been no Revolution
> so indicative of a transformation in the popular character of the nation
> that has effected it.

Isabella's fall was not only due to her personal unpopularity but
also to the failures of parliamentary liberalism.

The early promise of Spanish liberalism, expressed first in the
reforms of the Enlightenment and then in the Cádiz *Cortes* of 1810–
12, was blighted by the restoration of Ferdinand VII. The experiment of constitutional monarchy between 1820 and 1823 had
shown that the Liberals were an almost insignificant minority. It
was not until after Ferdinand VII's death and the return of the
exiles that parliamentary liberalism revived in the unpropitious
atmosphere of the struggle for the throne between Don Carlos,

---

[1] *La Igualdad*, 18 Jan. 1870, quoting an earlier letter to the *Neue Freie Presse*.
[2] *The Times*, 1 Oct. 1868.

Ferdinand's clerical brother, and María Christina, the Queen Mother, acting on behalf of her small daughter Isabella. Six years of civil war conditioned the future development of liberalism by introducing the sale of Church lands, consolidating a *rentier* class from which the Liberals drew their main support, and by enabling army generals to become arbiters in the struggles between Carlists and Liberals and between the two rival Liberal parties, Moderates and Progressives.[1]

The Moderates were right-wing Liberals who in the *Estatuto Real* of 1834 modelled government on the French Charter of 1814, favouring a strong executive and the restriction of political power by a high franchise qualification and a second chamber. The Progressives were nominally adherents of the 1812 Constitution with its single chamber, universal suffrage, a monarch subject to close parliamentary control, and a national militia to safeguard constitutional guarantees. Neither party represented exclusively industrial, landed, or commercial interests and, although the Moderates might be roughly classified as a party of the upper-middle class and the Progressives of the lower-middle class, the distinctions between the two revolved more round questions concerning the monarch's influence, government patronage, and the powers of local authorities.[2]

The question of what powers should be granted to municipal and provincial governments rapidly developed into a fundamental issue between the two parties. The French-inspired Moderates had arbitrarily divided the country into forty-nine provinces in 1833 to facilitate centralized control and to break down remnants of regional particularism. Centrally appointed civil governors were to ensure that government candidates were returned at local and national elections. Throughout the Liberal period the *jefes políticos* in the towns and the *caciques* in the rural areas were the managers for the small group of professional politicians at Madrid whose

    [1] See the Progressive A. Pirala, *Historia de la guerra civil y de los partidos liberales y carlistas*, Madrid, 1853, 5 vols., and the Moderate J. de Burgos, *Anales del reinado de Isabella II*, Madrid, 1851, 6 vols.
    [2] L. del Corral, *El Liberalismo doctrinario*, Madrid, 1945, especially ch. xxii; J. Sarrailh, *Martínez de la Rosa*, Paris, 1930, pp. 193–8, 246–67; R. Barcia, *La Constitución de la Nación Española y la Constitución de 1812*, Madrid, 1869.

power was largely dependent on the enormous patronage at their disposal. Influence in the capital was an indispensable prerequisite for a successful career in all branches of public life. A spoils system of government on this scale made it difficult for the Progressives, wedded to the decentralizing tradition of 1812, to be consistent supporters of political devolution as they too had to satisfy the *empleomanía* of their followers. Nor, once in power, were they to prove any more consistent in their political radicalism when, in their Constitution of 1837, they instituted a second chamber and a franchise qualification.[1]

The break with their radical inheritance provoked a long debate within the party on the relevance of popular support. This was complicated by the increasingly important political role played by army officers after the end of the Carlist war. Civil war conditions had eroded the traditions of obedience to the State but their political pretensions increased with the return to peace. Fear of ex-officer discontent led to the retention of many in the Army as well as to the incorporation of ex-Carlist officers, so that Spain in mid-century had twice as many generals as the larger French army. With poor pay and slow promotion officers were attracted by the offers of politicians promising promotion for political services rather than military efficiency. It became impossible for the ambitious officer to remain politically unattached. The significance of army officers in mid-nineteenth-century Spanish politics was not that they defended either national or even group interests or represented a distinct social class, but that as members of an inflated military bureaucracy they were another facet of *empleocracia*. The Moderates' relationship to army officers is reflected in the fact that out of sixty-five members of the Senate in 1845, forty were generals. Although Progressive influence was stronger among junior officers, the party's fortunes were indissolubly linked to those of their two *caudillos* Espartero and Prim.[2]

[1] A. González Posada, *Evolución legislativa del régimen local en España*, Madrid, 1910, *passim*; J. M. Orense, *Treinta años de gobierno representativo*, Madrid, 1863, *La Empleocracia*, Madrid, 1872. Evidence on the *cacique* system is scattered, but see J. de Zugasti, *El Bandolerismo*, Madrid, 1876–9, 10 vols., and J. Costa, *Oligarquía y Caciquismo*, Madrid, 1902.

[2] Cf. the interesting analysis by R. Carr, 'Spain: Rule by Generals', in *Soldiers and*

Once army generals became a determining factor in politics it seemed less necessary to woo the masses. By the end of the Carlist war, when the Progressives had won over Espartero, both parties had military protectors. As a result, from 1840 the temptation increased for parties to attach less importance to purely parliamentary activities and to divide internally once in power, making the development of a stable two-party system impossible. Such divisions were often caused by differences between military and civil factions within the same party or by the effectiveness of electoral corruption by which the government party returned overwhelming majorities to the *Cortes* and then broke up through lack of opposition. Elections were often rigged so as to provide a nominal opposition, but deputies cast for this role of keeping the government party united often refused to take their seats. Ostensibly, this *retraimiento*, or withdrawal from the *Cortes*, was a protest against government corruption and a tactical move to accelerate the break-up of the dominant party, but it came to be interpreted as a prelude to the use of force. 'In the political language of our day', a Carlist declares,[1] '*retraimiento* has a clear, precise and evident meaning, armed revolt.'

The cardinal importance of the *retraimiento* is well illustrated by the part it played in Progressive politics after the fall of Espartero in 1843. Outmanœuvred by the Moderates and rebuffed by the young Queen, who refused to become a Progressive puppet, the party split over tactics. They were unable to decide whether to rely on urban mob support and favourable generals or to return to power by establishing their influence over the Queen. When the chances of 'forcing the closet' diminished as Isabella came more and more under the influence of clerical palace advisers, the *retraimiento* became the key issue in party debates. It caused severe

Governments, ed. M. Howard, London, 1957. The memoirs of F. Fernández de Córdoba, *Mis Memorias íntimas*, Madrid, 1886–9, 3 vols., give a good insight into the soldier-politician.
[1] *El Pensamiento español*, 20 Apr. 1872. The main source for electoral corruption are the *Cortes'* debates when the *actas* or formal admissions presented by deputies at each new *Cortes* were challenged. Six elections between 1846 and 1858 have been analysed in L. M. Pastor, 'Las Elecciones', *Revista ibérica*, vi, 1863, showing 255 cases of direct government coercion and 564 cases of illegalities by electoral committees supervising the polls. Between 1834 and 1868 there were 57 ministries, 14 under the regency of María Christina, 6 under Espartero, and 37 under Isabella II.

internal dissensions and eventually led, in 1849, to the emergence of a new party, the Democrats.[1]

The success of the February Revolution in Paris, contrasting with yet more failures in the early spring risings of 1848 in Madrid and Seville, underlined the Progressives' isolation from the masses, and their dependence on backstairs intrigues with foreign diplomats and disgruntled army officers. To remedy this Rivero, a dynamic deputy from Seville, set up a junta of disaffected Progressives in Madrid with the purpose of organizing a new party whose aim was to attract the Progressives back to the radical inheritance of 1812 by persuading them that their departure from it had been the cause of all the party's subsequent failures.[2]

Rivero pursued his policy of 'attraction' by casting his programme in the broad Progressive tradition. He demanded freedom of the press, speech, and religion, a national militia, free and obligatory primary education, a liberal higher education, and the establishment of the jury system. The programme appealed to commercial and professional classes, frustrated by an antiquated administrative and fiscal system, and to an acquisitive land-hungry middle class demanding a more extensive disentailing policy of Church and common lands. But in spite of many echoes, the Democrats' programme, by including universal suffrage and the abolition of conscription, implied a complete reversal of Progressive tactics. So long as the latter preferred to work through their military contacts it was unlikely that they would be attracted to a party whose primary aim was to undermine the Army's power and to substitute the revolutionary enthusiasm of the populace for the *pronunciamiento*. The Progressives were also dubious about the radical group of utopian socialist journalists who were constantly embarrassing Rivero by trying to force the new party into a socialist and republican mould.

The early division of the party into an ex-Progressive and a socialist wing was reflected in the failure to produce a party paper because of the rivalry between Rivero and the socialist Sixto

[1] A. Pirala, *Historia contemporánea*, Madrid, i, *passim*.

[2] Vera y González, *Pi y Margall y la política contemporánea* (hereafter referred to as Vera), Barcelona, 1886, i. 428–32; E. Rodríguez-Solís, *Historia del partido republicano*, Madrid, 1892–3, ii. 383–401 (hereafter referred to as R.-Solís, op. cit.).

Cámara, whose money was to finance it. Without an official organ, the Democrats were unable to gain much support outside Madrid. Even the Catalan radicals tended to develop independently, divided from the Madrid Democrats by their own regional problems of cultural revival, expanding industrialism, and the growing demand for protection for which the ardent free-trade Democrats had no sympathy. The most constructive aspect of early Democrat activity was outside the field of politics in the establishment of the Madrid *Fomento de las Artes* in 1850 where, in the night schools, contacts were made between workers and radical intellectuals.[1]

However, Rivero's main aim failed. The Progressives did not respond to Democrat advances. After Narváez's fall from power in 1851 they preferred an understanding with their Moderate rivals in a movement of Liberal conciliation to overthrow the *camarilla*. Progressive preference for working with the Army was strikingly shown during the 1854 Revolution. This began as a purely military coup by Progressive and Moderate generals, but when their victory over the Government's forces at Vicalvaro, outside Madrid, produced no response in the capital, O'Donnell's civilian adviser, Cánovas del Castillo, drew up the Manifesto of Manzanares. By broadening the narrow range of the generals' complaints a military rising was turned into a popular revolution. The Madrid Democrats tried to exploit the revolutionary situation but the Progressives dominated the capital by reconstituting the 1843 militia of small property owners which guaranteed that the poorly organized mob support of the Democrats would not push the revolution to extremes.[2]

During the fighting at the barricades the Democrats lacked co-ordinated leadership. No one drew together the various radical juntas in different parts of the city: the Democrats' central

[1] F. Garrido, *Historia de la clases trabajadores en Europa*, Madrid, 1870, pp. 916–17, and his *Biografía de Sixto Cámara*, Barcelona, 1860; Vera, op. cit. i. 431–2; R.-Solís, op. cit. ii. 423–46. The best survey of social and economic development is J. Vicens Vives, *Historia social y económica de España y América*, Barcelona, 1959, vol. iv, part ii. For the Democrats' tenuous links with the United States and Mazzini see A. Ettinger, *The Mission of Pierre Soulé to Spain, 1853–6*, Yale, 1932, pp. 306–7, 326; Mazzini, *Scritti*, Imola, 1906–43, vol. 45, pp. 238, 240, 320–3.

[2] Pirala, op. cit. ii. 174–232; Vera, op. cit. i. 437–72.

committee, surprised by a police raid in February, were in prison when the fighting started and the party lacked the nucleus for organized resistance provided by the Progressives' militia. They therefore followed the Progressives' initiative. Their leaders believed that the camaraderie of the barricades would survive the fighting and that the popular nature of the rising would give substance to their arguments for a return to the old radical tradition. The programmes drawn up by Democrat extremists found little support among Democrat followers once Espartero had openly declared for the revolution in Zaragoza and there could be no doubt about his popularity among all sections of the capital when he made a triumphal entry on 29 July.

With Espartero in Madrid the Progressives could conjure with his name to keep down the radicals. Even Democrats like Garrido, who had no Progressive affiliations, hailed him as the 'saviour of the revolution'.[1] 'The coming of the Messiah', another wrote,[2] 'has never been so anxiously awaited by the people of Israel as was the arrival of Espartero by the people of Madrid.' Democrat effusiveness, however, did not prevent Espartero and O'Donnell from creating the Liberal Union in September. This alliance between the two forces which made the revolution excluded the Democrats from a share of power, forcing them to fight the elections on the terms of the new alliance under the electoral law of the 1837 Constitution. The result was a foregone conclusion. Deprived of popular support, unable to rally provincial feeling, they returned a mere sixteen ex-Progressive deputies to the new *Cortes* where their opposition, in face of overwhelming Liberal strength, was purely nominal.

The failure of the Democrats to influence the outcome of the revolution emphasizes the importance of the first political work of Pi y Margall, a literary journalist of working-class origin from Barcelona, whose *La Reacción y la Revolución* was published in November 1854. He had originally come to Madrid in 1847 to further his career as a literary critic and writer on art. Already a political radical and a religious heterodox, the frustrations of

---

[1] Garrido, *Espartero y la Revolución*, Madrid, 1854, pp. 71–79. Cf. his *El Pueblo y el Trono*, Madrid, 1854.   [2] *Las Jornadas de julio: por un hijo del pueblo*, Madrid, 1855, p. 338.

censorship, poverty, and lack of influence forced him, as it did so many other provincials, into political activity. But press censorship and financial difficulties made radical journalism a precarious profession. Disillusioned by his experience of Democrat politics in the early 1850's, Pi returned to literary work and was engaged in the unrevolutionary task of editing texts for the Madrid publisher Rivadeneira when the 1854 Revolution gave him his opportunity to become the spokesman of the Democrats' radical wing.[1]

His views first took shape in a fly-sheet issued on 21 July where he analysed the causes of popular discontent as being the burden of the *consumos*, the unjust *quinta* system, government extravagance and franchise limitation, and urged the people not to surrender the initiative they had won by their own efforts during the fighting.[2] Another fly-sheet, more radical in tone and, although anonymous, closely reflecting Pi's views, called for the creation of a federal republic.[3] But the extremism of these programmes, implying a complete break with the Progressives, was an embarrassment to the official Democrat leadership whose eager acceptance of Espartero's promises suggests that they welcomed the shelter of his name to escape the demands of their own extremist wing.

The collapse of Madrid radicalism in face of the Moderates' generals, the Progressives' militia, and the acquiescence in Espartero's leadership by the Democrats' central committee, stimulated Pi to complete a critique of Spanish politics before the end of the year. The genesis of *La Reacción y la Revolución* must be sought in his disgust at Democrat vacillations and inconsistencies. The party's behaviour had followed the familiar pattern of internal rivalries and political opportunism instead of firm adherence to principles derived from philosophical premisses. He advocated a new evaluation of politics based on the application of the 'scientific laws' of

[1] Vera, op. cit. i. 17–24, 171–85, 283–321. See also Rovira i Virgili, 'La juventud de Pi y Margall', *El Sol*, 17 Dec. 1930; C. Capdevila, 'Pi i Margall', *Annuari dels Catalans*, 1924–5. Two short lives are J. Roca y Roca, *Francisco Pi y Margall*, Barcelona, 1921; F. Caravaca, *Pi y Margall*, Barcelona, 1935. His political sympathies are made clear in his introduction to his edition of J. Mariana, *Obras completas*, Madrid, 1854.

[2] Printed in Vera, op. cit. i. 444–6. See Glossary for *consumos* and *quintas*.

[3] Printed in Marx, *Revolution in Spain*, London, 1939, pp. 131–3; cf. the more moderate draft federal constitution of 1832 by Xaurado y Fabregas in R.-Solís, op. cit. ii. 424–30.

historical development, stressing that the Democrats must have a firm doctrinal basis if they were to escape the inner fragmentation typical of the major Liberal parties. The book was primarily a long political pamphlet designed to convince the Democrats that they must cut themselves free from all Progressive affiliations and base their thinking strictly on an ideology derived from premises about the nature of freedom and historical progress:[1]

> I would like to awaken in you a belief and even more than a belief, a philosophical activity which unfortunately we lack in Spain. In other places this activity has engendered the Revolution and has made it irresistible: here, as it does not exist, we still have a revolution which lacks a base. Let us hasten to give it one.

In arguing the need to break away from the Progressives he attacked their doctrine of the 'sovereignty of the people'. This 'fiction', modified at will by the party in power (as it had been in 1837), was to be replaced by the principle of the 'inalienable sovereignty of the individual':[2] 'I have changed the starting-point and object of modern politics. For the sovereignty of the people, I have substituted that of the individual, for the idea of power, that of contract.' Obsessed by the iniquity and abuse of power by ambitious politicians he developed a theory of the autonomy of the individual from which he deduced that the only valid exercise of power was that sanctified by free contract between individuals whose liberty could only be restricted by their own physical limitations. Already in 1854 he was arguing for the continual reduction of power by the widest possible decentralization, in some measure anticipating both Proudhon's contractualism and later anarchist theories.

By demonstrating the inevitability and continuity of revolution he hoped to convince the established parties of the uselessness of trying to prevent it and also to buoy up the Democrats with an optimistic ideology. In developing his argument he showed the influence of all the foreign thinkers whose ideas were to determine the future course of Spanish radical thought. Proudhon's was

---

[1] *La Reacción y la Revolución*, p. 237. It appeared in Nov. 1854. All references are to the *Revista Blanca* edition. See Appendix for a fuller treatment of Pi's ideas in this book.

[2] Ibid., p. 224.

marked in his emphasis that the revolution was the emanation of
the principle of justice, Herder's in the pantheistic undercurrent
of his thought and in his development of the idea of progress,
while from Hegel he accepted unquestioningly the dialectical
interpretation of historical development.[1]

The second part of the book developed suggestions for practical
administrative and political reforms. Pi believed that eradication
of the spoils system was inseparable from political devolution by
which offices would no longer be in the gift of a handful of
Madrid politicians but would be distributed by the separate
governments of the reconstituted historic provinces. Proposals for
a drastic overhaul of the Army were central to his reform scheme
as he diagnosed that so long as promotion could be won by political
services the Army would remain part of the spoils system, fulfil-
ling a political and not a military function. The new Government
forbade the publication of a third part planned to deal with
economic reorganization, but he had already made it clear that
his concept of revolution implied social as well as political change.
Although hastily written, unfinished, and cluttered with a mass of
superficial learning, the book remains a landmark in Spanish
political thought, not only as a source-book for later Spanish
anarchists and Left-wing Democrats, but because it presaged a
new phenomenon in Spain—that of the ideologist whose political
activity is determined by intellectual theory. Pi argued that in a
corrupt and politically immature society, the absence of highly
developed and clearly marked group interests made ideas the
only genuine touchstone for differentiating between parties. Arguing from Hegelian premisses, he saw each party representing
a phase in the dialectic of historical development. He accepted the
necessity of party politics—only from the clash of ideas could
progress occur—but this clash could only be fruitful once party
distinctions had hardened.[2] Only by digging up ideological roots
could politics escape from continually shifting party lines where
loyalties were determined by whim, personal rivalry, and private
profit, enabling the monarch to be the ultimate political arbiter.

[1] *La Reacción y la Revolución*, pp. 37, 77, 175.
[2] Ibid., pp. 30–32; cf. Pi's article in *La Discusión*, 9 Sept. 1857.

Pi's emphasis on the generating force of ideas is the most extreme example of the intellectual in politics provided by nineteenth-century Spanish history. It was common enough for writers, poets, philosophers, and historians to take an active part in politics, but his single-minded and severe rationalism marked him out in an age which was distinguished by flamboyant oratory and undisciplined emotional exuberance. Where party loyalties were determined by *personalismo* and where *caudillismo* had been encouraged by bribing military adventurers into politics, an addiction to ideas rather than to personalities was a new challenge. Had Pi merely remained a product of Barcelona's Romantic revival of the 1830's and 1840's he might not have been distinguished from his contemporaries, but the shock of events there between 1840 and 1843, and the uncongenial conditions of intellectual life in Madrid, stimulated his interest in politics, turning him from a sensitive descriptive writer into an unemotional political analyst.

Even among Democrats, though, he was an isolated figure, whose aloofness and self-dedication often puzzled those who admired him most.[1] His personality contrasted sharply with the intellectually brilliant but temperamental Rivero (a man who owed his advancement from the slums of Seville to discerning patrons and his *entrée* into Madrid politics to a judicious marriage, and who accepted the easy familiarity of Madrid café politics, relishing the intrigues of *Cortes* lobbying), or with the vain Castelar, whose first speech at an electoral meeting in 1854 had singled him out as the party's most brilliant orator. Pi deliberately avoided publicity. He had few intimate friends and led a frugal and austere existence in a closed family circle after his marriage in 1854. The height of luxury for him was said to be an occasional lump of sugar soaked in liqueur. His slender income, derived from the sale of books and articles and from his *bufete* after family commitments forced him into legal practice, owed nothing to the spoils of office.[2]

[1] J. M. Sanroma, *Mis Memorias*, Madrid, 1887, i. 23–24.
[2] Pi y Arsuaga, 'Pi interno' in *Pi y Margall: ciclo de conferencias en la escuela moderna*, Madrid, 1924. His son only ever heard him use the familiar *tú* with two politicians—Duran y Bas, a conservative lawyer friend from the 1840's, and Figueras, the Democrat

In his youth, and after many years' vacillation, he broke with the Church. He was never again assailed by religious doubts— 'faith like virginity, once lost, is never recovered'.[1] His attack on Christianity which first gained him public notoriety was the prelude to a constant anticlerical campaign in the interests of free-thinking, which embarrassed many Democrats like Castelar, whose opposition to catholicism was political and aimed at weakening the influence of priests rather than at destroying the dogmas of the Church. Similarly, Pi's radical sympathies did not stem from the exaggerated emotionalism so common among the Democrat followers of Castelar, but from a logical analysis which owed much of its effectiveness to lucid exposition, economy and clarity of style. His fixity of purpose and intellectual honesty soon established the myth of his personality—the incorruptible in a corrupt society. Dry, humourless, imperturbable, the picture of him in the *Cortes*, so often described later, sitting motionless with his arms crossed, is the antithesis to the stock image of the excited Latin politician.

Pi's analysis, emphasizing the need for more rigid definition of party principles and for generalizing politics by universal suffrage, was not the only reaction to the failure of the 1854 Revolution to break the monotonous political pattern. Sterile party conflict over the distribution of the spoils of office and rivalry between Espartero and O'Donnell paved the way first for a ministry under Narváez in 1857 and then a court reaction, but in 1858 Isabella was compelled to call back O'Donnell without whose influence government had become impossible. Where Pi's solution was that of the intellectual, O'Donnell's was that of the practical politician. He remained in power for the next five years with his remarkably long-lived and successful 'Liberal Union'.[2] O'Donnell's aim, like

lawyer-politician from Tarragona who introduced him into the law. Pi married a Basque woman from Vergara in 1854. Experience of living there in 1856–7 confirmed his federalist views. There is no life of Rivero (1814–78). Cánovas had a very high opinion of his intellectual calibre: see *Problemas contemporáneos*, Madrid, 1884, ii. 202–3.

[1] *La Réaccion y la Revolución*, p. 50. Rovira y Virgili, 'Pi y Margall, los orígenes de su heterodoxia', *El Sol*, 19 Dec. 1930. His earliest and best-known anticlerical work is his *Historia de la Pintura*, Madrid, 1851. The anger of his clerical subscribers prevented publication of the second volume. His rationalist interpretation of Christianity was reprinted as *Estudios sobre la Edad Media*, Madrid, 1873.

[2] *La Discusión*, 5 Jan. 1859, Pi's article 'La necesidad y imposibilidad de la Unión Liberal'. Cf. E. Castelar, *La Fórmula del Progreso*, Madrid, 1857, pp. 30–34.

Pi's, was to prevent the continual disintegration of parties, but by the simple expedient of extending patronage so widely as to nullify the main motive force behind party activity. Advised by Cánovas, O'Donnell's system was a dress rehearsal for Cánovas's own period of political dominance during the Restoration period after 1874. With the skill of Posada Herrera, the 'Great Elector', O'Donnell made sure of rigged oppositions in the *Cortes* while critics outside were bought off with administrative posts or given lucrative concessions during the boom period of the late fifties and early sixties. O'Donnell also saw the danger of the soldier-politician to internal stability but, by canalizing the Army's energies into imperialistic expeditions abroad, he avoided the unwelcome implications of the Democrats' solution of reducing the Army's power. Significantly, the period of greatest internal stability in the fifty years after 1833 was the five years of O'Donnell's Liberal Union between 1858 and 1863 when for the first time since the end of the Carlist wars, the Army was engaged on its legitimate occupation of fighting—in Morocco, Mexico, in the Pacific war, San Domingo, and Cochin China.

Only three elements were excluded from the new dispensation —the Democrats; the 'pure' Progressives under Olózaga, who tried to retain their party's identity and keep alive its traditions, and the new clerical party of the neo-Catholics, which drew some of its main strength from the disintegrating Moderates. O'Donnell had little to fear from the opposition of either Progressives or Democrats. The Progressives were split over the alternative of co-operation with the Democrats, *retraimiento*, and expectations of being called to power, and the Democrats were divided over the implications of democracy and the desirability of co-operation with the Progressives. The main threat came from the neo-Catholics, whose influence on the Queen through the *camarilla* exposed the Liberal Union's main flaw; ultimately it was dependent on Isabella's goodwill. When O'Donnell refused to pander to her clerical susceptibilities he fell from power.

The fall of the Liberal Union and the subsequent reversion to party politics posed the fundamental question of Isabella's influence. The lack of clear party distinctions forced her, as it had earlier

compelled the regents María Christina and Espartero, to exercise
personal choice in the selection of ministers. The Progressives,
rebuffed in their expectations of being called to office, were faced
with the crisis of decision. Their *retraimiento* of 1863 was to be the
prelude, not to political futility, as in 1844, but to full-scale revolution directed against the throne itself. In 1844 Isabella's youth
might be pleaded in exoneration of her action when she refused to
accept dictation by the Progressives, but in 1863 she deliberately
rejected Progressive advice in favour of the *camarilla*. It was no
longer possible to escape the implications of the arbitrary exercise
of the Queen's will. However, before the Progressives could take
any action against the throne itself, it had first to be morally
isolated from the country. In this the Democrats, and particularly
their leading publicists Pi y Margall and Castelar, played a significant role in their journalistic activity after 1856.

(2) DEMOCRAT POLEMICS, 1856–66

The failure of the Democrats to influence the course of events
either during the Revolution of 1854 or in the two following years
only widened existing divisions within their ranks over policy.
Pi's book did not convince the party of the need to abandon the
policy of attracting the Progressives to a more radical programme.
To the initial division between the ex-Progressives in favour of
this and the radicals, who wanted to turn the Democrats into
a mass popular party by social and economic reforms, was now
added an extremist wing, led by Sixto Cámara, who had begun
to advocate terrorism after the disillusion of 1854. Both Pi and
Castelar had condemned this as sterile and wanted to educate the
party out of the immaturity of conspiratorial activity, which was
still the stock response of Spanish radicals when out of power.
But Espartero's fall after O'Donnell's coup in July 1856 and Narváez's return to power in January 1857 brought some support
for Cámara's views. The appointment of the clerical Nocedal as
Minister of the Interior and his vigorous press law of July led to
active insurrectionary outbursts in the late summer of 1857. At
this moment, Pi made his début as a regular political journalist.

In the previous year Rivero had found a financial backer for *La Discusión*, which he aimed to make the official party paper. As the Democrats were excluded from the *Cortes* their opposition was confined to the press, but Nocedal's press law put them under financial threat and compelled their opposition to take a mild form. Democrat journals, therefore, tended to concentrate on defining their own dogmas and arguing over their policy. The history of the party until 1866 is to be found in its press, where a continual debate was in progress between two main groups—one led by Pi, extending ideas foreshadowed but not developed in 1854, and the other, led first by Rivero and later by Castelar, beginning with a defence of the policy of attraction and continuing with a defence of 'individualism' against the 'socialistic' implications of Pi's group. What began as a political debate was turned into an analysis of the underlying social, economic, and philosophical premisses of democracy itself.

At the beginning of July 1857 Rivero invited Pi to help edit his new paper.[1] We do not know the terms on which Pi agreed to co-operate with someone so dissimilar, but it was soon evident that they still differed over the aims of the party. An article in the Progressive *La Iberia* had argued that further disentailing of Church land could solve the growing pauperization, which was causing public concern.[2] Pi replied that, on the contrary, disentailing had produced the exploiting *rentier* class which had been mainly responsible for this social problem. The article was mild; he had already rejected the extremist views of St. Simon, Fourier, and Owen on property distribution and now suggested a Proudhonian *mutuelliste* scheme of mutual exchange banks as the best solution to this particular problem.[3] The aim of the Democrats must be to distribute property as widely as possible, but, although critical of past speculative buying of entailed lands, he was careful not to commit himself to a policy of redistribution.

---

[1] R. Castrovido, 'Pi periodista', *Pi y Margall: ciclo de conferencias*, &c., p. 24. Pi wrote 154 articles for this paper as assistant editor between July 1857 and Mar. 1859, and Sept., Oct. 1860, and as director after Rivero's retirement, from Apr. to Sept. 1864.

[2] *La Iberia*, 26 July 1857; *La Discusión*, 30 July 1857, 'El partido progresista y la cuestión social'.

[3] Ibid., 21 July 1857, 'La democracia y la propiedad'; 4 Aug. 1857, 'Una nueva potencia'.

But any criticism of the underlying social assumptions of the Progressives seemed to Rivero a deliberate attempt to undermine his policy of attraction. His angry reply was also understandable as the paper was to be fined 10,000 *reales* for 'advocating a new agrarian law'.[1] After this incident, which indicates some of the perils of Democrat journalism, Pi's articles were confined to academic discussions of the various solutions to social problems, thus serving one useful purpose by disseminating current foreign socialist doctrines.[2]

The confusion about party aims was clearly brought out again during the Garrido–Orense quarrel in 1860, after the publication of Garrido's pamphlet on Sixto Cámara, who had died the previous year on a revolutionary mission in Andalusia.[3] Orense and Garrido were two of the most active Democrat propagandists, representing the opposite wings of Democrat thought. Orense, the democratic Marqués de Albaida, had been a rebel Progressive as early as 1844. A wilful individualist with ambitions to lead a radical party, he was one of the few Democrats of independent means. In favour of a *rapprochement* with the Progressives, his public life was one long campaign against the evils of *empleocracia* and in favour of an extreme *laissez-faire* liberalism. Garrido, in contrast, was an impecunious writer from Cádiz whose early interest in Fourier predisposed him on his arrival in Madrid, to join the radical circle round Sixto Cámara, whose money financed various ephemeral socialist journals in the late 1840's. Garrido was a tireless researcher, had contacts with European republicans, and after a visit to Rochdale became the leading Spanish advocate of co-operatives. He called himself a socialist and his purpose in writing about Sixto Cámara was to argue that the Democrat party had been socialist from its inception and that its aim was the emancipation of the workers through the practice of free association in consumers' and producers' co-operatives.

[1] *La Discusión*, 19, 21 Aug. 1857—this in spite of both Orense's and Rivero's angry repudiation of Pi's views in ibid., 8, 9, 12 Aug. 1857.
[2] Fourteen articles between 3 Nov. and 4 Dec. 1857 reprinted as *Las Clases jornaleras*, Madrid, 1915.
[3] *La Discusión*, 8, 9, 10 Oct., 7, 8 Nov. 1860. For Orense see R. Labra, *J. M. Orense, estudio biográfico*, Madrid, 1882; R.-Solís, op. cit. ii. 332–4, 403. For Garrido see *La República*, 31 May 1884.

Orense's refutation of this 'socialist' interpretation of the party was supported by Rivero who rejected government pressure in all spheres of public or private activity.[1] He was unconcerned with theoretical implications except to stress that democracy need not inevitably imply a progression towards socialism, as Donoso Cortés, the Catholic apologist, had asserted in his famous *Essay* of 1851, which had become the intellectual inspiration of the new neo-Catholic party. Confusion about the implications of socialism and an elastic use of the word were common in the 1850's throughout Europe, but any justification of state intervention would have destroyed the main appeal of the Democrats and encouraged the fear that they might redistribute lands bought for speculation. The gap separating Orense and Garrido was not as wide as the quarrel seemed to indicate. Garrido insisted in using the word 'socialist' but he was and remained a Mazzinian associationist, agreeing with Orense in his repudiation of state intervention. The difference was mainly one of emphasis. Garrido wanted the Democrats to formulate a positive social programme aimed to encourage association and to concentrate less on purely political activity: Orense saw universal suffrage as the panacea which would solve all social and economic problems.[2]

The quarrel aroused wide interest and the divisions seemed wide and public enough for Pi to draw up in November 1860, on his own initiative, the 'Declaration of the Thirty' in which he laid down the fundamentals of the Democrat creed:[3]

Those who subscribe declare that they consider as Democrats, without distinction, all those who, whatever may be their opinions on philosophy and economic and social questions, profess in politics the principle of human personality or of individual liberties, absolute and inalienable, and of universal suffrage as well as other fundamental principles written in the Democrats' programme.

This, however, was not an effective compromise. Rivero and

[1] *La Discusión*, 12 Oct. 1860.
[2] Garrido, *El socialismo y la democracia ante sus adversarios; con un prólogo de Mazzini*, London, 1862. Orense, *La Democracia tal cual es*, Madrid, 1862. Cf. also A. Joarizti, *Los Progresistas, los demócratas y los individualistas*, Madrid, 1861; C. Tressera, ¿ *Los Anarquistas, los socialistas y los communistas, son demócratas?*, Barcelona, 1861.
[3] *El Pueblo*, 16 Nov. 1860.

others refused to sign it. Further exchanges of pamphlets in the next two years showed how the lines within the party were hardening. But the Declaration was significant for Pi as it was the first time he had acted as arbiter between two factions, a role he was to repeat many times later. After this unsuccessful attempt to smooth over differences, he took no further part in active journalism until April 1864 when he accepted an offer to take over the directorship of *La Discusión*. He held this post for only six months but it was the most significant phase of his early career and of cardinal importance for the future development of the party.

When Rivero retired for so-called 'reasons of health' it was evident that his undisputed leadership of the Democrats was over. In 1860 the appearance of a new Democrat evening paper, *El Pueblo*, made him apprehensive that it implied further internal divisions, but a greater challenge to his position was the foundation, in December 1863, of *La Democracia* under Castelar's direction. It was true that Castelar's spectacular entry into Democrat journalism strengthened the anti-socialist wing, but his growing reputation threatened to make him, rather than Rivero, the leading figure of Spanish democracy. The son of a Liberal Cádiz merchant who had died when he was a child, Castelar was brought up by a doting mother.[1] After a brilliant university career at Madrid, he discovered his real talent for oratory during the electoral campaign for the 1854 *Cortes*. In spite of an unprepossessing appearance and small stature he was a spell-binding word spinner. His popularity among the students at Madrid University, where his lectures as professor of history were perorations on the ideals of democracy, the wide attention caused by *La Fórmula del Progreso* of 1858, with its scarcely veiled republicanism, his reputation as an orator at the *Ateneo* as well as his popularity outside Madrid, all combined to make him a formidable rival for the leadership of the anti-dynastic forces. It was, moreover, his journalistic flair and the ability of his staff which made *La Democracia*

---

[1] There is no detailed balanced study of Castelar (1832–99), whom many considered the greatest nineteenth-century Spanish orator. The best analysis of his character is B. Jarnés, *Castelar o el hombre de Sinai*, Madrid, 1935.

a serious rival to *La Discusión* and enabled the proprietor, Cañizares, to choose Pi as the new director to revive its waning popularity. Rivero's retirement left the stage clear for the rivalry between the two convinced republicans, Pi and Castelar.

By founding his own paper at the end of 1863 Castelar hoped to seize the initiative in the confused situation which had developed after the fall of O'Donnell's Liberal Union in February. Many Progressives had been beneficiaries under O'Donnell's system, but a small group had remained faithful to their party's principles—the 'pure' Progressives. These saw their opportunity to get into office on O'Donnell's fall, but Isabella, in spite of listening to their advice, would not call them into power. Denied office, they refused to play the part of a rigged opposition for which Miraflores had cast them in the October elections. Instead, a group including Olózaga, Sagasta, and Ruiz Zorrilla issued a manifesto on 8 September declaring the party's *retraimiento*. This split the party and raised the question of its leadership. Discontent at Espartero's incompetence during 1854–6, when he had been outmanœuvred by O'Donnell, predisposed many to support Olózaga's repudiation of his leadership at a meeting in May 1864, because of his reluctance to accept the implication in the *retraimiento* of acting against Isabella. But others were still bemused by Espartero's name or, like Madoz, rejected Olózaga's action as untimely, for Prim, whose reputation from the Moroccan war made him Espartero's obvious successor, had not yet, by May 1864, received the final rebuff which was to turn him into the Queen's implacable enemy.[1]

Castelar's début may be interpreted as an attempt to rally the Progressives, broken and divided over the October *retraimiento*, under the Democrats' programme. But to do this he must show their hostility to any socialist tendencies. Hence his insistence that the main object of the new paper was to combat all aspects of socialism.[2]

[1] Pirala, op. cit. iii. 12 et seq.; R. Muñiz, *Apuntes históricos sobre la revolución de 1868*, Madrid, 1884–6, i. 5 et seq. See also the detailed study by R. Olivar Bertrand, *Así cayó Isabella II*, Barcelona, 1955, which prints useful documents in the appendixes. For Madoz's Esparterism see his letter to Balaguer, 16 Nov. 1863: Espartero's dislike of Olózaga in App. 54, and for splits over the *retraimiento*, Apps. 56–61. O. Bertrand has also written the best study of Prim—*El Caballero Prim*, Barcelona, 1952, 2 vols.

[2] *La Democracia*, 1 Dec. 1863.

Pi's purpose, once in control of *La Discusión* four months later, was very different. He now accepted the failure of the 1860 truce and in a series of articles in which he spoke unequivocally as leader of the socialist faction, precipitated a polemic with Castelar which divided the party into 'socialists' and 'individualists'. In his first article he developed his ideas on the Spanish revolution which he interpreted as a class war between a land-hungry middle class and the aristocracy allied with the clergy. From this struggle the middle class, enriched by the sale of Church and common lands and bolstered by the Army, had become a 'second aristocracy' unwilling to dispense with Church or Monarchy so long as they did not challenge its political dominance. The essential feature of this revolution was the Liberals' disentailing policy and it was on this that his analysis centred. The Liberals, he argued, had thrown away the opportunity to turn the *jornaleros* (day-labourers) into a property-owning class, for instead of establishing a system of emphyteutic tenure they had sold the disentailed land on the open market. Apart from determining the course of politics this policy had failed in two of its avowed aims, to increase productivity and to reduce the National Debt.[1]

Pi felt that those Democrats who refused to admit the need for radical land legislation were no better than Progressives in disguise. Their solution to all problems was universal suffrage: they did not believe it was the function of democracy to solve social and economic problems—these, in Rivero's words, would be solved by 'science and liberty'. Unlimited freedom would benefit workers as much as capitalists. Pi attempted to show the falsity of the assumption that universal suffrage alone would bring the Democrats into power—on the contrary, it would merely widen the *caciques'* sphere of activity. In Spain, democracy could only become a reality if an independent peasantry were established, bolstered by cheap state credit. The Democrats must commit themselves to a social programme and this must imply legislating on property distribution. This referred specifically to landed property. After all revolutions the dominant class had legislated on property to its own advantage. Why should the property laws of

[1] *La Discusión*, 1 Apr. 1864, 'La revolución actual y la revolución democrática'.

the Progressives be final? His continued emphasis on the need for a new land settlement can be related to the deteriorating agrarian situation of the late 1850's and early 1860's when the results of disentailing policies were being acutely felt.

Agrarian discontent had increased after Madoz's disentailing law of 1855. Although by this law, peasants could buy land on reasonable terms, paying a small initial deposit and the rest over a series of years, it did very little to ease agrarian distress because, in addition to Church lands, common lands were to be sold on the open market. It is true that *Ayuntamientos* could have applied for their common lands to be exempted but because many were dominated by local landowners who saw an opportunity to expand their own estates, very few did so. Discontent, caused by loss of long-established communal grazing and foraging rights and fanned by agitators like Sixto Cámara, had broken out in 1857 at Utrera and El Arahal, near Seville, where agricultural workers had burnt the records of sales in the local archives. In 1861 a much more serious rising occurred at Loja involving thousands of armed peasants. Though this soon petered out, it caused considerable alarm and was attributed to the influence of the Democrats working through secret societies of the *carbonario* type.[1]

The Democrats strenuously denounced these charges through fear of government suppression but the majority of the party were uninterested in the causes behind the revolt. Even Garrido supported free disentailing unhampered by government control. This lack of interest betrayed the mentality of an urban party brought up on English and French economists for whom the problems of a dry farming area and a landless proletariat were marginal to their main interests. In contrast, the crux of Pi's articles in 1864 was to make the Democrats alive to this agrarian problem, and to show its relationship to the political structure. His analysis certainly owed something to Fermín Caballero's recent detailed study of agrarian conditions, but Loja had been particularly significant as being the first large-scale rising in which

[1] J. Díaz del Moral, *Historia de las agitaciones campesinos*, Madrid, 1929, pp. 61–62; R.-Solís, op. cit. ii. 555–9.

the military had played no part whatever.[1] In attacking the Progressives Pi hoped to canalize this discontent into political channels, arguing that their party had been responsible for causing it,
that disentailing had only helped to consolidate the power of
the *caciques*, and that by isolating themselves from the masses the
Progressives must increase their dependence on the Army and perpetuate military rule.

Pi's conception of the ideal society emerges clearly from his
articles in 1864. Hostile to the concentration of landed property,
to monopolistic industries, and to the monopoly of credit facilities
by the big financiers, he wanted an independent small-holding
peasantry existing by the side of small industries run by workers'
co-operatives linked together in loose federations with the State
providing cheap credit. In common with Proudhon, he tended
to see cheap credit as the key to social reform. 'Usury', he wrote
in 1854,[2] 'is the origin of all Spanish ills', and again later, 'If the
State has any function to perform, it is patently that of providing
credit.'

These views were not original, for beyond the obvious influence
of Proudhon he was echoing many arguments of the eighteenth-
century reformers and of Flórez Estrada, who had criticized disentailing policy in its early days in the 1830's. By initiating a
scramble for Church lands, the Liberal revolution had increased
the size of the great estates, particularly in the south, which the
eighteenth-century reformers had tried to break up. Whereas the
Liberals followed the classical free-trade views of Jovellanos, Pi
returned to the forcible state action of Aranda and Olavide, who
favoured splitting up big estates into small holdings.[3]

Pi argued the case for the Democrats being a socialist party with
the deteriorating agrarian situation in mind. His socialism did not
spring from any desire to increase the power of the State but from
a recognition that unlimited freedom, unless backed by some
economic guarantees, would inevitably lead to an economic

[1] Fermín Caballero, *Fomento de la población rural*, Madrid, 1863. Díaz del Moral refers
to Loja as the first example of 'indigenous socialism' in Spain. The nature of the rising
caused considerable speculation at the time in the Madrid press.

[2] *La Reacción y la Revolución*, pp. 340, 343; *El Pueblo*, 10 Sept. 1860.

[3] J. Costa, *Colectivismo agrario en España*, Madrid, 1898, pp. 13 et seq., 115 et seq.

tyranny. He tried to clarify his meaning of socialism by contrasting it with *laissez-faire*, political economy, which he described as 'mere social physiology' concerned with facts not rights and which, by taking the contingent for the absolute, had often been converted into a weapon of tyranny and social injustice. Political economy was fatalist. Socialism was true liberty, for where political economy meant class struggle, socialism meant order in class relationships.[1] He still held the views of 1857 when he had rejected all socialist systems except Proudhon's, which alone seemed to prevent the absorption of the individual by the State and gave due importance to the family unit. By 1864, though, he had changed his views to the extent of admitting the autonomy of collective groups concerning interests affecting society as a whole. The State as the depository of these rights was therefore justified in intervening in economic affairs and in the administration of matters of general interest. State intervention in economic activity could be justified in order to secure social justice. Again, following Proudhon, the desire for social justice was the driving force behind his socialism:[2] 'We want purely and simply the application of the idea of justice to the social order and equality in the conditions of work by means of successive reforms in the civil as well as in the economic spheres.' The State's main function would be that of a regulating mechanism ensuring the balance between collective and individual rights.

It was the implied threat to the free market and to absolute property rights, as two letters by Orense clearly show, which rallied support behind Castelar's refutation of Pi's thesis.[3] Much of the hostility to Pi was because, like Garrido in 1860, he was jeopardizing any hope of attracting the Progressives. Castelar, however, tended to ignore the realistic basis of Pi's arguments and attacked the theoretical assumptions, pointing out inconsistencies in his theories.

Castelar and the individualists had unquestioning faith in the free play of economic forces. The State must not interfere with

---

[1] *La Discusión*, 17 May 1864.
[2] Ibid., 22 May 1864.
[3] *La Democracia*, 3, 18 June 1864.

the providential laws of the natural harmony of interests:[1] 'We want society with its natural and divine laws: you want society with your artificial and arbitrary combinations.' The emancipation of the workers could only come from their own efforts. The sole aim of the Democrats, therefore, must be political action to remove the barriers to freedom of association.[2] The influence of Bastiat, the French popularizer of free trade, is felt throughout the whole of Castelar's arguments. In the *Ateneo* debates on free trade of 1863, in which Castelar had played a prominent part, Bastiat's influence had been very marked, and his books enjoyed great popularity among both the individualist Democrats and the Progressives. Particularly relevant in 1864 was his condemnation of socialism during the Second Republic, while the issue between him and Proudhon over free credit in 1849–50 was echoed sixteen years later in the conflict between Pi and Castelar.[3]

In September Pi resigned from his directorship of *La Discusión* without giving any reason.[4] It may have been that it distracted him from his legal work or that he was content to retire once he had expressed his economic ideas. But Castelar was less charitable in an article which sounded like an obituary notice on Pi's reputation as a political thinker:[5] 'And in this final hour when Señor Pi retires to his house, perhaps with rancour in his heart and with the conviction that his idea is ruined, we declare that if we have often seen him as an adversary, we have never seen him as an enemy.'

The discreet veiling of personal animosity behind the impersonal exchange of ideas was a familiar aspect of Democrat polemics, but the dispute exposed the contradictions within the party and in doing so laid bare the struggle for leadership. Castelar accused Pi of splitting the Democrats into two hostile camps (the bitterness can be seen in letters published by both sides) but the disagreement

---

[1] *La Democracia*, 26 May, 10 June 1864. A recent discussion of the controversy can be found in C. Martí, *Los Orígenes del anarquismo en Barcelona*, Barcelona, 1959, pp. 22–28.

[2] *La Democracia*, 18, 26 June, 3 July 1864, 'Cartas a los trabajadores democráticas de Cataluña sobre la democracia y el socialismo'.

[3] L. M. Pastor (ed.), *Conferencias libre-cambistas*, Madrid, 1864. See the rhapsodic Democrat appreciations of Bastiat in Echegaray, *Recuerdos*, Madrid, 1917, iii. 71, Sanroma, op. cit. i. 88. The bulk of Bastiat's most popular writings had been translated into Spanish by the late 1850's.

[4] Vera, op. cit. i. 755.   [5] *La Democracia*, 17 Sept. 1864.

had helped to clear away some of the confusion about socialism.[1]
There was no doubt that Pi wanted more state intervention than
the associationists would tolerate. Once the storm had broken,
however, Pi was the more conciliatory. He reprinted the Declaration of 1860 as a basis for agreement, but Castelar was determined
to secure the outright rejection of socialists from the party. He
tried unsuccessfully to set up a directing committee of 'individualists' but Rivero refused to be associated with it, presumably
because this would have meant yielding to Castelar's leadership.
Nor could he carry his editorial staff with him, for after Pi had
defended his viewpoint in a meeting chaired by Orense, a number
of the staff of *La Democracia*, the most important of whom was
Salmerón the young professor of philosophy at Madrid, resigned
and declared their support for Pi. More important, though, was
the reaction which Castelar's move provoked throughout the
country—shown by the flood of letters asking why the party as a
whole had not been consulted.[2] The polemic had helped to turn the
Democrats from a small group of Madrid writers and politicians
into a national party whose opinions could not easily be dis-
regarded.

However, the struggle for leadership had not been resolved;
Rivero had broken with Pi and the division between Castelar and
Pi remained. The polemic was the first trial of strength between
possible leaders of a future republican party. Although press
restrictions forbade discussion about republicanism, it was well
known that neither were monarchists. Rivero in common with
many Democrats was an opportunist as far as forms of government were concerned, but his eclipse during the polemic showed
him that his only hope for retaining leadership would be for the
Democrats to remain a monarchist party.[3]

[1] Ibid., 1 June 1864. Letters were printed in both *La Discusión* and *La Democracia* from
May to June 1864.

[2] Ibid., 25 June 1864. F. Pi y Arsuaga, *Historia de España en el siglo XIX*, Barcelona,
1902, iv. 318. Salmerón (1838–1908), the rising light of Spanish Krausist philosophy, was
the son of a country doctor at Alhama la Seca near Almería. He refused a chair at Oviedo
and was to remain at the centre of republican politics until his death.

[3] In a letter in *La Época*, 25 Feb. 1869, quoted in Fernández Almagro, *Historia política de la
España contemporánea*, Madrid, 1956, p. 158, Rivero declared his republican faith but believed that Spain was not ready for a republic in 1869. He had lost face with many Democrats by accepting a civil governorship in 1854.

Finally, the polemic did more than anything else before 1868 to popularize socialist ideas in Spain. Pi had for long been a prominent figure at the *Fomento de las Artes*, but it was the events of 1864 which gave his socialist ideas wider currency and enhanced his popularity among the workmen attending the *Fomento*, and those in Barcelona whom the polemic had helped to make politically conscious.[1] It was partly Pi's defence of the social aims of the Democrats which enabled the Federal Republicans to win working-class support after 1868.

The legacies of the polemic as well as acute differences over co-operation with the Progressives can be seen from the great variety of Democrat juntas with conflicting viewpoints which sprang up in Madrid in late 1864 and 1865.[2] A compromise solution based on Pi's Declaration of the Thirty and accepted by the central committee was only superficial; the intense personal rivalries remained. But whatever their internal disagreements, the Democrats' popularity continued to increase as ideological issues sharpened after the publication of the Syllabus of Errors in 1864. Their unequivocal hostility to the intolerant and aggressively anti-liberal neo-Catholics, also their outspoken criticisms of the Queen and the clerical *camarilla*, were evidence of the vitality of a party which was drawing its main support from the younger generation for whom the Progressives with their tired clichés and unsuccessful past held no attraction. It was clear, for example, where the loyalties of many Madrid University students lay after Castelar had written his brilliant scathing article attacking Isabella's 'magnanimous gesture' alienating two-thirds of her estates to relieve the country's financial situation. Their demonstration in favour of the Rector, who refused to dismiss Castelar, was turned into a riot in which several people were killed and which forced the Government to resign.[3]

But this new popularity could not offset those deep divisions

[1] A. Lorenzo, *El Proletariado Militante*, Mexico, n.d., p. 11; J. Morato, *Historia de la Asociación del arte de imprimir*, Madrid, 1925, p. 38. For repercussions in Barcelona see Martí, op. cit., pp. 30–38.

[2] F. Leiva y Muñoz, *La Batalla de Alcolea o Memorias políticas y militares de la Revolución Española de 1868*, Córdoba, 1879, i. 178–87, 217–34.

[3] Vera, op. cit. i. 767–72.

over policy and personal rivalries which deprived the party of firm leadership at a time when the Progressives, now committed to Prim, were angling for Democrat support after a series of unsuccessful risings.[1] The failure of the *pronunciamientos* at Valencia in June 1865, and at Villarejo in January 1866, convinced Prim of the need for the popular support which only the Democrats could provide. It was eventually agreed by those Democrats who favoured a tactical alliance that the ex-Progressive Becerra should represent the party at meetings in Paris to plan yet another rising. In return for this support Prim promised that he would accept universal suffrage should the revolt succeed.

This rising, planned for the summer of 1866, counted on the adherence of garrisons from Valencia to Valladolid. In addition to the popular backing of the Democrats in Madrid were added the regiments of artillery in the San Gil barracks where the long-standing grievance of artillery sergeants, prevented from promotion to officers by the aristocratic traditions of the corps, had been skilfully exploited. The Democrats hoped to use the artillery regiments and their own popular following to establish their position in the capital as a bargaining counter in their relations with Prim after the revolt had succeeded. But this never happened. Delay, indecision, internal rivalry, the failure of committed regiments elsewhere to rise, and the loyalty of the Liberal Union generals doomed Prim's coup and the sergeants' revolt to a bloody fiasco and, although the Democrats took to the barricades, they were easily routed. Stringent action was taken against those implicated. Democrat papers were closed down, their leaders condemned to death. There was no alternative to exile except possible garrotting and certain imprisonment. July and August therefore saw an extensive exodus of Progressives and Democrats to Portugal, France, Belgium, and Switzerland. This exile, by dispersing the Democrats, divided them even more effectively than their bitter polemics and personal rivalries.

[1] Muñiz, op. cit. ii. 48–54, chs. iii–viii; Pirala, op. cit. ii. 54 et seq.

2

Exile and the September Revolution, 1866–8

ALTHOUGH a few who were implicated in the San Gil revolt, like Rivero and Salmerón, took the risk of remaining in Madrid, the greater number were scattered across Europe for two years of exile. Paris soon became the focus of these expatriates and the centre of revolutionary intrigue. Olózaga, Sagasta, Ruiz Zorrilla, and other prominent Progressives, and the Democrats Martos, Becerra, Castelar, and Pi made it their home. In spite of continual plotting and the threat which a Spanish revolution might bring to Napoleon III, the exiles were left in comparative peace, subject only to police surveillance. Prim alone, rightly regarded as the major threat, was expelled from France and was forced to divide his time between the other exile gathering places, Brussels, Geneva, and London.[1]

Pi played little part in the political discussions of his fellow exiles and during his stay in Paris from August 1866 until February 1869 lived a solitary life with his family, dividing his time between caring for the legal affairs of his fellow exiles, writing articles for the South American press, attending lectures by the positivist Laffitte, and studying Proudhon.[2] Neither he nor Castelar played any active part in the preparation of the revolution which broke out in September 1868. Their main contribution to it had already been achieved by their oblique criticism of monarchy before 1866 which had helped to prepare public opinion for Isabella's overthrow. Castelar's role in this had been confined to spreading a

[1] The main printed source for the exile are the *Cartas de conspiradores*, Madrid, 1929, compiled from Zorrilla's papers by Alvárez Villamil and R. Llopis. Napoleon's attitude is discussed in W. A. Smith, 'Napoleon III and the Spanish Revolution of 1868', *Journal of Modern History*, Sept. 1953.

[2] Vera, op. cit. i. 831; García Ruiz, *Historia de la Internacional y del federalismo en España*, Madrid, 1872, p. 40; N. Estévanez, *Fragmentos de mis memorias*, Madrid, 1903, p. 244. There were approximately 2,000 Spanish exiles.

sense of dissatisfaction and frustration among the university youth and the educated public at the tyrannical restrictions of Isabelline government. In exile he held aloof from active politics. Pi, on the other hand, made a significant theoretical contribution. It was during his Parisian exile that he found, in studying Proudhon, the confirmation of ideas which he had felt after but not developed in 1854. Proudhon's influence had already been marked in the development of his views on Progress, in his concept of revolution, and in his economic ideas. He had been attracted to the social ideas of Proudhon rather than to those of other socialist thinkers and, in his views on credit in particular, he had seen the safeguard protecting the independent peasant who, with the credit provided by the State, would be relieved of economic and political dependence on middle-class moneylenders. Whereas in France Proudhon's economic arguments were based on his desire to make the existing peasantry the main bulwark against the expansion of monopoly capitalism, in Spain his arguments could only be applied after an agrarian revolution had created an independent peasantry from a redistribution of Church and common lands. Pi's failure to convince the Democrats of the interrelation of political and social revolution in *La Discusión* accounts for the increasing interest he took during exile in the purely political aspects of Proudhon's thought.

Both Progressives and Democrats, appreciating the strong currents of local feeling, had incorporated administrative decentralization in their programmes but this decentralization was merely a concession granted at will by the party in power and could as easily be revoked. Pi denied that constitutional guarantees in written law were adequate safeguards: what was needed to transform Spanish society was a reconstitution of the country dictated not by geographical or historical criteria but by the logical necessity of the devolution of power through a federal system.[1] In exile, therefore, he was primarily concerned with the political problem of how to ensure that the great strength of local feeling, which had been dissipated in the failure of sporadic and uncoordinated earlier revolts, could be canalized. By utilizing local

---

[1] Pi y Margall, '¿ Cual debe ser nuestra forma del gobierno?', article in *La Razón*, quoted in Vera, op. cit. i. 503–8.

feeling the chances of political revolution would be enhanced and, after the power of the centralized government with its vested interests had been broken, social reform could follow.

It was in Proudhon's last major work, *Du principe fédératif*, written in 1863, that Pi found the theory which he was to apply to Spanish conditions. When a Madrid publisher suggested he should translate Proudhon's book into Spanish he seized the opportunity, and in the summer of 1868 the translation appeared in Madrid, by coincidence only a few months before the September Revolution. This translation did no more than add intellectual justification to the separatist instinct which, Pi explained, had always led provinces to organize themselves during national crises. But this did not detract from its importance, as it immediately became a handbook for local republican revolutionaries as Pi had hoped in the Introduction:[1]

. . . through this book towns can acquire consciousness of their aspirations and learn the way of stating them and realizing them. . . . Are not perhaps towns and provinces, although of an inferior order, at least as natural and spontaneous as nations at a later date?. . . . Towns instinctively love federative régimes.

His success in giving an ideological framework for nascent republicanism provides a marked contrast to the failure of his earlier book to do the same for the Democrats in 1854.

The essence of the federal polity, which Proudhon advocated and Pi echoed, lay in the Pact or Social Contract:[2]

Not the lawyers' fiction of Rousseau, Robespierre and the Jacobins but a positive, effective pact which has really been proposed, discussed, voted, adopted and which is regularly modified at the will of the contracting parties. Between the federative contract and that of Rousseau and of 1793 there is all the difference between reality and hypothesis.

Proudhon's definition of this contract was taken directly from the Civil Code (Article 1101), which stated that: 'A contract is

---

[1] *El Principio federativo*, Madrid, 1868, p. 10.
[2] Proudhon, *Du principe fédératif*, Paris, 1868, pp. 64–66, 67. Proudhon's federal ideas are discussed in E. Dolléans, *Proudhon*, Paris, 1948, pp. 441–7, 470–3; M. J. Chevallier, 'Le fédéralisme de Proudhon et de ses disciples', in *Le Fédéralisme*, ed. G. Berger, Paris, 1956. See especially the Introduction to *Du principe fédératif*, ed. G. Scelle, J.-L. Puech, T. Ruyssen, Paris, 1959.

synallagmatic and bilateral when the contracting parties are reciprocally obliged one towards the other.' In order for a political contract to be synallagmatic and commutative: 'The citizen must keep all his liberty, his sovereignty and his initiative, less what is relative to the special object for which the contract is framed.' Pi did little to elaborate Proudhon's book and, although he expanded his federal theory later in 1876, in his translation he did no more than add a short introduction.[1] He made no attempt to anticipate criticism or to suggest how it could be applied practically in Spanish conditions. Much of the book's effectiveness lay in its oversimplification and in its uncritical acceptance by those who wanted a justification for resisting the central power. The popularity of the federal pactist theory of the State as a structure organized from below (*abajo-arriba*) was that it gave to towns and provinces which had enjoyed wide measures of autonomy in the past a juridical basis and justification for resisting the abuse of power by self-interested party groups at Madrid. When the federal movement became a reality in October 1868 it did so with a theory which emphasized in the most literal terms the contractual nature of government.

Proudhon's federal theory had developed under the cloud of French republican failure. The Second Republic had shown that not only monarchies end in tyranny. The pactist theory seemed to provide a safeguard for republicanism in Spain against falling into the errors of the French and to provide as well a theory to counteract the inevitable concentration of power in political societies. It also suggested a political form to correspond to Pi's idea of the individual's autonomy as outlined in 1854:[2] '. . . all power is an absurdity. Any man who extends his hand over another is a tyrant . . . between two sovereigns there can be only pacts . . . contract must replace authority as the Basis of Society.'

After adopting the pact Pi became more doctrinaire and inflexible: the pact was the acme of political wisdom, the only solution to the problem of Spanish government, and his strength of

[1] Pi y Margall, *Las Nacionalidades*, Madrid, 1876. For Pi's version of the pact see his *Lecciones del Federalismo*, Barcelona, 1923, pp. 69 et seq. See Appendix for a fuller consideration of Pi's views.

[2] *La Reacción y la Revolución*, p. 178.

will was later to be used to enforce this theory on the emergent republican movement in order to give to it the rigid discipline which he considered necessary in a fluid post-revolutionary situation. As far as we know, he made no attempt to win over the Democrats during exile, although a handful including Orense, García López, Garrido, and Castelar were sufficiently convinced to call themselves Federal Republicans before 1868. The most significant adhesion was Castelar. In a more mature political society Pi and Castelar might have been found in opposing parties but in a corrupt society addiction to ideas and abhorrence of opportunist politics forced them to be allies. Violently opposed in temperament and on most matters of policy the strange co-operation between the strong-willed Pi and the vacillating Castelar began in exile.

Although Castelar was often in Paris, the two potential leaders of Spanish republicanism rarely met or corresponded.[1] Castelar had no family ties and, in contrast to Pi, spent much of his exile travelling outside France. He visited Italy and Switzerland where, in 1867, he represented Spanish democrats at the meeting of the League of Peace and Freedom under the presidency of Garibaldi. When he was in Paris he used to stay with his friend, the monarchist Martos. His sociability, too, was in marked contrast to Pi's seclusion. He was on intimate terms with Girardin, Gambetta, Ollivier, and Jules Favre. Because of his contacts with European republicanism his movements were closely watched by the police. It seems clear that foreigners regarded him as the leader of Spanish republicanism, but it is more difficult to ascertain what his relations were with the other Democrat exiles and to what extent his political views had crystallized. As neither Pi nor Castelar left any precise account of their political views in exile we have to rely on third-party evidence which, in the case of García Ruiz, was not altogether disinterested. According to his account, Castelar took the initiative in building up republican solidarity by going to Pi at the end of 1866 and suggesting that they should forget the controversy of 1864 and work together in the interests of republican

---

[1] B. Jarnés, op. cit., pp. 116–41, gives an account of Castelar's life in exile built up from his correspondence with the Marqués de Grijalba.

unity. It was then, according to Ruiz, that Pi made his adhesion dependent on Castelar accepting the federal principle.[1] It is impossible to determine the extent of Castelar's conversion. It seems that he accepted Pi's federalism in principle, but whether by force of Pi's personality or, as Sagasta suggested later, through admiration of Swiss democracy after his stay there in 1866, or even, as Azorín suspected, through reading Considérant and Strada, must remain conjectural.[2] Nor do we know if he understood the implications of the federal pact; in common with all Democrats he had spoken and written in favour of wide administrative decentralization and of the aim of democracy being the 'autonomy of the municipality and the province', but there is nothing to suggest that he ever accepted or realized the far-reaching implications of the theory of the pact.

Castelar's adhesion to Pi's federalism did not provoke the split among the Democrats in exile, but, on the contrary, was a consequence of the divisions of the Democrats and of their failure to declare themselves unequivocally republicans. Democrats had not yet clarified their attitude to the form of government which should follow a possible overthrow of the Bourbon monarchy. The failure of Prim's attempts in 1865 and 1866 had convinced him of the necessity for Democrat support and popular backing. For the Democrats to commit themselves finally to republicanism might jeopardize their chances of winning Prim over to the principle of universal suffrage. Rivero, the nominal leader of the party, was still in Madrid and as a result there were divisions among the exiles about who should represent the party at the various conferences called by Prim in order to build up a revolutionary alliance. Accounts of different meetings among the exiles vary considerably according to the viewpoint of the writer, but it is possible to reconstruct the framework of the meetings from their published letters.

Prim convened for 16 August 1866 a meeting of prominent exiles at Ostend at which Becerra was elected by some fifty

---

[1] García Ruiz, op. cit., pp. 41–43.
[2] Pi y Arsuaga, op. cit. iv. 474; *Gaceta*, 9 June 1869, Sagasta's speech; but against this see Castelar's introduction to Garrido, *La República democrática federal*, Madrid, 1856. Cf. Azorín, *De Granada a Castelar*, Buenos Aires, 1944, pp. 139–40.

Democrats to represent them on a committee of action of three members which was to be established at Brussels to co-ordinate revolutionary activity.[1] Originally Prim had intended to hold the conference at Geneva where he had gone after being expelled from Vichy by the French police. From here he had written to Castelar inviting him to attend, and Castelar had accepted, but when Prim decided to change the meeting-place to Ostend it is not clear if another invitation was sent or not. In any case, Castelar was not present and refused, moreover, to regard Becerra as truly representing the interests of the Democrats. In this his views were shared by Orense, who wrote to Prim from Geneva that he did not regard Becerra as sufficiently qualified to represent the Democrats. Orense, it should be noticed, did not object to Becerra on political grounds. Prim was at a loss to understand Becerra's unpopularity as to him he seemed *todo abnegación*.[2] The most likely explanation would seem to have been his incompetence during the San Gil rising, his disagreements then with Moriones, who had the confidence of the military, and his factious opposition to Rivero. It was at this time, at the end of 1866, according to García Ruiz, that Castelar, presumably disillusioned with the outcome of the Ostend conference, approached Pi with a view to sinking differences between them in the interests of republican unity.

At the meeting at Ostend agreement had been reached between Progressives and Democrats to destroy the existing régime in Spain and to set up a constituent assembly to be elected by universal direct suffrage. Prim himself was dissatisfied with the outcome of the conference, for the agreement could only be nominal so long as Olózaga, the elder statesman of the Progressives and barely reconciled to Prim's leadership, had not been won over and so long as the Democrats did not regard themselves as being bound by Becerra's word. Prim's difficulty in dealing with the Democrats was to know who exactly could speak for the party as a whole. So long as Orense, Castelar, and Pi remained aloof

[1] Alvárez Villamil, op. cit., p. 168. Both Vera and Pi y Arsuaga are unreliable in their chronology of these meetings.
[2] Ibid., pp. 193, 204; cf. Pi y Arsuaga, op. cit. iv. 364.

he could not be sure of rallying Democrat supporters still in Spain. If he regarded the republican wing as unimportant from the point of view of their small following, he was nevertheless anxious to secure their co-operation, possibly because he valued their international connexions.[1]

The first task, that of winning over Olózaga, had been achieved by March 1867, although his dislike of the Republicans, expressed at a meeting at Mons in that month, and his insistence on the acceptance of Fernando of Portugal as the future king, threatened the unanimity of the earlier Ostend meeting.[2] He was willing, nevertheless, to work for agreement between the Progressives and the Democrats in the hope of achieving Iberian Union through a Portuguese candidacy. By June 1867 Prim felt that the time for the revolution had come but, with the Republicans still uncommitted, he deputed Olózaga to make one more effort to win them over. A meeting was held in Olózaga's house in Paris at which all sections of revolutionary opinion among the Parisian exiles were present. This was the only meeting which Pi attended.[3] To the Republicans it was a failure: Olózaga was still talking of the Portuguese candidacy and they insisted that they could take no part in a revolution of which the only aim was to replace one dynasty by another. Olózaga, however, seemed satisfied as he was convinced that his friendship with Orense, *antiguo cliente mio*, and Martos, who still seemed undecided, would wean them away from the Republicans.[4] A compromise solution between Democrats and Progressives was accepted in which both agreed to postpone the form of government to a popular referendum. Two days later at a final meeting with Prim in Brussels he accepted the terms agreed to in Paris.[5] The position after this meeting of July 1867 was similar to that after the Ostend meeting of the

[1] Alvárez Villamil, op. cit., p. 191. These were not worth much judging from a letter of Mazzini dated 8 Oct. 1868 in *Scritti*, vol. 87, p. 189, where he writes: 'All contact with the republican leaders was out of the question up to this moment: I did not know where they were, nor did they know about me.'

[2] Letter from De Blas to Zorrilla, 11 Mar. 1867, in Alvárez Villamil, op. cit., p. 246.

[3] Ibid., p. 325.

[4] Letter from Olózaga to Cirera, 11 Aug. 1867, in Olivar Bertrand, *Así cayó Isabella II*, Barcelona, 1956, Appendix 82.

[5] Alvárez Villamil, op. cit., pp. 280, 326.

previous year except that, in the meantime, Olózaga had been drawn into the revolutionary conspiracy. As neither Pi nor Castelar was present at the Brussels meeting it must be assumed that they were not party to this agreement and that from now on they remained aloof from the active planning of the revolution. The only Republican to remain within the conspiratorial circle was the anti-federal García Ruiz, a close friend of Olózaga.

In August Prim launched his attack. The original plan for *émigrés* to invade Aragón and Catalonia was suddenly changed on a report that the garrison at Valencia would be ready to second the rising. Governmental foreknowledge and divisions between Moriones and Pierrard, who had been left to cross the Pyrénées independently of Prim according to the original plan, caused the rising to collapse.[1] As popular response had been negligible, Prim was relieved to find that the gradual disaffection of the Unionists after O'Donnell's death in November 1867 promised other more reliable allies. By the summer of 1868, when he was assured of Unionist support after González Brabo had exiled their leading Generals Serrano and Dulce to the Canary Islands, Prim could afford to be less dependent on the Democrats. When final plans for the revolution were laid in the summer of 1868 neither republican nor monarchist Democrats took part. Castelar wrote to the Marqués de Grijalba at the beginning of September that he had heard of preparations being made for a new rising but that he would remain totally removed from political life, devoting himself to literature.[2] It was this exclusion of the Republicans from the planning of the revolution which later made them indebted to Paul y Angulo, a swaggering, boastful *señorito* from Jerez, who, although he had no political affiliations, offered his services to Prim to prepare the ground in Andalusia where Prim's agents had proved untrustworthy. It was only after the revolution that Paul, disappointed in his expectations, turned against Prim and became a violent Republican. It was through him alone that the Republicans could claim any active co-operation in the revolution.[3]

[1] For the 1867 rising see the letters in Alvárez Villamil, op. cit., pp. 355–405, 451–9. See also Pirala, op. cit. iii. 149–60; Muñiz, op. cit. i. 169 et seq., and C. Roure, *Recuerdos de mi larga vida*, Barcelona, n.d., i. 76–86.   [2] Jarnés, op. cit., p. 141.

[3] Paul's version is in his *Memorias de un pronunciamiento*, Madrid, 1869. See Rivas,

By the beginning of September Prim's contacts with the
Unionist generals guaranteed him overwhelming support in the
Army while the adhesion of Admiral Topete brought in that of
the fleet at Cádiz. On 19 September, after preparatory manifestoes,
Prim and Topete landed at Cádiz where agents had been working
to ensure the coup's success. On the 20th González Brabo, President
of the Council of Ministers, resigned and was succeeded by
Concha. For nine days Concha, deserted by Isabella, tried to
defend a losing cause. It was not until the morning of the 29th,
when news came to Madrid of the previous day's defeat of the
loyal army at Alcolea, that the repercussions in the capital of the
action at Cádiz were really noticeable. Concha, realizing that his
cause was hopeless, requested the revolutionary committee of
Unionists and Progressives, set up in the summer to co-ordinate
revolutionary activity after the Unionist generals had been exiled,
to take over. It was the revolutionary situation created by this
voluntary relinquishment of power by Concha which enabled the
Democrats to emerge as an independent political force.

Concha had handed over to Madoz, who, as interim Civil
Governor, had named an executive junta consisting only of Progressives and Unionists. The Democrats, with memories of 1854,
determined not to be excluded from a share of power again, and
formed their own junta under the presidency of Prim's old adjutant
Escalante.[1] On the same day as Madoz formed his junta, Escalante
opened the Arsenal in Madrid, distributed arms to the people, and
occupied the Ministry of the Interior. Faced with this demonstration of Democrat power backed by the populace, Madoz yielded
and the two juntas were fused, issuing a manifesto in their joint
names. As neither junta had legal standing, elections under universal
suffrage were held on 30 September for a new junta. Because of the
suddenness of this decision, and the fact that it was raining heavily,
few people voted, but the Democrats nevertheless won eight out

Anecdotario, Madrid, 1945, iii. 293 et seq. One of Paul's ambitions was to become Spanish
ambassador in London.
[1] Pi y Arsuaga, iv. 435–6. This consisted of the leading Democrats, with the exception
of Salmerón, who were still in Madrid. Cf. *The Times*, 14 Oct. 1868. The reports of *The
Times* correspondent constitute one of the fullest records of the first three months of the
revolution.

of twenty-eight seats.[1] Their numerical minority did not at first seem important as Rivero, the vice-president of the junta, with a large popular following in the capital, largely determined its policy. On 3 October, the day on which Serrano entered Madrid, the junta published a manifesto giving him the task of creating a provisional ministry (in accordance with an earlier agreement with Prim) to govern until the meeting of a constituent *Cortes*. Although there was opposition to this decision Rivero signified his agreement with Prim's policy by publicly embracing Serrano. On the day after Prim's own arrival in Madrid on 7 October the Provisional Government was finally constituted, consisting of five Progressives and four Unionists with the key Ministries of War and the Interior in Progressive hands. Rivero refused a post in this ministry because Serrano had been unwilling to admit Martos and Becerra as well, but as mayor of Madrid he still had an important position in the capital.[2]

The implications of the Madrid Junta's decision were far-reaching and played an extremely important part in stimulating the rapid growth of republicanism in the provinces. In every town of any size the news of the Cádiz coup and of Isabella's flight had been greeted with the setting up of juntas consisting of prominent local Democrats and Progressives. In response to popular demand these juntas, like that of Madrid, had been replaced by others elected by universal suffrage. They could claim, therefore, to be the expression of popular sovereignty. The Madrid Junta, by appointing Serrano the president of a provisional ministry, was arrogating to itself powers which belonged to the sum total of all the juntas and by this action made itself an accomplice of agreements reached by Prim and Serrano, irrespective of popular opinion. This was yet another example, so the Federals were to argue, of Madrid dictating to the rest of the country. Yet this argument, valuable though it was in creating resentment against the Provisional Government when it failed to pursue a popular policy, ignored the fact that by far the majority of local juntas,

---

[1] Vera, op. cit. i. 901.
[2] *The Times*, 13 Oct. 1868; Pirala, op. cit. iii. 227. For Rivero see Rivas, op. cit. i. 161 et seq.

dominated by Progressives, acquiesced in the Madrid Junta's decision. Only one in fact, that of Barcelona, following the precedent of the *centralista* agitation of the 1840's, protested against Madrid and refused to dissolve until it was clear that no one else would support them. Rivero's part in pursuing a policy which played into the hands of the Progressive–Unionist coalition was never forgotten by those who believed that he could have proclaimed a republic in September and so have turned a *pronunciamiento* into a revolution. The immediate consequence of Rivero's 'apostasy' was to make him the scapegoat for early republican failures: he became the most bitterly attacked figure in the republican clubs.[1] Long-term consequences were more profound, for it bred a deep distrust of Rivero and his supporters Martos and Becerra which prevented any reconciliation between the two halves of the Democrats after they finally split in November.

Because of the proscription of the party since 1866 and the scattering of their leaders in exile the Democrats now found themselves leaderless and without a programme. What Democrat activity there had been between 1866 and 1868 had been on a local rather than a national basis. Neither Pi nor Castelar was in Madrid to exploit the revolutionary situation. Pi, in fact, did not return to Spain until early February 1869. In view of his later dominance of the republican movement it is remarkable that he should have remained in the background at such a critical time, but scepticism over the revolution, unsureness of his own popularity among Democrats, their attempt to use his name without consultation, and even more prosaic personal reasons of having to support his family, may account for his delayed return of five months.[2] Apart from his translation of *Du principe fédératif* his only contribution to the first days of republicanism was an open letter to *La Federación* of Bilbao in September calling for the declaration of

---

[1] F. Flóres García, *Recuerdos de la Revolución*, Madrid, 1913, p. 59. Among many other attacks on Rivero's role see *La Igualdad*, 29 June 1869, 5 Mar. 1870. For his part in the junta see Reclus's article 'Comment on réveille un peuple' in *La Revue politique et littéraire*, 22 Nov. 1868; Estévanez, op. cit., p. 266.

[2] Pi's letter to *El Diario*, 3 Oct. 1868, pointing out his disagreement with a manifesto published under his signature but without his knowledge is printed in E. M. Vilarrasa and J. I. Gatell, *Historia de la Revolución de Septiembre*, Barcelona, 1875, i. 416–17.

a federal republic.[1] Even Castelar, whose popularity had never been in doubt since the *Rasgo* article, was slow to return, protesting his political neutrality until the enthusiastic welcome which greeted him on his arrival in Madrid in late October changed his mind, when in the vanity of his own words:[2]

As soon as he returned from exile Emilio Castelar dedicated himself to republican propaganda. An orator not merely loved but idolized by the Spanish people, as O'Connell by the Irish, he declaimed speeches before 20,000 and 30,000 people in open air meetings, raising his voice to all corners. The reception given him in Zaragoza, Valencia, Barcelona, Alicante, Alcoy, Reus, Valladolid and even Madrid itself on his return from exile had not been granted in Spain to any civilian.

But even Castelar's impassioned oratory was now echoing republican opinion rather than originating it.[3] In the absence of the other leaders Rivero was able to gain the upper hand and because of his immense popularity in the capital was at first accepted as the leader of the Democrats. It must be remembered too that it was Rivero, with his following in Madrid, who was the guarantee that Prim would not go back on his earlier promise of universal suffrage. By refusing office in the Provisional Government he appeared to be putting party interests before personal ambition and his action was interpreted as an example of Democrat solidarity. It was only during the course of the Democrat reunions in October and more particularly after the monarchist manifesto of 12 November which had been signed by Rivero, Martos, and Becerra that the breach between republicans and monarchists became apparent and it was realized that the strain of revolution had finally broken the party and made irreparable the breach which had been exposed by the controversies of the early sixties.

It was clear, at least after the Government's manifesto of 25 October, that although it was willing to leave the final decision of the form of government to a constituent *Cortes* to be elected by universal suffrage, the Government itself was in favour of a

---

[1] Reprinted in *La Igualdad*, 12 Nov. 1868. Cf. *The Times*, 21 Sept. 1868, for a Federal Republican manifesto printed in the Paris press and signed by Orense.

[2] Quoted by Jarnés, op. cit., p. 140.

[3] See the fly-sheets *Cartas de Emilio Castelar a los republicanos*, dated 8 Nov., and *Discurso pronunciado en la inauguración del comité republicano*, 13 Nov. 1868.

monarchy which implied that its influence would be exerted to ensure a monarchical majority in the forthcoming election. There was, however, to be a wide divergence over the actual monarch. There were two main dynastic claimants, the Orleanist and the Carlist. The first was the Duke of Montpensier, who had married Isabella's sister Luisa Fernanda in 1846 and was the Unionists' candidate. He had been expelled from his palace at Seville in July 1868 for suspected intrigue but returned after Isabella's expulsion. He and his money became one of the major causes of disturbance during the next two years. Isabella's fall also revived the Carlist claim now strengthened by the neo-Catholics. The Progressives were divided. Both Olózaga and Prim wanted Fernando of Portugal, reflecting their ambitions for Iberian Union. A smaller group looked nostalgically to Espartero, while more radical Progressives like Zorrilla wanted the Duke of Genoa.

The exclusion of any Democrats from the Government stimulated the republican feeling which was a marked feature of the first three Democrat reunions held on 11, 18, and 25 October. At these meetings, attended by 'between four and five thousand well-dressed Democrats' the tone was distinctly republican.[1] All the four secretaries elected, García López, Sorní, Tressera, and Vizcarrondo, had republican sympathies, while Orense, elected president, whatever his views may have been before 1868 now declared himself unequivocally republican ('I prefer a bad republic to the best of kings') and was hailed as the *decano* of republicanism in spite of his lingering Progressive sympathies, shown in his proposal that Espartero should be declared president of a federal republic. No one at these meetings tried to defend a monarchy. Martos, in the absence of either Rivero or Becerra, confined his remarks to a plea for union between all revolutionary parties. Nobody paid much attention to him as the tone of the gatherings was one of naïve, excited optimism with the implicit assumptions that the Democrats were a united party, that the party would be bound by the decision of the majority of its members, that Rivero was

[1] *The Times*, 19 Oct. 1868. For these meetings see the three fly-sheets *Primera (Segunda and Tercera) reunión pública que el partido democrático de Madrid ha celebrado después de efectuada la revolución de Septiembre de 1868*, Madrid, 11, 18, 25 Oct. 1868.

a republican and that, in spite of his 'abnegation' in refusing a post in the Government, the Democrats would still be in a strong position through his being mayor of Madrid.

No attempt was made at these meetings to defend a unitarian republic, and after Salmerón's speech on the 18th when he gave distinction to the debate with a philosophical defence of federalism, republicanism began to be accepted as synonymous with it. Neither Castelar nor Pi was mentioned during these debates and it was Salmerón who more than anyone clinched the federal argument, linking the intellectual justification of federalism with the popular acceptance of it.[1] At the third reunion it was decided to hold elections in Madrid for thirty members of a republican committee. From these elections dates the break up of the old Democrat party and the emergence of the first organized Republican party in Spanish politics.

In this election 13,735 people voted.[2] Orense headed the poll and was followed by Figueras, Castelar, Blas Pierrard, García López, Joarizti, Guisasola, Roque Barcia, Sorní, Pico Domínguez, Pi y Margall, Córdoba y López, Santiso, Vizcarrondo, and others less well known. Of these all were Democrats of long standing except for Blas Pierrard, whose notorious antecedents sullied the political purity of this first republican committee. His democratic leanings dated only from the failure of his attempts to raise Aragón in 1867 as part of Prim's coup. His inclusion showed how republican sympathizers voted for colourful personalities as well as for fixity of political conviction, but more important, he was the first general to declare himself a Republican—'the founder of a new race'.[3] A simple-minded hothead, he was evidence of the political immaturity of the new party welcoming the support of any general without scrutinizing his motives in joining a movement one of the main aims of which was the destruction of the Army's political influence. He was, however, some use as a

[1] N. Salmerón, *La forma de gobierno*, Madrid, 1868. Cf. R. Giralti-Pauli, *El cerebro de la Revolución: Carta al Sr. Salmerón*, Málaga, 1868.

[2] *La Igualdad*, 12, 14 Nov. 1868. This paper, founded by Figueras and to become the leading republican paper, first appeared on 11 Nov.

[3] Vilarrasa and Gatell, op. cit. i. 341. For Pierrard see C. Rubio, *Historia filosófica de la Revolución de Septiembre*, Madrid, 1869, i. 364 et seq.

symbol—his military rank, his age like Orense's, and his flow-
ing white beard—all enabled those with short political memories
to think of their movement stretching far back into the past.

The other members, whatever their inner motives, had at least
suffered exile and persecution for their democratic convictions.[1]
Orense, the Marqués de Albaída, was a wilful individualist whose
age and industry (he is reputed to have addressed 150 gatherings
in three months), untiring assault on *empleomanía*, political experience and possibly his wealth, made him attractive as a figurehead in spite of differences of opinion over his early convictions.
García López, prominent in the reunions and later a leader of the
extremists, was an old-vintage Democrat, a lawyer who had sat
in the *Cortes* of 1854, and with Orense had voted against Isabella
in the famous 'vote of the twenty-two'. It was mainly due to his
influence that Huesca later became a stronghold of republicanism.
Joarizti, a young Barcelona journalist of good family seeking his
fortune in Madrid, soon rose to an important position as editor
of *La Igualdad*. Guisasola, a Madrid doctor, combined his medicine
with a violent turn of phrase on the platform and on paper. Roque
Barcia, from Seville, was a flowery writer, philologist, and self-
styled philosopher; Sorní, a staid Valencian lawyer who had sat in
the 1854 *Cortes*. Pico Domínguez was a frustrated littérateur from
Cáceres. Córdoba y López, from Ciudad Real, a soldier who had
turned to novel-writing and the law. Santiso, a grocer, came from
the Plaza Anton Marín, the centre of Madrid working-class
radicalism. Vizcarrondo, an idealistic poet, had been forced to
leave Puerto Rico through his championship of slavery abolition
and, coming to Madrid, had devoted himself to humanitarian
works.

This first organized republican body reflected the professional-
class character which was to be the mark of federal republican
leadership. Salmerón was a significant absentee; he had been a
member of the Democrat central committee in 1866 but, although
in favour of federalism, he had recommended caution in its

[1] For biographical details see R.-Solís, op. cit., vol. ii, *passim*; and the two compilations
La asamblea constituyente de 1869: biografías de todos los representantes de la nación, Madrid,
1869, and *Los diputados pintados por sus hechos*, Madrid, 3 vols., 1869–70.

application. Disappointment at his lack of revolutionary fervour
raised a suspicion of the genuineness of his federal convictions which
clung to him until 1871.[1] Few, in fact, were willing to question
the implications of the federal idea. Republican feeling expanded
on the exploitation of a few known discontents and flourished on
a widespread but inarticulate feeling of resentment against Madrid.
It was easy to pose as a regenerating movement trying to unite all
social groups in resistance to the tyranny of over-centralized
government, but when it came to formulating a policy the desire
to placate all discontented elements prevailed over the need to base
themselves on specific social groups. The old splits within the
Democrats lingered on in the new republican movement. The
Democrats had been predominantly free-traders—Castelar and
Orense followed that precedent and so did Garrido, but his
embarrassed hedging in a speech at Sabadell in October showed
how any party to be popular in industrial Catalonia, had to
declare itself protectionist.[2] The republican attitude to catholicism
wavered between a doctrinaire anticlericalism and a desire to
exploit its emotional appeal for their own ends.

On one aspect, however, they were united—the abolition of the
quintas. This had figured prominently in the Democrats' programme, but it had become an increasingly important issue since
the early 1860's when O'Donnell embarked on imperialist ven-
tures. The Republicans' only tangible claim to be a mass movement
derived from their championship of *quinta* abolition. This was
based on their criticism which Pi had voiced in 1854, that political
reform was inseparable from military reorganization.[3] By 1868
Prim had acquired genuine political convictions; he wished to be
regarded as a civilian not as a soldier as he showed by his dis-
pleasure at Régnault's fiery equestrian portrait of him. Foreign
observers recognized the change; his manner, Hay wrote,[4] was

---

[1] Estévanez, op. cit., p. 281. Cf. Garrido, *Historia de los últimos Borbones*, Barcelona,
1869, iii. 1220.

[2] *La Igualdad*, 11 Nov. 1868.

[3] *La Reacción y la Revolución*, pp. 291-7.

[4] J. Hay, *Castilian Days*, London, 1897, p. 315. Hay was an eye-witness of the events of
1869-71 from his post in the U.S. embassy at Madrid. Cf. Layard, B.M. Add. MS. 38932,
ff. 20-22—Layard had met Prim in London during his exile. The Régnault portrait
incident is in M. B. Mariño, *El viaje del pintor Henri Régnault a España*, Madrid, 1948,

'sober and clerical ... like a pious and sympathetic undertaker ...
a born ruler'. But in spite of his success in obliterating the romantic
image of the fearless leader of the Moroccan war and the colourful
revolutionary, he could not conjure away the logic of having made
a revolution with the aid of officers. Genuinely wanting to lessen
the Army's political influence he was nevertheless condemned to
continue the system of political promotion to retain its loyalty,
nor was he able to honour promises to abolish the *quintas* because
of the Cuban insurrection. Thus he was exposed to the full force
of virulent republican propaganda. By championing *quinta* abolition the Republicans enlisted the mass support of the poor, who
were most heavily penalized by the system, being unable to afford
redemption payments. From an early date they concentrated their
propaganda on *quinta* abolition and on plans to reform the Army
by creating a volunteer force which, by reducing its size, would
both cut the national budget and enable better pay and conditions
to attract those who wished to make soldiering a genuine professional career.[1] But it failed as a vote-catcher in the elections in
January as Prim's promise to abolish the *quintas* as part of the price
of Democrat support was not broken until after the election was
safely won. It was not, in fact, until Prim had called for 25,000
men on 24 March to reinforce the depleted Cuban garrison that
they began to reap the full harvest of their campaign. Also, the
Government's decree limiting suffrage to men of twenty-five and
over meant that they were unable to utilize the voting strength of
those most affected by the system.[2]

The limiting of the voting age was a bitter blow as the Republicans claimed that they were the party of youth, comparing
themselves to the young enthusiasts of the French Revolution. It
was among students particularly that they made their strongest
appeal. After the municipal elections in December *La Igualdad*

pp. 49–50. Proclamations to the Army to abstain from politics are in *Gaceta*, 24 Oct.,
6 Nov. 1868. The vested interest of officers in revolution can be gauged from the 1,635
officer promotions after the revolution had succeeded (*El Correo Militar*, 24 May 1869).
 [1] *La Igualdad*, 19 Nov., 5 Dec. 1868. It cost approximately £60 to be exempted.
 [2] *Gaceta*, 10 Nov. 1868; *La Igualdad*, 13 Nov., 10 Dec. 1868. The Republicans wanted
twenty as the limit. Even the Second Republic had a limit of twenty-three. See also *The
Times*, 22 Jan. 1869; *Revue des Deux Mondes*, 15 Jan. 1869; M. Klapp, *Revolutionsbilder aus
Spanien*, Hanover, 1869, p. 253.

claimed that at least 800,000 potential supporters had been excluded by the electoral decree. Later *El Pueblo*, with slightly more
pretension to accuracy, calculated that 647,000 people between
twenty and twenty-five had been excluded from the general
elections.[1]

Despite this handicap, in the municipal elections they claimed
majorities in twenty provincial capitals.[2] These elections, the first
in Spain under universal male suffrage, constituted a moral defeat
for the Provisional Government and brought home to it in a
forcible manner the republican menace. But provincial success
was in marked contrast to their complete failure in Madrid.
Foreign observers confirm the monotonous republican and Carlist
descriptions of the capital as a city where political society was
dominated by regular and reserve army officers, by *pretendientes*,
empleados, and *cesantes*.[3] *The Times* correspondent estimated,
with some exaggeration, that 30,000 persons were more or less
dependants of the Government. It was hardly surprising in these
circumstances that a new party was unable to find much support
in the capital. Inability to increase their numerical following in
Madrid was to be a constant factor during the next five years, forcing them to rely increasingly on the well-tried device of the earlier
Spanish radicals—manipulation of the Madrid mob. The implications of this profoundly modified early expressions of republican
policy based on the efficacy of propaganda and legal opposition.
Unable to compete against government influence in the capital,
they resorted to bribery and intimidation, attracting to the movement doubtful characters of the Madrid underworld. The danger
of this mob manipulation was that it could be used as effectively
by discontents in the movement against their own leaders as
against their political opponents.

The figures for the municipal election in Madrid exposed
Republican weakness. Whereas 13,750 had voted in the committee

[1] *La Igualdad*, 23 Dec. 1868; *El Pueblo*, 19 Jan. 1869.

[2] Alicante, Barcelona, Castellón, Córdoba, Coruña, Huelva, Huesca, Jaén, Lérida,
Málaga, Murcia, Orense, Santander, Seville, Tarragona, Teruel, Toledo, Valencia,
Valladolid, Zaragoza. They also won at Cádiz but the December rising postponed the
election to January.

[3] *La Igualdad*, 20 Jan. 1869; *El Pensamiento español*, 14 Apr. 1869, to quote only two
examples. *The Times*, 22 Jan. 1869; *La Revue politique et littéraire*, 26 Dec. 1868.

election of 13 November only 3,600 voted in the municipal election in December. In the national elections to the *Cortes* in January the position was better, the Monarchists polling around 30,000 while the only Republican, Figueras, polled 16,295.[1] As all the popular leaders of the revolution stood in Madrid this result was hardly remarkable, but the gulf was nevertheless great considering the Republicans thought that they would be the main beneficiaries from universal suffrage. The notable feature about their first electoral campaign was their reluctance to exploit the very great social discontent which followed the disastrous crop failure of the summer. Mendicancy had shown such a marked rise that it was forbidden by decree in an effort to stop the flow of starving peasants into Madrid, and the corn situation had become so critical that in December its export was forbidden.[2] Reluctance to appear as rabble-rousers was due to the dominance of the anti-socialist wing of the ex-Democrats and their wish not to alienate potential middle-class supporters.[3] Republicanism in Madrid in 1868 was characterized by its respectability.

After the opening of the Arsenal between 40,000 and 60,000 rifles were in the possession of the populace, many of whom formed themselves voluntarily into detachments of 'Volunteers of Liberty'. This, combined with social discontent, created an inflammatory situation which could have been exploited by determined revolutionary leadership. The Volunteers' commander, Escalante, was hardly the man; promotion and inclusion in the junta were sufficient to mollify his revolutionary ardour.[4] Nor were any of the other Democrats ready to incur the odium of being disturbers of the social order. Energetic action by the Government insured that the revolution would not become more radical. Muñiz had tried to persuade Madoz to mobilize the militia of 1856 to defend property against the threat from the 'Volunteers of Liberty'. Madoz had refused, but Sagasta, the new Minister

---

[1] *La Igualdad*, 14 Nov. 1868, 20 Jan. 1869; *The Times*, 26 Dec. 1868. The total Madrid electorate was 82,724; of these, 54,662 voted (*Gaceta*, 4 Feb. 1869.)

[2] *Gaceta*, 23 Dec. 1868; *The Times*, 29 Sept., 30 Oct., 28 Nov. 1868; H. Régnault, *Correspondance*, Paris, 1904, p. 225.

[3] *La Igualdad*, 1 Jan. 1869.

[4] Estévanez, op. cit., p. 250; *The Times*, 12, 25 Nov. 1868.

of the Interior, sensing the danger, decreed the formation of a militia in November in which the absence of payment would ensure its conservative complexion.[1] Under threat of social disorder the junta created a precedent by providing work for the unemployed and, yielding to popular pressure, agreed to the abolition of the *consumos*. Rivero, the anti-socialist, admitted the need for a scheme comparable to the national workshops of 1848 to prevent the Volunteers from getting out of hand. On 6 November the Government offered thirty *reales* (equivalent to four days' pay) for any rifle returned to the *Ayuntamiento*, and work at seven *reales* a day was offered to anyone provided that he had a rifle.[2] It is difficult to know how many of the arms were recovered. Motives for keeping them varied from self-defence to using them for hunting and resale. Nor is it easy to say how many people were in receipt of government money, though estimates put it at between 13,000 and 15,000.[3] With no funds at their disposal the Republicans could offer no alternative to wean away these dependants of Rivero's charity. There were repercussions as well on the Government's economic policy with this drain but the important point was that, whereas the Government at Madrid had the financial resources to deal with a menacing situation, municipal councils in the provinces, faced with a similar problem, lacked the funds to buy off the unemployed. Figuerola, the Finance Minister, hoped to raise ten million *reales* to pay the unemployed by means of a loan, the interest on which would be covered by selling building plots in the city.[4] Social revolution in Madrid could be averted by alienating municipal property.

By the end of November the success of republican propaganda, even in Madrid, was alarming the monarchist Democrats and in early November *The Times* correspondent forecast with sombre prescience that within a month the extremists would have to be put down by force. On 6 December, in fact, there was a rising in

[1] *Gaceta*, 18 Nov. 1868; Muñiz, op. cit. ii. 243. The militia question is discussed in *The Times*, 26 Nov. 1868.

[2] *Gaceta*, 6 Nov. 1868.

[3] I. A. Bermejo, *Historia de la interinidad y guerra civil de españa de 1868*, i. 141–2, 386; *The Times*, 5 Nov. 1868. There had been a similar buying back of arms after the 1854 Revolution.

[4] *The Times*, 14 Oct. 1868.

Cádiz followed by one at Málaga on 1 January. These risings surprised both the Government and the Republicans of the capital
with the strength and independence of political feeling in the
south. Neither of these risings had been instigated from the centre
and each was independent of the other. Republicans at Madrid
believed, in common with sections of the press, that the Cádiz
rising was merely a Montpensierist or Bourbonist plot. Garrido
denied that his propaganda visit to Cádiz a few weeks before the
revolt had any relation with it. These risings contrasted the republicanism born of the barricades of Cádiz and Málaga with that
of Madrid, fed on the optimistic hyperbole of the masters of
European republicanism, who, as Mercier, French ambassador at
Madrid, reported, were hoping to exploit the Spanish revolution
in the interests of international republicanism.[1] Reclus, who had
accompanied Garrido on a propaganda tour from Barcelona to
Cádiz which ended in Madrid, gave a damning picture of the
'insouciance and naïveté of the Republicans of the capital' and in
a letter to his brother he remarks that 'only by revolutionary
audacity' can the Republicans triumph. This however, was exactly
the quality lacking in those at Madrid, conditioned by political
events in the capital and by their own preconceptions about the
nature of revolution. From the very beginning, therefore, may be
traced a difference in approach between the Republicans of the
capital and those of the provinces—a difference which was to
grow continually greater until, to the provincials in 1873, there
was nothing to distinguish those of Madrid from the parties which
they were claiming to replace.

---

[1] O. Bertrand, *El Caballero Prim*, ii. 206. For the reactions of European republicans see
Mazzini, *Scritti*, vol. 87, p. 187, letter to Castelar, Oct. 1868; Garibaldi from Caprera in
Lauser, op. cit. i. 81. Victor Hugo from Jersey in *Actes et paroles*, Paris, 1938, ii. 269, letter
of 22 Oct. 1868. Elie Reclus speaking for the 'Universal Republic' at Sabadell in *Correspondance*, Paris, 1911, i. 307. Alexandre Dumas *fils* to the Federal Club at Barcelona in *La
Igualdad*, 12 Nov. 1868. Cf. also Mistral from Provence, letter to A. de Quintana, 4 Oct.
1868, in *Revue de Catalogne*, 25 Mar. 1929.

3

The September Revolution in the Provinces

IN three months the Republicans became the most serious threat facing the Provisional Government. Within this time it had to crush two bloody revolts and to disarm forcibly the militias in the four towns of Seville, Jerez, Cádiz, and Málaga. These conflicts expressed the disillusion felt after the juntas had been dissolved before many points in their programmes had been put into effect. Hopes had centred on the local juntas, the traditional Spanish reaction to revolutionary situations, and an analysis of their actions and their programmes reveals the extent of popular hatreds and ambitions.

The juntas' programmes showed remarkable consistency.[1] Anticlericalism, led by the many masons in the juntas, was common to all and varied only in intensity. It was the expression of hatred against a church which had been a willing ally in enforcing political uniformity. This hatred was particularly strong against the Jesuits, who as in 1836 and 1854 were immediately expelled, and other orders which had been infiltrating since the Concordat of 1851 were disbanded; convents were demolished, usually as a means of providing work for the unemployed, religious liberty was proclaimed, permission was ostentatiously granted to Protestants to build chapels, cemeteries were secularized, and in the more extreme juntas at Seville, Málaga, and Cádiz, separation of Church and State was demanded.

[1] For junta activities see Bermejo, op. cit. i. 154 et seq., 349–54; Pirala, op. cit. iii. 230–3; Rubio, op. cit. ii. 345 et seq.; the clerical Vilarrasa and Gatell, op. cit. i. 459 et seq. J. Tassara González, *Apuntes para la historia de la Revolución de Septiembre en Sevilla*, Seville, 1919; C. Roure, op. cit. i. 232–46. Religious toleration and Protestant activity during and after 1868 is dealt with in J. D. Hughey, *Religious freedom in Spain*, London, 1955, chs. iii et seq. The reports of British consuls in F.O. 72/1190, 1191, 1192 are useful for the economic aspects. No detailed work has yet been done on either the juntas' composition or their programmes.

There was conformity, too, in most of the juntas' economic decrees. Abolition of the *consumos*, as in 1854, removed an unpopular tax which had led to high prices for essential foodstuffs. The abolition of duty on tobacco, salt, and stamped paper not only reduced prices but was a direct assault on *empleocracia*, for the administration of these taxes was associated with the Government's need to provide offices for their supporters. The first act of the revolutionary juntas was to declare these tax officials *cesantes*. The lowering of port dues and of taxes on imported goods was common to all ports from Santander to Barcelona and was designed to attract foreign shipping and stimulate trade. Barcelona reluctantly followed the lead of the other ports, not wanting to be at a disadvantage, but would have preferred to have had the free port issue linked to that of protection. The declaration by the Barcelona Junta of the trade with the Antilles as *cabotaje* (coasting trade exempt from customs duties) was a significant indication of the importance attached to it.[1] Finally, the demand for complete disentailing reflected the ambition of acquisitive buyers. There was, however, no mention in the juntas' programme of redistributing common lands for, although it was an issue in rural areas, it did not interest the urban radicals at this stage.

Every junta proclaimed the basic freedoms of reunion, association, the press, and teaching, and reforms desired in common were the abolition of the *quintas*, the *matrículas del mar*, unity of *fueros*, the independence of the judiciary, the jury system, penal reform (including abolition of the death penalty), educational reform; and, because of high unemployment, many juntas recognized the right to work. All these were accepted by the Provisional Government in principle, but its attitude was equivocal with reforms which might affect revenue or the basic social structure. The most popular of the juntas' decrees had been those abolishing unpopular taxes, but inevitably this posed the problem of finding alternative sources of revenue. By replacing the *consumos* with an equally unpopular poll-tax (*capitación*), and by restoring the duty on

[1] *El Boletín Oficial Revolucionario de la Provincia de Barcelona*, 9, 10, 20 Oct. 1868; *El Diario Mercantil* (Valencia), 6, 7 Oct. 1868. The most astringent attacks on *empleocracia* are Orense, *Ventajas de la República Federal*, Madrid, 1869, and *La Empleocracia*, Madrid, 1872.

salt and tobacco in November, the Government built up strong resentment. The vaguely worded clause on administrative de-centralization, common to all juntas and accepted in principle by the Government, was another cause of friction, for Prim's dis-tribution of the new civil governorships and captain-generalships to his supporters seemed an ominous return to the old state of affairs. In acquiescing in popular anticlericalism the Government showed certain misgivings. The demolition of convents was a useful means of providing work for the unemployed, but when it threatened to become too radical, as at Málaga, the Civil Governor tried to put a stop to it. Demands for the separation of Church and State found no support even with the fiercely anticlerical Ruiz Zorrilla, whose attempts to sequester the movable wealth of the Church were designed to break its financial power before the *Cortes* met and a possible Catholic reaction set in. But even for him separation was too extreme a measure and it was left to the Republicans alone to champion.

In addition, therefore, to the political factors, to be discussed later, discontent with the Government was stimulated by failure to accept the juntas' programmes in their entirety. For a moment it had looked as if the Progressives, dominant in most of the juntas, would recapture their lost claim to be the popular revo-lutionary party, but, largely under mob pressure, they had to embody points in junta programmes which were too radical for the revolutionary coalition at Madrid.[1] It was the report of the programme of the Seville Junta which first emphasized to the Provisional Government at Madrid the radicalism of the pro-vinces.[2] Faced with the choice of casting off loyalty to their party or gaining from the hand-out of offices, the majority sided with authority, accepted the decrees of the Provisional Government, and abandoned the more extreme claims to which they themselves had been originally party. It was after the resignation of the Madrid Junta, followed by that of the provincial juntas at the end

[1] As at Seville, where the Progressive Machado, a member of the junta, became Civil Governor of the province. For an example of Progressive doubts about radical extremism see Balaguer, Civil Governor of Barcelona, writing to Mistral, 1 Dec. 1868, printed in *La Revue de Catalogne*, 25 Apr. 1929.

[2] Pi y Arsuaga, op. cit. iii. 441–2.

of October, that federal republicanism began to be the new revolutionary force, driving the Progressives on to the defensive and
forcing them into closer co-operation with the Unionists. Although the radical minority in the provincial juntas had to accept
dissolution their reluctance was shown in their forming 'vigilance
committees'. It was in these radical rumps of the juntas that federal
republicanism was to find its first practical expression.[1]

Two main areas of republican activity outside Madrid merit
attention—Andalusia, together with the Levante, where it was
coherent and haphazard, and Catalonia, where it showed its
greatest maturity. Elsewhere federalism was an isolated phenomenon. There was a small federal minority in Galicia centring on
El Ferrol and La Coruña, but it does not invite comparison with
the main areas of federal activity. In the south and south-east
republican feelings spread most rapidly in the seaboard towns,
Valencia, Alicante, Cartagena, Málaga, Cádiz, and Seville. All
these towns had been foci of earlier Progressive or Democrat
radicalism and it was from these parties that the Federals drew
some of their support after 1868. But their main appeal was to the
lower-middle class and workers previously excluded from political
life by the franchise qualification. In some cases, particularly in
Málaga and to a lesser extent elsewhere in the south, federalism
appealed to those peasants who had been driven to the towns by
bad rural conditions. Among the *pueblos* of Andalusia—Carmona,
Utrera, Loja, Lorca, Antequera, Arcos de la Frontera, and Montilla
—the Federals secured a following, but it was difficult to establish
themselves in the rural areas which were still dominated by the
caciques and permeated by a whole network of caciquist relationships.

Federalism in Andalusia may be characterized as a reaction of
the urban middle and lower-middle classes against the continuing
political and economic predominance in national government of
the Andalusian landowners who had little interest in stimulating
industry or trade. A distinction, however, may be drawn between
two different types of federalism—that of Valencia, Seville, Cartagena, and even of the small boom mining town of Linares—which

---

[1] F.O. 72/1192, 14 Nov. 1868, report of Cádiz consul.

was a reflection of strong regional and local feeling supported by economic interests demanding a greater share in their own government. Resentment in these cases might be voiced either against Madrid, as at Seville and Valencia, or against towns like Baeza or Murcia, the political predominance of which was resented by their economically growing neighbours, Linares and Cartagena. On the other hand, the federalism of Málaga and Cádiz was a product of economic stagnation and decay.[1]

In Málaga, the most unruly of the southern towns during the next six years, this was particularly noticeable. For nine months of the year British ships bringing imports left Málaga empty.[2] Apart from the Larios textile factory, a few sugar refineries, and the Heredia ironworks, employing in all about 4,000, the economy centred round the grape and olive harvest and thus suffered from the disadvantages of seasonal employment. Mineral resources were left unmined because of the lack of native capital and the reluctance of foreign capital to invest in them. The labour problem was well illustrated when a British company started mining at Marbella in 1869; the number of workmen flocking into the town from outside threatened to depress wages and led to the demand by local labour to prohibit immigration.[3] In Málaga itself, radical extremists always had at their disposal a mob of unemployed landless peasants driven to the town looking for work. Perhaps this not only explains why Málaga's federalism was more volatile than elsewhere but also why the moderate Federals at first tried to find allies among the other political parties. In Cádiz the position was similar although not so acute; where in Málaga the Federals could be assured of an easy majority, in Cádiz this majority was only obtained through the abstention from politics of a large number of the electorate.[4] Cádiz's instability contrasted with

[1] For the economic stagnation and general decay of trade in Cádiz and Andalucía see the consular reports in *Parliamentary Papers* (*P.P.*), 1867–8, vol. lxviii, pp. 536–59.

[2] F.O. 72/1191, no. 38, 2 Dec. 1868, report of Málaga consul. Guillén Roblés, *Historia de Málaga y su provincia*, Málaga, 1873, pp. 689–90. In 1873, 109,988 out of the province's 446,659 inhabitants lived in Málaga.

[3] F.O. 72/1219, no. 12, 16 Oct. 1869, Málaga consul to Layard. Bermejo, op. cit. i. 440–2, writes that 800 of those captured in the 1869 rising were landless labourers.

[4] F.O. 72/1207, no. 21, 16 Jan. 1869, Cádiz consul describing the elections there. For Huelva see the Cádiz consul's report in F.O. 72/1218, 12 Nov. 1869. Huelva returned four monarchists in the 1869 elections.

Huelva where rapid development of the near-by Rio Tinto mines might help to account for its lack of sympathy with the general trend of Andalusian political feeling after 1868.

Whereas in Málaga the Federals were split into extremists and moderates and in Cádiz they were an organized minority, in Valencia they had good relations with other political parties. The distinguishing feature of Valencia federalism, revealed by the immediate acceptance of the Provisional Government's decrees, was its moderation and the degree of co-operation between political parties prompted perhaps by the presence of a Carlist minority. In the 1869 revolt and again, though to a lesser extent, in the 1873 canton the revolutionary junta included non-federals among its members. Without a landless proletariat the strength of Valencia federalism lay among the lower-middle class artisans; there the organization of industry was based on small workshops in which there was a considerable degree of co-operative enterprise.[1]

In Cartagena, to become by 1873 the most prominent Federal centre in Spain, the problem was different again. The Arsenal and the lead-mines of near-by La Unión provided employment, while many of the rural population earned a living by transporting coal up from the port to the mines. In addition, some of the population pressure was eased by emigration to North Africa, in contrast to the Andalusian provinces where emigration seems to have been less common.[2] Cartagena federalism tended therefore, like that of Valencia and Seville, to be rooted in a feeling of self-sufficiency.

Seville was the main centre of self-conscious Andalusian regionalism finding expression in the daily *La Andalucía* which had been calling for the union of the Andalusian provinces in a *Unión Bético-Extremense* since 1860.[3] A significant feature of nineteenth-century Spanish politics was the increasing influx of Andalusians into public life. 'At no period of Spanish history', wrote Hannay,[4]

[1] Pérez Pujol, *La cuestión social en Valencia*, Valencia, 1872. See also Pirala, *El Rey en Madrid y en las provincias*, Madrid, 1871, pp. 220 et seq.

[2] P.P. 1868-9, vols. lx and lxviii, reports of Cartagena consul. F.O. 72/1237, 7 Dec. 1870, Layard to Granville, enclosures on land tenure.

[3] *La Andalucía*, 13 Nov. 1860, 1 Jan. 1869. F. M. Tubino, *Esto matará a aquello*, Seville, 1864.

[4] D. Hannay, *Emilio Castelar*, London, 1896, p. 45. Hannay was consul at Barcelona in

'have the Andalusians been so conspicuous as in the last sixty years. Bullfighters, smugglers, journalists and politicians flowered in the age of parliamentary eloquence.' Like Catalan regionalism Andalusian self-consciousness may be partly explained by increased cultural awareness. Andalusian self-esteem had been flattered by the attention paid to the south by foreign writers; the romantic imagination had created the stereotyped image of the Andalusian as the typical Spaniard, while in Spain the development of *costumbrismo* writing also emphasized the peculiarities of the region. Intellectuals like Tubino, Machado, and Rubio figure prominently as leaders of Sevillano federalism, and Seville University, a centre of Hegelianism and Krausism, played a similar role to that of Madrid in fertilizing political radicalism.[1]

Narváez's brutal repression after the El Arahal riots of 1857 together with the Loja revolt of 1861 stimulated some radical activity by showing the Democrats how the base of their political movement could be broadened by exploiting rural discontent. The core of the Sevillano Democrats consisted of the lawyers Díaz Quintero Carrasco, Torres y Gómez, and Sánchez Silva, aided financially by the banker Calzada, all tried revolutionaries who, in the 1860's, had formed working-class contacts both in Seville and, through Leiva, at Córdoba.[2] Useful contacts had also been made with surrounding pueblos by Pérez del Alamo, who, since the failure of his rising at Loja, had settled in Seville where, as a veterinary surgeon, his links with a mule-owning peasant society were invaluable to the Democrats.

Seville occupied a key position in the September Revolution because Prim had failed to make sure of its garrison and it was mainly due to this very active nucleus of Democrats that the garrison there pronounced in favour of the Cádiz rising.[3] In

the early 1870's. See S. de Mas, *La Iberia*, Barcelona, 1856, p. 51, for figures illustrating the dominance of Andalusians in governments and the army in relation to other regions. Cf. Ortega y Gasset, 'A Theory about Andalusia' in *Invertebrate Spain*, London, 1937.

[1] P. Jobit, *Les Éducateurs de l'Espagne contemporaine*, Paris, 1936, ii. 54. Tubino became director of *La Andalucía* in 1870. His *Patria y federalismo*, Seville, 1873, was one of the best-written Federal pamphlets. Machado edited a cultural Federal review *El Hispalense*. Rubio was a surgeon and lecturer at the University.

[2] Leiva, op. cit. i. 89 et seq.; Rivas, *Anecdotario*, ii. 179 et seq.; Mendez Bejarano, *Idealismo jurídico-político*, Madrid, 1919.

[3] Vasallo, *Un capítulo para la historia del alzamiento de Sevilla*, Madrid, 1869.

September it had been the Democrats rather than the Progressives who prepared for the rising. After the garrison had been won over, the Democrats, aided by advanced Progressives, were able to dominate the provisional junta and to publish a programme, the repercussions of which in Madrid have already been mentioned. The fear there of Sevillano radicalism was stimulated by wild rumours of social revolution throughout Andalusia, where the overthrow of Isabella was seen as a prelude to a return of the common lands and to a break-up of the large landed estates. These fears found some justification as Federals argued that under a federal republic Andalusian proprietors would have to prove the titles to their properties.[1] On 22 October the Governor of Seville had to put down an attempt to divide some landed property near the city and at Vejer de la Frontera attempts were made to seize old common land.[2] How far these expressions of agrarian discontent were a result of deliberate republican incitement or how far just a natural corollary to the breakdown of central government is extremely difficult to determine. In their clubs the Federals talked about a *reparto de bienes*, but they were very careful not to stress this too strongly in their programme, for some prominent Andalusian Federals were themselves landowners. In the case of Córdoba province there was little repercussion of republican propaganda except in the two Progressive strongholds of Montilla and Montoro.[3] Pérez del Alamo, on the other hand, had no qualms about stirring up agrarian discontent and conducted a propaganda tour to Carmona, Ecija, and Antequera, towns which were natural foci for the rural unemployed. The municipal elections established that Seville was an overwhelmingly republican city, with 14,938 republican votes against 1,967 monarchist, and this was confirmed at the *Cortes* elections when four out of five deputies were Federals.[4] This increased the pretensions of the Sevillanos to regard themselves as the natural leaders of Andalusia but it was a claim which

[1] *La Discusión*, 23 Dec. 1868.

[2] J. Guichot, *Historia de la ciudad de Sevilla y los pueblos importantes de su provincia*, Seville, 1885, p. 335. *El Progreso Democrático* (Cádiz), 30 Oct. 1868.

[3] Díaz del Moral, op. cit., p. 67. For Córdoba and Montilla see Leiva, op. cit. i. 311 et seq., ii. 249 et seq.

[4] *La Andalucía*, 28 Sept. 1868; *Efimérides malagueñas*, 2 Oct. 1868; Guichot, op. cit., pp. 353–5.

was to be strongly disputed later when it became apparent that local pride and the desire for independence were not confined to the large cities alone.

Republicans argued that the September Revolution had had a predominantly republican character in Andalusia; a view popularized but only to a very slight extent confirmed by Paul y Angulo, who claimed that Prim's coup owed its success to the mass of the people 'in the greater part republicans' rather than to the minority of Progressives and Unionists.[1] But the actual participation of the 'masses' was confined to some hundred of 'democratic' peasants from Jerez who, paid and armed by Paul, were introduced into Cádiz to provide some element of popular support for the coup. To argue, as Paul did later, that his motive in doing this was to prevent the coup from being a purely military rising seems to be little more than a rationalization after the event. The absence of any mention of his name in the Federal press at Cádiz suggests that his relations with the Cádiz Democrats were tenuous. It is true that there was an increase of vague republican feeling when the Democrats were not included in the Provisional Government, but it is quite untrue to talk in terms of specific 'republican' participation in the September Revolution. Only after the revolution had succeeded did the masses become a consideration of any importance. The part played by the small nucleus of Democrats in Seville in winning over the garrison was much more important than any mythical mass rising.

The nature of republicanism in Andalusia and its dependence on local factors and conditions was shown by the events of December and January. The complete absence of co-ordination between the various republican centres was seen on the news of the revolt at Cádiz on 6 December, when the republican reaction, even at Seville, was one of confusion and incredulity. There was little reason for this as the genesis of the rising was made perfectly clear in newspaper accounts written a few days after the event.[2] An explanation could be their fear of being thought too extremist;

---

[1] *La Igualdad*, 11 Dec. 1868.
[2] *El Porvenir* (Seville), 11 Dec. 1868, supplement quoting *El Comercio* of Cádiz the previous day. Cf. Bermejo, op. cit. i. 422–32.

this might explain why they, in agreement with others, tended to attribute it to Montpensier's money. The immediate cause of the rising, however, was social and economic. Unemployment in Cádiz and surrounding towns was very high—one estimate put it as high as three-quarters of the population, while the torrential rains of September had ruined much of the grape and corn harvest. The *Ayuntamiento* was accused of slowness in demolishing convents, a stock method of employment, and of being too interested in the coming elections to bother about social problems.[1] At a demonstration on 29 November to protest agaist the *Ayuntamiento*'s inability to solve the unemployment question, evidence of strong republican feeling was particularly marked among the Volunteers who had been armed in the days immediately after the coup. Local councils, following Madrid's lead, provided money to prevent the unemployed from getting out of hand. In Puerto Santa María, across the bay, the money, mainly contributed by gifts from the richer inhabitants, soon ran out as the *Ayuntamiento* had to pay from five to six *reales* a day to 500 unemployed. Because of the threatening attitude they adopted, soldiers were sent from Cádiz and the Governor there declared a state of siege and ordered the militia's arms to be handed in. The weakening of the garrison and the threat of being disarmed decided the Cádiz militia to rise and for three days there was street fighting. The leader of the rising and the force behind Cádiz federalism until 1873 was the ascetic Salvochea, who although of middle-class stock himself was the hero of the Cádiz unemployed.[2] This revolt was caused by the inability of local authorities to solve the unemployment question and also by the attempted disarming of the militia. This, together with exaggerated emphasis on Cádiz's part in the revolution, and the leadership of Salvochea, combined to produce the first of the revolts which, because of the desire of the Madrid Republicans to appear respectable, was disowned by them and

[1] *El amigo de los pobres* (Cádiz), 13, 30 Nov. 1868.
[2] Very little is known about this legendary figure who became a member of the Federal Directory, leader of the Cádiz canton of 1873, and a prominent early Andalusian anarchist. See Bermejo, op. cit. i. 454; Rivas, op. cit. i. 322. González Prada, *Anarquía*, Santiago de Chile, 1936, has a brief sketch of him and there is a fictionalized study of him in Blasco Ibañez's novel *La Bodega*.

petered out with few repercussions elsewhere. There were slight disturbances at Jerez and Seville on 26 December, when the militias there were disarmed, but there was no attempt to co-ordinate republican activity.[1]

If Cádiz came as a surprise, the far more serious rising at Málaga on 1 January was less unexpected. From the beginning of October Málaga had been in a state of turbulence. The Democrats secured a majority in the junta, but politics there were soon resolved into an internal conflict between moderate Democrats like the Valencian lawyer Palanca, who tried to join with the Progressives in basing their support on the reconstituted militia of the 1850's, and the radicals, backed by the clubs and extremist papers and whose strength lay in the 'Volunteers of Liberty' formed from the unemployed.

The main problem facing the junta was to solve unemployment. The municipal funds contained 42,129 *reales*, which would not go far towards paying the 8,000 who paraded before the *Ayuntamiento* expecting payment merely by virtue of being armed or partly armed. Peasants from the country, released smugglers (about a hundred who, with the abolition of tobacco duty, saw their livelihood vanish), and discontented town workers were the unruly element. In the confusion the workers at the *Industria Malagueña* attacked the owner's private house compelling him to grant a rise in wages and finally forced him to flee to Gibraltar.[2]

The factor which decided the moderate Democrats to declare themselves Federal Republicans was not so much the pressure exerted by the extremists as the assertion of the Provisional Government's power by the new Civil Governor, Sanguinetti, who arrived on 20 October and who immediately dissolved the junta and attempted to stop the demolition of convents, to protect the Church, and to purge the militia of its radical elements. By mid-November tension between the Governor and the *Ayuntamiento* had become

---

[1] *La Igualdad,* 27 Dec. 1868. F.O. 72/1207, 3 Jan. 1869, Crampton to Clarendon quoting French consul at Cádiz. Bermejo, op. cit. i. 443–6, prints letters between Caballero de Rodas, the Unionist Captain-General of Andalucía and Peralta, Military Governor of Cádiz, which show how the military were determined to suppress radicalism even without prior consent of the Government.

[2] *Actas Capitulares,* 26 Sept. 1868; *Efimérides,* 29 Sept., 18, 20, 22, 23, 27, 28 Oct., 8, 11, 14, 15 Nov. 1868.

acute. After the failure of the Democrats to find any common ground with the Progressives, who supported Sanguinetti, Palanca, leader of the moderate Democrats, joined with the radicals in signing a federal republican manifesto on 19 November. Six days later Sanguinetti resigned after the new Federal-dominated *Ayuntamiento* had flouted his authority.[1]

The arrival of Garrido in the city on 29 November, only four days after Sanguinetti had left, and his speech there violently attacking Rivero and Olózaga, clinched the republicanism of the Democrats. A great open-air meeting held at Alora, to which cheap train excursions were run, may have helped to link the urban movement with rural agitation, for, despite attempts to limit the flow from the countryside, peasants still continued to come into the city.[2] On 29 December, when it was rumoured that the Government was sending Caballero de Rodas to disarm the militia after the successful disarming of those at Cádiz, Jerez, and Seville, a further 1,500 peasants entered the city to be immediately organized by a renegade priest, Enrique Romero. On the 29th Lafuente, a hardened conspirator since his friendship with Cámara, was elected, seemingly against his will, to be in command of the militia. In the same way as the Federal leaders had been unable to control the political development in the town, so now they were unable to control the rising indignation of the militia. At a meeting in the *Ayuntamiento* on the 29th the battalion commanders were divided over whether to resist or not. Lafuente himself was in favour of negotiation but, overruled by those who favoured resistance, he put himself at the head of the rebels.[3] All attempts at a compromise between Pavía, the Captain-General, and the Federals were cut short by the arrival of the Unionist Caballero de Rodas, who stiffened the determination to resist by his demands for the militia to disarm. On 1 January fighting began and continued bitterly for three days, at the end of which only those who protested their loyalty to the Government were allowed to keep

---

[1] Ibid., 19, 25 Nov. 1868.

[2] Ibid., 29 Nov., 6 Dec. See also *La Revue politique et littéraire*, Réclus writing from Alora on 6 Dec.

[3] *Efimérides*, 30 Dec.; R. Lafuente, *Málaga y sus opresores*, Oran, 1869, p. 7; Flóres García, op. cit., p. 3.

62   *The September Revolution in the Provinces*

their arms. The Federals were disarmed and their leaders driven into exile—Lafuente for the eighth time. The loss of fifty soldiers and eighty-eight rebels killed brought home vividly to the Government the importance which the Federals laid on being allowed to keep their militia, and the alleged brutality of the troops, written up in a series of atrocity stories by Garrido, created a gulf between Federals and the Government, showing the former that organization and not merely fine words was a requisite for survival.[1]

At Valencia the Republicans gave the Government much less cause for alarm and the disarming of the militia was postponed until the rising of October 1869. There had been a nucleus of Democrats at Valencia since the early 1850's under the leadership of Guerrero, who, as a practising Catholic and landowner, was a guarantee that, provided Valencia was not faced with similar problems to Málaga, republicanism there would be moderate and not extremist. The *Renaixença* had had some influence in Valencia but the absence of a large expanding industrial and commercial class tended to limit its political repercussions. The Democrats were in a minority on the junta in which Guerrero was vice-president, but his popularity led it to elect him as Governor of the province. When the Provisional Government appointed the Progressive president of the junta, Peris y Valero, to the post, Guerrero immediately resigned and a week later, on 24 October, the junta unanimously dissolved.[2]

This junta faced similar problems as elsewhere and the unemployed were put to work on pulling down part of the city wall and demolishing convents, payment being made by wealthy citizens anxious to avoid social disturbances. Towards the end of October the harmony which had existed between Democrats and Progressives began to dissolve, notably after the visit of Orense on 20 October, when he expounded the Federals' programme and showed dissatisfaction with the candidates proposed for the *Cortes*. On 31 October the Federals held a meeting to elect their committee

[1] F.O. 72/1207, no. 13, 2 Jan. 1869, report of Málaga consul. *Efimérides*, 29 Dec.–4 Jan. 1869. Garrido, *Historia*, op. cit., vol. iii.
[2] *El Diario Mercantil*, 30 Sept., 11, 13, 22, 25, 27 Oct., 1, 6 Nov. 1868.

and a week later brought out their first paper. The sudden quickening
in republican activity was perhaps due to the re-establishment of
the monopoly of salt and tobacco and discontent with the Government's economic policy.[1] The Government was strongly criticized
for ignoring the junta's decrees and for appropriating the income
from the re-established taxes. When Garrido arrived in Valencia
on 22 November, meeting Orense on his second visit, the Federals
gave them a rousing reception complete with flags in their colours
of red, yellow, and purple, but although the Federals were to
confirm their strength in Valencia by returning all four candidates to the *Cortes*, their behaviour did not justify government
interference, and so, preserving their militia intact, Valencia remained quiescent but at the same time a potential threat to any
monarchist government.[2]

In contrast to the vague federalism of the south, implying freedom from the restrictions of centralized government and political
domination by landowners, Catalan republicanism was more
mature in outlook, more complex in structure, and more sophisticated in practice. There were a variety of reasons for this.[3] Barcelona's industrial development had been accelerating since the
introduction of steam-driven machinery in the 1830's so that by
1868 it had both a large politically conscious middle class and a
working class with a far more developed concept of solidarity than
elsewhere. Industrial and commerical interests clashed with the
prevailing trends of Madrid politics as reflected both in free-trade
policies, which seemed to threaten Barcelona's economic survival,
in the political dominance of large landowners and in the spoils
system which was less applicable to Catalonia where the preva-
lence of traditional tenure systems, like the *rabassaire*, *masovería*,
and *parailisme*, had excluded Andalusian-style *caciquismo* and had
encouraged political independence among the rural community.
The Catalans also had a particular interest in the worsening Cuban

[1] Ibid., 25 Nov., 13 Dec. 1868.
[2] *La Revue politique et littéraire*, 22 Nov. 1868.
[3] More work has been done on nineteenth-century Catalonia than on any other region.
See especially J. Vicens i Vives, *Els Catalans en el segle XIX*, part I of *Politics i industrials*,
vol. xi in the Biografies catalanes series, Barcelona, 1959. J. Carrera Pujals, *Historia política
de Cataluña en el siglo XIX*, vol. v, Barcelona, 1958.

situation as the Cuban market was of paramount importance to the Catalan economy. This was emphasized in a petition by Barcelona merchants to the *Diputación* in January 1869, urging the retention of Cuba, and by their financing of Catalan volunteers sent to Cuba.[1] These political and economic antagonisms to Madrid had helped to encourage the regional awareness already created by the *Renaixença* of the Catalan language and literature which, in the revival of the *Jochs Florals* in 1859, in historical writing from a Catalan viewpoint as in Balaguer's *Historia de Cataluña* of the same year, in the *felibrige* movement of Catalan poets and in the work of philological scholars, reflected the cultural awakening of a prosperous middle class. But the political implications of this linguistic revival should not be exaggerated, as the serious exploitation of it for political purposes did not come till the 1880's.[2]

However, it is important to keep these strands in mind when considering Catalan, and more particularly, Barcelona politics after 1868 because every political grouping tried to exploit various aspects of regionalist feeling. There were three active political groups, the Progressives, the Carlists, and the Federals. The Progressives were led by Balaguer and supported from Madrid by Madoz.[3] Both realized that without concessions to the industrialists' demands for protection the party would have no future; in this they had a certain amount of sympathy from Prim, himself a Catalan from Reus, an important industrial town, but they always had to face hostility from the free-trader intellectuals of the party who rightly argued that Figuerola's free-trade policy had had beneficial effects on the Catalan economy, which had been depressed since the financial crash of 1866.[4] Many Catalan Progressives could be characterized, like Balaguer, as 'federal monar-

---

[1] *P.P.* 1870, vol. lxiv, p. 74; Carrera Pujals, v. 347–8, 357.

[2] There is a good survey of the various currents of the *Renaixença* in J. Pabón, *Cambó*, Barcelona, 1952, pp. 140–9. For details see F. M. Tubino, *Historia del renacimiento literario en Catalonia, Valencia y Baleares*, Madrid, 1880.

[3] Letter of Màdoz to Balaguer, 17 June 1863, printed in Olivar Bertrand, *Así cayó Isabella II*, p. 326.

[4] Vicens, op. cit., p. 106. M. Pugés, *Como triunfó el proteccionismo en España*, Barcelona, 1931, discusses the whole protection issue in the nineteenth century. See especially pp. 116 et seq.

chists'; fearing the social implications of federal republicanism they wished to retain the monarchy and a strong army but with a large measure of political devolution.[1] But this was a minority wing distrusted by the party as a whole, as their treatment of Balaguer later in the *Cortes* amply revealed.

The strongest support for the Carlists in Catalonia came from the peasantry of the mountainous interior who had been adversely affected by the Liberals' disentailing of Church lands and who lacked the security of tenure enjoyed by the *rabassaire* of the coastal region.[2] Carlist promises to restore the *fueros*—especially the exemption from conscription—thrived on the resentments engendered by the Moderates' centralizing policies of the 1840's. But attempts then and later to link rural discontent with that of the towns became less realistic as the economic expansion of the manufacturing towns, Barcelona, Igualada, Manresa, Reus, Sabadell, and Tarrasa, threatened rural domestic industry and created a politically ambitious and violently anticlerical lower-middle class and a vocal industrial working class from which the Federals drew their main support. Catalan Carlism remained predominantly a rural movement located in areas where a traditional way of life was threatened by economic change.

Federal strength was based not only in the industrial towns but also in the prosperous rural areas of the Catalan littoral—Ampurdan, Tarragona, and the Ebro valley. Emphyteutic tenure, a boom in the wine trade, and a protected market in Cuba had created a thriving rural class closely linked to the towns, on which they largely depended for their economic prosperity. There was, too, an element of continuity in Catalan republicanism which was lacking in the south. The *centralista* agitation of the 1840's, the legendary Abdon Terradas, republican mayor of Figueras in 1842, the *Foc de Llers* of 1856 when republican Ampurdan had resisted O'Donnell's coup, gave them martyrs and a tradition of resistance to the central government —well exemplified in the career of the popular Tarragonese leader Xich de las Barraquetas.

[1] *Gaceta*, 14 May 1869, Balaguer's speech.
[2] Vicens, op. cit., pp. 37, 263–6, 278. Cf. V. Almirall, *Las Leyes forales y el Carlismo*,

The main elements of Barcelona republicanism consisted of professional men resenting control and influence from Madrid, a lower-middle class seriously affected by the financial crash of 1866, and the textile workers who since 1857 (except for a brief period in 1864–6) had been denied the right of association. Although the leadership as elsewhere was largely in the hands of professional men there was also a working-class element which was lacking in both Madrid and Andalusia.[1] The textile operatives were the most highly organized section of Spanish labour: their prevalent attitude in the 1860's and early 1870's being one of democratic reformism.[2] Even the Catalan Workers' *Ateneo* tended to be under Progressive influence in the 1860's in contrast to the strong socialist influence in the Madrid *Fomento de las Artes*. Although there had been violent revolutionary outbursts at times of economic depression—in 1835, 1844, and during 1854–6—the textile workers' political attitudes were largely determined by an almost uninterrupted boom after the recovery of the cotton industry in the mid-1860's which reached a climax during the Franco-Prussian war and continued into the 1880's. With favourable economic circumstances they were concerned to increase wages, reduce working hours, and improve labour conditions—demands which were later to be incorporated into the Federals' social programme. After the September Revolution they were reorganized in the amalgamated union the *Tres Clases de Vapor* and in October the basis for the wider co-operation of workers was laid with the founding of the *Centro Federal de las Sociedades Obreras* which claimed the support of 195 workers' societies throughout Spain, of which 38 were in Barcelona. In December representatives of 61 of these societies in Catalonia declared their support for the Federals and with the acceptance in January 1869 by the Barcelona Federal election committee of Pablo Alsina, their nominee

Barcelona, n.d. Considerable research is needed before the precise relationship between economic factors and Catalan Carlism can be established.

[1] *El Federalista*, 29 Feb. 1869, gives an occupational analysis of candidates in the Federal committee election: 1 silversmith, 3 writers, 2 lawyers, 1 musician, 3 manual workers, 3 business men, 1 printer, 2 doctors, 2 painters, 1 dockyard worker, 1 foreman, and 1 tailor.

[2] M. Reventós, *Els moviments socials a Barcelona durant el segle XIX*, Barcelona, 1925; C. Martí, *Los orígenes del anarquismo en Barcelona*, Barcelona, 1959. The latter is a useful corrective to Reventós.

for the *Cortes*, the Federals aligned themselves with the newly organized force of working-class opinion.[1]

This mass support gave Barcelona republicanism a stability and strength in marked contrast to that of either Madrid or the south. The close relationship between the professional middle class and workers was merely a continuation in political form of the firm association which had sprung up in the 1840's and 1850's when surplus working-class energy had been canalized into educational and cultural activity, either in the workers' *Ateneo* or in Clavé's choirs. In these, Democrat intellectuals like the Cabetian Monturiol, the atheist doctor Suñer y Capdevila, and the writers Robert and Altadill had acted as mentors to workers denied a political outlet. Hence by 1868 not only were there strong links between the two groups but also a nucleus of literate workers who were ready to take an active part in politics. The best evidence of the strength of this relationship was the difficulty experienced by the International later in trying to win over the textile workers. It seems probable that migrant labour proved the most susceptible to Internationalist influence and to Bakuninist ideas of abstention from political activity—as in 1873 when unsettled rural conditions during the Carlist war speeded up migration to the towns.

To these three main political groupings must be added another group which cannot be easily classified—the big industrialists. No single party represented their interests; they must be seen rather as a pressure group trying to use each party for their own purposes. There was, in fact, a strong tendency for them to withdraw from politics altogether. Bosch y Labrus, one of their leading spokesmen, said in a speech in the *Ateneo Catalán* that economic rather than moral and political measures were needed to solve the problem of increasing national production.[2] To achieve this the *Fomento de la Producción Nacional* had been founded at the end of 1868 with its own paper *El Protector del Pueblo*. A *Liga Proteccionista* with branches in other towns was later set up so as to escape the

[1] Roure, op. cit. ii. 177. Lorenzo, op. cit., p. 34, gives a hostile picture of Alsina, who exemplified the old associationist tradition of the Catalan workers in contrast to the new revolutionary wing.

[2] P. Bosch y Labrus, *Escritos y Discursos*, Barcelona, 1929, xii. 4. *El Protector del Pueblo* first appeared on 11 Feb. 1869.

accusation of particularism. The *Fomento* rather than any political party represented the interests of the Catalan industrialists. Symbolic of the wider support given to the protectionist cause was the public embrace of Madoz and Almirall at a demonstration staged by the *Fomento* on 21 March at which the workers' *Centro Federal* were also present, carrying banners calling for protection and the Federal Republic.[1] A month later Alsina presented a petition in the *Cortes* signed by 120,000 workers calling for protection. But neither the Progressives nor the Federals could be relied on by the industrialists; the Progressives because of their free-trading sympathies; the Federals because of a free-trade wing and also because of their unequivocal support for slavery abolition and autonomy for the Antilles. There remained the possibility of Unionist support, but it was here that division was most marked. *El Diario*, the leading conservative Barcelona paper and generally reflecting the industrialists' viewpoint, was edited by the Unionist Mañé y Flaquer whose views on the Cuban problem were diametrically opposed to those of the industrialists, besides which the Unionists, finding much of their support among the landowners, had little or nothing in common with the industrialists except the desire to preserve the 'integrity of the territory'.[2] It was when the Federals showed themselves unable to preserve order and defeat the Carlist menace which began to affect production in 1873, that the industrialists returned to political activity as ardent Alphonsists.

Catalan regional feeling, whether rooted in culture, economics, or politics, was not the preserve of any one political party or social group. But it was the Federals who were the most effective in canalizing this feeling into specifically political channels. In this process the wealthy lawyer Valentín Almirall played a prominent part.[3] It was he rather than Tutau—whose reputation in 1868 as a

---

[1] *El Protector del Pueblo*, 22 Mar. 1869—Almirall spoke in Catalan. *La Alianza de los Pueblos*, 21 Apr. 1869. Cf. Roure, op. cit. ii. 133–45.

[2] The economic arguments are summarized in Carrera Pujal, op. cit., ch. viii. Mañé's views on Cuba are in *El Diario*, 15 Aug. 1869. For Mañé see G. Graell, *Mañé y Flaquer*, Barcelona, 1903. J. Maragall, *Obres completas*, Barcelona, 1930, pp. 119–91. Two industrialists' viewpoints on Cuba were Guell y Ferrer, *Rebelión Cubana*, Barcelona, 1871, and 'El Maquiavelismo cubano' by Puig y Llagostera in *El Imparcial*, 19 Oct. 1869.

[3] J. Roca y Roca, *Valentín Almirall*, Barcelona, 1915. His Catalanist interests were first roused through his friendship with the founder of the Catalan theatre, Federico Soler.

local politician rated him as the most likely leader—who emerged as the more forceful personality. Tutau became a deputy in 1869 but Almirall did not accept a candidature until 1873 and devoted all his energies to building up republicanism in Barcelona and Catalonia. He was in Roure's phrase the 'soul and oracle of federalism in Barcelona' and it was he who organized the Pact of Tortosa of May 1869 which gave the impetus to the national organization of the Federal party.

Nevertheless it was Tutau, a business man who in 1854 had been one of the district mayors of the city and an old member of the Terradas group, who first assumed control and who organized the street demonstrations of early October after Orense's programme for a Federal Republic had been hailed as the panacea for Catalan grievances. He was elected vice-president of the junta, in which he was supported by only two other Democrats, Clavé and Rubaudonadeu.[1] Hence they were unable to prevent the junta from expressing its approval of Rivero's action in handing over power to Serrano. But outraged republican feeling forced the junta to protest to Madrid when Prim did not include any Democrats in the Government on 8 October. When, on the 18th, the Madrid junta announced its intention of dissolving and invited others to do the same, Barcelona's reply was to refuse and to dispatch Tutau to Madrid to protest. This protest was useless as no other junta was willing to back it up.[2] On the 28th, therefore, the junta dissolved itself. In spite of their numerical strength the Federals had been unable to secure more than three members on the junta and it was only street demonstrations which had shown the extent of republican feeling of which Dumas *fils* was an enthusiastic witness. It was the attitude of the majority of the junta to street demonstrations on the 15th and lukewarmness in pressing for a central junta which caused Clavé and Rubaudonadeu first to resign from the junta and then to welcome its dissolution.[3] Apart

---

[1] *Boletín oficial*, op. cit., 1, 2 Oct. 1868. Three Democrats were elected to the *Diputación Provincial* and three to the *Ayuntamiento*. Orense had been the first person to call for a Federal Republic—at Figueras and Gerona at the end of September. He then visited Barcelona.

[2] See *El Diario Mercantil*, 23 Oct. 1868, for strong Valencian disapproval; Roure, op. cit., pp. 123–41.

[3] *La Vanguardia*, 30 Oct. 1868.

from the attitude to the Madrid Junta, the junta's programme had been a popular one, but the failure of Tutau's commission gave added force to federal propaganda.

The Federals were quick to exploit the new press freedom. Whereas Madrid had to wait until November for its first republican paper, in Barcelona three had already appeared before the end of October with another to follow soon in November.[1] Very little coherent policy was expressed in these early papers. It was not until the founding of Almirall's *El Estado catalán* in July 1869 that it is possible to talk of an official mouthpiece of the Barcelona Federals. At this time little attempt was made to clarify the federal idea. The main purpose was to exploit the misuse of the Madrid Junta's powers in overruling the provincial juntas. By playing on this and exaggerating the weak attitude of the Barcelona Junta the Federals were able to rally opinion in the municipal elections in December. The results of 18 December showed how little the revolutionary institutions represented popular feeling. Out of 47,000 people who voted in Barcelona only 17,000 voted for monarchists. This overwhelming victory was attributed by Roure to the Federals' better voting discipline and to the absence of government pressure through over-optimism, though he considered that the majority would have been even greater had more workers been able to get to the polls.[2] The Federals' voting strength was about 30,000, exactly twice that of Madrid with a bigger population. On the other hand, the poll for their committee in Barcelona was far lower than in the capital, for out of a nominal strength of 30,000 only 2,562 voted. This low figure revealed a serious rift. Clavé, in his paper, accused the organizers of rigging the elections so as to secure men who would be willing to accept the decrees of Madrid.[3] He was suspicious of Tutau whom he believed responsible for the Federals' weakness on the junta, and accused him of having imposed his candidates on the committee without first consulting the party. He also attacked the choice of

---

[1] *El Federalista*, directed by Almirall, first appeared on 24 Oct. 1868, in July 1869 it became *El Estado catalán*. *El Cohete* appeared on 1 Oct. *La Vanguardia* on 10 Oct. was Clavé's paper. *La Alianza de los Pueblos* on 23 Nov. 1868 stressed the international aspect of republicanism and had a column written in French.

[2] Roure, op. cit., pp. 182-6.   [3] *La Vanguardia*, 4, 22 Nov. 1868.

candidates made by the electoral committee for the *Cortes* elections. Until Clavé's paper closed down it consisted of little but violent attacks on the new committee.[1] Clavé represented the extreme wing of republican opinion and although Federal successes in the municipal elections took much of the force out of his criticisms he was a significant figure in this early period as his popularity among the working class and his championship of their claims to be fully represented on the committee helped to bring them into the orbit of republican politics.[2] Whatever Clavé's faults they were due to a sincere desire to better the condition of the working class. This sincerity marked him off from another group of republican sympathizers who appeared in Barcelona in these early months—associated with the name of an ex-Carlist sergeant Viralta, the president of one of the many political clubs which sprang up at the end of 1868. Viralta was a political opportunist and a conspirator who still thought in terms of secret societies rather than open propaganda.[3] It was he who later founded *El Tiro nacional*, which developed into a secret society within the Federal movement. From an early stage, therefore, any Federal leadership in Catalonia had to take into account a body of professional conspirators whose aim 'the emancipation of the Fourth Estate' was merely an opportunist phrase to attract to themselves desperadoes and social misfits.

The predominance of the Federals in Barcelona was repeated throughout most of Catalonia. At the national elections in January, out of thirty-five deputies returned twenty were Federals. In Barcelona itself they won all six seats. Without any clear-cut economic or social programme they had achieved an astonishing success. A new party, drawing its strength from the professional classes, the lower-middle class, and the workers had seized the initiative in the most politically and economically advanced city in Spain. Conscious of their power, they were willing to wait for developments in the *Cortes*. How long they would be able to

---

[1] Ibid., 15, 29 Jan. 1869.
[2] Ibid., 7 Nov. 1868: 'El partido republicano y los obreros.' Roure, op. cit., pp. 76 et seq.
[3] Bermejo, op. cit. i. 525; Roure, op. cit., p. 231. The Barcelona Federals frowned on Viralta's activities, such as his attempt to stage a rising on the night of 24–25 Feb. 1869. Pierrard was, significantly, made honorary president of Viralta's club in Feb. 1869.

retain their unity and cohesion would depend on the quality of their local leaders. By the beginning of 1869 Almirall was already the most prominent figure of Barcelona republicanism and the movement's future in Catalonia largely lay with him.

By the beginning of 1869 federal republicanism had taken root in the peripheral towns of the Mediterranean coastline. But because of differing conditions and varying motives it lacked cohesion and unity. The need in 1869 was to unify disparate and scattered forces. For this the movement needed leadership, a unifying belief, and a programme which would turn it from a group of agitators bound together only by resentment and disillusion into an organized political party. How did the preconceptions of their leaders, their views on revolution and on society, their ideas on organization, and the technique of propaganda affect the subsequent course of the movement's history?

4

Federal Republican Ideology

THE remarkably quick growth of the federal republican idea was due mainly to the efficient propaganda of a handful of publicists, especially Garrido, Orense, and Castelar, who, exploiting the disillusion of October, popularized federalism as the solution to endemic misgovernment.[1] The junta tradition, the stirring of regional aspirations, and the absence of an obvious successor to Isabella, assured them of wide support but, in a country where only 30 per cent. were literate and with a low level of political consciousness, their efficacy was due more to their playing on popular passions and prejudices than to constructive policies and it was only in the course of debates in the *Cortes*, in press polemics, and in club discussions that clearer ideas were formulated. Even so, republicanism never represented a homogeneous and coherent body of doctrine, but incorporated all the various strivings which had been frustrated by earlier misgovernment. A few basic concepts were accepted by the vast majority of Spanish republicans but there was also a mass of ancillary aims and ambitions which tended to confuse the main issues and to involve republicanism in a series of contradictions which it never succeeded in resolving. These aims stemmed from their leaders' preconceptions about the nature of federal republicanism and if an analysis of republican ideology concentrates on the intellectuals it is because the leadership of the movement remained largely in their hands and it was from them that Spanish republicanism took its shape.

The basic concepts were simple, consisting of the belief that the 'republic' was the antithesis to monarchy, that it was inseparable

---

[1] The best account of early republican propaganda is in the articles of Reclus in the *Revue politique et littéraire*, Nov. 1868 to Jan. 1869. Cf. Lauser, *Geschichte Spaniens*, i. 83 et seq. Lauser was the Madrid correspondent of the *Neue Freie Presse*; cf. also his *Aus Spaniens Gegenwart*, Leipzig, 1872.

from decentralization and that it was completely secular. Without adhering to these three dogmas it was impossible to be a Federal Republican.

Monarchy and equality were antinomies; a democratic monarchy was a contradiction in terms, for popular sovereignty could not be surrendered into the hands of an hereditary ruler. It was an irrational survival from the past, buttressing authoritarian ideas and resting for its support on that 'second aristocracy' of political and financial speculators who were replacing the old landed aristocracy as the governing class. The doctrinaire element in republican thought was often coloured by biological analogy in which the form of government determined the degree of liberty which a society enjoyed. When Castelar[1] declared, 'the essential question consists in form because form and essence are inseparable as are animated life and the organism', he marked them off from other political groups. To both Progressives and Unionists the personality of Isabella was the main obstacle to good government. Once she was removed, and with her the 'traditional obstacles'—the pernicious influence of a clerically dominated court—good government could follow. They did not, therefore, make the revolution against the monarchical principle but against a monarchy where the influence of the *camarilla* had gradually squeezed them from power. The attitude of the Democrats towards monarchy, on the other hand, was entirely opportunist; they believed the form of government was immaterial to the enjoyment of political liberty, which could be assured equally well under monarchies or republics. Their opposition to republicanism in 1868 may be attributed both to personal factors and to a genuine belief that the rigid application of doctrinaire federalism to a politically immature country could only lead to anarchy.[2]

The fundamental tenet of Spanish republicanism, with the exception of a very small group of Unitarians, led by García Ruiz, director of *El Pueblo*, was that monarchy was synonymous with political and administrative centralization which they believed, as a self-evident historical truth, had been responsible for all Spanish

---

[1] Castelar, *Discursos políticos dentro y fuera del Parlamento*, Madrid, 1873, p. 319.
[2] Echegaray, *Recuerdos*, iii. 191, 265. Cf. Rivero's letter above, p. 25, n. 3.

misfortunes since the accession of Charles I. The Federals adopted
and extended the romantic Liberal interpretation of Spanish history
since 1500 as a series of regionalist risings against the expansion of
tyrannical royal power. They identified themselves historically
with the *Comuneros*, the *Germanías*, the defenders of the Liberties
of Aragón against Philip II and those of Catalonia against Olivares
and Philip V.[1] The need for some measure of decentralization was
widely recognized; the Federals were not alone in their plea for
political devolution. Both Progressives and Democrats talked of
this but in both cases the attributes of local government were to
be decided by the central power and hence could be revoked at
will.[2] The Progressive Balaguer could argue for a democratic
decentralizing monarchy, the Independent Romani y Puigdengolas
for a federal monarchy, but the motives in one case were primarily
cultural and in the other determined by keeping catholicism as the
binding link in the federal state.[3] Yet a third possibility was reversion to a 'traditional monarchy' in the Carlist line in which the
Catholic Church, assisted by a revived Inquisition, would be the
unifying factor, thus allowing a greater measure of regional devolution. This Carlist solution was the rural equivalent of urban
federal republicanism and was rooted in a contented peasantry
in Navarre and the Basque Provinces, though the pretender Don
Carlos tried to extend its appeal to the rest of Spain, promising, as
did the Federals, to clean up the administration and to suppress
inequality of privileges between provinces.[4] The originality of the
Federals' contribution lay in their tacit acceptance of Pi's view that
in an 'age of doubt' like the nineteenth century religion was no
longer a cohesive social force and must be replaced by a new
principle sanctified by modern philosophy and science.[5] It was

[1] M. Fernández Herrero, *Historia de las Germanías de Valencia*, Madrid, 1870.
[2] F. M. Tubino, *Patria y Federalismo*, Seville, pp. 124–5.
[3] F. Romani y Puigdengolas, *El Federalismo en España*, Barcelona, 1869; and 'A los
demócratas federales de Igualada', 1 Dec. 1868. Cf. Mañe y Flaquer, *La República federativa*,
Barcelona, 1869.
[4] R. Oyarzún, *Historia del Carlismo*, Madrid, 1939, pp. 308–13, quoting Don Carlos's
letter to Don Alfonso; L. M. Llauder, *El Desenlace de la Revolución Española*, Barcelona,
1869. The fiery religious spirit of Carlism is well conveyed in V. Manterola, *El Espíritu
carlista*, Madrid, 1871, and *Don Carlos o el Petroleo*, Madrid, 1871.
[5] *Enciclopedia republicano federal*, edited by Díaz Quintero, Madrid, 1872, *passim*.

argued that the federal principle was not only eminently suitable to Spanish conditions but was also a logical deduction from purely rational premises.

In the 'republic' the Catholic Church was to be reduced to the level of an ordinary association and shorn of all its privileges. When, in the republican *Cortes* of 1873, Pi announced that the clergy could be tried in civil courts like any common criminal, he was enthusiastically cheered. Both education and the conduct of policy must be divorced from religious considerations. An edge of bitterness was given to this anticlericalism after the neo-Catholic reaction of the 1860's and the apparent subordination of foreign and domestic policy to the interests of the Church. But the formulation of republican anticlericalism was also to be traced to the prevailing cult of positivism and the exaggerated claims made for science by their intellectuals. Influenced by this, the Federals consistently underestimated the resilience of Carlism, attributing it only to political and economic factors and underestimating the genuine religious fervour which gave the movement much of its dynamism.[1]

These three elements provided the basis on which a republican policy could be built, but they were stock radical responses and required considerable elaboration before a positive political programme would emerge. The problem inherent from the beginning in republican policy-making was how to prevent their supporters from forcing the movement into the mould of traditional Spanish politics. Although the belief that universal suffrage might bring them into power accounted for much early enthusiasm, it was soon made clear that this was a delusion and that the aim of the republican leaders was to break the spoils system by creating a 'republic for all'. By depriving themselves of one of the main incentives for attracting supporters they were faced with a choice of either trying to become a 'party' by appealing to specific interests and basing themselves on the support of a homogeneous class or of being a 'movement' and so widening their programme as to appeal to as broad a section of the country as possible. The failure to resolve

[1] *La Igualdad*, 6 July 1869, 'El fiasco carlista', 8 Sept. 1871, 'La muerte del carlismo'; Orense, *Los Fueros*, Madrid, 1869, p. 13.

the conflict between a 'party' and a 'movement' concept of republicanism was a major cause of vacillation and weakness.

In the 1860's Pi had favoured the 'party' concept, arguing for winning over the rural and urban masses by promise of tangible economic and social reforms. His failure to persuade the Democrats then, convinced him that it was not practical politics, a conviction which was reinforced after republican failure at the polls in January 1869 to secure more than sixty-nine seats, when it was clear that the obvious backwardness of the masses and the continued domination of the *caciques* in rural areas argued for a policy of conciliation between 'individualists' and 'socialists' so as to unite all shades of republican opinion on as wide a programme as possible. By accepting this 'movement' concept Pi reflected the peculiar composition of federal republican leadership, its weaknesses and its limitations. It was a concept which came to rely more and more on those myths which were part of the luggage of every nineteenth-century republican—the emphasis on 'national regeneration', on the solidarity of international republicanism, on false analogies with the United States and Switzerland, and for the Spaniards, on Iberian Union. These myths helped to cover irresolution in domestic politics over the social question, vacillation on economic issues and reluctance to face up to the implications of the lack of political experience among their supporters, and of the adherence of political adventurers to the movement. At the same time they revealed the lack of a firm basis in any particular social class and the domination of the leadership by intellectuals. Their ideas on politics were determined by preconceptions about the nature of historical development, but the failure of their predictions tended to discredit intellectual leadership at an early date and helped to open the way for a more traditional approach to political action. Federal republicanism owed its initial expansion to instinctive reactions to a revolutionary situation, but as soon as it became a political force the intellectuals started to impose European categories on this particularly Spanish phenomenon and, by fitting it into an abstract intellectual scheme, failed to understand the change in the balance of forces inside the movement or even to understand the motives behind peoples' adherence to it.

Who were the men who determined republican policy and what were the presuppositions on which it was based? The federal republican leaders were drawn from those who wished for complete political and, in rarer cases, complete social change. They were professional men, lawyers, doctors, university lecturers, journalists, writers, and school teachers, with a sprinkling of small business men. They were drawn mainly from the middle and lower-middle class and the two most numerous groups were the lawyers and the writer-journalists. The study of law had always been a training for politics and a legal practice could easily be combined with a political career. Pi, Figueras, Palanca, Sorní, Maisonnave, Carvajal, to mention only a few, ran a lawyer's *bufete* at the same time as they were active politicians. Pi himself had been persuaded to enter the law by his friend Figueras in 1856—enabling him both to earn a living and to make useful contacts such as the Marqués de Pallarés, who financed some of the Democrats' early activities. Over a third of the university population in 1868 were studying law, and federalism with its web of contracts must have had a considerable attraction for the legal mind.[1]

Only second in importance to the lawyers were the aspiring writers and journalists. Political centralization had its cultural counterpart. Cultural stagnation in the provinces drove many aspiring writers, as it had Pi in 1847, to Madrid. Once there, the small literate public made a living difficult to obtain and the impecunious writer was soon tempted to put his talents at the service of a political party. Even Valera once confessed that he had never earned enough by literature to keep himself for six months and what he did earn came almost entirely from political journalism.[2] Political involvement was further caused by the repressive influence of the Church, shown by its condemnation of Pi's *Historia de la Pintura* in 1851, and Roque Barcia's *Progreso y Cristianidad* in 1861, but this influence is seen most clearly in the factors leading

---

[1] Fermín Caballero, *Reseña estadística de España*, Madrid, 1868, p. 25. The total university population in 1868 was 9,704. Of these 3,406 were reading law, 2,040 letters, 1,841 medicine, 508 pharmacy, 288 theology. Madrid had 4,194 students, Barcelona 1,365, and Seville 887. The Ministers of the Republic in 1873 included 2 professors, 2 business men, 2 doctors, 1 schoolmaster, 2 soldiers, and 14 lawyers.

[2] J. Valera, *Disertaciones y juicios literarios*, Madrid, 1890, p. 269.

to the emergence of Madrid University as a breeding-ground of political radicalism and religious heterodoxy from the late 1850's. Castelar, professor of history since 1857, had used his neo-Hegelian lecture courses to popularize the idea of progress and the inevitability of revolution at the same time as Krausist infiltration under Sanz del Río, who became professor of the history of philosophy in 1854, threatened religious orthodoxy. This dual threat to the established order prompted the neo-Catholics in the 1860's, and particularly after the 1864 Syllabus of Errors, to agitate for stricter control over the political and religious opinions of professors. The threat to their freedom of expression forced non-political Krausists into active politics.[1] Their participation in political discussion brought a moralistic idealizing element into Spanish politics. Canalejas declared in 1861 that politics must be based on rigorous moral principles, and the foundation of a new review, *La Revista Ibérica*, in that year to fulfil this need was evidence of the reaction against the philosophical influences of French eclecticism against which Sanz del Río had railed in the 1840's, and which, according to Canalejas, had been responsible for 'corrupting Latin Europe by encouraging opportunist politics without rigorous principles or superior morality'.[2]

In reacting against French influence intellectuals were echoing popular feeling, but German thought suited the radicals' purpose for a number of reasons. Strauss and Feuerbach fostered a rationalist criticism of catholicism; Krausist moralism gave a criterion for judging 'immoral' doctrinaire Liberal political thought, its panentheism provided a religious alternative to catholicism, and its legal implications a criticism of the whole legal structure. But above all Krausism with its doctrine of *armonismo* provided an all-embracing ideology, making it a potent force for moral regeneration.[3] Although the Krausists did not have any specific political affiliations, many of them saw republicanism as a vehicle for

[1] P. Jobit, *Les Éducateurs de l'Espagne moderne*, Paris, 1936, i. 48–53. For the Krausists see López Morillas, *El Krausismo Español*, Mexico, 1956; J. B. Trend, *The Origins of Modern Spain*, Cambridge, 1934.

[2] *La Revista ibérica*, 15 Oct. 1861. Cf. Castelar's *Semblanza* on Cousin, Madrid, 1871.

[3] Jobit, op. cit., ch. v; López Morillas, op. cit., pp. 142–63. For their organic theory of politics see Giner de los Ríos, 'La Política antigua y la Política nueva' in *Obras completas*, vol. v, Madrid, 1921.

imposing reforms on the country. They never enjoyed wide popularity in the movement, as the career of Salmerón showed, and their terminology restricted their audience, but they were important as a pressure group in championing women's education, slavery abolition, legal and penal reform, while some able republican journalists such as Ruiz Chamorro and Manuel de la Revilla were drawn from Salmerón's Krausist students at the university.

Hegelianism was more important as a direct intellectual influence because of its easier political application.[1] Both Pi and Castelar applied Hegelian historicism to their criticisms of Spanish politics in the 1860's, combining it, in the case of Pi, with the views of Comte and Proudhon in order to foster belief in the inevitability of revolution. Because of their lack of influence in the Army, of any following outside certain areas, and because of governmental repression, the Democrats had tended to over-exaggerate the power and influence of ideas. Although they had played little part in the revolution they saw it as the natural climax to a lifetime's agitation and, more important, as confirmation of their theories about the inevitability of historical processes—as Castelar expressed it:[2] 'Revolutions do not come when an individual wishes them, nor when a party wishes them. . . . they are forged, like lightning, in the laboratory of the Universe, revolutions are in the spirit of the century.' According to him two elements had made the revolution of 1868, Force and Ideas; the Force was popular and military, the Ideas were republican. The view that 'ideas' had played the main part in overthrowing Isabella seemed to find confirmation in the ease and bloodlessness with which this had succeeded.[3] Now, it was argued, with the assurance of basic liberties nothing could prevent a republican victory: 'The republican idea has planted itself. That idea has conquered intellects by

---

[1] M. Menéndez y Pelayo, *La Historia de los Heterodoxos Españoles*, iv. 353–8 (vol. xl of *Obras completas*, Madrid, 1948).

[2] Castelar, *Discursos*, speech at Alicante 18 Sept. 1872.

[3] Régnault, op. cit., letter of 29 Sept. 1868, contrasted the bloodlessness of Spanish revolutions to those of the French. Cf. the popular rhyme quoted in Rubio, op. cit. ii. 458:

> Ni un solo crimen empaña
> Nuestra gran Revolución.
> Ser libres sin un borrón
> No se hace mas que en España.

its own logical force.' And again later:[1] 'The law of necessity is a draconian law; what is necessary is inevitable and unavoidable. The federal republic comes imposed by necessity.' The cult of ideas was reflected in many aspects of republican ideology—not only in the myth of the permanency of revolution but also in the view that revolutions not inspired by the force of ideas inevitably ended in dictatorship.[2] There was also an undercurrent of fatalism which could be traced to pantheistic tendencies in the thought of both Pi and Castelar encouraging the belief that the individual had no responsibility for his ideas:[3] 'There is really no responsibility for ideas: each man obeys the voice of his own conscience and remains a slave of that voice which, to a certain extent, is divine.'

The first disillusion came with the collapse of the juntas and Rivero's 'betrayal', but greater than this was the shattering of the dream of universal suffrage and association and the recognition that these alone were insufficient to secure a republican victory. When, as a natural corollary to low republican returns at the elections in January 1869, they were unable to affect the course of debates in the *Cortes* there was a revival of another republican idea—that of spontaneous revolution generated and sustained by popular enthusiasm and the reassertion of the revolutionary tradition which had already found expression in the Málaga and Cádiz revolts. All the presuppositions of Mazzinian republicanism, which had been largely discredited after 1848 in Italy, remained popular currency among Spanish Republicans. The lessons of the failures of 1848 were lost on Spanish radicals, who clung to their belief in spontaneous revolution. The naïve faith in popular enthusiasm was accompanied by the belief that democracy was not a party but the expression of the generating idea of progress and that to struggle against it was to struggle against destiny. These attitudes led to a reluctance in admitting the need for strict organization, centralized leadership, or even for the forming of policies to win over supporters. Much of the idea of spontaneous revolution had been encouraged by intellectual theorizing, but once the

[1] *La Igualdad*, 1 Jan. 1869, 14 May 1870, 'Querer es poder'.
[2] *El Combate*, 1 Nov. 1870.
[3] *Gaceta*, 15 July 1869, Castelar's speech. Cf. Pi, *La Igualdad*, 26 May 1870, 'El Soldado y el Hombre-Humanidad'.

intellectuals had been proved wrong at the beginning of 1869 and the Republicans emerged as a mere minority opposition group, the idea of spontaneity was used as an argument against control of the party by intellectuals:[1]

At times of crisis the people have a superior instinct, which is the logic of its honest heart and excels in its ability and profound morality the judgment of the intellectual who only sees life through his books and only represents humanity with the abstraction of a geometrical problem.

Central to republican belief was the assumption, which none of the leaders did anything to dispel in the early days, that the political interests of the radical middle class were identical with those of the mass of the people. This assumption was valid so long as the working masses were forbidden the right of association and the radicals were excluded from the franchise or not allowed freedom of expression. Before 1868 the two groups complemented each other, the form of their co-operation usually being educational activity. But after 1868 identity of interests broke down as the workers with the right of association could reject the radicals' leadership if they were not offered tangible social and economic benefits. For the majority of Republicans, however, the myth persisted; they continued to see identity of interests where these no longer existed. This was the significance of the introduction of the International into Spain at the end of 1868. Just at the moment when the radicals thought they were coming into their heritage, the workers were offered the alternative of Bakuninist doctrines which, in scorning politics, were drawing a logical deduction from the corruption of parliamentary life. The majority of Republicans, however, continued to nurture themselves on the illusion that in the ultimate instance an appeal to the barricades would rally the masses and bring them into power. Only gradually did a few become aware that mass support could not be taken for granted. Faced with this situation a possible policy would have been to contract out of a 'movement' concept by drawing up a social programme radical enough to offer a

[1] *La Igualdad*, 21 Oct. 1872.

practical alternative to the unrealistic promises of the Bakuninists
—such a policy in fact as advocated by Lafargue when he arrived
in Spain as Marx's emissary at the end of 1871. But this was exactly
what the Republicans were precluded from doing by virtue of
their social origins and their preconceptions about social organization.

The social views of the Democrats and the Republicans of the
1860's and 1870's were directly influenced by the social romanticism
of the 1840's in France. The time-lag between France and Spain
is best illustrated by the way in which the stock reading matter
among Spanish Republicans was Eugène Sue and his Spanish
imitators, the early Hugo, Lamartine, and Lamennais.[1] Moral
regeneration was still considered a necessary antecedent to political
action and it was the duty of the intellectuals to undertake their
preparatory task 'in the same spirit', according to one writer,[2] 'as
Jesus sought his disciples among the poor and ignorant fishermen
on the beaches of Tiberias'. It was in such a spirit that the *Centro
de Lectura* at Reus was founded by Democrats in the early 1860's,
where workers were to be taught morality and good habits,
where gambling was condemned and where harmony between
capital and labour was preached, and where, in 1863, the audience
wept as Castelar intoned a 'hymn to the liberty of oppressed
people holding out to them the hope of redemption'.[3] This
lachrymose religiosity, reminiscent of Lamennais, was particularly
marked among those who had been influenced by Castelar, but
it was an attitude shared by others as well who believed that
Republicans were propounding a new religion of love and returning to the moral precepts of Christ Himself. Proudhon had described Christ as a 'moraliste, réformateur social, justicier en un
mot'.[4] The atheist Clavé described Christ as 'that worthy apostle

[1] Sue enjoyed immediate popularity in Spain. Between 1843 and 1845 there were twelve
editions of *Les Mystères de Paris*. The Federal Altadill wrote his own version *Los Misterios
de Barcelona*, Barcelona, 1862. The reading habits have been deduced from the frequency of
advertisements, the stories serialized in their press, and the influences reflected in their
articles.
[2] Güell y Mercader, *Cosas de Reus*, Reus, n.d., p. 127.
[3] Ibid., p. 86. Cf. Lamartine, addressing the *Athenée ouvrière* at Marseilles in 1847,
H. Guillemin, *Lamartine et la question sociale*, Paris, 1946, pp. 210–17.
[4] Dolléans, op. cit., p. 466. Cf. Clavé in *La Vanguardia*, 25 Dec. 1868; Paul y Angulo,

of democracy', Paul y Angulo called him 'that great socialist', and
the rationalist Garrido during the debate on the International in
the *Cortes* in 1871 described Internationalist agents as 'new Jesus
Christs who wish to redeem the world'. In the same way, for the
Portuguese republican Antero de Quental, 'the Revolution was
nothing but the Christianity of the modern world'. These were the
sentiments of men who regarded republicanism as a selfless movement of redemption, like the writer at Cádiz referring to the
rising of December:[1] 'If the man of God was crucified on Golgotha
to redeem the human race, the heroic people of Cádiz were crucified also on that memorable and imperishable day of December,
to redeem humanity in the nineteenth century.'

In considering this religion of humanity the influence of
Castelar's oratory must not be underestimated. Florid and rhetorical, he was the greatest orator in an age of parliamentary eloquence.
Octavio Picon, one of his pupils, wrote:[2] 'From the time when
I heard him I have always seen History through the prism with
which he made me see it on that first day—as the march of humanity
guided by progress towards the still distant promised lands of
liberty and justice.' Even foreigners unaccustomed to the flights
of Spanish oratory had to admit the compulsion of his style. The
'nightingale of democracy', as Clavé called him, symbolized the
opposite facet to Pi's severely rationalist and unemotional approach
to political problems and it was primarily for this reason that
Castelar rather than Pi occupied the front of the republican stage
in 1868 and 1869. Vain, fecund, and exuberant, Castelar's oratory
required little intellectual effort from his listeners—any uncer-
tainty, as Valera scornfully noted, was hidden by the vagueness
and splendour of his metaphors. Castelar was in the direct tradition of utopian republicanism, finding his heroes in the pre-1848
era. Lamartine, Quinet, Michelet, and Victor Hugo were his
favourites. He fired the imagination of university youth and set
the fashion for the republican writer as the *cantor del pueblo*, self-
consciously following in the tradition of Byron, Béranger, and

Verdades revolucionarios, Madrid, 1872, p. 1; Garrido, *La Legalidad de la Internacional*,
Madrid, 1871.
  [1] *El Pacto federal* (Cádiz), 4 July 1869.
  [2] Jarnés, op. cit., p. 86.

most of all Victor Hugo, 'the great poet who suffers exile for liberty and is sacrificed in serving the cause of the people'.[1] A writer from Cádiz, Castelar's home town, gives us a clear insight into the Castelarian cult which grew up rapidly after the September Revolution. Describing him as a descendant of Christ, he wrote:[2] 'Always when humanity faces a crisis, Providence gives life to a privileged being who understands what the multitude does not, who has greater power, greater intelligence, more faith, more hope and more love than the remainder of society.' After the cynicism of doctrinaire liberalism and the glacial indifference of materialism, Grimaldi saw Castelar following in the steps of Lamartine, releasing 'the springs of emotion and love'. To Republicans like Grimaldi, as to some early Jacobins, theirs was a religious movement and could only be described in religious terms.

The humanitarianism which sprang from this attitude crystallized in their desire to abolish slavery (which they shared with the Democrats), their demand for the abolition of the death penalty, and for penal reform.[3] But, characteristically, they shared with Concepción Arenal, the penal reformer, an approach which emphasized moral rather than institutional problems.[4] Concepción Arenal was herself a symbol of the way in which women were beginning to take a part in Spanish public life and one of the most original features of republicanism was its attempt to win feminine support. This was partly an offshoot of its social romanticism and partly an acute perception of the subtle influence indirectly exerted by women on political opinion. Women could be described together with workers as 'the two disinherited classes of society' and more extreme Republicans talked of the September Revolution as having 'emancipated women' and there was even talk of

[1] H. Juretschke, *España ante Francia*, Madrid, 1948, pp. 62–64. Cf. Pi in *La Discusión*, 19 July 1857, 'Béranger'; 29 Sept. 1857, 'De la decadencia de la arte'.
[2] A. Grimaldi, *Emilio Castelar: Semblanza moral, intelectual y política*, Cádiz, 1868, pp. 19–22.
[3] Castelar, *La Redención del esclavo*, Madrid, 1859. *El Abolicionista*, the organ of the *Liga Abolicionista* founded by Vizcarrondo, first appeared in July 1865.
[4] Concepción Arenal, *Obras completas*, Madrid, 1894–1902; F. Córdoba y López, *Cuatro páginas acerca de la pena de muerte*, Madrid, 1864. See also C. Saiz, *La Revolución de 1868 y la cultura femenina*, Madrid, n.d.

the 'equality of the sexes'.[1] But there was little question of weakening family ties—civil marriage, for example, was seen as part of the trend towards the complete secularization of the state and not a granting of equal rights to women. It was widely assumed that the majority of them were under the influence of the Church and hence perpetuated in the home the clericalism which their children imbibed at school. Women were foremost in presenting petitions protesting against the granting of religious toleration in 1868.[2] The Republicans therefore made a determined effort to wean them from the influence of priests. Garrido stressed the importance of enrolling them in political clubs and a republican women's association was founded in Madrid to discuss their role in the new society and to undertake charitable work formerly under the charge of religious orders. The growing awareness of the feminine social role was reflected in the series of Sunday lectures of 1869 in which various republican intellectuals lectured women on their social duties. But these attempts did not altogether meet with the desired results. The rate of literacy among them was low and doubts about the efficacy of discussion groups for them were expressed when it was discovered that literary rather than scientific topics were more popular in the new women's *Ateneo*.[3]

A much more effective way of appealing to women was through the highly emotional *quinta* campaign. Women vied with men in writing lachrymose articles deploring the whole system of conscription.[4] The effectiveness of this aspect of republican propaganda was shown by the number of female demonstrations at the time of the *quinta* draws, as in March 1869, at Cádiz, outside the *Cortes* at Madrid and at Sans, and during the republican revolt at Barcelona in 1869, when women helped their men-folk build barricades, and again during the Gracia riots of April 1870.[5] There

---

[1] *El Progreso democrático* (Cádiz), 28 Oct. 1868. See Appendix for Pi's attitude.

[2] Vilarrasa and Gatell, op. cit. i. 526–9; Hughey, op. cit., p. 34.

[3] *La Ilustración republicana federal*, 28 Mar., 16 Aug. 1872; *La Igualdad*, 1 July 1869; *La Justicia social*, 28 Apr. 1871.

[4] *La Igualdad*, 16 Dec. 1868, 'No mas quintas', by Isabella de Llorente. For male lachrymosity see Clavé in *La Vanguardia*, 12 Dec. 1868; Castelar, *Discursos*, pp. 332 et seq.

[5] *La República federal* (Cádiz), 14 Mar. 1869; Masriera, op. cit., pp. 354, 358; Serraclara, *La Nueva Inquisición*, Barcelona, 1870, p. 11.

were even occasional examples of women taking active part in political meetings like Trinidad Pérez or Guillermina Rosa and later Concha Boracino, the woman leader of the canton of Torrevieja in 1873, but although *La Igualdad* pointedly adapted Michelet's *Women of the French Revolution* as a *folletín* there were few who wished to emulate Mme Roland.

Castelar's romanticized vision of the manual worker demonstrated some other aspects of republican ideology. He referred to them as 'the true kings of creation' and as 'models of love and order' echoing the clichés of the social romantics. In an essay on Clavé's choirs he writes of the Catalan worker spending his nights in learning songs, and enthuses[1]—'when the soul feels those lyrical raptures it cannot be vitiated'. Here again he betrays that sentimentality which was the mark of so much republican writing about the class they were claiming to bring into political life. Both Clavé and Castelar popularized the notion that the workers, uncorrupted by politics, would be the regenerating force of the republican movement after 1868. The idea of their political innocence and moral virtue was continually contrasted with middle-class immorality in pamphlets and in poems which were dedicated to *trabajadores virtuosos* and *obreros honrados*. It was their 'mission' to introduce the workers into political life and to 'emancipate the Fourth Estate'.[2] But underlying this sense of mission was the unquestioned assumption that it was the intellectuals, unsullied by personal interests in their pursuit of abstract truth, who were their natural leaders. The workers, uncorrupted and enthusiastic, needed guides of 'upright purpose and honest intentions'.[3]

Tearful romanticism, combined with a moralistic attitude to the working class, was very largely a literary and rhetorical convention echoed by those conservative Republicans who, like Castelar, had come under the literary influence of Lamartine and the economic

---

[1] 37. Castelar, *Perfiles y bocetos de ideas*, Madrid, 1875, pp. 254–6.

[2] Paul y Angulo, op. cit.; *La Ilustración republicana federal*, 27 Aug. 1871; *La Justicia social*, 7 Nov. 1871; *La Legalidad de la Internacional*, op. cit., p. 63.

[3] *La Igualdad*, 9 Aug. 1873; Orense, *Ventajas de la República Federal*, Madrid, 1869. Cf. A. Pavía, *Solución práctica de la cuestión social*, Madrid, 1871. Although calling himself a 'social republican', Pavía illustrates an aspect of *empleomanía* among those under-employed 'intellectuals' who prefer an alliance with the downtrodden masses to humiliating dependence on the patronage of politicians.

influence of Bastiat, but it was effective in making the bulk of
Republicans cling to the myths of class harmony and association.
Their social policy remained conditioned by an outlook which
gave primacy to political over social revolution. This was partly
due to the need to attract support from those whose discontent was
primarily political, but also to their belief that, owing to wide
variations in social structure throughout the country, social problems might be better solved after the establishment of separate
federal states.[1] It was also due to unawareness of what social conditions were really like. Only a few Republicans like the workers
Alsina, Clavé, Lostau, Rubaudonadeu, Roca y Gales, and the
doctor Suñer y Capdevila (from his experience in the Barcelona
slums) appreciated what these slum conditions were or the sharpening of class antagonism which Internationalist propaganda, the
unjust *quinta* system, disease, and overcrowding had encouraged.[2]
What mass support the Republicans managed to retain was in
spite of the opinions of the majority of their leaders rather than
because of them. Believing in class harmony, they disapproved of
strike action, and even Pi, whose unromantic vision enabled him
to see economic class struggles determining political behaviour,
adhered to these ideas and rejected strike action as wasteful and
irrational.[3] Nowhere in any republican paper or pamphlet was
strike action encouraged. Both Pi and the party advocated the
mixed jury as the solution to labour disputes. Their social programme, when it was formulated in 1872 after much delay and
in response to the challenge of the International, consisted mainly
of proposed factory legislation to protect women and children,
greater educational opportunities for workers, easier credit facilities, and the setting up of consumer co-operatives.[4]

Castelar was mainly responsible for linking Spanish federalism
to the main current of European republicanism. International
republicanism, which had been discredited since the failures of

[1] *Gaceta*, 20 May 1869, Pi's speech; Orense, op. cit., p. 30; Paul y Angulo, op. cit.,
pp. 73, 90; Tubino, op. cit., p. 202.

[2] F. Suñer y Capdevila, *Dios*, Barcelona, 1869, p. 3. Tuberculosis and cholera were
endemic—there were three great outbreaks of cholera in Barcelona, in 1854, 1865, and
1870. The last was politically exploited in *La Federación*, 18 Dec. 1870.

[3] Pi y Arsuaga, op. cit. v. 326-33.

[4] Vera, op cit. ii. 295-8.

1848, began to revive in the late 1860's under the stimulus of changing international developments. The revival was expressed in the 1867 Congress of Peace and Freedom which met at Geneva under the presidency of Garibaldi and which canvassed the idea of a United States of Europe, modelled on Switzerland and the United States of America to be achieved through a confederation of European republics.[1] The new republicanism in the tradition of the Abbé de St. Pierre, Kant, and Considérant was anti-militarist, pacifist, and anti-dynastic, believing that nationalism was too dangerous to be exploited by a single man whether a Napoleon or a Bismarck. In France Proudhon, Strada, Lemonnier, Renan, Mistral, and Victor Hugo; in Spain Castelar, Pi y Margall, and Salmerón; in Portugal Braga and Antero de Quental; in Italy Cattaneo, Garibaldi, Pisacane, Ferraro, and Mario were, or had been, representatives of this current of opinion, all for a variety of motives seeking a counterbalance to bellicose nationalism.[2]

The attractions of international republicanism to a minority group like the Spanish Federals were obvious—international solidarity might be compensation for internal weakness. Castelar, furthermore, used his simplified Hegelian mythology to argue that the 'republic' was the synthesis of the nineteenth-century historical process.[3] The September Revolution, the first successful revolutionary outburst in Europe since 1848, gave him the opportunity to open up a vista of a regenerated Spain taking over the leadership of a Latin republican confederation of France, Spain, Italy, and Portugal. The frequency of similar sentiments in the republican press between 1868 and 1871 is evidence of the popularity of this aspect of federal ideology. Although Spanish federalism must be seen primarily in terms of a native tradition, the fact that the leadership of the movement was almost entirely

---

[1] P. Renouvin, *L'idée de Fédération européenne dans la pensée politique du XIXᵉ siècle*, Oxford, 1949; *Movimento operaio*, 1946 (4), A. Saitta, 'L'Idea d'Europa dal 1815 al 1870'. Admiration for the U.S.A. and Switzerland was common to all Federals. Chao translated extracts of de Tocqueville's *De la Démocratie en Amérique* in 1854. The only critical work on Swiss democracy published in Spain was Molina, *Los Cantones suizos* Madrid, 1869, pointing out false analogies made by the Federals.

[2] See especially: 'Strada', *L'Europe sauvée et le fédéralisme*, Paris, 1868; C. Lemonnier, *La Ligue internationale de la paix et de la liberté*, Paris, 1869.

[3] Castelar, *Historia del movimiento republicano en Europa*, Madrid, 1874, 9 vols., *passim*.

in the hands of intellectuals trying to break down Spain's isolation from Europe meant that there was a tendency to impose European categories on a particularly Spanish situation which led them to lose touch with the realities of domestic politics.

Castelar's vision of Spain's role as leader of a Latin Union of France, Spain, and Italy derived from a sense of frustrated nationalism and from a vague and ill-defined concept of 'latinism'. He had expressed 'latinist' ideas in the *Ateneo* in 1859 and was still doing so in the *Cortes* in 1870.[1] In an interview with a French journalist in 1872 he argued that an alliance of the Latin races was necessary to combat 'Germanism', which he equated with absolutism—'it is the only way of rejuvenating these old peoples and restoring the West'. Whatever the flaws and contradictions in his latinist views, the idea of a union of Latin countries to defend the values of 'Mediterranean civilization' enjoyed some popularity among Left-wing radical and Right-wing clerical intellectuals both in Spain and in France. It was, however, essentially a literary idea divorced from practical politics. This racialist concept, with its echoes of Social Darwinism, was given a stimulus by the Franco-Prussian war and was used, particularly after the declaration of the Third Republic to foster a sense of international republican solidarity.[2] The illusion was sustained until after the defeat of the Paris Commune in May 1871, when, with the establishment of Thier's conservative unitarian republic and Mazzini's unequivocal condemnation of federalism, the ideas of racial and republican solidarity were exposed as republican myths. Although the lunatic fringe of Spanish federalism continued to embrace the hope of republican confederation the republican leaders, and even Castelar himself, turning to the possible material and moral benefits of North American aid, began to give up the task of trying to reconcile political reality with racial latinism.

One facet of the 'latinist' idea though was retained—the idea of *Iberismo* or the political union of Portugal and Spain. Iberian Union

---

[1] Speech in *Ateneo*, 5 May 1859; *Gaceta*, 7 June 1870; Castelar, op. cit. viii. 381 et seq. Juretschke, op. cit., pp. 66–67, discusses his latinism. L. Teste, *Viaje por España*, Valencia, 1959, 'Una entrevista con Castelar'.

[2] *La Igualdad*, 29 Sept., 15 Aug. 1870, 'El Pacto de los pueblos latinos'. Cf. *La Revista de Andalucía*, 1 Sept. 1874; Tubino, 'Latinos y Germanos'.

was an ideal shared by many Spanish intellectuals and politicians in the nineteenth century.[1] It reached a peak in the 1840's when Isabella attained marriageable age, but, after her marriage to Francisco de Asis in 1846, Pan-Iberians began to look to republicanism to achieve union. The September Revolution revived hopes of a monarchical solution, but the humiliating rejection of Prim's offer to Fernando of Portugal in April 1869 was ample indication of Portuguese mistrust of Spanish intentions and lukewarmness in Portuguese monarchist circles to the idea.[2] The Republicans could now claim that only through federalism and its guarantee of autonomy could the Portuguese be won over to the idea of union. In Portugal desire for union was echoed only among a handful of Republicans, mainly intellectuals of the 'Generation of Coimbra' under Teofilo Braga and Antero de Quental, whose purely literary criticism had broadened under the influence of Proudhon and the French positivists into a criticism of the whole Portuguese social structure. The September Revolution was hailed by these writers, who tried to turn their renovating movement into political channels by renewing contacts made by the Spanish Democrats in exile in 1869.[3] But Iberian Union, the least impracticable of the schemes for federation, was politically unrealistic, for not only did it find little echo in Portugal but both Britain and France were resolutely opposed to any such union and even Portuguese Federal Republicans shared monarchist suspicions of Spanish motives when they omitted Iberian Union from their programme in 1873.[4] When Castelar became Foreign Minister in 1873 he had the humiliation of denying one of the cardinal points in the Federals' programme when he assured Layard that the federal revolution was a purely national one and that no scheme

[1] From a mass of Iberist pamphlets see S. de Mas, *La Iberia, Memoria sobre la Conveniencia de la Unión pacífica y legal de España y Portugal*, Barcelona, 1856; A. de Paz, *España y Portugal*, Madrid, 1861.

[2] B.M. Add. MS. 38997, private letter from Sir Charles Murray, ambassador at Lisbon, to Layard, 20 Jan. 1870: F.O. 63/969, 24, 26 May 1870, Murray to Clarendon. The whole question of Iberian Union is dealt with in Fernando de los Ríos, *Mi Misión en Portugal*, Paris, 1877, *passim*.

[3] Antero de Quental, *Portugal perante a revolução de Hespanha*, Lisbon, 1868; T. Braga, *As Ideias modernas na literatura portuguesa*, Oporto, 1892, i. 287 et seq., ii. 462 et seq.; Luis de Montalvor (ed.), *Historia do regimen republicano em Portugal*, Lisbon, 1932, 2 vols.

[4] *A Rebate*, no. 1, 1873.

for Iberian Union was contemplated.[1] *Iberismo* was linked in republican arguments with the return of Gibraltar and, like other aspects of international republicanism, was useful as a rallying cry for frustrated nationalism, useless as a programme for practical politics.

On the other hand, if federation was impractical in Europe, it seemed to be a possible solution to the problem of the Antilles, which had been a constant distraction ever since separation had become a serious issue after the revolt of Narciso López in 1849. Creole discontent stemmed from the economic and political predominance of the *peninsulares*, as the Spaniards were called, and the subordination of Cuban economic interests to the Spanish protected market. A difficult problem was complicated by the increasing interest shown by the United States. From the period of 'Manifest Destiny' and the notorious 'Ostend Manifesto' of 1854 American motives were always suspect.[2] After the Civil War and emancipation, humanitarian desires to free the Cuban slaves mingled with political and economic interests. The creoles found allies in the United States and among the slaves. In 1867 Spanish-Cuban relations worsened as plans for slavery abolition and fiscal reform petered out. A bare fortnight after the news of the September Revolution, Céspedes, a lawyer-rancher from Oriente province, declared the Cuban Republic at Yara and the ten years' war had begun. From the refusal of successive Spanish Governments to undertake reform until the rebels laid down arms, stemmed a deadlock which the Republicans thought they could break by the granting of autonomy to Cuba as a province within a Spanish federation. It is very doubtful if they ever grasped the real complexity of the problem, which American interest, by stimulating nationalist agitation inside Spain, did nothing to ease. There was little evidence either to show that the rebels reciprocated the idea of Cuba remaining in a Spanish federation. Republican politics seemed, as to the Puerto Rican Hostos, to be entirely opportunist.

[1] F.O. 72/1338, nos. 248, 253, 28 Mar. 1873, Layard to Granville.
[2] The best survey of Cuban history in this period is in R. Guerra y Sánchez, *Historia de la Nación Cubana*, La Habana, 1952, vol. iv. See also B. Rauch, *American Interest in Cuba, 1853–5*, New York, 1948; A. Ettinger, *The Mission of Pierre Soulé to Spain, 1853–4*, Yale, 1932; F. E. Chadwick, *The Relations of the United States and Spain*, London, 1911, vol. i.

It is true that, studying in Spain at the time of the September Revolution, he had said in the *Ateneo* in December 1868:[1] 'I am a Puerto Rican: I am, therefore, a federalist . . . the bonds of liberty which can still unite us with Spain are federal bonds.' But when he left Spain in 1869 he did so completely disillusioned with the Republicans and this was later echoed by *La Revolución*, the mouthpiece of Cuban and Puerto Rican exiles in New York, which accused the Republicans of 'barbaric patriotism and putting Spanish interests before humanity'. By 1873 both Céspedes and Martí, the hero of Cuban independence, had despaired of republican good intentions.[2] Cubans and Republicans were complementary to each other not because they had the same political aims but because the Cubans could use the Republicans to prevent troops from being sent to Cuba by financing them to stage revolts inside Spain. The charges accusing the Federals of being in the pay of the Cuban rebels[3] are difficult to prove one way or the other, but they repeat the similar charges brought against the Liberals after 1814 during the revolt of Spain's other American colonies.

The most striking feature of early republican activity was not so much their ideology, most of which could either be traced back to the Democrats or be accounted for by eclectic borrowing from foreign thinkers, but the means which they adopted to put these ideas over to the public. Their originality in Spanish politics lay in the combination of their ideology and their propaganda techniques which exploited the potentialities of the press, clubs, and the stage. The 'club' soon became the characteristic unit of their social life in Madrid and the provincial capitals. Flóres García, an ebullient Malagueño, whose memoirs give a vivid picture of the Federal journalist, found the Madrid clubs more 'fanatical and barbarous' than those of the provinces.[4] The very use of the word

[1] *Caribbean Historical Review*, Dec. 1953, T. Mathews, 'Confederation of the Greater Antilles'.
[2] A. Nevins, *Hamilton Fish*, New York, 1936, p. 637, quoting Céspedes's letter to Grant, 22 Mar. 1873; for Martí see Baeza Flóres, *Vida de Jose Martí*, Habana, 1954, pp. 161–222, and Martí's own pamphlet, *La República española ante la Revolución cubana*, Madrid, 1873.
[3] See the anonymous pamphlet proving collusion—*Los insurrectos de España y los de Cuba*, Habana, n.d.
[4] Flóres García, *Recuerdos de la Revolución*, Madrid, 1913, p. 53.

'club' with its French revolutionary overtones instead of the more
sedate *tertulia*—still used by the Progressives and Democrats—was
an indication of their radicalism to which the names of some gave
added confirmation—*El Club Rojo, La Montaña*, and *Los Hijos de
Padilla*, imitating radical forerunners of the 1820's and 1850's.
These clubs usually met in hired rooms, the most famous being
those in the Calle de la Yedra and the Calle del Lobo, and the
most notorious in the Plaza Anton Marín, the centre of working-
class radicalism. In addition to serving as centres for discussion, the
clubs, with newspaper offices, were focal rallying points for the
republican militia. More informal were the cafés, such as the
Imperial in the Carrera de San Jerónimo, which were the meeting-
places for republican journalists from the provinces who, living
in cheap pensions, eked out monthly allowances from their families by concocting articles for republican papers.[1]

The clubs debated policy and played a considerable part in
formulating republican opinion. They claimed to represent the
purity of republicanism in their demands for government by
direct democracy and, by canalizing discontent in the capital, they
became the most vocal centres of opposition to the Government
and a serious embarrassment to republican leaders; but, as it was
pointed out at the time, without the clubs to relieve their feelings
the people would have become ungovernable. They were patron-
ized mainly by journalists, office seekers from the provinces, professional men, and workers from the *Fomento de las Artes*. Joarizti
was the first president of the *Club Anton Marín*, Guisasola of *El
Club Rojo*, Luis Blanc, a bizarre revolutionary from Barbastro and
writer of propagandist plays, of *Los Hijos de Padilla*, Cárceles
Sabater, a medical student, was president of the *Asociación de la
juventud republicana*, Araus, an extremist, of the *Asociación librepensadora*, and Pi was president of the more select republican
Ateneo.

The provincial clubs, often meeting in the open air or in empty
convents, followed a similar pattern, although some had a more
specialized appeal. At Cádiz, for example, there was a *Centro de
Obreros*, a republican club for women, a republican youth club,

---

[1] García, op. cit., p. 158; Estévanez, op. cit., pp. 302–3; Echegaray, op. cit. iii. 52–58.

and, an educational club named after a schoolmaster, Bohorquez, a martyr of the 1869 revolt, which gave free schooling to children and evening classes to adults. Many small towns had their *casino republicano*, as at Montilla which had been a radical centre since before 1868. Most of these clubs served an educational as well as a political function.[1] In Málaga, Cádiz, Seville, and Barcelona the clubs were influential in framing local political action, but it was only at Barcelona that an attempt was made to control and organize them as part of a general policy of building up the strength of Catalan republicanism. As envisaged by Almirall, clubs were to have a dual purpose, political and educational.[2] In the political sphere they were to examine and criticize governmental acts at all levels in the light of Federal principles. Great emphasis was laid on mutual help between clubs and on the creation of new centres. It was on their club records that candidates for the various committees, for local and even national government, were to be selected. All elections within the club were by universal male suffrage from the age of twenty. The importance given to club activity may be gauged by the stipulation that the presidency of a club was incompatible with the holding of any other party post. This attempt to co-ordinate the activity of the Barcelona clubs was in marked contrast to the haphazard organization of those at Madrid and the greater discipline of the Barcelona Federals may be partly attributed to this.

By stressing educational activity Almirall was merely following the Democrat tradition, but the way in which the Catalan Workers' *Ateneo* expanded after 1868 suggests that the old Democrat monopoly of educator of the masses was breaking down as it tended to come under Internationalist influence, although many Federals continued to lecture there on such topics as Proudhonism, Comte's positivism, and the utopian socialists.[3] The educational tradition was equally strong at Madrid, especially in the *Fomento de las Artes*,

[1] *La Justicia social*, 20 Aug. 1869, 'Los Clubs en Andalucía'; *La República federal universal* (Cádiz), 1 Jan. 1870; *Efimérides malagueñas*, 4, 19 Nov., 30 Dec. 1868; Leiva, op. cit. i. 342 for Montilla.
[2] *El Estado catalán*, 21–29 Dec. 1869, a series of articles covering all aspects of club organization. Cf. *La Revista de Catalunya*, Apr. 1926, M. Font, 'El Club dels Federalistes'.
[3] *La Justicia social*, 19 Aug. 1869, *La Federación*, 19 Sept., 25 Dec. 1869, 21 May, 14 Aug. 1870.

founded in 1850, while women were catered for in *La Fraternidad*, which gave evening classes from 1869. The importance of the *Fomento* in creating a literate section among the working class, and especially printers, cannot be over-emphasized.[1] After 1868, though, educational activity declined in proportion to the increase in political activity and after the visit of Bakunin's agent, Fanelli, to Madrid in October 1868 it could no longer be taken for granted that the Federals' guidance in education would be repeated in politics. Alsina, a self-educated Federal deputy, stressed another aspect when he pointed out, in striking contrast to Castelar's romanticism, how difficult it was for a worker to go to a library in the evening after twelve, fourteen, or even sixteen hours' work a day.[2] In fact, the Federals over-estimated their educative function and although the demand for better educational facilities figured in every working-class programme, politics were beginning to prove a greater attraction. When Cervera had founded his night school in 1850 he enrolled 500 students. When in 1873 the Madrid authorities set up eight evening schools they were forced to admit after five months that total enrolment had only reached 530.[3] The decline in the number of the Clavé choirs in Catalonia was another aspect of the same phenomena, as Clavé himself and his singers were drawn into political activity. The falling off in the educational drive was due as well to the deliberate repudiation of middle-class leadership encouraged by such Internationalists as the deraciné intellectual Sentiñon, and was expressed most forcibly in the famous debate in Valencia University and in the Bolsa at Madrid where Internationalist spokesmen challenged all comers in open debate.[4] The implication of the entry into politics of workers who were illiterate or had only had a minimal education was of cardinal importance in the development of Spanish working-class politics, making it even more susceptible to anarchist utopianism.

[1] Lorenzo, op. cit., pp. 11–16.
[2] *La Justicia Social*, 5 Aug. 1869. The 10-hour day was a leading labour demand at this time.
[3] Garrido, *La Cooperación*, Madrid, 1879, p. 30; *Ayuntamiento* posters, 10, 13 June, 1 Nov. 1873.
[4] *La Emancipación*, 25 Sept. 1871; *La Justicia social*, 5, 12 Aug. 1869. See also Lorenzo, op. cit., pp. 32–33, 43–53, 127–36, 292–3.

As the clubs owed their existence and expansion to the right of association after 1868 so the freeing of press restrictions, the abolition of deposits and of responsible editors combined with a lowering of the duty on paper, led to a rapid expansion in the press throughout Spain. The small literacy rate did not seem to affect the number of papers in circulation, although it might account for the ephemeral life of many of them in this highly competitive market. In 1867 the number of political papers in Madrid, including periodicals, was only seventeen.[1] By the end of 1870 the number of political dailies and weeklies alone was twenty-eight and by the beginning of 1873 this had risen to forty-three. It was true that the Madrid press merely stultified itself with papers plagiarizing each other and Layard's comment that 'there was probably not a more venal or unscrupulous press in the world' was scarcely an exaggeration.[2] The press was no more than another example of *empleocracia* providing a meagre living for a proletariat of needy journalists who hoped to pick up through journalism some of the plums of office.

The career of Flóres García may be taken as a typical example of the Federal journalist. After a spell of revolutionary journalism and political activity in Málaga he came to Madrid in 1869 with a number of introductions including one to Garrido, who until he went abroad in 1870 employed him as a secretary. Failing to get a job on the notorious *El Combate*, he became a leader writer on *La Discusión* until the Republic when Figueras rewarded his faithful service with the Civil Governorship of Ciudad Real. The career of another journalist, Roque Barcia, in contrast, was an extreme example of the disillusioned and frustrated office-seeker. A self-styled philosopher, with a muddled intellect and inflamed imagination, he was the most highly regarded of the extremist journalists, a strange mixture of bombast and sentimentalism—'a democrat in white gloves' in a contemporary's phrase. He became more unbalanced after his imprisonment without trial for his

---

[1] E. Hartzenbusch, *Apuntes para un catálogo de periódicos madrileños*, 1661–1870, Madrid, 1894, appendix. In 1855 there were 151 papers of all types in the capital, in 1864, 198; 1868, 246; 1870, 302.

[2] F.O. 72/1313, no. 338, 5 Nov. 1872, and F.O. 72/1336, no. 7, 6 Jan. 1873, Layard to Granville. L. Teste, op. cit., pp. 89–93.

supposed complicity in Prim's murder, and failing to secure an ambassadorial post in 1873 he finished his active career as a leader of the Cartagena canton. Most of the prominent Federal journalists, however, were more fortunate by being appointed to civil governorships or to ambassadorial posts during the Republic.[1]

The Carlist and republican press showed the most rapid expansion; both were distinguished from the other parties by their combination of principle and scurrility. The most important republican papers were the newly founded *La Igualdad*, which, after its merging with *El Amigo del Pueblo* in 1869, became the leading Federal daily with a circulation of 12,000. *La Discusión* and *El Pueblo* were both refounded under their old directors, Bernardo García and García Ruiz. *La Discusión* was rather colourless and did not have a wide circulation; it was moderate and usually reflected the views of the current leadership. *El Pueblo* was the only unitarian republican paper and voiced the views of a very small minority which were often barely distinguishable from those of the Democrat *El Imparcial*. It enjoyed a wide circulation simply because it was one of the very few republican evening papers. *La Igualdad* soon established itself as the semi-official mouthpiece of the Federal party and its importance stemmed from printing all the decrees and manifestoes of the party leaders whether it agreed with them or not.[2] In this way policy was transmitted to the provinces but it was a constant complaint that the Government deliberately withheld copies in the post so as to prevent instructions from reaching the provinces until it was too late for them to be effective. One of the main difficulties encountered by the Federal leaders was their inability to get complete control of *La Igualdad* and to turn it into an official party paper. In 1870 Pi succeeded in getting one of his supporters appointed as director, but this arrangement was only short-lived and the Directory continued to contend with difficulties stemming from eight changes in the directorship of the

[1] Among civil governors were Flóres García, Altadill, Tressera, Clavé, and Del Val. Diplomatic appointments included Mellado, Martra, Robert and Bernardo García. Garrido accepted a post in the Philippines.

[2] *La Igualdad*, 1 Jan. 1873, contains a full review of the history and administration of the paper.

paper within five years. It is difficult to account for these changes; we do not know, for example, how far the views of the proprietor, Pérez Luzano, a monarchist sympathizer, determined policy changes. There was in fact a general conspiracy of silence about how papers were financed. *La Discusión* was an exception among Federal papers as Bernardo García, director from 1866 to 1873, had married Sixto Cámara's rich widow and hence the finances were independent of any outside proprietor.

In the notorious abuse of press freedom after 1868 the Federals were the worst offenders with papers like the infamous *El Combate* of Paul y Angulo, *El Tribunal del Pueblo* of Córdoba y López, and *La Justicia Federal* of Roque Barcia which constantly incited Federals to violence. It is a moot point whether these papers were financed by political opponents who wished to discredit the Federals. Outside Madrid there were only two influential Federal papers commanding attention beyond their own immediate area— Almirall's *El Estado catalán* in Barcelona and Tubino's *La Andalucía* in Seville. In common with the rest of the Spanish political press all these papers concentrated on political affairs to the virtual exclusion of other interests. The Federals did make a concession by introducing *folletines*, but these serials, which included Voltaire's *Zadig* and *Candide*, Lamartine's *History of the Girondins* (the Federal classic), Strauss and Renan's *Life of Jesus*, seemed designed to improve the mind and not, like those of Girardin from whom the idea was copied, to increase circulation. High moral earnestness combined with vindictive abuse at the expense of political rivals were the main ingredients of their daily press.

In addition to their dailies the Federals had their weeklies aimed at a more cultivated audience. With the exception of the Sevillano *El Hispalense*, they were all edited at Madrid. The most important and the one which best reflects the various strands of Federal ideology was *La Ilustración republicana federal*. It aimed to disseminate culture in the widest sense—from articles by Pi on Italian painting and Pompeii to poems praising machines and the wonders of modern science. The heading of the title-page—a locomotive and machinery against a rising sun—symbolized the march of Science and Progress to which the review devoted a great deal of

its space.[1] This attempt to stimulate interest in the sciences reflected
the positivist influences in federal ideology though the articles
were always written in the exaggerated and effusive style which
was the hall-mark of so much federal journalism. An earlier review,
La Federación española, continually stressed that 'social emancipation' would not come merely by releasing the springs of emotion
but from a deeper understanding of the scientific laws underlying
historical development. A third review, *La Justicia social*, specialized
in social questions and in reporting the activities of the Madrid
and provincial clubs. These periodicals reflect the Federals' admiration for 'science', but the language of their admiration still betrayed
their literary upbringing and their romanticized view of scientific
development. Apart from doctors such as Guisasola, Pérez Costales,
Zabala, Suñer y Capdevila, and the surgeon Rubio, Monturiol,
inventor of the submarine *Icteneo*, was the only practising scientist
who was also a notable Federal.

The great number of Federal papers not only gave employment
to importunate journalists but was also evidence of the Federals'
belief in the power of discussion and in their eventual triumph
through the dissemination of their ideas. This reflected the idealism
of both Pi and Castelar with their belief that from the dialectical
clash of ideas truth would emerge, but in practice it merely led to
the perpetuation of artificial polemics. In contrast to this idealistic
approach there was that of the professional revolutionaries to
whom revolution did not mean the dialectical revelation of Truth
but conspiracy, secret organization, and violence. Freemasonry
had been the typical secret organization of Spanish radicals and
secret societies of the *carbonario* type had flourished under the
government repression after 1856. But, Pi argued, where liberty

[1] Edited by Rodríguez-Solís, the historian of Spanish republicanism. The following
poem, one among many, illustrates the admiration for 'Progress':

La Locomotora

Agua y fuego; resultante
Vapor, potencia, presión;
Por un milagro gigante
Audaz, alzará triunfante,
El Rey de la creación.
Progreso . . . su mejor propagandista
Será la locomotora.

of the press was assured, as it was with few exceptions after 1868, the Federals must seek to persuade by the supremacy of their propaganda. For this reason he was opposed to secret societies although he had himself been a member of the *carbonarios* in 1858.[1] However, this was not a view shared by many in the party. Lafargue commented unfavourably on the Spanish addiction for secret societies and saw this as one of the main barriers to the growth of the International in Spain.[2] Secrecy had become an ingrained habit with Spanish radicals which those who had been masons largely for anticlerical reasons found difficult to break even when anticlericalism was no longer the main political issue.

The extremely important part played by masonry in Spanish liberalism, particularly between 1815 and 1823, has led to an over-exaggeration of its influence after 1868 when it has been blamed for the Montpensier duel, Prim's assassination, and the Cuban imbroglio. It is true that the leading Progressives continued to be masons as did many Federals, but not Pi, Salmerón, Almirall, or Castelar. Nevertheless, it seems that the secret society *El Tiro nacional* developed as an offshoot of freemasonry in response to the demands of frustrated revolutionaries who found the myths of republicanism being shattered and the official leadership of the party too cautious. Paul y Angulo became its leader in 1870, establishing a Central Directory in Madrid with contacts in Aragón and Catalonia. Although it is hard to find details of it, it seems to have been a *carbonario*-type secret society working within the framework of republicanism but owing little to the basic pre-conceptions of the official leadership.[3] Its leaders were opportunist, impatient, and believers in the virtue of violence. Unconstructive and rooted in a myth of violence, it was a denial of all the Federals' preaching in the press and by their leaders. Its rapid expansion was itself a comment on the failure of the leadership to satisfy their

[1] Roure, op. cit. i. 255.

[2] P. Lafargue, *Correspondance*, Paris, 1956, p. 10, letter of Lafargue to Engels dated '2, 8 bre 1871', commenting on *El Tiro nacional*.

[3] The 'masonic plot' interpretation of nineteenth-century Spanish history still has a frenzied partisan in Comin Colomer. See his *Historia de la Primera República Española*, Barcelona, 1957. Roure, op. cit. i. 232–55, discusses masonry immediately after 1868. The details on *El Tiro nacional* in Tirado y Rojas, op. cit. ii. 185–6, were taken from an article on it which appeared in the Progressive paper *La Iberia* in mid-1870.

followers. It was attractive because it promised immediate revolution and the prospect of a quick share-out of office. It was popular because it appealed to a conspiratorial tradition which had become ingrained through years of government repression and it thrived on the resentment felt against all types of professional Madrid politician.

Much of the internal strain in the Federal movement between 1868 and 1874 was due not so much to the conflict between the two unresolved facets of Federal ideology represented by Pi and Castelar—between the rational and the emotional—but to the conflict between the beliefs represented by these two idealists who, whatever their differences, shared the basic conception of an open society, and the secret machinations of a group of desperate adventurers who, learning from the disappointments of 1868-9, turned to violence and secrecy to obtain what discussion and theorizing had failed to achieve.

5

Opposition Politics, the Pacts and Revolts, 1869

THE political problem facing the Republicans in 1869 was how to organize from the centre a minority movement depending for its momentum on peripheral provincial enthusiasm. Their failure to solve this problem during the first six months was a direct cause of the collapse of the revolts of September and October. This failure can be attributed to a variety of factors; the revolutionary legacy of September 1868 and the feeling of betrayal stimulated by the idea of republican participation in the September Revolution; the imprecise definition of republican aims and confusion over the implications of federalism; the difficulty experienced by many Federal deputies with a revolutionary past to submit themselves to the discipline of a minority opposition party, and finally the absence of clear undisputed leadership during the critical immediate post-revolutionary period.

The Federals' dilemma was well illustrated by their two main activities between February and July. On one side there was the attempt to make themselves a compact opposition party in the *Cortes*. On the other, was the provincial organization exemplified by the signing of the federal pacts of May and June. The main feature of federal republicanism in 1869 was the failure to co-ordinate these two activities or to define the relationship between the elected representatives in the *Cortes* and the new organization set up by the pacts. Two viewpoints conflicted; one, represented unequivocally by Pi, stressed the importance of parliamentary opposition by a small compact Federal Republican party exploiting the differences in the revolutionary coalition, combined with 'the greatest moral agitation' in the press and the clubs. The other, representing purely local interests, repudiating any sort of direction from centralized leadership and traditionally distrustful of Madrid, believed that the nature of parliamentary government had not changed with the revolution and that only by relying on the spontaneous enthusiasm of the provinces could the Federals' strength be best utilized and a Federal Republic made a reality. This view stressed particularly the importance of a republican militia as the best safeguard for civil and political liberties—hence the importance of the militia issue during 1869.

The elections for the *Cortes* were held in the second week in January. The results were not as good as the Republicans had expected after the encouraging municipal successes in December, but their very success then may have convinced Sagasta of the necessity to revert to traditional methods of government influence to ensure an overwhelming monarchist majority. Nevertheless, their victories were impressive if only for the concentration of their strength. Half the total number of their deputies came from Andalusia and Catalonia, while in Barcelona, Seville, and Cádiz, in spite of Progressive governors, republican majorities were overwhelming.[1] Their press referred to the elections as a 'moral victory' and attributed the absence of larger numbers to the continued predominance of the *caciques* in rural areas, to the *empleados* dependent on the Government, and to direct government pressure and intimidation.[2] Other factors which were not mentioned was their novelty, the coinciding of many points in their programme with the promises of the Progressives, and their comparative lack of interest and absence of organization outside certain well-defined areas.

When the *Cortes* met on 11 February they were able to muster 69 deputies, but in view of the overwhelming numerical predominance of 159 Progressives, 20 Democrats, and 69 Unionists and the combined determination of these parties, at least in 1869, to preserve the revolutionary coalition, the Federals were condemned to the role of a minority opposition party able to rely only on the rather dubious support of the 2 Unitarian Republicans, the small Carlist party of 18, and the independent Isabelline oppo-

---

[1] A. Carro Martínez, *La Constitución española de 1869*, Madrid, 1952, p. 111; Guichot, op. cit., p. 355; Roure, op. cit., ii. 194.   [2] *La Igualdad*, 20, 23 Jan. 1869.

sition of 14. This did not prevent the Federals from becoming an extremely energetic opposition, constantly criticizing the Government, exposing its weaknesses and inconsistencies, disputing *actas*, and continually adding amendments to clauses of the Constitution. Partly because the debates on the Constitution were academic in tone the Federals were able to make a far greater impression than their numbers warranted. Figueras, a lawyer from Tarragona, who had moved in Madrid political circles since the 1850's and who had already had some parliamentary experience between 1854 and 1856, was accepted as their unofficial leader in the *Cortes*.[1] A skilled debater, an astute tactician, and lacking the dogmatism of the republican intellectuals, he was an ideal parliamentary man although, all observers agree, a weak character whose practising catholicism and devout strong-willed wife sometimes led the rank and file to suspect the sincerity of his republican convictions. He was ably supported by Pi and Castelar, who, although rivals in the inner councils of the party, complemented each other in the *Cortes*. The rhetoric and sweep of Castelar's historical generalizations did much to enhance the prestige of the Federals in a *Cortes* of poets, philosophers, and connoisseurs of oratory. But Pi provided the main impetus behind the party's criticisms of the Government. He soon established himself as their economic expert, attacking Figuerola's free-trade policy and his reliance on foreign loans to relieve the worsening financial situation.

Weaknesses in the financial system such as poor credit institutions which led to the spectacular crash on the Barcelona exchange in 1866—'the mother of the 1868 revolution' in Vicens's phrase—had bequeathed a difficult economic legacy to the Provisional Government. Furthermore, out of a total income of £17,860,000, it was estimated that £6,700,000 had been lost during the last three months of 1868 when the reaction of revolutionary juntas to the increasing expenses of an overloaded system of government patronage had been to abolish the *consumos* and to reduce the price of state monopolized salt and tobacco.[2] Figuerola attempted to

---

[1] E. Castelar, 'Figueras', *Fortnightly Review*, Mar. 1872.
[2] *The Times*, 5 Nov. 1868, 15 Mar. 1869. F.O. 72/1210, no. 78, 22 July 1869, Ffrench to Clarendon, report on the previous nine months.

replace lost revenue by an unpopular poll-tax and by the unsuccessful expedient of a 'patriotic loan' which, significantly, was only covered in Barcelona. This had led to the gradual raising of salt and tobacco prices which, with rumours that the *consumos* were to be reimposed, added to popular discontent. Discouraged by the failure of the internal loan and warned by popular feeling, Figuerola resorted to raising further foreign loans at high rates of interest.

Pi criticized this policy by exposing its political roots, arguing that economic reform was inseparable from a complete overhaul of the existing state structure.[1] Resorting to foreign loans and the poll-tax indicated two things: the country's lack of confidence in the new régime and the Government's reluctance to increase the tax burden of its main supporters. In this way the future of the country was mortgaged to a policy which ensured the continued political predominance of the parties represented in the coalition. By resorting to a poll-tax rather than an income-tax the Government favoured the *rentier* at the expense of those with little or no capital. When Pi went on to argue that Figuerola's policy towards agrarian banks favoured capital rather than labour he was echoing his arguments of the 1860's and was again attacking the political groups whose power derived from the dominance of the rural areas by the big landowners. Without a complete revolution economic progress was impossible, hence he argued for a drastic reduction of the over-staffed conscript Army and its replacement by a cheaper, small professional force, for stringent economy in the administration, and for the separation of Church and State on financial as well as rationalist grounds.

Even before these attacks the Government had played on Federal weaknesses. On 17 February Sagasta set the tone by accusing them of being socialists. Pi's speech on the 24th had elicited a similar response from the Progressive *El Imparcial* which, a month later, repeated the Government's attempts to reopen the divisions which had split the Democrats in the 1860's:[2] 'Who are the republicans?

---

[1] *Gaceta*, 25 Feb., 25, 30 Mar., 21 June 1869, Pi's speeches. Out of a total expenditure of £21,210,861, the Army's budget was £3,966,712; the Ministry of Justice, which paid the clergy, £2,110,940; and the largest single item, payment on the Public Debt, £6,735,583 (*The Times*, 5 Nov. 1868).   [2] *El Imparcial*, 25 Feb., 19 Mar. 1869.

Are they Unitarians or Federals, protectionists or free-traders, individualists or socialists, supporters of direct or indirect taxation, are they those of *La Discusión* who respect the decisions of the *Cortes* or those of *El Rojo* who reject them.' The disturbances at Jerez at the beginning of March which brought the anti-*quinta* campaign to a climax encouraged opponents to accuse them of spreading socialistic doctrines among the rural population of Andalusia, some of whom had been agitating for the return of common lands sold in the 1850's. Rubio, a Sevillano deputy, had defended seizure of old common lands because this was only a 'revolutionary antecedent to what must inevitably come from the *Cortes*'. Conversely, two other Andalusian deputies, themselves landowners, Paul y Angulo and Moreno Rodríguez, indignantly rejected the socialist charge.[1] But it did not need a Federal deputy to point out that the revolution had immediately been interpreted in Andalusia as a legal return to communal habits which had remained ingrained in Spanish custom. Although the exact relationship of the Federals to these rural outbreaks cannot be established, they had to bear the consequences of Pi's ideas, for which he had achieved notoriety in the 1860's and, even in 1869, his assurance that the *reparto de bienes* only referred to common lands was little relief to those who had bought them. Realizing the divisions of Federal opinion Pi deliberately played down the controversial aspect of socialism. On 19 May he said that socialism was being deliberately used to divide the Republicans, but he continued:[2]

One can be a republican and accept or reject the theories of socialism. . . . So long as liberty serves me for the resolution of questions I will accept it in preference to any other solution; but from the moment when liberty cannot solve them I will want and ask for the intervention of the State, because I believe that when one is dealing with the evils which afflict peoples it is necessary to remedy them by whatever means are at our disposal.

A further aspect of this division and one related to the socialist issue was the difference of opinion over free trade with the indi-

---

[1] *Gaceta*, 4 Apr. 1869.   [2] Ibid., 21 May 1869.

vidualists, particularly the Andalusians, who wanted cheap foreign textiles, following free-trade Democrat precedents, and the Catalans remaining ardent protectionists. This issue cut across party lines so that when the Catalan Progressive, Balaguer, spoke for protection he was supported by the Catalan Federals.[1] Although the Progressive protectionists were only a very small minority in the party Pi was still able to use the protection issue as a means of widening the differences in the Government, knowing Prim's own sympathy with Catalan demands.

It was in the debates on the Constitution that the Federals were most active in their opposition. 'Their uncompromising consistency', wrote Hay,[2] 'was inexplicable to the old parties . . . they were a solid phalanx in the *Cortes*.' The three articles which they contended most fiercely were those on religion, the form of government, and the militia issue. The general tenor of republican anticlericalism was far more rationalist and uncompromising. Pi and Garrido attacked the establishment of Church and State on rationalist and economic grounds. Pi's analysis was particularly resented for his exposure of the way in which those loudest in their defence of catholicism had benefited from the sale of Church lands and were now using religion to bolster property rights. But the speech by Suñer y Capdevila set the tone for republican anticlericalism which they never succeeded in dispelling. It is difficult to convey the hysterical reaction to his *Guerra a Dios* speech in which he attacked the doctrine of the Immaculate Conception, yet its importance as a factor in nullifying later appeals to Catholic opinion cannot be over-emphasized.[3] 'The Republic has become impossible,' commented *El Pensamiento español* two days later, 'no Catholic can now be republican.' Suñer's militant atheism was endorsed as enthusiastically and uncritically by the republican press as Castelar's liberal ideal of a free church in a free society

---

[1] *Gaceta*, 4, 9 Mar. 1869. On 4 May all Catalan deputies united in a petition for the reduction of port dues (the declaration of the Antilles trade as *cabotaje* by the junta had been revoked by the Madrid Government on 22 Nov.). Yet another petition was presented on 26 June 1869. Cf. Pugés, op. cit., pp. 140, 156.

[2] Hay, op. cit., pp. 366–8.

[3] *Gaceta*, 4, 5 May 1869, Pi and Suñer's speeches. See also *La Igualdad*, 6 June 1869, Suñer's article 'Una carta sobre la madre de Jesus' and his pamphlet *Dios*, Barcelona, 1869. Cf. J. L. Esquirol, *La Idea nueva del diputado: D. F. Suñer y Capdevila*, Madrid, 1869.

which he thought could revivify catholicism.[1] But ardent
Catholics, like the Carlist deputy Manterola, regarded the poetic
splendours of Castelar's oratory and liberal catholicism as insidious threats. Both Federal attitudes were anathema to ortho-
dox opinion.

Inevitably the main opposition was concentrated on the form
of government. All the amendments to Article 33 were presented
by the Republicans and they forced the *Cortes* to debate the issue
for eight days.[2] Their thirteen amendments ranged from Garrido's
demand for a plebiscite, basing his arguments on the assumption,
as the Carlists did, that only they represented the mass of the
nation, to specific criticisms of the hereditary principle of democratic monarchy and to justifications of federalism. The assumption was implicit in these arguments that the *Cortes* did not
represent the nation because of the corrupt election and the arbitrary fixing of the age limit. The only amendment with a tactical
purpose, one by Garrido stating that the head of the State must
be a Spaniard by birth, was aimed at exploiting the unpopularity
of the Unionist candidate Montpensier.[3] Finally, on 20 May, in
spite of republican opposition, the monarchy was voted the form
of government by 214–71.

But perhaps the most significant amendments were those to
Articles 28 and 107 on the liability of all Spaniards for military
service when the Federals failed to get the principle of a national
militia accepted. It now became abundantly clear that their main
popularity in the country lay in their unqualified support for
quinta abolition. A demonstration of women outside the *Cortes*
on 22 March and riots at Jerez accentuated this. After Prim broke
his promise with the decree of 25 March calling for 25,000 men,
the Federals could not resist the temptation to foment popular
discontent. The parliamentary Federals were anxious to give the
impression of orderliness, and republican *ayuntamientos* at Seville,

---

[1] *La Igualdad*, 12 May 1869; *Gaceta*, 13 Apr. 1869, the famous exchange between
Castelar and Manterola. Cf. Manterola, *Don Carlos o el petroleo*, Madrid, p. 26. For
Castelar's religious views see García de Castro, *Los Intelectuales y la Iglesia*, Madrid, 1934,
pp. 46 et seq.
[2] *Gaceta*, 13–21 May 1869. These are summarized in Carro Martínez, op. cit., pp. 261–8.
[3] Ibid., pp. 244–6, 374–5.

Málaga, and Barcelona avoided disturbances by raising loans to redeem conscripts, but the broken *quinta* promise made it difficult to restrain extremist agitators.[1] This popular passion, combined with the inability of the minority to affect either the course of legislation or modify the Constitution and the continued use of traditional methods of governmental patronage, began to change the nature and emphasis of the Federal movement. By the middle of May, at the time of the signing of the Pact at Tortosa, they were beginning to show a disposition towards *retraimiento*.[2] However homogeneous they might be as a voting body in the *Cortes* their impotence there brought latent disagreements to the surface and increased differences over tactics.

As early as March Pi had written pessimistically to a friend that there was a notable falling off in enthusiasm.[3] It was hard, too, to deny Sagasta's remark that the Federals' appeal had lain in their originality. Once the novelty had worn off there was the need for an agreed policy and firm leadership, both of which were absent. When the Constitution was finally voted on 1 June by 214–55 with the Federals signing it as individuals although not accepting it as a party, they were forced to face up to problems which they had postponed during the debates on the Constitution and to come to terms with the prevailing mood of frustration and disillusion in the country and among their own supporters. Although their achievement had been remarkable both in terms of the quality of their speeches and their discipline as a new and untried party, even many of their deputies now began to share the frustration of the rank and file and started to look to the new pactist organization in the provinces to provide the action which parliamentary activity had failed to generate.

On 18 May with the signing of the Pact of Tortosa, the first practical expression of pactist federalism, the initiative in the movement passed from the parliamentary party to the provincial Federals. Followed by similar Pacts signed at Córdoba, Valladolid, Eibar, and Coruña, a national organization was set

[1] *Actas capitulares* (Málaga), 23 Apr. 1869; Guichot, op. cit., p. 359; Carrera Pujal, op. cit. v. 195, 204. For *quinta* articles see *La Igualdad*, 16 Mar.–1 Apr. 1869.

[2] Ibid., 13 May 1869.

[3] Letter of Pi to Segundo Flóres, 6 Mar. 1869 (appendix 122 in Olivar Bertrand, op. cit.).

up.[1] The initiative for this came entirely from the provincial
Federals and only one deputy, Bes y Hediger from Tarragona,
played any part in their organization. At Tortosa twenty-two
representatives from the three provinces of the 'Ancient Crown
of Aragón'—Catalonia, Aragón, and Valencia with the Balearics,
called together on the initiative of Almirall and under the Presidency
of Bes y Hediger—signed on 18 May the first federal pact. The
favourable reception accorded to it both by the Federal press and
deputies encouraged other local committees to follow its example.
Although the wording of the various Pacts differed in details
that of Tortosa set the pattern. The purpose of it was succinctly
stated: 'to turn the rising of September from a *pronunciamiento*
into a revolution' and to perfect the federal organization of provinces united by geographical similarities and a common historical
past. This attitude to a common historical past was shown by the
appeal to the old provinces rather than to the arbitrary administrative creations of 1833 and to the interpretation of their history as
a struggle against despotic centralized power. In addition to emphasizing the cohesive ties of common historical experience, all
the other Pacts followed Tortosa in their agreement on the role
of the Federal party, following Pi in emphasizing the efficacy of
the power of ideas and propaganda. Although the Pacts recognized
the role played by the parliamentary party, they argued for a
greater participation of the provinces in the work of propaganda
and organization. They all specifically rejected the use of force:
'We feel natural repulsion towards solutions of force . . . we are
confident in the powerful virtue of our ideas; our principles have
conquered all intellects, and it will not be long before they direct
wills.' But it was added, although the *Cortes* vote for monarchy
did not in itself justify an appeal to arms: '. . . convinced of the
evils which the monarchy must inevitably produce we decline all
reponsibility for what might happen with its establishment'. This
alienation of reponsibility was the loophole which, under pro-
vocation in September, was to turn the pactist organizations into
revolutionary committees.

[1] Vera, op. cit. i. 889–1009; R.-Solis, op. cit. ii. 630–8. *La Igualdad*, 25 May, 13, 17,
18, 27 June 1869; *El Pueblo*, 16, 21 June 1869.

Under the stimulus of the voting of the Constitution on 1 June other pacts soon followed. With an Andalusian flair for publicity that at Córdoba attracted the widest attention, La Andalucía, organ of the Sevillano Federals, claimed, with exaggerated local pride, that Córdoba was of far greater significance than Tortosa not only because of the wider interest shown by outsiders and even foreigners, but because the Pact came as the climax to a campaign waged by the paper since the early sixties for a union of all the Andalusian provinces.[1] One of the clauses here made the right of insurrection more explicit. Revolt would be justified if 'the principles of the Spanish Revolution' were subjected to any 'attack of a general character' and if legal means were not sufficient to ensure the progress of the revolution. Three days later, at Valladolid, this was repeated in a slightly different form: 'All attacks of a general character against the individual rights proclaimed by the revolution will be considered as legitimate cause for revolt if no reparation is made by legal means.' Both other Pacts included a similar reservation of the right to rebel. In none of them was any attempt made to outline what might constitute 'attacks' nor was any attempt made to define the relationship of the Pacts to the parliamentary party or to each other. Expressions of regional cohesion, they failed to provide an answer to the problem of either leadership or co-ordination and as a result were unable to curb, canalize, or guide later outbursts of enthusiasm.

Pi, especially, recognized the need for providing some body to direct general policy, particularly in view of the coming recess when deputies would disperse to the provinces and be less controllable. With this in mind he took the initiative by inviting representatives of the Pacts to Madrid where on 30 June they signed a National Pact which 'would establish among the new groups of states a common bond which would give them vigour and force'.[2] This Pact would determine the general conduct of the party but would have no power to compel assent from the regional Pacts. Here reference to revolt was, if anything, less cautious: '. . . with the free practice of individual rights revolt is a crime; without it a duty, as much or more than a right. To embody

---

[1] *La Andalucía*, 1, 3 June 1869.   [2] Pi y Arsuaga, op. cit. iv. 547–52.

this duty in the Pact has seemed to us to-day not only convenient but from all points of view necessary.' The National Pact did not state what its action would be should these rights be violated in one single Pact area. It was hardly surprising that the National Pact did not provide a more definite lead because of the strong distrust of any central body. Only after Pi had brought pressure to bear on Bes y Hediger and Guerrero, who had both opposed the idea of a central Pact at Tortosa, were they willing to accept the need for one. The new Pact set up a central assembly composed of three representatives from each of the five regional Pacts. The members of this *Consejo* were to be responsible to their own committees and could be replaced by them at will. This organization might have been suitable in an existing federal system, but for organizing opposition it was singularly inefficient. Its main weakness lay in making the representatives responsible to their own committees; this meant that the organization of the Pacts was confederal with no surrender by them of any of their sovereignty. In addition, it isolated the party in the *Cortes*, for there the deputies, by the very act of being deputies, were committed to a policy of legal opposition which, at any moment, one or all of the Pact committees might disown depending on local conditions.

The legacy of the Pacts was confusion between the Pacts themselves, between them and the National Pact, and between the minority and the whole Pactist organization. This confusion in attributes and in responsibility was increased by the fact that many deputies with an eye to the regional committees sought mandates from them rather than from those who had elected them. The National Pact was the first attempt by Pi to control the new movement but it was a compromise solution imposed by force of circumstances. Reluctant to alienate provincial feeling, he had to make concessions which left the National Pact weak and ineffective. The whole organization, with its lack of clear definition of responsibilities and its reluctance to place too much power in the hands of a central body, was the first halting step towards practical federalism, but its weakness and impracticability were only exposed after the fruitless uncoordinated revolts of the autumn.

Hostility to any sort of central control, even towards the

compromise of 30 June, was immediately expressed by Almirall
in Barcelona where, on 15 July, he brought out a new paper pro-
vocatively named *El Estado catalán* in which he declared that he
did not recognize the committee set up by the National Pact.[1]
He intended that his new paper should be the official Federal
party paper in Barcelona and emphasized its independence of
La Igualdad and Madrid. He claimed a more important part for
Barcelona in the life of the nation arguing that the opening of the
Suez Canal would increase its economic importance.[2] Later, on
1 August, two more papers appeared in Barcelona—*El Pacto
federal* and *La Federación*. Although the latter was not a specifically
Federal paper but the official organ of the Catalan workers'
societies, it declared that 'the Federal Republic is the form of
government which would most conduce to the workers' emancipation'.[3] These three papers, appearing within a fortnight of each
other, indicated a quickening in Barcelona's political life. The
impetus of the pactist organization had come originally from the
Catalan Federals and now they were continuing to take a line
increasingly independent of Madrid. In view of these developments the need for a strong central leadership was more than ever
apparent, but at Madrid policy was still divided. In the course of
a ministerial crisis in early July over finance, the protection issue,
and public order, Prim had offered Pi and Castelar, through
Zorrilla, the two Ministries of Finance and Development. The
opinion of the parliamentary minority was divided. Garrido and
Castelar were in favour of acceptance but as Pi refused to take
part in a ministry which would compromise him in the eyes of
the provincials the offer was rejected.[4]

More important than divisions of opinion over Prim's offer
was the absence of organization at Madrid. The National Pact
had set up, on paper at least, a council of three delegates from
each Pact, but there is no evidence of this having been set up or,

[1] *El Estado catalán*, 16 July, 3 Aug. 1869.
[2] Ibid., 15 July 1869, prospectus, 5 Aug. 1869.
[3] *La Federación*, 1 Aug. 1869. *El Pacto federal* described itself as a 'workers' paper'.
[4] Vera, op. cit. i. 1013–14. Ffrench reported that Silvela, a Unionist minister, told him
that Zorrilla had made the offer without consulting Prim, who was forced to deny that an
offer had been made in the Council of Ministers (F.O. 72/1210, no. 62, 8 July 1869, Ffrench
to Clarendon).

if it was formed, of its members remaining in Madrid. Parallel with this absence of leadership was the increasing belligerence of the Federal press. This was not only confined to Barcelona but was also apparent in Madrid where, on 23 August, *La Igualdad* came under the direction of Paul y Angulo whose series of articles *Memorias de un pronunciamiento* gave wide currency to the myth of republican participation in the September Revolution.

In July Carlist disturbances in Catalonia had given Sagasta the excuse to revive the decrees of 4 April 1821 which gave discretionary powers to civil governors. Federals felt that this was aimed at them as much as at the Carlists. The dispersal of deputies to the provinces in the summer recess made it difficult to keep any control from Madrid over increasing tension fanned by the Madrid and the provincial press and by propaganda speeches like Castelar's at Zaragoza on 19 September where his enthusiastic welcome 'eclipsed Espartero's'. The incident which brought the uneasy tension to a climax was the murder at Tarragona on 21 September of the secretary of the Civil Governor during disturbances on the arrival of Pierrard. Republican papers deplored the incident but their tone of self-righteous indignation changed to fury when the Government imprisoned Pierrard and began to disarm the militia at Tarragona and Tortosa as a precaution against further excesses. Sagasta, alive to the possibilities, published a decree forbidding republican demonstrations of any sort. It was this decree, with its apparent threat to the Federals' very existence, which provoked a reaction in Barcelona. When the news of Tarragona had first arrived there, the provincial committee had met and declared that the Barcelona militia had given no cause to be disarmed. From the 23rd to the 25th the Civil Governor temporized, but in the afternoon of the 25th the mayor was summoned to the Governor and told to send the militia commanders to him as the Government had decided to disarm them. This was the signal for barricades to be set up, but even then negotiations continued until suddenly, according to Roure, a chance shot led to the outbreak of fighting.[1]

---

[1] *El Estado catalán*, 25, 26 Sept. 1869; Roure, op. cit. ii. 142–4; Serraclara, *La Nueva Inquisición*, Barcelona, 1869—written protesting against his trial by a military court.

Lacking any plan, resistance was short and by the 28th the revolt had been crushed. The *Ayuntamiento* was dissolved, the Federals' papers suppressed, and the leaders imprisoned. On the 28th the provincial committee resigned its powers into the hands of a revolutionary junta which undertook the task of raising the rest of Catalonia and, in the name of the Tortosa Pact, to appeal to the other Pacts for support. Catalonia answered immediately as members of the junta put themselves at the head of local Federals— Joarizti at Vilanueva y Geltru, Lostau at Igualada, and Suñer y Capdevila in traditionally republican Ampurdan. Discontent with the *quintas* and social and economic discontent predisposed a few people in these towns to join the revolt, but the general reaction seems to have been apathetic.[1] Certainly the military found no difficulty whatever in putting down the revolts. Unlike the Carlists, the Federals centred their resistance on towns where troops and artillery could be easily concentrated. Only in Ampurdan did the revolt last longer than a week, and even there at the first appearance of the military Suñer's band melted away and he was forced to flee to France. If it was true, as Vera estimated, that the Federals had 8,000 men under arms in Catalonia their complete failure is a damning comment on their leadership and lack of organization. Suñer de Capdevila was the only leader of the revolt to draw the lesson that the Federals had more to gain from legal opposition than from armed rising.[2]

Meanwhile, at the beginning of October, Federals were appealing to arms in the south where a rising had been most feared by the Government. As the large towns had been heavily garrisoned, the risings focused on smaller towns like Utrera, Carmona, and Puerto de Santa María. Seville and Cádiz, where the militia had been disarmed, were unaffected by the revolt and in Málaga there was only a small undirected riot. At Seville the provincial committee, in conference with the city's deputies, decided on revolt but planned first to raise surrounding towns, concentrate on Utrera, and then advance on Seville after cutting communications

---

[1] F.O. 72/1211, no. 16, 7 Oct. 1869, Ffrench to Clarendon, quoting the Barcelona consul.

[2] Vera, op. cit. ii. 33. Suñer's manifesto is in Olivar Bertrand, op. it., p. 265 and p. 283 note. Cf. Masriera, *Barcelona isabellina y revolucionaria*, Barcelona, 1929, pp. 247 et seq.; P. Cariño, *Sucesos de la Bisbal*, Barcelona, n.d.

with Cádiz and Córdoba. After cutting the line to Cádiz, the Sevillano rebels dispersed even before the military had taken the field. Five deputies were implicated here but no contact seems to have been established with Paul and Guillén, who were working farther south. The rising here degenerated into a pursuit into the hills. At Carmona on 4 October the Federal Republic was proclaimed but a detachment of the Civil Guard sent from Seville snuffed it out. In the south-east the rising of 2 October at Alicante failed to develop because of the reluctance of local Federals to rise, and the leaders here, with a few supporters, fled to the country.[1] An attempt by Orense Rispa and Estévanez to raise Bejar petered out through lack of support and because of the opposition of the local Federal militia. The local Federal leader here was Brigadier Peco, an ex-Carlist, but apart from him and Pierrard the Army nowhere seems to have been touched by republicanism.[2]

The two most formidable risings were those at Valencia and Zaragoza. What distinguishes these risings from the others was the fierceness of the resistance, the concentration of the Federals' forces in the two cities aided by peasants from the countryside, and the fact that, in both cases, the risings originated in the decision of the captains-general to disarm the local militias after the suspension of the guarantees announced on 5 October. These risings were occasioned neither by orders from a central committee nor by the desire to assist Federals in other parts of the country but by the resistance of local Federals to the threat of being disarmed. On 6 October there was considerable unease among the militia at Valencia. They accepted the promise of the captain-general that they would not be disarmed, but when soldiers began to occupy strategic positions on the 8th fighting broke out and lasted for six days, when Ocon, a Federal participant, estimated that some 6,000 Federals fought 23,000 soldiers. At Zaragoza the situation was complicated by a rift among the Federals, many of whom were opposed to a rising, and hence the revolt lacked some of the unanimity of Valencia, but at Zaragoza

[1] R.-Solís, ii. 648, 653–7—he took part in the rising near Alicante. Guichot, op. cit., p. 366.
[2] Estévanez, op. cit., pp. 314–23; F. Rispa y Perpiña, *Cincuenta años de conspirador: — memorias político-revolucionarias, 1853–1930*, Barcelona, 1932, pp. 123–37.

peasants who had come into the city provided the nucleus of resistance in the fierce fighting which broke out on the 7th and lasted five days.[1]

The subduing of Valencia and Zaragoza meant the end of risings which, through lack of organization and a naïve belief in spontaneous revolution, had enabled the military to snuff out one centre of resistance after another. Although the stimulus to revolt undoubtedly came from local causes, from the attempt to disarm militias or to replace republican *ayuntamientos*, from social causes as at Zaragoza, and from distrust of the Government's general intentions, there remains the question of the extent to which plans had been made for a general rising after the failure of the Federals to prevent the Constitution from being passed in the *Cortes*. Evidence of a rather dubious character was produced later showing how a rising had been planned for 1 November but that the events at Tarragona had forced the date to be moved forward, but exact evidence on this point is impossible to obtain.[2] Federal accounts of the genesis of the rising are unsatisfactory; their concern was to find a scapegoat.[3] It is nevertheless possible to advance a hypothesis pieced together from the various accounts which exist. Federal arguments advanced for the failure of the revolts centre on the assertion that a central committee gave the order for a general revolt to take place after the suppression of the Barcelona rising. The responsibility therefore rested with this committee to decide on the extent and timing of the revolt. This central committee, variously called the 'Directory' or the 'Triumvirate', consisted in most accounts of Castelar, Figueras, and Orense, but there is no evidence to show that these three had ever obtained a mandate from the party which would bind it to obey their directives.[4] What seems definite is that the National Pact was not functioning when the news of Tarragona reached Madrid. When

---

[1] J. D. Ocon, *Los Héroes de Valencia*, Marseilles, 1869; Gimeno y Cabana, *El partido republicano de Valencia ante la Historia*, Valencia. n.d. F.O. 72/1211, 10, 18 Oct. 1869, reports of vice-consul at Valencia, See the full account in Bermejo, op. cit. i. 696–716, and R.-Solís, ii. 651, 657–60. Federal estimates of their total number involved in the risings vary from 30,000 to Paul's wildly exaggerated 90,000.   [2] See below, p. 123.

[3] Vera, op. cit. ii. 17–47; Pi y Arsuaga, op. cit. iv. 554–70; Paul y Angulo, *Les Assassins du maréchal Prim et la politique en Espagne*, Paris, 1886.

[4] Cf. Paul, p. 144; R.-Solís, p. 654; Vera, ii. 46; Estévanez, p. 314.

the Government issued its decree of the 26th the Federals' manifesto of the 28th protesting against it was not signed by any committee of the Pact but by an arbitrary selection of deputies still
left in Madrid. Pi's name does not appear on this document. This
was because he had left Madrid on private business just after the
news of Tarragona arrived. He suspected that some sort of general
rising was being planned. During the course of his business trip
he found local Federal committees in Ciudad Real and Alcazar
San Juan preparing to rise on receipt of a general order signed by
Figueras. When Pi arrived back in Madrid some time after the
28th the rising was already a fact. The discrepancy in the various
accounts of this 'signed order' raises doubts as to whether an order
had ever been signed at all.

None of the sources is completely reliable but accounts by
Estévanez and Rispa, both participants in the revolt, indicate the
existence of an inner revolutionary body working independently
of any official leadership.[1] According to Rispa, a *Centro de acción
revolucionaria* had been set up under the presidency of Pierrard,
who had already in February been elected to the presidency of
Viralta's extremist club in Barcelona. Pierrard, it seems, had
wished to go to Andalusia to raise extremist elements there but,
being dissuaded from this, he went to Catalonia instead. At
Tarragona he defied his colleague's instructions not to hold any
public meetings and, by doing so, precipitated Sagasta's arbitrary
measures. These events in Catalonia now forced the hand of the
extremists at Madrid. When it was clear that the Federals there
were not unanimously in favour of an armed rising (Rispa refers
to a meeting of an 'Assembly' at which Castelar and Figueras
supported a rising and Pi and Orense remained neutral), a group
began to prepare for one. Preparations were made to rise in Madrid
where the garrison had been depleted but, when these fell through
due to inability to win over the military, it was decided to concentrate on Extremadura and Andalusia. It was presumably this
decision, reached according to Rispa by a group including Castelar, Figueras, Orense, Guisasola, and himself, to which Estévanez,
refers in his account. He says that he rose from a sick-bed as soon

[1] Ibid., pp. 314 et seq.; Rispa y Perpiña, pp. 105 et seq.

as he heard of the order for a general rising and, in accordance with agreements reached with the extremists Guisasola, Pierrard, Joarizti, Rispa, and Guillén, left Madrid to raise Bejar.

What emerges is that there was no recognized fount of authority at this time, no 'Directory' to which Paul refers which had a mandate from the party; the only officially recognized body, and even that was not recognized by the Catalans, was the National Pact, but this, as has been pointed out, was not functioning at the end of September. Figueras, Castelar, and Orense, whom Vera blames, could not be held responsible as no one was under any obligation to obey them. But, by using their names, the extremists could be assured of wide support at the same time as they freed themselves from responsibility and, in the case of failure, the scapegoats would be to hand. The onus for failure did in fact rebound on those who were supposed to have signed some order for a general revolt, while those who died, were exiled, or imprisoned became martyrs to the cause. Because Orense had risked his life at Bejar he survived the opprobrium while Pi's convenient absence from Madrid for private reasons made it possible for him to plead ignorance and to escape some of the resentment felt towards Castelar and Figueras, although it must be noticed that the general attitude of the leadership condemning the armed revolt discredited the Federals with the International's leaders at Barcelona and influenced them later in their decision to abstain from political activity.[1]

The failure of the revolts underlined the inefficacy of the pactist organization in providing an answer to the problem posed at Tarragona—when should abuse of the powers by civil governors constitute a justification for a general rising and who should be responsible for initiating it? The course of events had clearly shown that where the stimulus to revolt came from local causes— the decision of captains-general to disarm local militias, as at Barcelona, Valencia, and Zaragoza—resistance was largely spon-

---

[1] *La Igualdad,* 27 Dec. 1869; Bermejo, op. cit. i. 820. Pi categorically denied that he was implicated (Pi y Arsuaga, op. cit. v. 522). Cf. T. von Bernhardi, *Aus dem Leben Theodor von Bernhardis,* vol. ix, Leipzig, 1906, pp. 205 et seq. Bernhardi was Bismarck's personal agent in Spain. He travelled widely and was well informed about republican activities. *La Federación,* 12 June 1870, 'Las clases trabajadores y la política', quoted in Martí, op. cit., pp. 113–14.

taneous, but elsewhere, as at Málaga, Cádiz, and Seville, where the militia had already been disarmed or was sympathetic to the Government, it was impossible to raise more than a handful of adventurers. The failures discredited the idea of spontaneous revolution, emphasized the need for obtaining foreign support before another revolt was attempted, and underlined the necessity for the Federals to clarify their aims and to reorganize the whole basis of the party.

The six months after October 1869 saw a degree of self-analysis which had been noticeably absent during the previous year. Three main problems deserve attention: how the revolts affected the role of the parliamentary minority, their effect on the party leadership, and the diverging views among Republicans on federalism itself. The revolts forced them to examine their role as a parliamentary party and to determine their attitude towards *retraimiento*. When the *Cortes* had reassembled on 1 October only nineteen Federal deputies were present and these stayed until the suspension of constitutional guarantees on 5 October, when they withdrew from the *Cortes*, making their return conditional on a restoration of the guarantees. A conditional *retraimiento* condemned the Government's action without implying complicity in the revolts, but it was an anomalous situation illustrating the dilemma of a party whose main effectiveness as an opposition seemed to rest on its extra-parliamentary strength. But their deputies had little alternative to withdrawal if they were to placate revolutionary opinion, although by itself *retraimiento* could be no more than a sterile protest. Prim himself was anxious to prevent the Federals from withdrawing. This may have been due to his fear that removal of their opposition would hasten the break-up of his coalition ministry. Although rumours that he was actually planning a coup to consolidate his own position with the aid of the Federals seem implausible his attempts to play down Sagasta's impetuous desire to force the issue with the Federals might be explained by his wish to keep as many lines open as possible.[1]

---

[1] Martí, op. cit., pp. 206, 236; *La Igualdad*, 29 Sept., 20 Dec. 1869; Hay, op. cit., pp. 318–19. Silvela denied the unlikely rumour in a conversation with Ffrench (F.O. 72/1211, no. 169, 14 Oct. 1869).

When, in fact, the coalition did break up in November with the resignation of two Unionists the Federals' *retraimiento* had outlived its usefulness and Pi argued for the minority's immediate return. His success in overcoming resistance to this course in a policy meeting of 22 November was a personal victory for his reiterated policy of legal opposition.[1] By practical demonstration of effective parliamentary opposition he hoped to break the tendency of *retraimiento* and to build the Federals into an effective parliamentary party which could eventually come into power by legal means. The press reaction to his speech on 27 November on the party's return to the *Cortes*, in which he probed the differences dividing Progressives and Unionists, was ample evidence of how effective this policy could be.[2]

Pi's growing ascendancy was also illustrated by his defeat of Castelar in a meeting of the minority on 24 November. At this meeting Castelar had attempted to create a united republican front aimed to attract the Unitarians by excluding any mention of federalism in a draft policy manifesto. It was the first expression of Castelar's disillusion with federalism, but he only succeeded in obtaining the support of seven of the deputies against thirty-three who supported Pi's reaffirmation that the doctrine of the pact remained a cardinal point in the republican programme.[3] It was, in fact, clear by November 1869 that Pi's personal position in the party had been strengthened and not weakened by the revolts' failure. But the small minority who supported Castelar was a dangerous portent as it exposed the threat of the Unitarians seizing the initiative in the republican movement by trying to exploit the disillusion after the revolts by blaming their failure on the pactist theory. The Unitarian *El Pueblo* had constantly attacked Pi, and the speeches of García Ruiz had been directed as much against the Federals as against the monarchists. In June he had written a well-argued anti-Federal tract.[4] Still more striking was the Unitarians' equivocal behaviour over the suspected relation-

[1] Vera, op. cit. ii. 52.
[2] *El Imparcial*, 28 Nov. 1869, accused Pi of playing into the Unionists' hands. Cf. *El Pueblo*, 29 Nov.   [3] Vera, op. cit. ii. 53–58.
[4] *El Pueblo*, 20 May 1869; *Gaceta*, 15 May 1869, Ruiz's speech; García Ruiz, *La República Democrática Unitaria*, Madrid, 1869.

ship of the Federals with the Cuban rebels. In November *El Pueblo* printed three letters written in the summer by a certain Miguel Pacheco, 'the revolutionary delegate of Cuba in Spain', and addressed to the rebel leader Céspedes. They referred to money for financing a Federal revolt, shipments of arms in an American ship at Cádiz, and named the leading members of Andalusian republican clubs, giving 1 November as the projected date for a revolt. The fact that they were printed in *El Pueblo* and, as a result, discussed in the *Cortes* four days later shows how the Unitarians were prepared to exploit the traditional Spanish resentment against rebellious overseas possessions by accusing their own political rivals of being in their pay.[1]

As Pi pointed out on the 17th, the Federals' claim to retain their militia had been the cardinal issue of the revolts. As with the Progressives at an earlier date, the militia was a party force with no legal standing and if left unsuppressed would soon become the focal point in their whole organization. The main result of Prim's energetic action had been to break the militia's power in the Federals' main centres. Future revolutionary activity would be dependent on obtaining armed help from either international republicanism or from the Cuban rebels. The breaking of the militia and the exiling of the extremists gave Pi the necessary breathing space to impose his leadership on the party. He favoured a stronger central organization—the National Pact showed this— but although he was able to summon an assembly of the party in March 1870 for this purpose he had to face opposition not only to his theories but also to his increasing dominance within the party. His problem was how to use the provincial Federals, whose independence he wished to curb but whose enthusiasm he wanted to retain, against those who were arguing for an abandonment of the pactist theory altogether.

How the republican movement would react to new developments would largely depend on Pi's ability to convert his growing influence inside the party into official leadership, trying to impose through it his own conception of revolution by propaganda and legal opposition controlled by a central organization inspired by

[1] *El Pueblo*, 19 Nov. 1869, 'Fiat Lux'. See *Gaceta*, 23 Nov. for the *Cortes* debate.

his own 'rational' principles. The main threats could be expected to come from the insidious attempts by the small but able group of Unitarians to exploit the growing divisions among the Federals, and resentment at Pi's increasing dominance and from a revival of revolutionary extremism should the exiled rebels return. This would be the greater danger as they would try to alter the emphasis of the party from the conception of expansion by propaganda and legal means of revolution by means of a closed conspiratorial group working secretly for the Government's overthrow. It was doubly imperative therefore for Pi to establish his own position before the extremists returned to work on feelings of disillusion and betrayal.

6

Challenge from the Right: Pi's Hegemony, 1870

DURING the first half of 1870 the Federal party was completely reorganized and by the end of May Pi had been accepted as its official leader. It was he, as President of the newly established Directory, who had to meet the changing conditions brought about in the latter half of the year by the declaration of a republic in France, by the election in the *Cortes* of Amadeo of Savoy as the new king of Spain, by the increase in the activity of the International which threatened to wean potential supporters away from the party, and by the revival within the republican movement itself of an extremist wing, with a secret organization and devoted to violent revolution.

From January until the end of May, when the new organization was established, three aspects of Federal activity are paramount. These are: the reaction of the party to the changing governmental situation; next, the first Federal Assembly, called to reorganize the party, which set up a central Directory under Pi's presidency; finally, the aftermath of decisions reached at the Assembly in which resentment at Pi's dominance led to an internal struggle for leadership and the demand for a restatement and clarification of federal theory culminating in the Declaration of the Press, the defeat of the Unitarians' attempt to capture the party, and the confirmation of Pi's position.

Although Prim had removed the immediate Federal threat by suppressing the autumn revolts his position in the Government was no stronger. If anything, the removal of opposition had enabled internal differences to assume a more vigorous form, exposing the divisions within the revolutionary coalition. His relations with the Unionists had deteriorated with his adamant

refusal to consider their candidate, Montpensier, for the throne—
a refusal determined by diplomatic as well as political considerations. Montpensier's appearance in Madrid in February, lavishly
distributing money, did not make matters any easier.[1] As Prim's
relations with the Unionists had worsened he had shown his
readiness to come to terms with the Democrats; in June 1869
Echegaray and Becerra had replaced two Unionists in the Government. Increasing difficulties with the Unionists in the autumn of
1869 had made him reluctant for the Federals to leave the *Cortes*
after 5 October, for their opposition, small though it may have
been, was a valuable factor in keeping the revolutionary coalition
intact. The way, too, in which the Government, in Catalonia
at least, had been far less severe with Federals than with Carlists
seemed further evidence of a desire not to alienate them more than
could be helped.[2] In November, during the Federals' absence
from the *Cortes*, there had been another ministerial crisis when
two Unionists were replaced by a Democrat, Martos, and a Progressive, Figuerola. Ten days before the *Cortes* reassembled on
3 January the breakdown of the Genoese candidacy led to further
changes when Zorrilla and Martos, ardent supporters of the Duke,
resigned. It was an indication of the extent to which Prim was
now dependent on Democrat and Left-wing Progressive support
when Rivero and Monteros Rios entered the ministry. Increased
Democrat participation meant stronger Unionist opposition as
well as conflict between Democrats and Progressives over the
distribution of offices.[3]

These were not the only worries facing Prim. In February it
was feared that the Carlists would revolt and that, with the
Government embarrassed in the north, the Federals in the south
would seize the opportunity to rise again. Catholic feeling was to
be further antagonized by a decree requiring the clergy to swear
allegiance to the Constitution, implying acceptance of the principle
of freedom of worship.[4] There was also the intractable Cuban

[1] Hay, op. cit., p. 378; Bernhardi, op. cit., p. 253.
[2] F.O. 72/1211, no. 16, 7 Oct. 1869; Layard to Clarendon, enclosure from Barcelona
consul.
[3] For this see Pirala, 'El decreto de un consejo de ministros', *La España moderna*, Apr.
1894.   [4] *Gaceta*, 17 Mar. 1870.

problem needing another *quinta* in March and bringing with it much unpopularity and rioting. National confidence in Prim had been severely shaken by the disclosure of his secret talks in the summer of 1869 with General Sickles, the newly appointed United States ambassador, and by his attempt then to try and negotiate a settlement of the Cuban problem.[1] The extreme touchiness of Spanish public opinion over the Antilles and Prim's secretive methods made it only too easy for the Unionists to accuse him of betraying Spanish interests to the United States. In addition to these troubles the frustration of his greatest ambition through the breakdown of his plans for Iberian Union with the failure of the Portuguese candidacy and the failure, too, of an approach to Britain to cede Gibraltar in return for Ceuta, emphasized his inability to recoup his waning popularity by measures which would have gratified national pride.[2] The most sinister feature, however, was that his main support, the army officers, were becoming restive. The appointment of the popular Unionist general, Caballero de Rodas, to be Captain-General of Cuba in June 1869 merely turned him from being a nuisance in domestic politics to becoming one of the bitterest critics of Prim's Cuban policy. At home, the discontent caused among Unionist officers by Prim's promotions after the Federal revolts compelled him in February to exile five colonels to the Canary Islands.[3]

By the beginning of March, therefore, the difficulties of finding a new ruler and embarrassments in domestic policy forced him into greater dependence on the Democrats and stimulated those Federals whose sympathies were closer to them than to their own extremists to try and attract Prim towards a *república templada*.[4] This policy cannot have appeared entirely fanciful to conservative

---

[1] R. Guerra y Sánchez, *Historia de la guerra de los diez años 1868–78*, La Habana, 1950, p. 384; Pirala, 'La Venta de Cuba', *La España moderna*, Dec. 1894. Sickles, one of the 'Young America' group of the 1850's, gave considerable moral support to the Federals in the next three years.

[2] C. W. Clark, 'Marshal Prim and the question of the cession of Gibraltar to Spain', *Hispanic American Historical Review*, vol. 19, 1939.

[3] F.O. 72/1230, no. 36, 25 Feb. 1870, Layard to Clarendon. As early as June 1869 Ffrench had reported that Prim was trying to recoup his waning prestige by army promotions. For promotions after the 1869 revolts see *Gaceta*, 2, 15 Nov. 1869.

[4] Pi y Arsuaga, op. cit. v. 721.

Republicans for although Prim had always been scornful about the depth of republican feeling in the country, acceptance of a republic might solve the vexed question of the succession with its diplomatic complications; it would free him from his equivocal relationship with the Unionists; it would guarantee republicanism itself against impractical federalism and growing radicalism, and, finally, Republicans and Prim were united in wanting Iberian Union. In June 1869, when there seemed a possibility that the Federals could enter a ministry, extremist opinion had precluded acceptance. Now, however, with the extremists in exile, with pactism discredited, and with the increased Democrat representation in the Government the chances of *rapprochement* seemed quite hopeful.

Before Prim could be expected to respond to any overtures it was first necessary to purge republicanism of federal and radical tendencies. Castelar's federalism was lukewarm as his behaviour in November had shown. Moreover, he had been in favour of accepting Prim's offer of the previous June and had only been dissuaded by Pi. Meanwhile García Ruiz and Ruano, in favour of an approach to Prim and suspecting Castelar's and Figueras's jealousy towards Pi's growing ascendancy, were trying to win over Federal opinion.[1] It is against this background that the opening of the first Federal Assembly on 6 March must be viewed.

It must have been with this in mind that at a meeting of the Pact representatives on 20 February Castelar's friend Morayta, a history lecturer at the university, editor of the conservative *La República Ibérica*, and a prominent mason, suggested that an Assembly of the Federal party should meet in Madrid in the following month. The aim of the projected Assembly—to provide a greater degree of centralized leadership so as to avoid past confusion—was shared by both Pi and those, like Morayta, in favour of *rapprochement*, but for different reasons. Out of sympathy with the October revolts and the use of violence, Pi wished to tighten control over the party so as to restrain extremism but at the same time retaining the pactist theory.

When the Assembly met Pi was unanimously elected president.

[1] M. Revilla, *Historia y defensa de la Declaración de la Prensa*, Madrid, 1870.

Forty-eight provinces were represented by delegations varying in size but each carrying a single vote.[1] It was the first national meeting with direct representation. The business of the Assembly was divided into two halves: organization and future tactics. The most important organizational change was the by-passing of the old Pacts and their ill-defined attributes by the setting up of a Directory of Five to direct policy and propaganda and to co-ordinate the activities of local committees. The Assembly was to determine policy, the Directory to put its decisions into practice. The convocation of a new Assembly was to be left to the discretion of the Directory or to any ten provinces demanding its recall. All republican juntas were to be renewed by universal suffrage and the right of provinces and even towns to form centres was recognized. Among the resolutions passed was a request for draft Federal constitutions to be submitted to the Directory, a message of fraternal goodwill to Portuguese Republicans, and the hope that the colonies would accept federalism as the solution to their problems. The election to the Directory of Pi, Castelar, Figueras, Orense, and Barbera showed that much of the rancour of the winter had died down, but Pi's ascendancy was further stressed when, in addition to the reaffirmation of pactist federalism, he was elected to be its President. For the first time he was officially acknowledged as leader of the movement—a position he was to hold with re-election until the end of 1872. It is significant to notice, though, that the emphasis on the efficacy of propaganda and the peaceful nature of the party stressed during the Assembly was in marked contrast to the letters from exiles, keeping alive the memories of 1869 and calling for revolutionary intransigence, which were appearing in the Federal press at the same time.[2] It underlined the fact that Pi's ascendancy was only made possible by the absence of the extremists.

It was soon apparent that those who favoured an approach to Prim had nothing to gain from the convocation of an Assembly dominated by provincial Federals for whom Prim's name was

---

[1] Pi y Arsuaga, op. cit. v. 717–29; Vera, op. cit. ii. 82–90; *La Igualdad*, 11 Mar. 1869. Twenty-seven provinces sent 3 delegates, 12 sent 2, 7 only 1, and Guipuzcoa 5.

[2] Ibid., 12, 16, 23, 31 Mar. 1869. Cf. the first cautious policy manifesto of the Directory quoted in Pi y Arsuaga, op. cit. v. 729–30.

synonymous with brutal repression. They remained unconvinced
by tactical arguments for *rapprochement* and were only willing to
agree to a centralization of control provided Pi remained in the
key position. In addition to the confidence he inspired and to his
obvious ability, he owed this new predominance to developments in late February and early March, which, unforeseen by
those in favour of an approach to Prim, considerably weakened
their arguments. If Prim were to be attracted to a republic the
conservatives must show that they were able to dominate the
radical elements in the party. This, however, they were unable
to do.

In February, unemployment in Madrid had led to demonstrations at which inflammatory socialist speeches had been made.
Demonstrations organized by Federal clubs were held demanding
work from the Government. Marches on the *Cortes* were planned
and a petition was presented to the Government by the deputy
Luis Blanc, the spokesmen of working-class Federals. Agitation
continued into March when rumours of a new *quinta* increased
their activity.[1] On 14 March Prim, out riding with his son, who
although only eight had been made an honorary captain, was
stoned by workers attending an anti-*quinta* meeting presided over
by Sorní, a prominent Federal deputy. On the 16th the funeral
of Isabella's cousin, the neo-republican Enrique de Bourbon, who
had been killed four days earlier in a duel with Montpensier, was
turned into a mass popular demonstration.[2] This show of radical
republicanism and anti-Prim feeling among the rank-and-file
supporters weakened the arguments of those who believed Prim
could be attracted to a republic, at the same time as the duel, by
discrediting Montpensier, strengthened Prim's hand in his dealings
with the Unionists. It was clear from the behaviour of the Federals
during the parliamentary crisis of 19–21 March, when the storm
between Progressives and Unionists broke over Silvela's amendment to Figuerola's finance Bill, that any idea of attracting Prim

[1] *Gaceta*, 30 Mar. 1870, *quinta* decree. For anti-*quinta* rioting see F.O. 72/1233, 8, 18
Apr. 1870, Layard to Clarendon, enclosure from Barcelona and Seville consuls. In the
Gracia riots Carlists and unpaid officers were exploiting anti-*quinta* feeling. See also *La
Igualdad*, 11, 14, 18, 24 Feb., 3, 22 Mar. 1869.
[2] Hay, op. cit., pp. 373–84.

had been jettisoned as the Federals saw the chance to become an effective parliamentary opposition for the first time.[1]

When the Assembly dispersed on 31 March, Pi's position as leader of the party seemed secure and the reaffirmation of pactist federalism in the closing manifesto was clear evidence of his ascendancy backed by the support of the provincial Federals and the Madrid clubs. But this did not mean that all differences within the party had vanished. There remained the undigested extremists still in exile and, more important, the party's right wing which had been routed in the course of the Assembly's debates. This group, disliking the political implications of pactist federalism and the threat of radical social extremism which seemed to accompany it, sought an opportunity to reverse the Assembly's decisions. Their Declaration of the Press on 7 May must therefore be seen as the corollary to Pi's success in the Assembly. This Declaration was the protest of a group of Madrid intellectuals and journalists against the increasing influence of Pi and his theories. It had its origin in a series of debates held in the *Ateneo* in March in which federalism in internal government and in international relations had been discussed. In the debates, Revilla, a young Krausist intellectual, and Tubino, a prominent Sevillano intellectual, had defended the Federal principle against the attacks of the Progressives.[2] In the course of the debate Revilla came to the conclusion that all that divided the Federals from the Unitarians was the doctrine of the pact—the cardinal point of Pi's Federal theory. After discussing his views with Tubino and Sánchez Ruano they agreed to collect the journalists, deputies, and directors of republican papers in Madrid whom they could trust and, by means of a surprise and unanimous anti-pactist declaration by all the leading republican papers, force Pi to yield. A meeting took place on 27 March which included leading Federal journalists and those deputies who had supported Castelar's first draft of the 20 November manifesto and who had been in favour of an approach to Prim.

Figueras, who as the nominal leader of the party in the *Cortes*

[1] Ibid., pp. 328–35; *Gaceta*, 20–22 Mar. 1869, debates on the proposed sale of the Rio Tinto and Almaden mines; F.O. 72/1232, no. 56, 21 Mar. 1870, Layard to Clarendon.

[2] *El Imparcial*, 3, 10, 15, 21 May 1870. Cf. J. Brandt, *Towards the New Spain*, Chicago, 1933, pp. 114–25.

was suspected of jealousy at Pi's new position, was also approached. He argued that Pi would not dare to oppose a unanimous declaration by the press. Castelar, however, after being worsted in November, would not commit himself, preferring to remain neutral rather than challenge Pi's newly established position. On 7 May the Declaration appeared in the leading Federal papers at Madrid.[1] The signatories declared that they, the 'true' Federals as distinct from the confederationists, were united in resisting the theory of pacts which they claimed would mean: '... a confederation of states and cantons, independent and only united by more or less arbitrary pacts and alliances'. They then defined their own conception of the 'republic', discovering that the difference between the 'true' Federals and the Unitarians was negligible. Both recognized the complete autonomy of the municipality and of the provinces in all that concerned their own internal affairs. They admitted that insurrection could be justified only in the face of a complete and systematic violation of natural rights. Finally, they repudiated all demagogic and anarchic tendencies. Socialism, they declared, was not an integral part of republican dogma. All socialist systems which did not run counter to the 'principles of Spanish democracy' could exist within the Republican party but authoritarian socialism was barred. The main criticism was, however, against Pi's contention that the pact was fundamental in order to give juridical form to federalism—the view which he had expressed in *La Igualdad:*[2] 'In federal organization the State, the province, the town are three entities equally autonomous linked by synallagamatic and concrete pacts. Each has its own sphere of action according to the interests which it represents and each can move freely without disturbing the other.' Pi's theory in fact made him a confederationist, but as only sovereign States could confederate, it would be necessary first to break the nation's unity and leave the decision to confederate to the wills of the new autonomous units. It was primarily this threat to the nation's unity which prompted the Declaration.

The Declaration was applauded in the Liberal press. *El Imparcial*

---

[1] Signed by the directors of *La Discusión, La Igualdad, El Pueblo, Gil Blas, La República ibérica, El Sufragio universal.*   [2] *La Igualdad,* 2 Apr. 1870.

particularly welcomed any clarification as 'federalism had only thrived so much because of its vagueness'.[1] Only two republican papers of any importance in Madrid disagreed with it, but, significantly, both the two most influential Federal papers in the provinces—*El Estado catalán* and *La Andalucía*—attacked it violently.[2] Pi's immediate reaction was to assemble the Federal deputies and to declare his disagreement with the contents of the Declaration. No record of this meeting survives, but the outcome was that Castelar and Figueras were persuaded to join Pi in signing a manifesto on 10 May disavowing the Declaration and reaffirming the federal principle based on the pact. Three days later nineteen deputies signed a manifesto declaring that without the pact federalism lacked any juridical safeguard.[3] For a moment it looked as if *La Igualdad*, the most influential Federal paper, would defy the Directory, but on 18 May Mellado resigned and Benot y Rodríguez, a close supporter of Pi, took it over. On the same day the paper announced its adhesion to the Directory.

The Declaration was the most serious crisis which Pi had to face until the El Ferrol revolt at the end of 1872. That he weathered it was due to his inflexibility of purpose and the miscalculation of the signatories, acting on the advice of Figueras, who should have known Pi better. Pi's insistence on a rigid, dogmatic theoretical basis for federalism again underlined his belief that the party's survival demanded strict adherence to doctrine in order to save it from political opportunism. Finally, the support of the two leading Federal papers in the provinces and the adhesion of provincial committees to the Directory showed that in resisting the Declaration he had behind him the weight of the provincial Federals who had voted for him in the Assembly.

The prominent part played by Ruano in preparing the Declaration showed again how the Unitarians were hoping to win over the movement, as some Federals were quick to point out.[4] Their

---

[1] *El Imparcial*, 8 May 1870.
[2] *El Estado catalán*, 9 May; *La Andalucía*, 9, 10 May 1870. In Madrid, *La Justicia Social*, 10 May, *La Federación española*, 13 May 1870.
[3] Pi y Arsuaga, op. cit. v. 735–9; *La Igualdad*, 13 May 1870.
[4] *La Federación española*, 13 May 1870; I. Domenech, *Idea práctica de la Federación española*, Madrid, 1870.

participation not only implied a rejection of pactist federalism but also the repudiation of its radical implications. Social as well as political factors motivated the Declaration. The growing importance of social questions is reflected in the thirteen new Federal papers with a marked radical and socialist bias to appear in Madrid between August 1869 and May 1870.[1] Revilla considered that the expansion of the International by posing the social question in a new form threatened to reopen the breach between individualists and socialists which had been partially healed by the manifesto of 1865. He considered that the pactist theory, by weakening the unifying bonds of society, was a deliberate incitement to social extremism and made the Declaration doubly imperative.

Pi's personality, too, was an important factor. There was growing reaction to what Revilla described as his 'infallible pontificate'. During the Assembly, García López had criticized the leadership being in the hands of intellectuals; he wanted to see men of action in the key posts.[2] *El Pueblo* described Pi:[3] 'He has little of the politician, much of the doctrinaire; he does not seem to be a deputy speaking in an Assembly but a professor explaining in a lecture room.' His unbending character, his aloofness and refusal to modify his ideas to meet a changing circumstances, were irritating to those like García Ruiz who preferred to work within the framework of traditional Spanish political behaviour. As a Catalan, Pi was considered by his opponents to be putting Catalan interests before those of Spain. The fact that the Tortosa Pact had been entirely due to Catalan initiative, that Catalans had sparked off the autumn revolts, and that Pi had supported the Catalan plea for protection in the *Cortes* all seemed to make this a plausible accusation. Raising the bogey of Catalan particularism was a well-worn political trick which Ruano, balked over the Declaration, used in the *Cortes* on 16 May. The next day *El Imparcial*,

[1] Hartzenbusch, op. cit. *La Solidaridad*, organ of the Madrid section of the International, appeared on 1 Jan. 1870. Revilla's fears were echoed with increasing frequency after the Barcelona Congress of the International in June which voted in favour of political abstention. The serious aspect was that the Barcelona *Centro federal de las Sociedades obreras* which in 1869 had declared its support for the Federals, declared itself Internationalist in September. See Martí, op. cit., p. 102. For Federal alarm in Barcelona, ibid., p. 100 n. 30, and in Madrid, *La Igualdad*, 10, 15 June, 18, 20, 27 July 1870.

[2] Ibid., 11 Mar. 1870.   [3] *El Pueblo*, 13 May 1870.

in commenting on this speech, accused Pi's Federals of being mere propagandists for a Catalan republic. These assertions echoing the pamphlet war of the middle years of the century had little justification in fact. It was not true to say that Pi was pandering to purely Catalan interests; the evidence suggests that he was out of touch with the general feeling of Catalan Republicans. It was, for example, on Pi's suggestion that the National Pact had been set up in July 1869 to co-ordinate the activity of local pacts, even though the Catalan Federals had refused to recognize it. The attitude of the Catalans may have been strengthened by Pi's theories, but much of Barcelona republicanism had an origin independent of Pi and the Catalan attitude often caused him acute embarrassment. To accuse him of Catalan particularism was to misinterpret the basis of his policy, which was that no province or group of provinces should act independently until all were in a position to do so. He was a federalist and not a regionalist, giving equal weight to each province.

Revilla argued that Salmerón was the leader of those Federals who believed that the nation was an organic whole in contra-distinction to the 'confederationists' of Pi's school, whose theory stemmed from the premiss of the autonomy of the individual. This was the first time that Salmerón's name had been used as a theoretician of federalism. This is not surprising in view of the affinity between Krausists—Revilla was one of Salmerón's brightest pupils—but Salmerón's popularity of 1866, when he had been elected to the Madrid Democrat committee, had declined rapidly after his cautious speech at the first Democrat reunion in October 1868. Later he had been attacked for his 'gradualism' and doubts were cast on his republican convictions.[1] Using Salmerón's name as the theoretician of the federalism which the party should adopt would scarcely find much support with the rank and file, but it was symptomatic of the isolation of the 'true' Federals from the currents of opinion within the movement.

The immediate effect of the Declaration was to strengthen Pi's

[1] *La Igualdad*, 13 Jan. 1870, 'A los electores republicanos de Madrid'. See also ibid., 15 Jan. 1870, for a letter from the Internationalists Rubaudonadeu and Cenagorta amplifying this article.

position. Benot took over *La Igualdad* and for the first time a central Directory, with a mandate from the provincial Federals and under Pi's control, had a semi-official mouthpiece through which orthodoxy could be impressed. Pi's immediate success in enforcing this orthodoxy after the Declaration was a considerable achievement, but, in consolidating his position, he had been largely dependent on the strength of provincial feeling. Herein lay a paradox, for he had established himself in a position to impose on the party a dogma which could only take power out of the hands of the central authority. His position would be assured only so long as a revolutionary situation did not develop in the country or so long as the revolutionary wing remained quiescent. But before the reorganization decided on at the Assembly had been completed, the Directory had to face the problems posed by the return of the exiles after the amnesty of 23 June and by the repercussions of the Hohenzollern candidacy.

On 23 June the *Cortes* adjourned after Prim had failed to receive a reply from Leopold of Hohenzollern in time to put his candidacy to the vote. Three days later Isabella finally abdicated in Paris, making over her rights to her son Alphonso, thus providing a formula for a possible Bourbon restoration. On 3 July reports of the Hohenzollern candidacy reached Paris, and the rest of the summer was dominated by its political and diplomatic repercussions and by the outbreak of the Franco-Prussian war on 19 July. After the failure of yet another candidate it might be expected that Prim would be more inclined to consider a republican solution. This impression was conveyed in a cryptic telegram to Saldanha, the aged Portuguese marshal (and like Prim an ardent Pan-Iberian), who had made a successful coup in Lisbon on 18 May.

In this Prim was reputed to have said that he 'had passed the Rubicon and that if the success of Leopold's candidacy were now prevented he would proclaim the republic'.[1] Too much importance should not be attached to this, as Prim's main aim was to persuade Fernando to accept the Spanish throne, which might be done by

---

[1] F.O. 63/970, no. 2, 10 July 1870, secret and confidential, Murray, ambassador at Lisbon to Granville.

threatening to declare a republic. Saldanha's reaction, in fact, was to advise Fernando to accept the Spanish throne to forestall a republic, and negotiations for this were resumed in the second week in July.[1] These came to nothing, British support was luke-warm; Fernando still feared the veto of Napoleon III, whose sudden collapse could not be foreseen in mid-July. In August a Portuguese solution and any republican ideas which Prim may have had in mind were finally shelved when, in response to renewed Italian interest, he decided to make another approach to Amadeo of Savoy, the second son of Victor Emanuel, and on the 20th wrote to Montemar, ambassador at Florence, to sound the prince.

Meanwhile the Federals were preoccupied with the consolida-tion of their new party organization and were concentrating on appeals for working-class support after the set-back from the International's Congress at Barcelona in June.[2] But an equally significant event for their internal politics was the return of the extremist exiles after the amnesty of 23 June. On 20 July Paul sold his proprietary rights in *La Igualdad*, marking his break with the official leadership. His efforts were now concentrated on trying to turn Viralta's secret organization, *El Tiro nacional*, into an instrument for violent revolution and the 'emancipation of the Fourth Estate' on the assumption that violent revolution would retain working-class support more effectively than the persuasion of the leader-writers of *La Igualdad*. But this new concern with the International's challenge to the Federals' claim to be a working-class party was overshadowed by events in France.

At first the Federals supported Prussia, so great was their hatred of the Empire, but they switched their loyalties once the régime was overthrown.[3] Enthusiasm reached a climax on the news of the declaration of the Third Republic in Paris on 4 September. An extraordinary supplement to *La Igualdad* on the 5th and the

[1] F.O. 63/970, no. 4, 16 July 1870, Murray to Granville. J. A. Smith, Count of Carnota, *Memoirs of the Duke of Saldanha*, London, 1880, i. 404–7. The diplomatic aspect is best studied in G. Bonnin, *Bismarck and the Hohenzollern Candidature for the Spanish Throne*, London, 1957.
[2] *La Igualdad*, 18 June 1870. Directory's manifesto reorganizing local committees.
[3] Lauser, *Geschichte*, op. cit. i. 250–2. P de Luz, *Los Españoles en busca de un Rey*, Barcelona, 1948, pp. 160–1.

devotion of the whole issue of the 6th to the new republic was the beginning of a nation-wide campaign in which the Federals reached the height of their popularity. The fall of the Empire, they argued, was proof of the decadence of the monarchical principle of which the war, 'inevitable between monarchies', was a condemnation; a Federal Republic would be the salvation of France and in achieving this, French Republicans were assured of Spanish support. A huge demonstration in Madrid on 8 September called for solidarity and meetings organized by students declared their sympathy for France. In September *La Igualdad*, for the first and last time, had the largest circulation of any Madrid daily. From Bayonne Orense called for a Spanish legion to assist the French and one of 400 men was was soon formed under his son Antonio. At Marseilles, where Garibaldi had arrived on 7 October, a Spanish 'socialist' Emilio Marros, an exile from the 1869 rising, carried away by the vision of a universal republic, offered 10,000 Catalan volunteers. But on reflection, the Federals thought it was wiser to remain in Spain and husband their resources for the struggle against Prim during the new session of the *Cortes*.[1]

By early October Federal enthusiasm was threatening to outrun the Directory's control. The Directory therefore decided to contact the French Republicans to try and enlist their support for a rising. Castelar, who had been on friendly terms with Gambetta during his exile, travelled to Tours to negotiate with the Provisional Government.[2] He achieved an oratorical success but little more beyond a vague promise of 3 million francs. As this sum was not immediately forthcoming and as the candidacy of Amadeo was gaining ground, Pi himself went to Bordeaux to emphasize the advantages to France of having a friendly Spanish republic on its flank instead of a monarchy linked diplomatically with Prussia. This mission, however, proved abortive. Pi could now argue with justification that there were insufficient resources to guarantee the success of a rising.

French reluctance to commit themselves to the Spanish Federals

[1] *La Igualdad*, 9, 27 Sept., 1, 23 Oct. 1870. Cf. ibid., 15 Aug., 'El Pacto de los Pueblos latinos'. A. Olivesi, *La Commune de 1871 à Marseilles*, Paris, 1950, p. 107.
[2] Castelar, *Historia del movimiento republicano en Europa*, Madrid, 1874, viii. 312 et seq.; cf. *The Times*, 13 Oct. 1870, account from Tours on 8 Oct.

may have been due to a true estimate of their strength but was probably determined by the hope of securing the more substantial support of Prim himself, particularly as Spain had been the first power to recognize the new republic. It was to try and secure this that Count Keratry, who had known Prim in Mexico, came to Madrid on 19 October.[1] The fall of Napoleon had removed one of the brakes on Prim's policy and it was Keratry's aim to offer French support for Prim in establishing a Unitarian Republic and, in return for Spanish help, to assist Prim in achieving his ambition of Iberian Union. Keratry also spoke with the Federal Directory, which, according to his own report, had promised its good offices in supporting Prim should he set up a republic, but the attempt of the Federals to make political capital out of the visit did not predispose the Government towards the mission. Prim's rejection of a republican solution broke up the negotiations and on Keratry's return Gambetta decided to dispense with the complications of Spanish aid.

Although Prim might have been more amenable to Keratry's suggestions a month earlier, by 19 October negotiations were already far advanced for the Savoyard candidacy. Montemar had his first interview with Amadeo on 12 October. Hence Prim's categorical rejection of Keratry's overtures. On 30 October Amadeo telegraphed his acceptance. Four days later the news was broken to the *Cortes,* which then adjourned for thirteen days. On 16 November, by a majority of 120, he was elected King of Spain.[2] The result of the elections, following closely on the failure of the Federals to get more than verbal support from France, posed new questions for the Directory and called for a reorientation of party policy.

In May the challenge to Pi's leadership had come from the Right; now it came from the Left. The Directory's instructions before the election called for peace and order. After Amadeo's

---

[1] Vera, op. cit. ii. 126–31; Pirala, op. cit. iii. 398–400; J. P. T. Bury, *Gambetta and the National Defence*, London, 1936, p. 162. B.M. Add. MS. 39122, 20 Oct. 1870, Layard to Granville. P. de Luz, op. cit., pp. 168–76.

[2] Pirala, op. cit. iii. 406–7. Out of 344 deputies 311 voted. The minimum of votes required was 172; Amadeo obtained 191; 60 voted for a federal republic; 27 for Montpensier (Serrano voted for Amadeo); 8 for Espartero; 2 for a unitarian republic; 2 for Alphonso; 1 for a republic; 1 for the Duchess of Montpensier; there were 19 blanks.

election its tone remained the same as if nothing had happened.[1] This was not good enough for the extremists. On 31 October Paul y Angulo had returned to the political scene and after violent abuse in the *Cortes* brought out on the next day his violent and libellous *El Combate*, preaching the doctrine of armed revolution. His extremism was echoed both by the radical clubs of the capital and the university students, who hooted down professors of known monarchist sympathies. A pacific policy became harder to enforce as the activities of the *partido de la porra*, organized by the impresario Ducazcal, supposedly with the connivance of the Government, started to attack Carlists and Federals alike.[2] The offices of *El Combate*, the *Teatro Calderón*, where a skit on Amadeo, *Macarroni I*, was being performed, and various Federal clubs were set upon by men armed with cudgels.

In an atmosphere of mounting violence *El Combate* attacked the Directory for lack of revolutionary zeal and in December defied it by calling for armed insurrection. It argued that the time to strike had come now that the Federals were organized and following the cool reception granted to Amadeo's election. It quoted the majority of the provincial press in support of its policy.[3] In Catalonia, Carlists and Federals had begun to plan a joint rising, but through lack of funds this did not materialize.[4] In Valencia the Federals had split into two groups, one refusing to obey the Directory's instructions and the other determined to rise when Amadeo arrived. Even in Madrid, the bulk of the Federal press supported Paul. This was only to be expected from such papers as Luis Blanc's *La República federal*, reflecting working-class republicanism, but more indicative of a swing of opinion was Morayta's normally conservative *La República ibérica*.[5] Only *La Discusión* had the courage to criticize *El Combate*. In this situation the Directory continued to call for patience and 'abnegation'

[1] *La Igualdad*, 16 Nov., 3 Dec. 1870.
[2] *El Combate*, 1, 3 Nov. 1870. Rispa y Perpiña, op. cit., pp. 149–57; Echegaray, op. cit. iii. 365. Flóres García, op. cit., pp. 86–87.
[3] *El Combate*, 13, 17 Dec. 1870.
[4] Pirala, op cit. iii. 593–7. J. de Bolós y Saderra, *El Carlismo en Cataluña*, Barcelona, 1930, pp. 39–45. B.M. Add. MS. 38998, letter from Dart, vice-consul at Valencia to Layard, 24 Dec. 1870.
[5] *La Discusión*, 22 Dec. 1870.

but, in view of hostile opinion and the decline in his prestige, Pi called a conference in his house on 27 December. Opinion was divided but, with Paul's absence and in spite of Luis Blanc, the dozen or so deputies present decided against armed insurrection.[1] What threatened to become a serious breach, leading to a possible rising when Amadeo arrived in Spain, was averted by Prim's death on 30 December after being shot three days earlier when leaving the *Cortes*.

In May Pi had been saved by the political miscalculation of the Moderates; now he was saved by the excesses of the extremists. Suspicion for the cause of Prim's death immediately fastened on the Federals—particularly as Pi had made a violent attack on him in the *Cortes* on the 25th. But the Directory and the Federals' press immediately deplored the crime and because of the Directory's antagonism towards the extremists, the Federal party as a whole was able to ward off the accusation of complicity. As *El Combate* had closed down on the day Prim had been shot and Paul had vanished, it was naturally assumed that he had been responsible for the murder.[2] The Government seized the excuse to imprison the more extreme Federal journalists like Roque Barcia, but this was an advantage for the Directory. Its position had in fact been strengthened as it was freed from the embarrassment of an en-thusiastic and short-sighted revolutionary wing, while Prim's death could not fail to strengthen the Federal minority in the *Cortes* by removing the one man who might have been able to give support to Amadeo. His death hastened the break-up of the coalition and left the leadership of the Progressive–Democrats open to doubt. Progressives who had been reluctant to accept the democratic concessions of Prim looked to Sagasta for leader-ship; those who accepted these concessions, and the Democrats

---

[1] Estévanez, op. cit., pp. 341–2.

[2] The responsibility for this has never been conclusively proved. Paul always denied complicity and accused secret police in Serrano's pay. Prim's wife believed Montpensier was responsible, while some see it as the result of a masonic quarrel. Evidence points to Paul being implicated although how far he was responsible for the planning remains uncertain. The enormous dossier compiled by the Government (which led to no specific charges) has still to be examined. The question is discussed in Olivar Bertrand, *El Caballero Prim*, ii. 314–22. Paul's apologia is *Les Assassins du maréchal Prim et la politique en Espagne*, Paris, 1886.

themselves, looked to Ruiz Zorrilla. The Directory could now argue that any rising could only lead these groups to combine in face of a common menace.

The political situation on Amadeo's arrival at the beginning of 1871 was fluid, with the Unionists still hankering after the discredited Montpensier, with the widening breach between Progressives and Democrats, and the rivalry between Zorrilla and Sagasta. Political stability would depend on how far Progressives and Democrats could sink their differences, on the extent to which the Unionists wanted the new monarchy to work, and the skill of the two largest opposition parties, Carlists and Federals, in exploiting the differences between the wings of the Liberal coalition. As in 1870, Federal politics would be determined by the success or failure of the leadership in keeping the party from an impractical and ineffective outbreak of revolutionary violence. The task was initially made easy by the temporary discredit into which the extremists had fallen but general policy would to a large extent be determined by developments outside Spain—by the Paris Commune, by the collapse of French federalism, and a subsequent increase in the activities of the International in Spain. Questions which had been postponed by events in France in 1870 would be brought into prominence by other events in France in 1871.

7

Challenge from the Left: Benevolents and Intransigents, 1871–2

FOR the next two years Spain was a democratic monarchy ruled by a king determined to give no cause for offence to national pride and by ruling constitutionally to avoid the accusation that he was a 'party King'. But, ridiculed and lampooned by Alphonsists, Carlists, and Republicans, he was forced to rely on those who had voted for him in the *Cortes*. He remained the 'King of the 191'. Among these were not only the 'pure' Amadeist supporters of the Progressive–Democrat coalition but the majority of the Unionists under Serrano, who, Montpensierists at heart, reconciled themselves to Amadeo and threw their energies into preventing him from becoming the tool of the Progressives. Serrano's policy, therefore, was to agitate for a ministry of conciliation in which the Unionists might be able to exert an influence out of proportion to their numerical strength. As this coincided with Amadeo's desire to prevent his subordination to any single party the first ministry of his reign was one of conciliation in which Progressives, Democrats, and Unionists were represented.

However, Amadeo's position was insecure from the outset because of mutual hatred among the Amadeist parties. Progressives and Democrats distrusted Serrano's intentions, but they were unable to ignore him because of his influence in the Army. Neither Sagasta nor Zorrilla, the two contenders for Prim's position as leader of the Progressives, had much influence among the officers; they were the civilian managers who found themselves tied by a promotion policy which Prim had been forced to adopt to keep the Army loyal. These promotions had irritated the older generals, who now found their champion in Serrano. He was a political opportunist, an inveterate intriguer, vacillating and dominated by

his Cuban creole wife and was to exert an important but baneful
influence on Spanish politics until the restoration of the Bourbons
finally put an end to his active political career.[1]

More significant for their immediate repercussions in 1871 were
the divisions among the genuine Amadeists. It soon became clear
that the Progressive–Democrat coalition was not going to survive
Prim's death as the breach widened between Sagasta and Zorrilla. Both men were hard-boiled professional politicians. Sagasta,
although charming and able, was unscrupulous and of doubtful
honesty. Conservative by inclination, he favoured a ministry of
conciliation, aware of his unpopularity with many Progressives
and recognizing the need to secure the support of the older
generals. Zorrilla was vain, uncultured, lacked personal charm,
was obstinate and intensely ambitious, but he was supported by
the Democrats and Left-wing Progressives. Unlike Sagasta he
was quite prepared to break the ministry of conciliation if this
would secure his own political hegemony and to do this he would
even form understandings with his political enemies. Far from
wanting a strong executive as Sagasta wished, he was in favour of
'as little king as possible'. In the same way as Serrano's inflated
self-importance as ex-Regent made him incapable of accepting
the limitations of constitutional monarchy, so Zorrilla's almost
pathological distrust of the Court and the Queen's clericalism—
the legacy of the old-time Progressive—made his genuine co-
operation with Amadeo impossible.

Zorrilla's breaking up of the ministry of conciliation in June
1871 and the subsequent split between him and Sagasta in the
following October made impossible the emergence of a stable
parliamentary system, as it meant that no Amadeist party was
strong enough to secure itself in power unless Amadeo was prepared to act unconstitutionally or unless it could secure the support
of opposition parties. Party government broke down as both
those in power and those in opposition split into personalist
factions. Zorrilla had to face bitter hostility from the old Democrat

---

[1] There are no good detailed studies of Serrano, Sagasta, or Zorrilla. Villaurrutia,
Marqués de, *El General Serrano, duque de la Torre*, Madrid, 1929; Romanones, Conde de,
Sagasta o el Político, Madrid, 1930, and Gómez Chaix, *Ruiz Zorrilla o el ciudadano ejemplar*,
Madrid, 1934, are all inadequate.

leaders, who resented his newly won hegemony, while Serrano,
with whom Sagasta was to be forced into coalition after his break
with Zorrilla, was interested only in his own future and was prepared to overthrow Sagasta as soon as it suited him to do so.[1]

With these divisions among the nominal adherents of Amadeo,
what were the alternatives open to the anti-Amadeo opposition,
the Alphonsists, Carlists, and Federals? The Alphonsists were
fortunate in being able to wait—in fact a waiting policy was the
best as their candidate was only thirteen in 1871 and any premature restoration would raise the complications of a regency, to
which both Montpensier and Serrano might aspire. Besides which,
Isabella had had great difficulty in finding a leader for the new
party with sufficient influence to rally both the civil and military
elements. Some believed that Serrano would emerge as Alphonsist
leader and it was not until the irrevocable break between him and
Isabella in July 1873 that she was finally willing to acknowledge
Cánovas as the party's director. Alphonsist strength lay in the high
aristocracy whose wealth could be used for bribery and whose
boycott of Amadeo's court helped to increase his isolation.[2] However, until Cánovas took over, the main sphere of Alphonsist activity
must be sought in the traditional suborning of army officers
and in augmenting the resentment caused by Prim's promotions.

Both Carlists and Federals, in contrast, immediately set out to
exploit xenophobic distaste for a foreign king whom the Carlists
described as a member of the anti-papal, masonic house of Savoy,
'son of the crowned eunuch of Florence' and the Federals as an
'English puppet'.[3] Both these parties were divided into parliamentary and revolutionary wings and as both depended for their

---

[1] The appearance of new names for the various political groupings illustrates the disintegration of parties under Amadeo. 'Pure' Unionist followers of Serrano became
Conservatives; those in favour of an understanding with Sagasta *fronterizos*. Sagasta's
followers were either *sagastinos* or, popularly, *calamares*, as they stuck to office under all
circumstances. 'Radical' referred both to the *zorrillistas* and the *cimbrios*, those ultra-
Democrats like Rivero and Martos veering towards republicanism.

[2] Letter of Barral, Italian ambassador, to Visconti Venosta, Feb. 1872, in O. F. Tencajoli,
La Nascita del duca degli Abruzzi e l'abdicazione del Re Amadeo, Rome, 1934, pp. 21 et seq.
For Alphonsist politics see Lema, Marqués de, *De la Revolución a la Restauración*, Madrid,
1927, 2 vols. Forty-three out of fifty-one Grandees openly declared their hostility to
Amadeo (*Cuatro palabras sobre la elevación del duque de Aosta*, Madrid, 1870, p. 15).

[3] *La Esperanza*, 21 Sept. 1870; *La Igualdad*, 16, 18, 20 Nov. 1870.

momentum on mass support concentrated in certain areas, their leaders had a common difficulty in restraining revolutionary enthusiasm from outrunning political realism and, at the same time, in stopping the evaporation of enthusiasm through a too-cautious policy.

The September Revolution had revived Carlism as a political force but this revival was due as much to an influx of neo-Catholics as to the efforts of the Old Carlists. These 'new' Carlists brought with them a highly developed press and the determination of their leader, Nocedal, to turn them into an effective national parliamentary party. The Old Carlists, with their romantic traditions of mass peasant risings based on the fierce local price of the Basque Provinces and Navarre, were suspicious of this new trend. Internal divisions had forced those in favour of revolt in November 1870 to enter into relations with the Federals but, as lack of funds precluded a rising, Nocedal's policy of legal opposition gained ground. But it was not until the Carlist reunion at Vevey in August 1871 that Don Carlos was prepared to appoint Nocedal as the party's leader, convinced this was necessary by the Carlist gain at the April elections and by his failure to persuade Cabrera, the legendary hero of the first Carlist war, to exchange the pleasures of retirement with an English wife at Virginia Water for the command of his forces in the field. Until April 1872 they were an active parliamentary party entering into electoral alliances and parliamentary agreements with the Federals.[1]

Both parties regarded themselves as part of international ideological movements and to a certain extent their policies were conditioned by events abroad, particularly in France. But, paradoxically, whereas events there tended to aid the Carlists, the establishment of a republican régime militated against the Federals. In this wider sphere the revolt and suppression of the Paris Commune played a cardinal role. Thiers was reluctant to add to his

[1] Pirala, op. cit. iii. 480 et seq., 556–61, 620–7. The neo-Catholic, *El Pensamiento español*, ably edited by Navarro Viloslada from its foundation in 1860, became the leading Carlist paper after 1868. Out of the six Madrid papers with the highest circulation, three were Carlist, *El Pensamiento español*, *La Regeneración*, and *La Reconquista*. The history of Carlism and Carlos VII is inadequately treated in R. Oyarzún, *Historia del Carlismo*, Madrid, 1939, and Rodezno, Conde de, *Carlos VII, Duque de Madrid*, Madrid, 1944.

troubles by forcing a breach with the Legitimists.[1] This meant in practice that the Carlists could continue to use France as a base for their operations and to receive aid from their French sympathizers whereas after the suppression of the Paris Commune the Spanish Federals saw the collapse of their hopes for the establishment of a friendly federal republic in France.

Deprived of the hope of French support, the Federals had to readjust their policy. The Directory had two alternatives: either to try and widen the basis of their support and become a genuine mass party or, by exploiting the fluid situation in the *Cortes*, to become an effective minority opposition party by forming tactical alliances with other discontented groups. This would inevitably imply playing the political game of bargaining in the lobbies, which the Federals had always opposed. Although a logical deduction from the changed balance of forces in the *Cortes*, such a policy was dangerous because of its repercussions on provincial opinion. But the alternative of widening their appeal would mean either returning to a revolutionary tradition which had been proved impractical although it still commanded widespread support, or making social concessions which, in the aftermath of the Commune, many Federal leaders were unwilling to sanction. Two factors would determine the issue; the results of the first elections of the new reign in March and the impact of the French 'federalist rising'.

At the beginning of Amadeo's reign Pi was strongly placed to restrain those in favour of armed revolt. Although he had sacrificed some popularity with the extremist rank and file his arguments against insurrection and *retraimiento*, given the lack of resources, convinced many that increased propaganda coupled with parliamentary activity exploiting the monarchists' divisions, would hasten the coming of a republic.[2]

The elections had been fixed for 9–11 March. Successes in the February municipal elections increased official optimism and it was confidently forecast that the Federals would double their

---

[1] *Theirs au pouvoir. Texte de ses lettres; annoté par G. Bouniols*, Paris, 1901, pp. 213, 217. Thiers had difficulty in getting the *préfet* of the Basses-Pyrénées to enforce his instructions.
[2] *La Igualdad*, 2 Feb. 1871, the parliamentary party to the electors.

representation, returning over a hundred deputies.[1] There was, therefore, considerable surprise when instead of gains they only won forty-eight seats while even the Carlists, with whom they had an electoral alliance, won sixty-two.

This failure was explained in terms of government corruption and intimidation—the ninety disputed *actas* spoke for themselves—but there were other reasons which they seemed reluctant to analyse.[2] The Directory's electoral instructions had been hesitant, dominated by the desire to keep a factitious unity rather than scare away potential supporters by a too definite or extremist programme. Electoral manifestoes were therefore vague, generalities without constructive policies. The Federals fought the election primarily on the issue of the monarchy and by playing on outraged national pride, although it was the Carlists, with their appeal to tradition, who must gain from this issue. Conscripts, workers, and 'rural proprietors' were the objects of ardent exhortations, but even if the benefits of voting Federal had been made more tangible the party's divisions would still have produced a similar result. Many felt that it was useless to vote in the face of government pressure. Electioneering was half-hearted or non-existent, as at Huesca, where the local committee under García López declared in favour of an armed rising with the result that a Federal stronghold which had returned six deputies in 1869 only returned two in 1871.[3] The electoral alliance with the Carlists and Alphonsists which had been proposed by the Directory was a weakness not a strength, as it was followed, modified, or neglected by local committees as each saw fit.[4]

The first reaction to the election results was desultory planning by Carlists and Federals for a rising.[5] Although this failed to

[1] *La Igualdad*, 13 Feb. 1871, Directory's manifesto. The numbers returned were: Ministerials (Progressive–Democrat) 237; Republicans (including 2 Unitarians) 48; Montpensierists (irreconcilable Unionists) 10; Alphonsists 12; Carlists 62. The numbers voting were Monarchists, 1,900,000; Carlists, 450,000; Republicans, 350,000 (*Gaceta*, 22 Apr. 1871).

[2] *La Igualdad*, 20 Jan., Directory's manifesto; 13 Feb., Directory's electoral instructions. See also ibid., 21, 25 Feb., 2, 5, 11, 16, 25 Mar. 1873. For the *actas* see *Gaceta*, 4 Apr.–17 May 1871.

[3] Vera, op. cit. ii. 225 note.

[4] *La Igualdad*, 5 Mar., electoral manifesto of the Madrid joint Carlist–Republican committee: see *La Esperanza*, 3 Mar. 1873, for a repudiation of the alliance.

[5] Pirala, op. cit. iii. 578; B.M. Add. MS. 38932, f. 168. Layard's evidence is useful for

materialize, the militant mood was reflected later on 30 April when the Second Federal Assembly met in Madrid to redefine policy. After Pi's tactics of legal opposition had been endorsed by a small majority, the Assembly re-elected him President of a new and expanded Directory in which concessions had been made to extremist opinion for, apart from Pi, Castelar, and Orense, the others, Pruneda and Salvochea, were notorious extremists, and Barcia, soured after his release from prison where he had been languishing for suspected complicity in Prim's murder, was rapidly becoming one. Further evidence of the Directory's desire to placate the extremists was shown in May when García López, their self-appointed leader, was made director of *La Igualdad*. The Directory was in fact no longer a homogeneous body, but its divisions merely echoed those in the Assembly where a defeat of the extremists on the *retraimiento* issue by the narrow margin of only two votes showed the flimsy nature of the support for a pacific policy.[1]

Much of this radical tone was caught from the example of the Communards who were fighting in the streets of Paris while the Assembly was in session. When the revolt had broken out the Federals interpreted it as a struggle to establish a free and independent commune—it was the prototype of the federal revolution. 'The Commune's aim', wrote a Barcelona paper,[2] 'is not an unrealizable utopia but simply the autonomy of the Commune.' Resolutions of solidarity were passed and a commission left for Paris to convey the moral support of the Federal movement. But later, towards the end of May, Right-wing propaganda began to work its effect. Influenced by lurid atrocity stories, republican ardour began to cool and for the first time in a *Cortes* vote (in a debate on granting asylum to political refugees) the Federal minority were divided; in spite of Pi's reasoned defence of the Communards, only twenty-five voted against the motion condemning them.[3] The Unitarians quickly exposed the Federals'

this period because of his close friendship with Serrano. Layard's house was one of the places in Madrid where political rivals met socially.

[1] *La Igualdad*, 15 Mar., 4, 5, 8, 10, 21 May 1871.
[2] *La Redención social*, 9 Apr. 1871. Cf. *Gaceta*, 23 Apr. 1871, Figueras's speech.
[3] *Gaceta*, 31 May 1871. The voting was 235–25, one of the largest divisions since 1869.

lack of agreement and Layard, commenting on their divisions, could say that 'the effect of events in Paris has been apparently to break up the republicans altogether'.[1]

Not only did the social implications of the Commune scare the Moderates, but its collapse seemed to spell the end of all hopes for international republican co-operation and of active help from France at the same time as the concept of international republican solidarity received a rude blow when its leading spokesman, Mazzini, condemned not only the Commune but federalism and socialism as well.[2] The myth of international federal republicanism, a key belief of the Spanish Federals, was finally shattered. Fear of federalism, now equated in people's minds with mob rule, was skilfully exploited by the monarchist press. Meanwhile in France, Thiers entertained no illusions about Spanish republicanism and appointed as the new minister to Madrid the anti-republican, ex-Orleanist Marquis de Bouillé, to reassure the Spanish Government, which in March had been fearing French republican propaganda more than anything else.[3]

The spirited resistance of the Communards was in sharp contrast to the vacillations inside the Federal party, whose internal divisions and sense of isolation were increased on receiving the news of the Commune's collapse at the end of May. The first indication of a reorientation of Federal policy came on 22 June when Castelar announced in the *Cortes* that although unwilling to serve in a Radical ministry he would be willing to give one his support. Coming from a member of the Directory this declaration of 'benevolence' towards a monarchical party was taken as a statement of official policy. This speech may have stemmed from Gambetta's advice, which, it was believed, had been given to the Federal leaders during a visit in April.[4] It certainly emphasized how at least Castelar had recognized the significance of the collapse

---

[1] B.M. Add. MS. 39122, 2, 12 June 1871, Layard to Granville. See R. Cala's favourably disposed *Los Comuneros de Paris*, Madrid, 1871, 2 vols, and M. Morayta, *La Comuna de Paris*, Madrid, 1872, where he dissociates federalism from Left-wing extremism.
[2] J. Guillaume, *L'Internationale: documents et souvenirs*, Paris, 1909, ii. 173; cf. an earlier disapproval of federalism in *Scritti*, vol. 87, p. 202, letter of 6 Nov. 1868.
[3] B.M. Add. MS. 38932, f. 176.
[4] Ibid., f. 161.

of French federalism and the unlikelihood of receiving any support
from the republican régime in France.

The speech was really a public announcement that the Federals
would be prepared to support Zorrilla if he wished to break the
ministry of conciliation by forming a ministry from his own
followers, which would not be possible unless he could be sure of
Federal votes. This assurance must have given Zorrilla added confidence in provoking the crisis which finally broke the ministry
of conciliation and enabled him to come to power on 25 July.[1]
Although the Federals' new policy of benevolence increased their
parliamentary importance it led to violent internal disagreements.
Provincial opinion, hostile at the lack of consultation and resenting
'dictatorship' by the Directory, forced *La Igualdad* to change its
first enthusiastic support of the policy to a reluctant and grudging
defence of it.

The debate within the party raged throughout the late summer
as the Directory tried to clarify its new policy. Benevolence, it
was argued, did not imply recognition of Amadeo: it was purely
a tactical move to hasten the disintegration of the Amadeist parties.
But this sounded too much like equivocation to the purists who
began to form an opposition within the party, calling themselves
the Intransigents. This division into Benevolents (*benévolos*) and
Intransigents (*intransigentes*) over political tactics was new, but the
use of these two words emphasized those differences of opinion
which had become increasingly obvious since Amadeo's election.[2]
The Intransigents were those who rejected any sort of understanding with monarchical parties. At Madrid they were a vociferous minority who saw benevolence as a watering down of
republicanism. They clamoured incessantly for armed revolt on
the unquestioned assumption that governments never respected
individual rights. They were the professional revolutionaries,
soured journalists, and frustrated office-seekers who saw in the
radical clubs and the unemployed of the capital the means with
which to offset their party's traditional weakness in Madrid and
by exploiting social discontent to force the hand of the cautious

---

[1] Pi y Arsuaga, op. cit. v. 10; *La Igualdad*, 23 June, 3 Aug. 1871.
[2] B.M. Add. MS. 38998, 24 Dec. 1870. Dart, vice-consul at Valencia, to Layard.

official leadership. Although champions of provincial independence they were themselves a product of the capital's environment, not daring to retire to the provinces in case they missed some opportunity for advancement in Madrid. Political antecedents did not worry them and it was the ex-Moderate, ex-Esparterist, General Contreras who eventually emerged as their leader. If they included social extremists like Córdoba y López and Luis Blanc they were joined later by the anti-socialist but naïve humanitarian Roque Barcia, the *enfant terrible* of the Intransigent press, whose motives were those of the misjudged and inadequately rewarded intellectual. Opportunistic, they promised anything which would buy them mass support and, less inhibited than the Benevolents, offered social reforms in which they had no real interest. Working in a conspiratorial tradition, they hoped to achieve their ends by secret organization, but incapable of learning by past mistakes they continued to cling to the myth of spontaneous revolution.

There was, however, a core of truth in their belief that enthusiasm among the Federal supporters would evaporate in proportion to the extent that they accepted legalism and parliamentary activity. But even here they misjudged the feeling of their followers. Although they deliberately appealed to the working-class members in the movement they could not compete with the International. Their leaders were not of working-class origin, their social backgrounds did not differ from those of the Benevolents, and the insincerity of their intentions was realized by the International, which never accepted them as more than passing allies. They consisted of men like the ex-officer deserter Estévanez who were temperamentally incapable of accepting any society which gave no opportunities for conspiracy and the *élan* of the barricades and who, like him, were prepared to try and make a revolution even though they knew it was bound to fail. The Intransigents constituted neither a homogeneous group nor succeeded in building up any party discipline. Intransigentism was an attitude of mind rather than a political or social programme. To the Intransigents federalism meant either the adventure of conspiracy or a means of widening the sphere of government patronage: it had no other purpose.

The provincial Intransigents, for their part, retained an instinctive distrust of Madrid politicians, whether republican or monarchist. All they had in common with their Madrid counterparts was a shared feeling of resentment against politicians in general and against the caution of their own leaders in particular. What they wanted was the control of local affairs and of the appointment to posts at present in the gift of the Madrid Government.

The Benevolents were more realistic; their conception of the Federals' role placed the main emphasis on their activity as a parliamentary opposition. They recognized that failure at elections could not be written off as solely due to government corruption for, as Pi admitted, republicanism still had no deep roots in the country. What was needed, therefore, was more comprehensive propaganda at the same time as deputies in the *Cortes* exploited differences between the monarchist parties.[1] The Benevolents' aim was to support Zorrilla with his near republican programme, and ultimately to make his power dependent on Federal votes.

The Benevolents' position though was complicated by personal factors. Castelar had much more in common with the Democrats than with Pi. He shared their views on property and economics: he was a close friend of Martos; he was only separated from them by the issue of federalism and, as their view on the form of government was entirely opportunist, Castelar believed they could be won over—provided it was not a 'red' republic. If benevolence was a reaction to changed internal and external circumstances it could also be interpreted as the Intransigents were to do in 1872, as a preliminary move towards a reconstruction of the old Democrat party in the guise of unitarian republicanism. Nor must it be forgotten that Castelar was not a doctrinaire Federal—as Cánovas prophetically remarked,[2] Castelar was closer to his own viewpoint than to that of his fellow Federals—and the experience of the Paris Commune could now be used as a warning of the dangers of a too-literal interpretation of federal theory.

By his speech of 22 June Castelar virtually put himself at the head of the Benevolents. It was in Pi's interests not to associate

[1] *La Igualdad*, 14 June, 'La propaganda rural', 8 Aug. 1871, Directory's manifesto.
[2] *Gaceta*, 4 Nov. 1871, Cánovas's speech.

himself too closely with this viewpoint for his social ideas, his protectionism, and his belief in the necessity to 'trust the people' put him out of sympathy with Castelar and his former Democrat associates, nor was he willing to yield to all on the doctrinal points of federal theory. Nevertheless, he aligned himself with the Benevolents because he disapproved of violence, did not believe that funds could support a revolt, and because he still trusted in the efficacy of propaganda rather than secret organizations. Benevolence gave the opportunity for the Federals to be what Pi had always desired—a compact party in the *Cortes* supported by a Directory guiding the policy of the provincial committees. Benevolence, combined with his personal ascendancy over Castelar, would help him to retain control of the movement. His position in the party remined centralist. Unwilling to commit himself too closely with either faction, his aim was to prevent the Benevolents from going too far right and the Intransigents from breaking into open revolt.

However, the real significance of benevolence was in its relation to the wider issues posed by events in France. The ingenuous and utopian optimism of 1868-9 evaporated in the aftermath of the Paris Commune, which, by helping to destroy the myth of international federal republicanism, constituted the real dividing-line in the party's history by making it face up to the social question which until then had been continually shelved. The Moderates, frightened by the 'socialist excesses' of the Commune, reacted strongly against any sort of social revolutionary activity and welcomed the prospect of safe parliamentary manœuvring promised by benevolence. The extremists, on the other hand, by trying to preserve the purity of the revolutionary ideal, aimed to exploit provincial distrust of the official leadership and parliamentary junketing and later to benefit from the outlawing of the International.[1]

After the Commune, Right-wing deputies in the *Cortes* were constantly expressing alarm that the banning of working-class organizations in France would make Spain the centre of the

---

[1] F. Córdoba y López, 'La Internacional' in the *Enciclopedia democrático federal*, ed. Díaz Quintero, Madrid, 1872.

International's activities. It was widely believed that French workers were primarily responsible for the great increase in the International's activity in Spain in mid-1871.[1] These fears were not wholly unfounded: many prominent organizers were to be French refugees and a cache of arms had been assembled at Marseilles for the purpose of fomenting revolution in Spain.[2] The Federals also showed alarm at the International's growing activity but for the reason that its propaganda, urging workers to turn their back on political activities, threatened to siphon off many potential supporters. This, combined with the realization that no help could be expected from France, emphasized the need for widening the party's appeal and provides an explanation for the marked increase in space devoted to the social question in the Federals' press from the middle of the summer onwards. *La Justicia social*, a Federal review specializing in social matters, referred to the great influence exerted by their clubs in winning over workers to federalism, but rather than being weaned away from the International, evidence suggests that they were being attracted to it.[3] The older workers might retain Federal sympathies but the younger ones appeared to be Internationalist enthusiasts. Certainly Pi's gloomy views, expressed to Lagargue at the end of 1871 on the impossibility of forming a workers' party in alliance with the Federals, do not suggest that their drive to increase their popularity had met with much success.[4] Attempts to appeal to workers seem to have been nullified by the Directory's adoption of the policy of benevolence and co-operation with bourgeois parties which the Bakuninists were specifically attacking. If also, as was suggested at the time, the main attraction of the International

[1] *Gaceta*, 23 May 1871, Sagasta referred to more than 8,000 French workers in Barcelona alone. Among refugees from France who played an important part in the International in Spain were Alerini and Bastelica, who had escaped from the Marseilles Commune, Brousse, later the French Possibilist leader, and Marx's son-in-law Lafarge, who crossed into Spain in Aug. 1871. See Martí, op. cit., p. 107 n. 53, for repercussions of the Commune in March and April.

[2] A. Olivesi, *La Commune de 1871 à Marseilles*, Paris, 1950, p. 154.

[3] *La Justicia social*, 15 June 1871; the *Eastern Post*, 21 Oct. 1871, report of the International's Spanish correspondent. Cf. Bermejo, op. cit. ii. 544.

[4] M. Nettlau, *Miguel Bakunin, la Internacional y la Alianza en España, 1868–73*, Buenos Aires, 1925, p. 105, quoting articles in *La Revista Social*, 24, 31 Jan. 1884. Cf. Lafargue's brief account in a letter dated 2/8 br., 1871, in *Correspondance*, p. 9.

was its organizing of strike action, then the Federals' lack of success is easily explained, for nowhere, in press or in pamphlet, did they recommend strike action or encourage resistance as a means of increasing wages.

The wide gap between the Federals' and the International's conception of the working class in politics can be clearly seen from their press. The tone was set as early as April when the Internationalists' committee in Madrid refused an invitation to send observers to the Assembly's debates because 'whereas the republicans only want to ameliorate the lot of the workers, the International wants to overthrow the existing social structure'.[1] Throughout the summer and autumn of 1871 the new organ of the Madrid section, *La Emancipación*, carried on virulent attacks against the 'bourgeois and authoritarian republicans' who 'like the Girondins were representatives of the middle class and who were only interested in palliatives'. Babeuf and Hébert were the revolutionaries to be emulated. Pi's panacea for labour troubles— the mixed jury—and Castelar's ideas of class harmony were both violently attacked. The Madrid Federals were accused of being out of touch with the provinces and uninterested in social problems. 'The Federals', it declared,[2] 'must choose between Mazzini the hero of *La Igualdad* and Garibaldi the hero of the International.'

In face of these and similar attacks the Federals did not change their attitude. Garrido, their leading propagandist, merely repeated arguments with which he had been flooding Federal journals for the past three years—platitudes about how the middle classes must be 'good brothers to their less fortunate fellows' and hymning the advantages of association. They show that the Federals were only prepared to make an alliance on their own terms. Without concessions and with the inevitable condescension of their dealings with the working class, Garrido's words were raindrops scattered on the ocean. The main object of the Federals was in fact not to offer an alternative social programme so much as to

---

[1] Guillaume, op. cit. ii. 275. See *La Emancipación*, 24 July, 'Porque combatimos el partido republicano', 31 July, 18 Sept., 8, 25 Oct.
[2] Ibid., 11 Feb. 1872, cf. 23 Mar., 6, 27 Apr. 1872, for continuing attacks.

persuade workers of the necessity of taking an active part in politics so long as they lived in a society where civil liberties were not guaranteed.[1]

The Federals' point was driven home in November when the *Cortes* voted to outlaw the International. It was clear that the three weeks' debate on this issue could not be explained merely by the academic desire to argue the case from first principles. Layard was quick to point out that the Government had almost unanimous support and that it could have been decided in a matter of minutes.[2] The aim of the weak stop-gap Malcampo ministry seems to have been to rally conservative opinion by exploiting the Internationalist menace; to split the Radicals and to divide the Federals. These aims were achieved as the Right built up the International as an immediate threat, as the Radicals abstained in order to avoid exposing their differences, and the Federals, although prominent in defending the legality of the association, with Salmerón arguing they were committed to 'emancipate the Fourth Estate', divided over the implications of openly supporting the International with twelve deputies refusing to vote against the motion.[3]

This climax to the Federals' attempts to woo the workers did not lead to any substantial results owing to the continuing predominance of the Bakuninists in Spanish Internationalist politics. Lafargue's arrival in Madrid as a refugee from the Commune at the end of 1871 offered a chance for the creation of a workers' party allied to the Federals, but it was a slender one. Lafargue had the backing of Marx and Engels, but they carried little weight in Spain. Undeterred by Pi's depressing assertion that Spanish workers were uninterested in political action, Lafargue set out to lessen Bakuninist influence, but his efforts met with little success and the majority of Spanish Internationalists continued to adhere

[1] *La Igualdad*, 29 Oct., 4, 5 Nov. 1871. See Lorenzo, op. cit., ch. xi, for his hostile picture of Garrido.

[2] B.M. Add. MS. 38932, f. 190. Cf. report of Barral, the Italian ambassador, on 27 Oct. 1871, quoted in Martí, op. cit., p. 107 n. 57.

[3] *La Legalidad de la Internacional*, Madrid, 1871, reports the speeches of Pi, Salmerón, Castelar, and Garrido. Other speeches attacking the International, such as Cánovas's, were also reprinted as pamphlets. The Internationalists' view is in Lorenzo, op. cit., pp. 195–214; the Radicals' in Echegaray, op. cit. iii. 53, and *Gaceta*, 11 Nov. 1871, Zorrilla's speech.

to the Alliance of Social Democracy, which Marx and Lafargue condemned.[1] This, however, did not deter the Federals themselves from trying to win over persecuted Internationalists, although attempts to do so only led to a further widening of the gap between Benevolents and Intransigents.

The main significance of the International in Federal politics was not that it deprived them of the support of the masses (most of whom remained a-political or under the control of the *caciques*), but that, by offering an alternative to the small group of educated and politically conscious workers, it prevented either Federals or Internationalists (quite apart from the latter's internal divisions) from presenting a united front and, by posing the social question in such acute form, facilitated the splitting of the Federals into two antagonistic groups. Although it had been the Benevolents who defended the International in the Cortes, it was the Intransigents who tried to fill the vacuum left by its demise. In February 1872 *El Combate* reappeared under Intransigent editorship with a violence reminiscent of its infamous forerunner, but with a completely new emphasis on the need for social as well as political revolution.[2] The Intransigents not only hoped to benefit from rank-and-file frustration with the policy of benevolence, but also from the Directory's hesitancy in formulating a social programme.

As President of the Directory Pi found himself increasingly in a false position, as the Benevolents, with whom he had associated himself, were reluctant to admit the need for the radical social concessions which he had always advocated and which he felt were now increasingly necessary if federalism was to become a mass movement rather than a mere appendage to Zorrilla's Left-wing Radicals. It was therefore planned that social issues would be the main topic for discussion at the Third Federal Assembly called to meet in Madrid on 25 February. But unfortunately the issue dominating all its meetings was electoral policy, as Sagasta's

[1] For Lafargue's intrigues see the hostile Nettlau, op. cit., ch. x. Engels's views are in Guillaume, op. cit. ii. 308, iii. 23, and his 'Bakuninists at Work' in Marx and Engels, *Revolution in Spain*, London, 1939. The only echo in the Federal press of Lafargue's views I have been able to find are two anonymous laudatory articles on Marx in *La Igualdad*, 12 Jan. 1872, and *La Ilustración republicano federal*, 28 Mar. 1872.

[2] *El Combate*, 11, 12 Mar. 1872. Rispa y Perpiñá, op. cit., p. 165. Rispa, one of Paul's old editors, was its new director.

inability to command a majority had made it necessary for him to call new elections for 2 April. Also, the establishing of separate committees of Benevolents and Intransigents at Barcelona and Valencia had weakened the Directory's moral authority and exposed it to the attacks of the Intransigent minority. The pattern followed by the debates was the one so familiar to Spanish electoral meetings, of whether to participate or abstain. As not even the most sanguine Federal believed the party would stand any chance by itself against Sagata's use of government influence, the issue resolved into a struggle between the Benevolent's support for a national coalition of opposition parties and the Intransigent demand for *retraimiento*. After the Intransigents had been defeated on this main issue by 57 votes to 25, and after failing to dominate the Assembly, they withdrew leaving it without the necessary quorum to conduct the further business of formulating their social programme.[1]

The Directory's support for the national coalition, which Zorrilla had reluctantly proposed as the only alternative to *retraimiento* and possible civil war, nominally committed the party to support official candidates appointed by a central committee of the opposition parties. But after the Intransigents' pique over their defeat and with the resignation of the Directory's three Intransigent members in March its electoral instructions did not promise to be very effective.[2]

No one was surprised, therefore, when the government parties returned a clear majority with 211 against 142 of the coalition consisting of 62 Radicals, 42 Federals, and 38 Carlists. The only surprise of this election was the extent to which the return of only 82 Sagastinos compared with 129 Conservatives confirmed the fact that Serrano had now replaced Sagasta as Zorrilla's main rival.[3] *El Pueblo* voiced the hostile reactions of the opposition

---

[1] Vera, op. cit. ii. 289 et seq. *La Igualdad*, 1, 4 Mar. 1872. There were 129 representatives from 43 provinces. Coruña, the Canaries, Valencia, Seville, Córdoba, and Jaén were unrepresented. As five of these were Federal centres, their absence suggests a deliberate boycott.

[2] *La Igualdad*, 7, 9–17 Mar. 1872, for the party's mixed reception, 30, 31 Mar. 1872, electoral committee's instructions. Rispa y Perpiña and García López, both Intransigents, in favour of *retraimiento*, had been elected to this committee!

[3] *El Imparcial*, 9, 11 Apr.; *El Pueblo*, 19 Apr. 1872.

parties to the most corrupt elections since the revolution by declar-
that 'everyone had lost faith and hope in the *Cortes*'.

Although the Federals lost only six seats, the Directory was
discredited, as it was felt that the coalition had put them at a disadvantage—at Cádiz, for instance, the other parties had refused
to vote for the Federal candidate and government pressure seems
to have been deliberately stronger in the predominantly Federal
areas of Andalucía.[1] Apart from the feeling of being cheated,
Intransigent anger and the demand for violent action was stimulated by the example of the Carlist reaction to the results. Nocedal's
policy of legal opposition in the *Cortes* had never been popular
with the Old Carlists and the drop in the party's deputies from
62 to 38 had given them a perfect argument for *retraimiento* and
armed revolt. On 15 April a manifesto from Don Carlos's head-
quarters at Geneva announced the Carlist *retraimiento* and six days
later they resorted to arms after mobilizing their bands in the
Basque Provinces and Navarre.[2] Serrano believed the Army could
be trusted against the Carlists but was much less sure about their
attitude should the Federals rise as well. The Government shared
his apprehension, assuming that they would immediately seize the
opportunity to revolt.[3]

In spite of brave words in their press they did not do so. Although even *La Igualdad* talked of *retraimiento* and revolution, no
one was willing to give a lead and Pi was not prepared to do so
without first receiving a new mandate from the party. The
Assembly was therefore recalled for 30 April in order to elect a
new Directory which lack of a quorum had prevented in March.
Because of the gravity of the situation the new Assembly surrendered its powers into Pi's hands—for the first time granting
him dictatorial powers to solve a crisis. His unequivocal condemnation of armed revolt was immediately followed by the introduction of a policy of conciliation in which he chose for his new
Directory the Benevolents Castelar, Pérez de Gúzman, Figueras,
and Sorní and the Intransigents Estévanez and Contreras. The

[1] *La Igualdad*, 20 Apr. 1872.
[2] *El Pensamiento español*, 20 Apr. 1872.
[3] B.M. Add. MS. 39122, 17, 21, 24 Apr. 1872, Layard to Granville, reporting conversations with Serrano.

price of this conciliation was heavy, as Estévanez, an ex-officer with a chequered military past, and Contreras, an incompetent general notorious for his opportunism and unreliability, were both adventurers whose loyalty was open to question.[1] At first Pi's policy of conciliation was successful; a Federal rising did not materialize. In some places, as at Barbastro, preparations had been made to join with the Carlists, but Pi refused to be stampeded. A cautious policy manifesto on 14 May declaring that nothing bound the Federals to the Carlists was accepted by the press in the interests of party unity.[2] In getting the support of Contreras and Estévanez (who both signed the manifesto) for the unpopular decision, Pi could, point to the advice of the French Republicans in favour of parliamentary activity, to the lack of resources for a rising, and most persuasive of all, to the fiasco of the Carlist defeat at Oroquieta on the 4th which showed only too clearly that their revolt had been premature.

Agreement, however, was short-lived. The two Intransigents' acceptance of Pi's policy was only temporary. Contreras, in touch with García López, played for time organizing provincial juntas for revolt and trying to use his position as a Director to overturn Pi's policy. The Intransigent press criticized Pi for using his dictatorial powers to condemn armed revolt. Few, in fact, had confidence in Pi's policy: *La Igualdad*, bravely trying to reflect the Directory's views, was becoming hypersensitive to Intransigent criticism, and even the moderate *Casino federal*, of which Pi was the President, joined with the radical clubs in demanding a *retraimiento*.[3] An increasingly important factor in this mounting hostility to Pi's policy after the April elections was the growing suspicion, fed by Intransigent propaganda, of the Benevolents' real intentions. So long as benevolence was limited to a purely

[1] Vera, op. cit. ii. 309–10. At the time of the San Gil rising Crampton, Layard's predecessor, had described Contreras and Pierrard as 'mere political adventurers who have at different times been the tools of every faction which have disturbed this country' (F.O. 72/1125, no. 171, 24 June 1866, Crampton to Clarendon). Contreras had been a Moderate, an Esparterist, and was to finish as a leader of the Cartagena canton.

[2] *La Igualdad*, 14, 15 May 1872; Pirala, op. cit. iii. 644. For French Republican advice to the Federals see B.M. Add. MS. 39122, 9 May 1872, Layard to Granville, and later, in February 1872, Barral to Victor Emmanuel in Tencajoli, op. cit., p. 23.

[3] *La Igualdad*, 15, 27 June 1872.

parliamentary function the two wings of republican feeling could complement each other with the Benevolents exploiting weaknesses in the *Cortes* and the Intransigents keeping provincial feeling alive, but from the middle of 1872 benevolence was suspected of being extended to include understandings between Radicals and Federals to overthrow the monarchy. It is not easy to say when these suspicions begin to have any substance in fact, although there is evidence that secret meetings were held in November 1872 between Martos, Rivero, Córdoba, Echegaray, and Becerra, and Figueras and Castelar.[1] But already in the summer of 1872 the deterioration of the political situation and the slowness of the Directory's response to it raised serious doubts as to their motives.

In June Zorrilla returned to power after Serrano, trying to exploit his position as peacemaker after the convention of Amoravieta at the end of May, had failed to coerce Amadeo. On 28 June Zorrilla dissolved the *Cortes* and fixed elections for 24 August. Once in power, he not only insured himself against a Conservative comeback by outdoing Sagasta in purging the Army and administration and by strengthening a revived militia, but also by stealing the Federals' thunder through the inclusion in his new programme of specifically Federal measures such as the *quinta* abolition and the separation of Church and State.[2]

What would the Directory's attitude be as its erstwhile ally prepared to consolidate its newly won position? An Intransigent reunion meeting in Madrid on 30 June, called by the firebrand García López, left no doubt about their attitude—unconditional *retraimiento*, outright opposition to benevolence, and the complete independence of the party from any further centralized control.[3] The success of this propaganda was shown on 15 July when only forty-two representatives appeared at a new Assembly called to consider electoral policy. Two days later, after fruitlessly calling for full attendance and urging unity at the coming elections, Pi

---

[1] Letter of Alcalá Zamora to Manuel Zorrilla, 24 Apr. 1873, in O. Bertrand, 'Puntualizaciones en torno al 73', in *Revista de estudios políticos*, 1956, no. 90; cf. Rispa y Perpiña, op cit., p. 189. The Federals were being described in the monarchist press as 'mere auxiliaries of the Radicals' (*La Época*, 24 June 1872).

[2] *Gaceta*, 26 June 1872, circular to civil governors.

[3] Bermejo, op. cit. iii. 793–4.

decided to dissolve the Assembly. For all practical purposes his influence seemed to have ended. But when the Federals returned eighty-seven deputies, their greatest number so far, it was clear that whatever the Madrid Intransigents might say, the provinces continued to support the Directory. This rather surprising result was not caused so much by a great increase in the number of Federal voters, although there was a rise of 38,000 over the 1871 figures, but because of the partial *retraimiento* of the Conservatives, only twenty of whom were returned, and the complete abstention of the Carlists.[1] Appeals to the Basque Provinces and an attempt to placate Catholics showed how the Federals hoped to benefit from their abstention. In Madrid the Radicals' dominance was insufficient to account for the extraordinarily low Federal poll there, which seemed to imply that the Intransigents, strongly entrenched in the radical clubs of the capital, had succeeded in partially enforcing the *retraimiento*. But even so, the fact that Contreras and Guisasola both stood as candidates in the capital is a comment on the inconsequence of Intransigent politics.[2] The August elections provide the first confirmation that the power of the Intransigent leaders hardly held outside the capital.

Although the Directory referred to the elections as a 'moral triumph', the disparity between 87 Federals and 224 Radicals enabled the Intransigents to argue that benevolence had only succeeded in putting the Radicals in an unassailable position. Furthermore, when Zorrilla went back on his election promise to abolish the *quintas*, they could claim that the Benevolents had been fooled as well. Radical strength, however, was largely illusory, for by his overwhelming majority Zorrilla encouraged his party to break up. It was another example of the too-successful election. His troubles did not come from Federal strength, although they gave the Government no respite, but from the split of the Radicals into a Right-wing group under Ruiz Gomez and Gasset

[1] The voting returns were: Radicals, 1,339,733; Federals, 386,734; Conservatives, 108,740; Alphonsists, 45,693 (Pirala, op. cit. iv. 154). Alphonsists may have voted for Federals in some areas, as they did at Córdoba in 1871, hoping that a republican anarchy would drive the Army to Alphonsism. Demoted Conservative generals were talking of 'making terms with the Republicans and establishing a well-ordered republic as in France' (B.M. Add. MS. 39123, 18, 22 June 1872, Layard to Granville, reports of conversations with Serrano).   [2] Contreras obtained 424 votes and Guisasola only 42 votes!

y Artime, the influential director of *El Imparcial*, and a Left-wing
group corresponding to the old Democrat party, the leadership
of which was contested between Martos and Rivero. Once the
Radicals dominated the *Cortes*, these two were far less inhibited
about intriguing with Conservatives and those Federals like
Castelar who were becoming alarmed at the growing volume of
extremist criticism of the Directory.

This criticism reached a climax after a revolt had broken out on
12 October among the garrison in the Arsenal at El Ferrol.[1] Both
the Government and the Federals were taken by surprise. It was
not a specifically Federal revolt, although the Intransigents hailed it
as one. It was, in fact, a small-scale *pronunciamiento* staged by
a Colonel Pozas, a disgruntled ex-Carlist officer, who used the
'Federal Republic' as a rallying cry. The revolt was confined to the
Arsenal and had no repercussions either in the town of El Ferrol
or in neighbouring La Coruña, which had a Federal *Ayuntamiento*.
In the *Cortes* on the 14th, Pi explicitly condemned the rising and
any armed revolt so long as basic civil liberties were guaranteed.
When the Government quoted his speech in an appeal to the
rebels to surrender, Intransigent anger was boundless. By 20
October the revolt had petered out, but Pi's condemnation and
the Directory's support for him had been sufficient to break it up
and to encourage the Intransigents to set up their own in opposition. As neither Contreras nor Estévanez had been able to influence
the Directory's policy, they both resigned; Contreras immediately
establishing a rival *Consejo Provisional de la Federación Española*
with himself as president and Córdoba y López's new *El Tribunal
del Pueblo* as its mouthpiece. In this the rival Directory called for
social revolution, rejection of Pi's leadership, and the setting up
of secret action committees.[2] Pi's response was to seek a new
mandate from the party at an Assembly called for 17 November.
He still retained a measure of the party's confidence as his unanimous election to the presidency of the Assembly showed, but the
boycotting of it by the Intransigents led him to refuse the office.

[1] *La Igualdad*, 13, 17, 21, 27 Oct. 1872; Bermejo, op. cit. ii. 832; Zorrilla told Layard he
believed Montpensier was behind it. For anger at Pi's stand see *La Igualdad*, 29 Oct., 9 Nov.
1872. Most of the protests came from Andalusia.
[2] *El Tribunal del Pueblo*, 25 Oct. 1872.

His policy of conciliation had failed and he had no wish to be the leader of a divided party. On 26 November the Assembly broke up with nothing achieved.[1] The decision not to elect a new Directory was due to recognition that it would no longer have the moral authority to impose its will, for on 24 November the much-vaunted Intransigent revolt broke out in the provinces.

The Intransigents hoped to achieve maximum effect by timing the revolt to coincide with the *quinta* draw on the 24th, although this decision, according to Ripsa y Perpiña, who was at Málaga preparing for a rising in February 1873, was made by Contreras, who succeeded in forcing his views on the reluctant Estévanez.[2] Their purpose in staging a revolt might have been to forestall a more comprehensive coup which they feared was being planned in the secret reunions between the Radical discontents, and Figueras and Castelar. The Intransigents' aim, according to their programme outlined in *El Tribunal del Pueblo*, was to seize key positions in the State, excluding from them all Radicals and moderate Federals at the same time as they rallied mass support by an extremist social programme. This was to include, in addition to the stock radical aims of the abolition of the *quintas* and *consumos*, and a volunteer army, the dismissal of all government employees, the revision of railway contracts, the nationalization of banks, price control, direct democracy, free justice, and land reform.[3]

After the wordy eloquence of the Intransigent press, the risings were a fiasco and an example of how revolutions should not be made. Agents were sent into the provinces to contact Intransigent committees. Contreras, heavily disguised, was picked up by the police at Seville. Ocon, a veteran of the 1869 revolt, at Valencia. Estévanez, with greater success, evaded the Madrid police and put himself at the head of a small band in the Sierra Morena where the cutting of the pass of Despeñaperros was to be the signal for a general revolt. There were repercussions throughout southern Spain. Unsuccessful attempts were made to exploit social

[1] Vera, op. cit. ii. 367 et seq.
[2] Rispa y Perpiña, op. cit., pp. 191–6. Estévanez, op. cit., pp. 384–9. Layard refers to Contreras being supplied with funds by an Alphonsist banker.
[3] Vera, op. cit. ii. 356–64. Cf. Paul y Angulo, *Verdades revolucionarias*, Madrid, 1872, *passim*, which shows this new interest in social revolution.

discontent in the notoriously volatile industrial towns of Bejar and Alcoy. At Murcia a popular local figure, Gálvez Arce, had a momentary success in whipping up *quinta* grievances. But these grievances had no repercussions in any of the traditionally republican towns. In Barcelona the *quinta* draw passed off more quietly than usual and it was probably the Government's heavy garrisoning of Cádiz and Seville which decided the rebels to concentrate their efforts on the smaller Andalusian towns. At Linares, for example, an attempt was made to build up the local grievances against Baeza. In twenty years it had risen from 5,000 to a flourishing mining centre of 30,000, but Baeza, a third of the size, continued to enjoy greater political influence in Jaén province.[1] Estévanez arrived to take control, loopholing houses and arming a local militia, but, at the approach of a squad of cavalry, resistance petered out and he decamped with municipal funds. Strangely enough no attempt was made to use Intransigent strength in the radical clubs of the capital to stage a coup there and, although there was a brief echo of revolutionary thunder on 11 December when troops quelled a riot in the republican working-class area round the Plaza Anton Marín, it seems that bribery by Cuban slaveholders, anxious to embarrass a government in favour of legislating against them, was the spur to this outburst rather than any belated attempt at an organized coup.[2]

These failures show that the Intransigents could not even rally support in those areas they claimed to be saving from dictation by the party leadership at Madrid. Intransigent incompetence and Pi's prediction at the Assembly that there were no resources for a rising led to press support for the Directory's past policy, but opinion was divided about whether to re-establish the Directory or to revert to the old Pacts. These divisions and mutual recriminations apportioning the blame wasted the party's strength as the events of December and January ushered in the political climax of Amadeo's reign.

[1] F.O. 72/1313, nos. 372, 373, 1 Dec. 1872, Layard to Granville, enclosures from consuls at Cádiz and Barcelona and vice-consul at Linares. The Cádiz consul believed the rebels were in Cuban filibusters' pay.
[2] Letter of Sickles to Cooper, 17 Dec. 1872, n A. Nevins, op. cit., p. 627; cf. Martos's similar claim to Layard in B.M. Add. MS. 39123, 14 Dec. 1872.

The flaring up of the Cuban question in December as a result of the Government's determination to proceed with the abolition of slavery in Puerto Rico now spotlights the United States ambassador at Madrid, General Sickles. His aggressive republican sympathies were no secret; Sagasta had already asked for his recall on this count. Sickles believed that American interests as well as Cuban freedom would be best served by a republican régime in Spain. Whatever the official United States policy in this matter, and evidence suggests that Sickles was forcing the pace, the publication on 9 January by Secretary of State Fish of his recent correspondence with Sickles helped to weaken the régime by undermining public confidence in Zorrilla, confirming the opposition's accusations that Zorrilla's decision to abolish slavery in Puerto Rico had been due to American pressure.[1] Important though the Cuban question was in rallying Right-wing elements round Serrano in the newly created 'League for the Defence of the Integrity of the Territory', Zorrilla's main trouble came from the dissatisfaction within the Army arising from the Hidalgo affair and the question of the artillery officers.

Hidalgo was an artillery officer who had been implicated in the San Gil rising in 1866 and was regarded by his fellow officers as an accomplice of the mutineers. He had gone into exile and had become Prim's secretary, but realizing his unpopularity Prim posted him to Cuba from whence he returned in 1871. In November, Córdoba, Minister of War, tactlessly appointed him to be Captain-General of the Basque Provinces although he knew from personal experience the susceptibilities of the artillery officers and had been warned by Amadeo that the appointment would be an unpopular one. The refusal of the artillery officers of the Pampluna garrison to recognize the appointment forced Hidalgo to resign. No government could afford dictation by the Army, but the situation was particularly inflammable as each party used the ensuing crisis for its own purposes. The Conservatives encouraged the officers in their resistance, especially at Madrid where

[1] Nevins, op. cit., pp. 628–34. Spanish colonial clubs in Madrid, Cádiz, Seville, and Barcelona, branches of the *Casino español* in Havana, were active in their support of Serrano's League. The Cuban issue provided Serrano with a perfect plank to make his political comeback.

Alphonsists were also fanning the discontent. Zorrilla and the Ministry made a stand in defending Hidalgo and their unwillingness to let the matter rest was shown by his subsequent appointment to a command in Tarragona at the end of January. Although precautions had been taken to remove artillery officers who might take offence, Zorrilla knew that any attempt to give Hidalgo another command would precipitate a crisis, but, ignoring the warning of both Amadeo and Pavía, Captain-General of Madrid, he persisted in the appointment and on 27 January Hidalgo left for Tarragona, whereupon 300 artillery officers immediately resigned.[1]

The expected crisis broke in the *Cortes* on February 7 when after accepting the resignations of the artillery officers the Government received a vote of confidence of 191–2. Wildly cheered by Federals, Córdoba announced the Government's intention of using the opportunity to democratize the artillery corps and to replace those who had resigned by sergeants. Although Amadeo signed the decree abolishing the privileges of the corps on the 8th, the deliberate flouting of his advice was the final action deciding him to abdicate in spite of the attempts of both Zorrilla and foreign diplomats to dissuade him.[2]

At this moment only Zorrilla among Spanish politicians had an interest in preserving the monarchy. Alphonsist encouragement of the officers was aimed at provoking a head-on clash between the Army and the Government. The Federals welcomed the crisis for the possibilities of overthrowing the monarchy. Serrano saw in the conflict between Amadeo and the Government a chance that Amadeo might turn to him, or failing that, the opportunity to come to an agreement with discontented Radicals to stage a coup and set up a unitarian republic. Zorrilla, unable to restrain either Córdoba or the majority of his own party, was finally ex-

---

[1] Bermejo, op. cit. ii. 847–52. Many strands in the Hidalgo affair need sorting out. Córdoba's motives are very obscure; he was speculating with an Alphonsist banker and was a close friend of Sickles, who told Layard he had urged him to persist in Hidalgo's appointment.

[2] Tencajoli, op. cit., p. 42; *Docs. diplomatiques français*, 1re série, i, Paris, 1929, no. 172, 13 Feb. 1873, Thiers to Bouillé; no. 171, 12 Feb. 1873, Rémusat to Fournier, French ambassador at Rome.

posed as an impotent figurehead with the real leadership of the Radicals being disputed between Rivero and Martos.

It was Serrano's return to political activity at the end of January which forced the hand of the Radicals, who now sought the slightest opportunity to pick a quarrel with Amadeo. One occasion was Amadeo's omission to invite the Radical ministers to witness the birth of his son on 30 January, but it was the *Cortes* crisis of 7 February and the enthusiastic reception of Córdoba's plan for the reorganization of the artillery corps which forced Zorrilla and Amadeo into open conflict.

During the crisis the Conservatives again offered their support to Amadeo as they had at the time of the Federal rising in Madrid on 11 December, but he refused it as he also refused to accept Zorrilla's resignation. The only solution which Amadeo would countenance was a ministry of conciliation, but this the other Radicals in the ministry, sure of their own strength, refused to consider. With the Federals' support and an overwhelming majority in the *Cortes*, Martos, Rivero, and Córdoba were able to exploit the artillery issue and force a breach between Zorrilla and Amadeo. Zorrilla's own solution, to set up a provisional government until new elections could be held, was supported neither by Amadeo nor Zorrilla's own ministers, whose intrigues with the Federals were aimed as much against him as against Amadeo.

When Amadeo finally abdicated on 11 February the bankruptcy of Zorrilla's leadership was fully exposed. In the final instance it was not American pressure, nor republican intrigues, nor those of the non-republican opposition which decided Amadeo to abdicate, but the jealousies and rivalries within that party which claimed to be his only real supporters. Failing to make him their puppet, the Radicals had no compunction in turning against him. It was the hour of vengeance for Zorrilla's rivals, Martos and Rivero, but, in their triumph and fighting over the spoils, they furthered and completed the decline of the Radicals which Zorrilla had begun. The Federals were to be the heirs of Amadeo's worldly kingdom and the Radicals were to be cast into outer darkness.

8

Radicals and Republicans, 1873

THE First Republic owed its existence to a shabby backstairs political intrigue. For eleven months the Federal leaders lived in the shadow of its origins. They did not come to power on the high-tide of revolutionary enthusiasm and, as they could not appeal to a mystique of the barricades, they never escaped from the initial sense of anticlimax.

It was true that when Amadeo abdicated on 11 February the predictions of the Federal leaders had, for once, been fulfilled. 'Nobody has destroyed the monarchy in Spain,' Castelar said,[1] 'it has died through internal decay.' But the fall of the monarchy was not sufficient in itself to ensure political initiative for the Federals. In February they were still leaderless, the Intransigent *Consejo* had not been dissolved, and although a new party Assembly had been called to meet in Madrid to discuss issues previously postponed, no one pretended that differences would then be smoothed over. It was only Amadeo's abdication which cut short the bitter sterile polemics which had characterized the first weeks of 1873.[2]

Inevitably, the Benevolents interpreted Amadeo's fall as the result of their policy. 'Benevolence', in Carvajal's words, was 'the most practically revolutionary act and the one most favourable to the triumph of the republic which the Federals up till then had realized.' But the comings and goings of Federal leaders with the

---

[1] *Diario de la Asamblea Nacional*, 11 Feb. 1873. The fullest account of the First Republic is in Vera, op. cit. ii. 404 et seq. Pi's own account, *La República de 1873*, Madrid, 1874, is reprinted in Pi y Arsuaga, op. cit. v. 278–344, to which references are made in the following chapters. Bermejo, op. cit. iii, is a full and useful account from an Alphonsist viewpoint. Pirala, op. cit. iv, v, are little use for the Federals but useful for the Carlists to whose papers he had been granted access. González Sugrañes, *La República en Barcelona*, Barcelona, 2nd ed., 1903, is a very useful account by a leading local Federal.

[2] *La Igualdad*, 1 Feb. 1873, manifesto of 27 deputies and 19 presidents of provincial committees repudiating here violence and any centralized direction. Cf. ibid., 4–7 Feb.

Radicals gave substance to the Intransigent fear that benevolence implied understandings between Radicals and the Moderates which might lead to a reunification of the Democrat party forged by common fear of the Intransigents' recent social extremism. This fear, real though it may have been to the Intransigents, was not in fact sufficient to merge Radicals and Benevolents because of their mutual distrust and hostility. Moreover, the distribution of power in the *Cortes* militated against any such merger. The Radicals there had no need of any alliance with the Benevolents who, committed to a policy of legality, had little alternative but to accept Radical supremacy unless they wanted to follow the Intransigents' lead. Under the monarchy Federal strength had lain in the parliamentary activity of their deputies. Amadeo was at the mercy of the Radicals, who were themselves becoming dependent on the Federals in the intrigues against him. After 11 February the position was reversed and when, rather than be excluded from power, the Radicals voted for a republic, the ground was cut from under the feet of the parliamentary Federals.

How did these new developments affect Federal policy and what was Pi's conception of their new role? The essence of Pi's criticism of the revolutionary wing of the party was that any use of force would deprive the Republic of legality. Castelar, Figueras, and Salmerón shared his belief that the Republic must be rooted in law. Legality did not mean the revolutionary justice of the barricades and yet, as Pi was to admit, many of their later troubles stemmed from the fact that the Republic had been introduced by a series of illegal acts to which they had all agreed.[1] Under the Constitution the *Cortes* should have been dissolved immediately on Amadeo's abdication—both the merging of the two Chambers into one body and the declaration of a new form of government by a *Cortes* not having constituent powers, were illegal acts. The legal course, as Zorrilla argued, would have been to appoint a provisional government until elections for a new *Cortes*, but Rivero and Martos were determined to use the immediate declaration of a republic as a means of ousting Zorrilla from the party leadership. After Zorrilla's resignation Rivero was the man of the

[1] Pi y Asuaga, op. cit. v. 283.

hour, as he had been in 1868. As President of Congress, he intended to join the two Chambers and declare a National Convention with himself as its first President. The foiling of this move by Martos, who secured his own election to the Presidency of the Assembly, was the first unedifying quarrel of a series between the two men which was to reduce the Radicals to impotence during the crises of the spring.

The Radicals had no real alternative but to declare a republic—they had no monarchist candidate and another interregnum was unthinkable as ugly crowds, waving republican slogans and agitated by club leaders, milling around the *Cortes* building, emphasized the dangers of delay and the threat of armed rising if the Republic were not immediately proclaimed. Mob pressure, combined with the Radicals' unsureness about Serrano and the Army's attitude, stampeded them into this unconstitutional step. The type of Republic declared on 11 February was left undefined—this was to be decided later by a constituent *Cortes*. Whereas the Intransigents clamoured for the immediate declaration of a Federal Republic, the parliamentary Federals refused to yield to their pressure and joined the Radicals in voting for an unqualified Republic. It was true that their vote made no difference, but this decision was in accordance with Pi's view that it would be fatal to declare a Federal Republic until a Constitution had first been voted and discussed. The question of the Constitution is a key to Pi's policy in 1873, believing, as he did, that any premature declaration would encourage provinces, towns, and villages to seize the initiative and create the Federal Republic from below (*abajo-arriba*). Once towns had declared their independence, the central authority would be powerless to fix the attributes of the Federal units except by force.[1]

This question of the Constitution provides the best illustration of the lack of clarity in republican thought. Although Salmerón and Chao had presented a draft Constitution to the 1872 Federal Assembly it had not been discussed or debated.[2] No one, therefore, had a clear idea what should constitute the Federal States. Debates

[1] Pi y Arsuaga, op. cit. v. 292–3.
[2] Printed ibid., pp. 357–64; cf. Díaz Quintero's draft, pp. 364–84; Castelar's, pp. 261–76, and M. Ayllon y Altolaguirre, *Proyecto de constitución democrático-federal de la República Española*, Madrid, 1873.

later were to reveal a fundamental cleavage on this vital point.
The 'Federal Republic' meant as many different things as it had in
1869 and the activity of the intervening years had done little to
clarify the issue.[1] Echegaray, Radical Minister of Finance, summed
up the confusion in the *Cortes* on 7 March:

I have asked for a definition . . . we've asked for a doctrine, an idea,
something in common in which we could join together and march
firmly to the solution of these great problems . . . it is impossible because
you have no federal republic, because you do not know what your
republic is. For the intransigent masses the federal republic is not even
a feeling nor the instinct of something noble and practical . . . for them
the federal republic is here a farm to be divided, a wood to be parti-
tioned, there the fixing of a minimum wage; in another province a
battering ram opening a breach in the forces of law and order so
that contraband may pass; poor against rich, the partition of property,
tax payer against the exchequer, all these momentary interests, all these
social utopias, deep yearnings, great needs, ardent appetites constitute
the essence of the republic among the people, but you will never find
among them a redeeming idea or the germ of a programme for society.

In 1873 as in 1868 the demand for a Federal Republic was a spontaneous reflex after the collapse of central authority and was largely
a shibboleth independent of the intellectuals' theorizing.

The problem facing Pi and others was how to canalize this
spontaneous feeling and to instil confidence in their provincial
followers to accept the idea of a revolution directed from above.
The drawback to this was that by 1873 benevolence, whatever its
other merits, had made the official leadership lose much of the
party's trust. Moreover, the office hunters were determined not
to be balked of their prey by Radicals masquerading as Republicans. They now demanded the rewards of past support; the cry
of the 'republic for the republicans' rapidly destroyed all traces of
republican idealism, that utopian 'republic for all' fostered and
proclaimed by Pi and his associates. Throughout the Federal
Republic every government had to contend with a small but
vociferous group of Intransigents in Madrid, who, by working
through radical clubs and playing on current discontents, were

[1] Cf. Vilarrasa and Gatell, op. cit. ii. 645, distinguishing between seven different prevalent conceptions of the 'Republic'.

able to stage demonstrations in the streets round the *Cortes* building and in this way to exert an influence out of all proportion to
their number. Their purpose if ambition was unsatisfied was to
make government impossible. The fact that once ambition had
been satisfied they became supporters of firm policies as did
Estévanez, Córdoba y López, and García López is a sufficient
indication of the motives behind their behaviour.

In the first period of the Republic, lasting until the Radicals'
unsuccessful coup of 23 April, power was uneasily shared between
Radicals and Federals in two ministries of conciliation. In the first
ministry formed on 11 February Figueras, the President of the
Executive Power, was supported by the Radicals because of his
lack of doctrinaire enthusiasm, his weak character, and his supposedly lukewarm republican sympathies. He was, however, an
able tactician and in Layard's considered judgement nearer to the
English conception of a parliamentary man than any of his contemporaries. Castelar was Minister of State; he was not only the
best known abroad but was an assurance of the new Republic's
moderation.[1] Although Pi was expected to take the Ministry of
Finance, he occupied instead the key post of the Interior where he
would have charge of electoral arrangements, of the republican
volunteers, and of the vital telegraph system. His tenure of this
post until his resignation on 18 July provides the one element of
ministerial continuity in the ever-changing ministries of the first
half of the Republic's life. Salmerón, who had not yet attracted
much attention as a politician, became Minister of Justice, a
guarantee that the much-publicized judicial reforms and anticlerical legislation would be put into effect. The five Radical
ministers were to be birds of passage lasting only thirteen days.

The untried Federals were at least given the benefit of being
more honest than the Radicals in the Ministry, who had already
been soiled by office. In his memoir, Layard amplified his earlier
impression of Pi, whom he considered to be:[2]

... the worst and the most dangerous. It was especially unwise to give

---

[1] Thiers, *Notes et souvenirs, 1870–3*, Paris, 1901, p. 378.
[2] B.M. Add. MS. 38932, ff. 325–6. Cf. B.M. Add. MS. 39123, 19 Feb. 1873, for Layard's
view of Figueras.

him the Ministry of the Interior. He belonged to the extreme red republican party, of a determined and resolute disposition whilst outwardly calm and impassive he was uncompromising in his opinions and ready to have recourse to whatever means required to carry them out. He belonged to that class of men who were responsible for the worst excesses of the French Revolution and who encouraged them and allowed them. . . . He was placed in the Ministry to satisfy the extreme section of the republicans.

Allowing for his bias and the fact that this was not based on personal acquaintance, the contrast he drew between Pi's strength of character, Figueras's weakness, and 'the egregiously vain Castelar who would be a monarchist if it would flatter his vanity', emphasizes Pi's inflexibility, which was to be a cardinal factor in politics until July. It was a divided and weak government which had to deal with the situation provoked by Amadeo's abdication.

The immediate reaction in the provinces to Amadeo's fall had been the establishment of revolutionary juntas, the deposition of non-republican *Ayuntamientos*, and scattered disturbances such as the burning of the customs offices at Málaga and widespread attacks on state property. The most violent outburst was at Montilla, the wine-producing town near Córdoba, the electoral history of which had been one of fraud and corruption by *caciques* working to preserve the political dominance of local landowners against a strongly organized local Federal party.[1] Tension built up in this atmosphere of violent coercion finally broke on 12 February on receipt of the news that the republic had been proclaimed. Local Federal chiefs, about to establish a revolutionary junta and republicanize the *Ayuntamiento*, found popular anger outrunning their control and in a day's rioting an armed mob, leaderless and inflamed by drink, sacked the *alcalde*'s house, fired the local archives, and killed a number of municipal employees, dispersing only when troops were called out from Córdoba.

The affair was lugubriously publicized by the monarchist press, providing confirmation for their worst fears of republican anarchy, but *La Igualdad* excused it as a natural reaction after the intolerable

[1] Díaz del Moral, op. cit., pp. 70–73.

domination of the *caciques*.[1] Charges of complicity in the riot brought by the authorities against local Federal leaders were later dropped through lack of evidence, for although they may not have been averse to the mob's action it seemed questionable whether in fact they had any influence over it. Nor were the International or the Alliance of Social Democracy implicated in a riot which Diaz del Moral characterized as a popular and spontaneous uprising—'an explosion of hatred of the poor against the rich'. Although the news of Amadeo's fall did not have such violent repercussions elsewhere the reaction of the socially oppressed at Montilla differed from other Andalusian demonstrations only in degree. The popular image of the 'Federal Republic' contained a messianic element which for the Andalusian *jornaleros* meant the satisfaction of their land-hunger and the replacing of *cacique* coercion by a reign of social justice. The breakdown of social restraints heralded by the new régime encouraged demands for retribution and social revolution, but the vast majority of these were divorced from precise political affiliations and were independent of local Federal activity, which continued to concentrate on the immediate political aim of republicanizing the administration and weeding out false republicans.

As Minister of the Interior Pi's reactions to all expressions of revolutionary fervour was to order the dissolution of the juntas and the reinstatement of the previous *Ayuntamientos*.[2] The damping down of revolutionary ardour was a clear intimation that the Government was not going to be stampeded into further unconstitutional steps, but if the Government thought that it could mollify provincial feeling by passing a series of radical decrees, such as re-forming the republican militia and making the judiciary independent, it was mistaken.[3] The Intransigents in Madrid were determined to exploit the disillusion of the provinces in order to force the Federals in the Government to resist the Radicals' attempts to turn their parliamentary majority to their own advantage.

It is clear that the Federal leaders hoped that their treatment of the Army would restore confidence in their good intentions, but

---

[1] *La Igualdad*, 15 Feb. 1873.
[2] Pi y Arsuaga, op. cit. v. 283.
[3] *Gaceta*, 15, 20 Feb. 1873.

if we examine their policy in this key question the full extent of their dilemma becomes apparent. Army appointments sharpened the clash between Radicals and Federals and were partly responsible for the break-up of the first ministry of conciliation on 24 February. The Army question also exposed the Federals to the blackmail of their own extremists at the same time as the breakdown of discipline as the Federals reaped the harvest of their anti-military propaganda posed the whole question of public order, the nation's confidence in the new régime, and was largely responsible for determining the attitude of foreign governments and capital towards the new Republic.

La Igualdad emphasized the paramount importance of the Army question when it called for the 'moralization' of the Army, the arming of the people, the immediate abolition of conscription, the establishment of a volunteer professional force, and the waging of a people's war against Carlists and all reactionaries.[1] By mid-February even *La Igualdad* had come to realize the gravity of the revived Carlist menace and the Government, through the importunity of the Catalans, recognized that the Carlist threat flaring up again on Amadeo's fall had assumed the proportions of a full-scale war. Unfortunately for the Federals the optimistic assumption that the Carlists would lay down their arms once Amadeo had fallen was soon shown to be false. Granting local autonomy in a federal State was insufficient to buy off the Carlists whose ambitions were now national and not regional. With the appearance of an avowedly anticlerical Republic the Carlist rising took on the aspect of a national crusade.

To prevent the decomposition of the Army and at the same time to retain the trust of their own supporters was the circle which the Federals in the Government tried to square. Only two generals were of known Federal sympathies—the equally incompetent Contreras and Nouvilas—both were despised by the regular officers and disliked for their Intransigent contacts. For lack of alternatives the Government was forced to trust them. Contreras was therefore appointed to the key command of the Army of Catalonia on 18 February. This had the advantage of removing

---

[1] *La Igualdad*, 14, 20 Feb. 1873. For the Carlist war see Pirala, op. cit. iv. 133 et seq.

a dangerous man from the centre of intrigue at Madrid and also appeased the Catalan Federals, whose feelings rose dangerously high after the attempt of the hated Gaminde, Captain-General of Catalonia, supported by Alphonsist sympathizers, to stage a coup in Barcelona on 21 February.[1] But the refusal of Contreras to leave for Catalonia until Córdoba, whom he disliked on personal grounds, had been dismissed brought to a head the division within the ministry over the distribution of offices and highlights the way in which the Intransigents could force the Government's hand.

Already squeezed out of several civil governorships, the Radicals disliked Contreras's appointment and even more the rumour that Nouvilas was to be given the captain-generalship of Castile, a key position controlling the Madrid garrison.[2] Martos's attempt to foil this by nominating Moriones to the post on the 23rd hastened the crisis. When Figueras resigned the next day, admitting the ministry's inability to agree, he was replaced by Martos but, although he tried to nominate a new government of conciliation, the attitude of the Madrid mob and reports from the provinces led the Assembly to agree to the appointment of a mixed commission to discuss the ministerial crisis. Mob pressure and the threat of civil war compelled it to agree that extremist feeling could only be assuaged by increasing Federal representation in the Government. Figueras was then empowered to form a second ministry in which the Radicals retained only the two posts of War and Marine.

Within thirteen days the Radicals, despite overwhelming predominance in the Assembly, had been forced by extremist pressure to agree to a more homogeneous Federal ministry. They had been forced to yield to a small minority faction because they lacked any substantial following in the Army, and also because they hoped by a policy of conciliation to win over the moderate Federal leaders like Castelar who were now realizing the full extent of the

[1] González Sugrañes, op. cit., pp. 63 et seq.; Vera, op. cit. ii. 439–49. Cf. B.M. Add. MS. 39123, 26 Feb. 1873, secret, Layard to Granville, giving Serrano's account from an officer involved.

[2] *Gaceta*, 16 Feb.–6 Mar. 1873, between these dates thirty-eight new civil governors were appointed to replace Radicals.

danger from their own left wing. There was irony in the Federals' victory, as Acosta the new Minister of War was one of Serrano's creatures.[1]

Ministerial changes alone, however, could not dispel the Army problem. The Intransigents knew that the Federals in the Government would not use the Army to suppress them for fear of alienating what little support they had in the country. So long as the Army problem remained, therefore, the Intransigents could exert pressure out of all proportion to their numbers. They also realized their value to the parliamentary Federals in intimidating the Radicals by aggressive street demonstrations and, indeed, there is little evidence to suggest that any of the Federal leaders were averse to this so long as their own position was not being threatened. But even the long-awaited abolition of the *quintas* by decree on 22 February failed to provide a solution. Once conscription was abolished, conscripts were urged by Intransigent propaganda to mutiny if they were not immediately released. Even more important, though, was the fact that after abolishing the *quintas* the Federals were no longer able to exploit the one grievance which could ensure them mass support.

The party and its leader regarded the rapid arming of the people as the touchstone of any government's good intentions. One of Pi's first decrees had been the establishment of a republican militia.[2] Controlled by the Minister of the Interor, it would act as a counterweight to the Army. But this militia was a party not a national organization. In Madrid the conservative classes boycotted it, showing their distrust by setting up the *vecinos honrados* —a vigilante organization centred on the wealthy *barrio* Salamanca.[3] Although the republican militia was to serve one purpose in Madrid when it saved the Government from the Radicals' coup on 23 April, it failed in its main purpose of giving Federal supporters confidence in the Government's good intentions,

---

[1] B.M. Add. MS. 39123, Layard to Granville; Serrano told this to Layard in confidence. This would account for much of Serrano's inside knowledge of ministerial divisions which he passed on to Layard. 'Officially' Acosta was a Radical.

[2] *Gaceta*, 15 Feb. 1873, decree re-establishing the Volunteers of Liberty dissolved in Oct. 1868.

[3] *La Igualdad*, 2, 5 Mar. 1873.

mainly because the Government found it impractical to arm the people sufficiently quickly. Lack of funds prevented rifles from being bought abroad and by mid-July only 16,000 out of 50,000 which had been ordered in March had been distributed.[1]

The Carlist war demanded the retention of a professional army, but the republican solution of a volunteer regular force had not been worked out in any detail. Until this had been done, they hoped to tide themselves over with the creation of eighty battalions of *cuerpos francos*.[2] *Quinta* abolition was based on the erroneous assumption that the 'people' would voluntarily flock to the colours to defeat the clerical reaction. But the *cuerpos francos* scheme was a complete fiasco through lack of response. Out of the projected 48,000 men only 3,000 had volunteered by the end of April and by mid-June the number had barely risen to 10,000. The attempt to bribe volunteers with the offer of better pay than the regulars led to army discontent and pay increases to equal that of the volunteers. No Federal doubted that the new force would be more efficient than the old conscript army, but the 'two-peseta patriots' were little more than an armed mob of unemployed who had joined up for loot. Failure to create an efficient popular force meant that the Government was compelled to rely on the regulars, who, riddled with discontent, were rapidly becoming a prey to Alphonsist propaganda.[3]

No understanding could be reached with the regular army until the question of the artillery officers had been solved. No genuine Federal would stomach their reinstatement and although Castelar and Figueras, after Serrano's advice, came to realize the crucial importance of reinstating them as a prelude to gaining the Army's confidence, Federal rank-and-file opinion, both in the

---

[1] Pi y Arsuaga, v. 321–2. Cf. Carrera Pujal, op. cit. v. 230; *La Igualdad*, 22, 23 Feb. 1873, complaining that the people were not being armed fast enough and reporting that the Sevillano deputies were making their own arrangements to obtain 6,000 rifles abroad.

[2] *Diario*, 4 Mar. 1873. App. 5 for the draft of this law; they were to be financed from the sale of the Rio Tinto mines.

[3] F. O. 72/1339, no. 317, 28 Apr. 1873, Layard to Granville; *The Times*, 25 June 1873. For examples of indiscipline see Pirala, op. cit. iv. 599–603; Mañé y Flaquer, *La Revolución de 1868 juzgada por sus autores*, Barcelona, 1876, ii. 188–200. B.M. Add. MS. 39123, 26 Feb. 1873, Layard to Granville, reporting Serrano's account of a talk with Figueras. Cf. letter of Grijalba to Isabella, 1 Apr. 1873. See also 11 Apr. 1873 (in *El Sol*, 6 Mar. 1924), where Grijalba recounts how Castelar was confiding each day in Grijalba.

Army and among the civilians, precluded any such *rapprochement*. While Carlist agents tried to bribe ex-artillery officers to join them, the Federals were forced to sacrifice any hope of winning over the Army to an impractical scheme for a volunteer force which never showed any sign of taking root. Loyalty to the Republic was to be achieved by expanding the budgetary deficit —such was the promise of cheap republican government. Discontent among the Army as men demanding immediate release, and inflamed by Intransigent propaganda, began to murder their officers forms a sombre background to the republican period.

The Republic's failure to find an early solution to the question of public order had a disastrous effect on diplomatic opinion and on foreign capital. The United States and Switzerland acknowledging their influence on Spanish republicanism were the only powers which immediately recognized the new régime. Other powers adopted a cautious waiting policy. In mid-February Bouillé told Castelar of Thiers's fear of federal republicanism and Serrano believed that the declaration of a Federal Republic might even lead to French intervention. Layard anxiously tried to ensure that the European powers would only recognize a conservative Republic.[1] Both Britain and France shared suspicions about the new Republic's intentions towards Portugal, whose ambassador, thoroughly alarmed by the new developments and by press descriptions of Spain's 'historic mission of Iberian Union', was constantly asking Layard's advice.[2] It was Castelar's experience as Minister of State which at last wakened him to a sense of political reality, confirming his belief in moderate policies and the need to restore discipline in the Army as a prerequisite for recognition by foreign powers and for attracting much-needed foreign capital.[3]

But the Government could do little to counteract the bad impression made on foreign powers or even to spend time debating

[1] B.M. Add. MS. 39123, 17, 22 Feb. 1873, Layard to Granville. Thiers wrote later to Serrano via the latter's wife at Biarritz, expressing the hope that he would remain in Spain and help to restore order (F.O. 72/1338, no. 262, 31 Mar. 1873, cipher, Layard to Granville).

[2] B.M. Add. MS. 39123, 26 Feb., 6 Apr. 1873, Layard to Granville; letter of Thiers to the King of Portugal, 16 Dec. 1872, in *Thiers au pouvoir*, pp. 288–9.

[3] B.M. Add. MS. 39123, 24 Mar. 1873, Layard to Granville, reports dissension in the Government over Castelar urging stronger measures.

foreign policy as it was distracted by increasing Intransigent opposition and by Radical opposition over the question of the dissolution
of the Assembly and elections to a constituent *Cortes*. Intransigent
pressure before the ministerial crisis of 24 February had not led to
their participation in the Government. On the contrary, it had
only strengthened the Moderates' position, as Tutau, Chao, and
Sorní took over the vacant ministries. These Moderate gains, however, were illusory as the Intransigents became even more importunate, petitioning the Government to dissolve the Assembly and
to republicanize the administration and local government.[1] The
marked change of feeling discernible in the more persistent demands in the Federal press for revolutionary changes seems to have
been stimulated by anger at the formation of the *vecinos honrados*,
whose existence was first noted in the press on 2 March. Until
23 March, when the Assembly was finally dissolved, the Government's efforts were concentrated on trying to resist this pressure
from federal extremists. Reluctance to yield to their own left wing
is well illustrated in the series of attempts made early in March to
come to a compromise with the Radicals over the question of
dissolution and the elections which the Radicals justifiably feared
would be managed by the Federals so as to exclude them from the
new *Cortes*. A committee was set up on 5 March to consider this
question. Radical in composition, it advised against dissolution
unless the Government promised not to work the elections and
to protect them against Intransigent intimidation. Negotiations
between the Government and Radical leaders to consider giving
the Radicals certain offices in the provinces so that they could
manipulate some elections broke down.[2] Exactly why is not clear.
Pi had never been in favour of these electoral bargains, which he
thought the Federals were committed to destroy; he may therefore have overcome Figueras's political realism or, more likely, the
Radicals, realizing the Government was in no position to honour
such arrangements, decided to harden their attitude on the committee, at the same time resisting the more informal attempts of

[1] *El Combate federal*, 5, 7 Mar.; *La España federal*, 1 Mar.; *La Igualdad*, 2–5 Mar. 1873.
[2] B.M. Add. MS. 39123, 8 Mar. 1873, Layard to Granville. For the Radical conciliators
see Bermejo, op. cit. iii. 325–7.

the conciliatory Radicals Vidart, Labra, and Canalejas to find a compromise.

On 8 March Figueras declared in the *Cortes* that the Government intended to accept an amendment by one of the committee, Primo de Rivera, proposing that the *Cortes* should be dissolved when outstanding legislation had been passed, that elections should be held in mid-May, and that the new *Cortes* should meet on 1 June. In the interim period between the dissolution of the Assembly and the new *Cortes* a permanent commission, drawn from all parties, should act as an advisory body to the Executive. By deciding to stand by Primo's amendment Figueras risked the Government's defeat by the Radical majority. The amendment was in fact carried by an overwhelming vote of 187–10, but only after Martos had tried to replace the Government by a homogeneous Radical ministry. The Government survived due to an intrigue by Rivero, anxious for revenge, which swung the Radicals against Martos and to the influence of the small group of conciliatory Radicals who joined Rivero in opposing Martos's bid for power. But internal factors were unimportant compared with the intimidating mob outside the *Cortes* armed with *trabucos* and harangued by club leaders, which was once again the decisive factor in unnerving the Radicals. Just how foolhardy Martos had been was shown by the violent provincial reaction to the rumour of a possible government defeat. Reports from the Andalusian cities indicated how the Federals were prepared to rise should the Government be defeated.[1] However, the most serious threat came from Barcelona, where the declaration of a Catalan State on 8 March by the newly formed Intransigent group, *El Estado catalán*, led by Lostau and supported by Internationalists, was only revoked after Almirall and Pi had independently thrown the weight of their prestige behind the Moderates in the *Diputación* in telegraphic conversations from Madrid on 10 March, and after Figueras had made a hurried personal visit to the Catalan capital on the 12th.[2]

During the early months of the Republic it looked as if

---

[1] F.O. 72/1338, nos. 166, 180, 186, 196 of 6, 10, 11, 12 Mar. 1873, Layard to Granville, quoting reports from consuls at Seville, Cádiz, Málaga, and Barcelona.

[2] Pi y Arsuaga, op. cit. v. 284–7; González Sugrañes, op. cit., pp. 97 et seq. Apps. I, J, K for the telegrams of Rubaudonadeu, a close Catalan friend of Figueras.

Barcelona would force the pace of political change. On two occasions prior to 8 March—on 12 February and again on 21 February after Gaminde's unsuccessful coup—the Barcelona *Diputación* had proclaimed the Catalan State.[1] And yet one of the striking features of the First Republic was the failure of Barcelona extremists to seize power and declare their independence of Madrid as other Federal centres were to do in the cantonalist risings of July. This can be largely explained by Carlist activity in Catalonia, which conditioned the development of Barcelona republicanism in 1873. Although extremists in the Catalan capital might agitate for independence from Madrid, the other three Catalan provinces, directly threatened by the Carlists, wanted no weakening of the ties with the central government. The persistent refusal of their representatives to be brow-beaten in the *Generalidad* was a major set-back for those demanding Catalan independence. Furthermore, Barcelona republicanism was firmly based on the lower middle class, who with the reformist textile workers constituted the backbone of the militia where even the Internationalist committees formed in each battalion failed to undermine its loyalty to the Moderates in the *Diputación* during the crises of 21 February, 8 March, 19 June, and 14 July. Also the dominant role played by Catalans in republican politics was a guarantee that Catalan interests would not be overlooked. Figueras's influence in Barcelona rather than Pi's prestige was the more important factor, as the former, unlike Pi, was in close touch with the two wings of Catalan Federal opinion, being a friend of both Almirall, now editing *El Estado catalán* at Madrid, and Rubaudonadeu, who in March was acting as Figueras's private secretary and who was himself an Internationalist sympathizer.

The price paid for averting secession during the March crisis was a high one—a decree by the *Diputación* dissolving the army in Catalonia. This apparent victory for the Intransigents, who had persistently undermined army discipline, left nothing between the Carlists and Barcelona but a mutinous army and the militia. But the collapse of discipline which led to immediate Carlist gains culminating in their capture of Berga at the end of March, only

[1] Carrera Pujal, op. cit. v. 224 et seq.

strengthened the arguments of the Moderates against weakening the links with Madrid.

The Government's victory soothed provincial feeling but Radicals and Intransigents maintained their pressure at Madrid. In the Assembly the Government's weakness was shown by its failure to replace Martos with its own candidate. This was a set-back as the new President, Francisco Salmerón (brother of the Federal), would also be President of the Permanent Commission. On this Commission, reflecting the distribution of parties in the *Cortes*, the Federals only had five members compared with eight Radicals, three Conservatives, and three 'Radicals of conciliation'. Once the Radicals had an assured majority on the Commission they agreed to dissolution and after outstanding legislation had been passed— the abolition of slavery in Puerto Rico and credits voted for the *cuerpos francos*—the Assembly was dissolved on 22 March after fixing the elections for 10–13 May and convoking the new *Cortes* for 1 June.

The Government was now spared the embarrassments of Radical hostility in the Assembly but the Radicals' interpretation of the Commission's function merely transferred the conflict from the Assembly to the Commission.[1] For the next month their clear policy was to establish the Commission as the representative of the Assembly with the Executive responsible to it, but, as the Executive had themselves been elected by the Assembly and as their respective constitutional positions had not been made clear, the Government regarded the Commission simply as a consultative body. Conflict between the two could only be avoided if the Government could instil confidence in its ability to conduct free elections. This, however, was exactly what the Intransigents, distrustful of conciliation and always suspecting the Government might do a deal with the Radicals, were determined to prevent. Hence their continual demand for the replacement of non-republican *Ayuntamientos* by trusted Federals—a necessary prelude to their own victory at the polls. A vigorous public demonstration on 30 March was aimed at adding emphasis to a commission which

[1] Brandt, op. cit., pp. 195–8; *The Times*, 26 Apr. 1873, has a full account of the Commission's meetings.

went to Pi again demanding the republicanization of local government. His refusal to yield to these demands and his mobilization of the Civil Guard to suppress an armed demonstration planned for 6 April was clear proof that he did not intend to be intimidated. It also seemed to give some assurance to the Radicals, who, appointing an electoral committee on the same day, spoke in terms of gaining a hundred seats.[1]

Although the Government might dominate Madrid by concentrating its forces, in the provinces where the elections would be fought its authority barely existed. Reports revealed that government there, so far as it was exercised, was in the hands of Federal-dominated *Ayuntamientos* or provincial Federal committees. Málaga was 'virtually independent' and its *Ayuntamiento* had levied a tax on retailers and merchants to offset the loss in revenue from the abolition of *consumos*. At Cádiz, Salvochea, now the mayor, refused to obey the Government's order to stop demolishing convents.[2] In Catalonia government troops were forced to evacuate Berga at the end of March. After this set-back, and faced by the mutinous spirit of the Army, Contreras recognized his incompetence and resigned. The Intransigents petitioned the Barcelona *Diputación* for his reappointment but he found a more congenial atmosphere for his talent for intrigue at Madrid.[3] Here his angling for the Ministry of War opened a more vocal phase of Intransigent activity as they now clamoured for the overthrow of the Permanent Commission.

The continuing inability of the Government to control the Intransigents spurred Radicals and Conservatives in the Commission to hostile criticism. On four occasions—27 March, 10, 17, and 23 April—the Commission met to review the Government's policy. In each of the last three meetings its failure to deal with disorder was strongly criticized. On the 17th, when Pi represented the Government, Rivero suggested that the state of the country

---

[1] F.O. 72/1333, no. 278, 7 Apr. 1873, Layard to Granville. Bribery and grants of office to the two leaders broke up the plans for the demonstration.

[2] F.O. 72/1338, nos. 268, 289 of 2, 14 Apr., Layard to Granville, enclosures from Cádiz and Málaga consuls.

[3] *Gaceta*, 31 Mar., 6 Apr. 1873. Carrera Pujal, op. cit. v. 229, for the Intransigent petition.

demanded the Assembly's recall and it was agreed that all ministers should attend on the 20th to justify their policy. In the absence of Figueras, whose wife had just died, Pi assumed the Presidency of the Executive Power and used the three days' grace to prepare for the struggle which the meeting would inevitably provoke.

The Radicals in the Commission had the support of Castelar in drawing up demands that the elections should be free, that social order must be guaranteed, and a Unitarian Republic proclaimed, but his influence was not strong enough to persuade the rest of the Government to accept them. Thus on the 23rd, when all the Government (except Pi, who remained at the Ministry of the Interior) were present at the Commission's meeting, deadlock was soon reached when Rivero declared that all understandings between Radicals and Federals had broken down and that, as the Government had lost the confidence of the conservative classes, elections would be a farce. The Radicals, anticipating the Government's obduracy, had planned for their militia under the orders of the Radical mayor of Madrid to stage an armed coup on the signal that the Government had refused the Commission's demands. The news that the Bull Ring had been occupied by the Radicals' militia brought the last meeting to a stormy close with the Radical members barely escaping the anger of the mob outside.

Although in retrospect the Radical coup can be seen as a last desperate attempt to recapture their lost power, the prospects of success must have seemed considerable at the time—the Alphonsist observer Grijalba, for example, failed to understand why the garrison did not support the coup.[1] The majority of the militia battalions, the Captain-General of Madrid, and the Minister of War were Radical sympathizers and a number of ex-Unionist generals had been won over by Serrano to the idea of a Unitarian Republic. But unfortunately for the Radicals they failed to achieve the element of surprise. Already on the 19th Pi had taken the precaution of transferring the control of the Civil Guard from the military to the civil authorities. Suspicions that an armed coup was being planned had been aroused sufficiently for a group of Intransigents to meet independently of the Government to plan counter-

[1] Letter of Grijalba to Isabella, 25 Apr. 1873, *El Sol*.

measures. The clubs declared themselves in permanent session and Estévanez, the Civil Governor, mobilized the republican militia.[1]

The fact that the Radicals allowed themselves to be taken off their guard by the prompt action of Pi and Estévanez may be explained by their two miscalculations of overestimating Castelar's influence in the Government and Serrano's influence among the officers of the Madrid garrison. Once Castelar had proved a broken reed the Radicals were left with Serrano and the possibility of an armed coup. But even apart from mutual distrust and the Radicals' reluctance to attribute the success of any coup to Serrano, they greatly overrated his influence. Acosta and Pavía found that the garrison had been assiduously worked by officers with Intransigent sympathies—Contreras, Pierrard, Carmona, Ferrer, and Asín —while the artillery detachments under Hidalgo's command and officered by ex-sergeants remained loyal to the régime which guaranteed their position and offered quick promotion. But it never came to the point of fighting, as the Government showed the greater energy in sealing off the Bull Ring with loyal troops and the republican militia, forcing the Radicals to capitulate with hardly any bloodshed. Not trusting the Government's ability to guarantee their safety, the majority of the Radicals and Conservatives fled into voluntary exile. Serrano took refuge in the British Embassy and was smuggled out of the country, disguised with false side-whiskers, by Layard himself.[2]

After the failure of 23 April the first phase of the Republic was over. The uneasy co-operation of Radicals and Federals had broken down. It was now the 'republic for the republicans', and the Federal leaders were left face to face with their own extremists, who, until the end of 1873, constituted the main opposition. Pi's success was again due to the Madrid Intransigents, although the victory did not mean that the administration was prepared to make concessions to them. Both friends and enemies now regarded the Government as a revolutionary dictatorship and the Intransigents expected it to match its revolutionary reputation

---

[1] *Gaceta*, 19 Apr. 1873; Vera, op. cit. ii. 491–506. See especially Estévanez, op. cit., pp. 423–5; Rispa y Perpiña, op. cit., pp. 208–22; Pi y Arsuaga, op. cit. v. 287–91.

[2] Serrano's account and his strong criticism of the Radicals is recounted by Layard in F.O. 72/1338, no. 305, 25 Apr. 1873.

with revolutionary action.[1] The press became more insistent that
the Federal Republic should be proclaimed immediately by decree
and Intransigent leaders together with militia battalion commanders petitioned Pi in person to replace all *Ayuntamientos* and to
push the federal revolution through to its logical conclusion before
the *Cortes* met.[2] For a moment Pi regained the popularity he had
lost by his leadership of the Directory, but this soon vanished in
the aftermath of 23 April. The behaviour of the Radical mayor of
Madrid in mobilizing their militia was an obvious argument for
replacing *Ayuntamientos* and *Diputaciones* with trusted Federals.
Pi did so by decree in the case of Madrid but refused to allow the
precedent to be followed elsewhere.[3] It was difficult to avoid the
inference that there was one law for Madrid and another for the
provinces.

The next phase of the Republic, until the meeting of the *Cortes*
on 1 June, was therefore one of frustrated revolutionary hopes as
provincial Federals taking their cue from Madrid tried to replace
non-republican *Ayuntamientos*. At Barcelona, which again set the
pace, it was only after a long telegraph conversation that the
Federals recognized Pi's authority and their reluctance to break
with Madrid can perhaps again be explained in terms of the dependence of Catalonia on the capital for help against mounting
Carlist activity.[4] Elsewhere, too, the action at Madrid was taken as
the cue for revolutionary measures. Salvochea at Cádiz followed
the precedent of Málaga in levying taxes on retailers to recoup
losses from the abolition of the *consumos*. This discrimination
against the shopkeepers alienated potential Federal support. In
Málaga there were demands for the resignation of Radical sympathizers still left in the *Ayuntamiento*.[5] Although these had the
support of the majority of the Federal militia, who were Moderates, they still thought it advisable to resign.

[1] Pi y Arsuaga, op. cit. v. 291.
[2] *La Igualdad*, 27 Apr. 1873; Rispa, op. cit., p. 22. Pi replied he that was morally
obliged to wait for the *Cortes*.   [3] *Gaceta*, 25 Apr. 1873.
[4] González Sugrañes, op. cit., pp. 240–1, App. J, telegrams between Pi and the militia
commanders. Pi described their request to depose the *Ayuntamiento* elected under Amadeo
as 'puerile impatience'.
[5] F.O. 72/1339, nos. 310, 312, 28 Apr. 1873, Layard to Granville, enclosures from
Cádiz and Málaga consuls.

When it was clear that Pi would neither be bludgeoned into a premature declaration of a Federal Republic nor would agree to administrative changes, the Intransigents switched their attack by trying to infiltrate into as many official posts as possible so as to influence the elections. An attempt was made to buy off Contreras as Estévanez had already been bought off, with the offer of the War Ministry, but his price was too high—he wanted three of his supporters given posts as well. The problem of the vacancy at the War Ministry after the Radical Acosta's resignation was solved by giving it to Nouvilas, but he only accepted on condition that he retained command of the Army of the North. In the forty-eight hours between his appointment and his arrival in Madrid, General Pierrard, brother of the Federal 'martyr' and Under-Secretary at the Ministry, made a clean sweep of all personnel there and promoted 145 officers who were Intransigent sympathizers.[1]

Meanwhile Pi and Salmerón were preparing for the elections on 10 May in a very untypical manner by sending circulars to all civil governors calling for complete freedom, refusing to nominate any official candidates, and ordering the judges to ensure that there should be no irregularities.[2] The circular to the electors expresses all the high hopes of republican idealism in its condemnation of electioneering abuses:

The electoral régime must be purified and the best way of purifying it is for public employees to stop considering their job as a way of gaining votes and the Civil Governors above all to stop considering their government as a ministerial agency. These elections must finish for ever the official candidate, the administrative pressure, the conversion of public employees into agents of power, the menace of armed mobs, the obstacles in the elctoral assemblies, the arbitrary distribution of voting slips, the falsifications and the miraculous resurrections of eligible voters in the voting lists.

Such a circular caused surprise, but the Radicals were sceptical after the dissolution of the Permanent Commission and declared

---

[1] F.O. 72/1339, nos. 318, 388 of 28, 31 May 1873, Layard to Granville.
[2] *Gaceta*, 3, 6 May 1873.

their *retraimiento* in a manifesto on 6 May. The certainty of a Radical *retraimiento* led the Government to approach the Conservatives with an offer of sixty seats as a bribe to participate in the new *Cortes*.[1] But negotiations begun with Rios Rosas and Ulloa had to be broken off because of protests from the rest of the party. It was nevertheless indicative of the lengths to which the Federals were prepared to go in order to ensure an opposition, but both Radicals and Conservatives knew their Spanish politics well enough to realize that the best tactics was to abandon the *Cortes* and leave the Federals to tear themselves apart through the absence of any strong opposition.

The much-boosted elections began on 10 May, but both in Madrid and the provinces they were characterized by apathy and lack of interest.[2] Much of this may be explained by the *retraimiento* of opposition parties, but even so, the lack of enthusiasm and the small number of votes underlined Federal weakness. Under the new electoral law, 97,307 had the vote in Madrid but only 21,088 figure in official returns and of these it was estimated that 8,000 were dependants in one form or another of the Government. The most popular candidate in the capital was the erstwhile Intransigent leader García López with 5,031 votes, whereas Figueras standing for *Centro*, the populous of the electoral districts, only polled 2,125 and was sixth in popularity in Madrid: even the comparatively unknown grocer Santiso, from the Plaza Anton Marín, polled more votes. At Barcelona the situation was similar. Out of 63,000 electors, only 17,500 voted. The highest recorded vote was at Cartagena where a nonentity, Lapizburu, polled 9,622 votes. In the Basque Provinces the elections were a farce. In six of the Northern Provinces conditions were so unsettled that no proper elections could take place, but deputies were nevertheless returned,

[1] *El Imparcial*, 9 May; *La Igualdad*, 10 May 1873.
[2] This paragraph is based on the analysis in F.O. 72/1339, nos. 358, 366 of 9, 16 May 1873, Layard to Granville; *La Igualdad*, 12, 13, 14, 28 May; *La Época*, 14 May 1873; Mañé y Flaquer, op. cit. ii. 88–89. Some idea of the large poll in Andalucía can be gained from a comparison between ten deputies in Málaga province who polled 83,636 votes and eighteen deputies in Catalonia who only polled 38,582 (about 17,000 of which were in Barcelona): from *La Época*, 14 May 1873. The official returns were Federals 348, Unitarians 1, Radicals 22, Conservatives 4, Alphonsists 2. Sixteen Puerto Rican deputies still had to be elected.

one with only nine votes being cast for him. When the *Cortes* met it was estimated that as many as forty deputies had been returned with less than a thousand votes each. Twenty-six out of the forty-nine civil governors were returned; should they choose to take their seats the Government would be faced with a serious problem in finding suitable men to replace them. Already it had been forced to rely almost entirely on men with no practical experience of public affairs such as the new Civil Governor at Pampluna whom Layard met—'a mere boy, a drawing master who had been earning forty pounds a year'. Opposition papers complained of intimidation and corruption, but as only a few opposition candidates were standing in a private capacity this was not really an issue. Out of a total electorate of nearly five millions, 1,326,810 people voted—or just over 25 per cent. of the electorate—which, although low, quadrupled the previous number of votes gained by the Federals—a rise which may be explained by the reduction of the voting age to twenty-one.

The overwhelming majority of those elected were Federals, although no one knew until the *Cortes* met exactly how many seats had been won by Intransigent sympathizers. But the general feeling was that they had suffered a severe defeat. They did not fight the election as a separate party, though there were examples at Barcelona of conflict between them and the electoral committees which had nominated official party candidates.[1] Even complete Federal victory did not mean that the threat of extremism was lessened; in fact the rest of May saw a sharpening of tension as the Intransigents began to realize their numbers were smaller than they had anticipated. The most violent attacks on the Government came from *La Justicia federal*, directed by Roque Barcia, who, failing to be appointed ambassador to Switzerland on Robert's death in April, ridiculed the notion that any Madrid *Cortes* would ever establish a genuine Federal Republic.[2] As Intransigent leaders like Estévanez, García López, and Córdoba y López were bought off with offices, Barcia and Contreras assumed greater prominence, although the one was unbalanced and the other incompetent.

[1] González Sugrañes, op. cit., pp. 248–52. Apps. LL,M,N.O.
[2] *La Igualdad*, 22, 25 May 1873.

But Barcia's verbal violence was a minor worry to the Government which, in spite of the election results, had no cause for optimism. Foreign encouragement still only came from the two-edged support of General Sickles and from the fringes of a defunct European republicanism. Antero de Quental's support from Portugal was conditional on the republic turning socialist. Felix Pyat sent a fulsome letter, utopian and apocalyptic in tone, and Charles Bradlaugh arrived with good wishes from English Republicans.[1] But even this caused dissension, as he disgusted the Intransigents by his moderation, embarrassed Castelar by his extremism, and terrified the Portuguese ambassador by going on to Lisbon to meet Portuguese Republicans. Castelar's care not to associate himself too closely with Bradlaugh's visit by stressing the purely national character of Spanish republicanism did not convince the Portuguese ambassador, who confided in Layard that the republican Marqués de Magalhães was in Madrid negotiating a loan through Pi with the Bank of Spain to finance another rising in Portugal.[2]

However, by far the most depressing news came from France where, on 24 May, Thiers was replaced in the Presidency by MacMahon. Although Thiers had been extremely distrustful of federalism he had become reconciled to the Spanish Republic, genuinely wanting good relations and hoping to see a conservative republic eventually consolidated under Castelar or even Serrano.[3] Thiers's fall was therefore an ominous sign. 'Carlists, Alphonsists and Radicals', noted *The Times* correspondent,[4] 'all agree that the victory of the Versailles Right has given the Federal Republic its death blow.' Although his prediction that the triumph of the conservatives in France would have a sobering effect on the new *Cortes*, overestimated its political intelligence, Thiers's fall confirmed Castelar in his disillusion about the chances of federalism succeeding. At the end of May he was seriously thinking of

---

[1] Ibid., 18, 21, 25, 26 May 1873; H. B. Bonner, *Charles Bradlaugh, His Life and Works*, London, 1894, i. 352–71; B. Carreiro, *Antero de Quental*, Lisbon, 1948, i. 448–9.
[2] F.O. 72/1339, nos. 368, 369, 22 May 1873, Layard to Granville.
[3] *Documents diplomatiques français*, no. 193, 26 Mar. 1873, Thiers to Bouillé.
[4] *The Times*, 2 June 1873.

retiring from politics and was sounding Maffei, the Italian ambassador, to see if he would be acceptable as Spanish minister in Rome.[1]

Public confidence after the election was sapped by the Right-wing press assiduously exaggerating every case of disorder and attacks on landed property, reported mostly from Andalusia and Extremadura. Public funds fell to the lowest recorded since 1868 and, most serious of all, there was a rapid deterioration in the Carlist situation, as their activity flared up in Catalonia and in the Basque Provinces, while their agents worked on army discontent in the capital. On 5 May Dorregaray won a victory at Eraul compelling Nouvilas to return to the front. Santa Cruz, the wild guerrilla priest, was terrorizing Vizcaya and in Catalonia the Carlists were again on the offensive. On the 13th one of their bands entered Mataro only twenty miles from Barcelona. For the first time the Carlist war threatened serious industrial dislocation. Because of interrupted communications with the interior, goods were beginning to pile up in the mills. Some had been forced to go over to short time and a close down was threatened for others. This was particularly serious as until now the textile workers had remained comparatively untouched by Internationalist propaganda. The dangers of threatened unemployment and the exploitation of discontent by their agents, the immediacy of the Carlist threat, and the pending release of conscripts at the end of May led Velarde to proclaim the *somaten* on 18 May calling to arms all able-bodied Catalans. This Catalan version of the nation in arms failed to produce any worth-while results because of the clause allowing exemption for a graded monetary payment which enabled Intransigents and Internationalists to whip up feeling against a measure said to favour the rich and which could easily siphon off their own supporters.[2] The failure of the *somaten* served once again to confirm moderate Federals in Barcelona in their reluctance to break with Madrid. In future, their attitude to the Government would

---

[1] F.O. 72/1339, no. 371, 22 May 1873, Layard to Granville.

[2] González Sugrañes, op. cit., p. 283, App. A, p. 286, App. D, pp. 288–9, Apps. E, F. The information on the International is in F.O. 72/1338, 28 Mar., 21 Apr., F.O. 72/1339, nos. 306, 377, 380 of 26 Apr., 24, 27 May 1873, enclosures from Barcelona consul which emphasize the lack of support for the International.

be determined by its ability to provide reliable troops and trust-worthy generals to take the field against the Carlists.

In the few days before 1 June the Intransigents made no secret of their intention not to abide by parliamentary decisions should they fail to dominate the new *Cortes*. In a meeting on 29 May at the *Centro Federal* lists of proposed legislation were drawn up to be submitted for immediate ratification when the new *Cortes* met, after which it would then be able to adjourn.[1] The enthusiastic speakers on this occasion had no idea that any difficulties faced the new *Cortes;* for them the *Cortes* was merely a gathering to give legal sanction to decisions already made in the really democratic assemblies—the radical clubs of the capital.

The Government showed its determination to resist any attempt by the extremists to exploit the opening of the new *Cortes* to their own advantage by moving troops into the capital. Its position there was to be strengthened by seriously depleting garrisons in the south—as at Seville where all reliable troops were sent to Madrid.[2] At the same time nothing shows better the Government's political bankruptcy as when yet another régime invoked the magic name of Espartero. When Salmerón was sent to investigate reports that Nouvilas could no longer be trusted, he went by way of Logroño to visit the old caudillo and to sound him about becoming the first President of the Federal Republic or at least to give the new régime his blessing. But it needed more powerful persuasion than the Federals could muster to win over the Cincinnatus of Spanish politics. Ironically, Salmerón's brother had made a similar pilgrimage in the company of Contreras in 1869 canvassing the charms of a democratic monarchy and they, too, had come away empty-handed.

[1] *La Igualdad*, 30, 31 May 1873.
[2] F.O. 72/1339, no. 364, 21 May 1873, Layard to Granville, enclosure from Seville consul reporting a conversation with the Civil Governor.

9

Pi in Power, June–July 1873

THERE was little excitement in Madrid on 1 June, which had been declared a public holiday to mark the official opening of the *Cortes* of the Republic. The occasion was celebrated by a military parade at which the enthusiasm of the volunteers was in marked contrast to the apathy of the regulars. The mood of the Federal press was one of optimism tinged with relief. It was felt that with a genuine republican assembly, unhampered by impostors, nothing could retard the establishment of the Federal Republic under a duly voted Constitution. This optimism was reflected in Figueras's inaugural address in the *Cortes* on the same day—an optimism justified neither by the events of the previous week nor by developments after 1 June. His claim that military discipline had been restored was in complete defiance of the facts and was refuted almost immediately by the mutiny at Igualada and the shooting of the colonel of an infantry regiment. Nor could Federals find any consolation in the volunteers who, aping the conscripts, revolted in their barracks at Vicalvaro, outside Madrid, on the 6th. Figueras's optimism over finance was no more justifiable. Now, he claimed, the Government could borrow at 12 per cent. compared with the 25 per cent. under the monarchy, but the failure of Tutau's finance scheme on the 8th, the financial panic caused by the rumour of an issue of paper money, and the deliberate postponement of budgetary proposals until the new Constitution had been voted again showed a baseless optimism. But most noticeable in this address was the glossing over of the Federals' differences.

At the end of May various Federal factions were beginning to organize themselves into groups. Three of these may be distinguished—the Right, Left, and Centre. The Right were moderates who shared the disillusion of Castelar, comprised the bulk of the old Benevolents, and looked towards him or even to Salmerón for leadership. Federals by habit rather than conviction, they were in favour of strong government and federalism only if this did not imply social revolution. On the Left were the Intransigents under Contreras and Barcia, who had been violently attacking the official Federal leadership by exploiting the unpopularity of lawyers.[1] In between these two extremes there was a fluctuating Centre which included those Intransigents like Estévanez, García López, who had been bought off by office, and others like Orense, Benot, Cala, and Díaz Quintero, who, although largely in sympathy with the Intransigents, were not men of action but the self-styled intellectuals of the movement.[2] It was to this group that Pi looked for his main support, but not representing any particular interest beyond adherence to dogmatic federalism, they had no power and little popular following. It was they alone who could provide a basis for a policy of conciliation, although there was the constant danger that any hardening of opinion on the Right would drive them to support the Intransigents.

The balance of forces in the new *Cortes* was well represented in the election of its officers. Orense senior (his son Antonio, a Moderate, was also a deputy) was elected President of the *Cortes*. The large number of votes cast for him was out of deference to his age and reputation as the 'grand old man' of federalism, but seventy years' deafness and total inability to keep order forced him to resign on the 9th, when Salmerón was elected in his place. Of the four Vice-Presidents, three were Moderates—Palanca, Cervera, and Pedregal—and one, Díaz Quintero, represented the Centre. Apprehension about the actual size of the Intransigents was laid to rest at the first division when a motion by them was defeated by 85–36 votes.[3] This early realization of their weakness drove them into vocal and riotous opposition in the second week of June, when the real business of the *Cortes* began.

The disabilities under which the new *Cortes* was to labour were evident during the first fortnight of its existence. The majority of

---

[1] *La Justicia federal,* 21 May 1873.
[2] *La Igualdad,* 30, 31 May 1873, manifesto of 'El Centro de la Asamblea'. Cf. *The Times,* 14 June 1873, 'Parties in the Cortes'.
[3] *Diario,* 1 June 1873.

the deputies had had no previous parliamentary experience: many had been club orators, but few made any attempt to adapt their style of debating to new conditions. The majority, too, were obscure provincials whose idea of Madrid had probably been gleaned from Federal propaganda. What *La Igualdad* regarded as the greatest strength of the new *Cortes*, the 'provincial spirit', was in fact its greatest weakness.[1] The deputies were mostly professional men; lawyers, doctors, and journalists were well represented, with a sprinkling of soldiers, schoolmasters, unfrocked priests, and business men. The staid social tone was set by the wearing of frock coats and even some uniforms—no worker's clothes were to be seen and attempts to use the address *ciudadano* did not find wide support.[2] The average age was younger than in previous *Cortes* although old age in itself, as shown by Orense was no guarantee of political maturity. Rarely more than half the 406 deputies were ever present at debates—often there were insufficient to provide a quorum for legislation, which led to a proposal that non-attendance by deputies should be penalized as treason. Nothing like all the deputies even presented their *actas* and quite a few who came to Madrid to do so must have then returned to their homes. There may have been material reasons for this. Most deputies were not wealthy men—Federals boasted they were 'men of the people' and the need to earn a living, combined with the cost of travel and high prices in the capital, must have raised problems for those, like Monturiol, whose fare even had been subscribed for by his constituents. But payment of deputies did not figure in any official programme, although in April the Catalans had petitioned for it.[3] The weather, too, was extremely hot and after the factious wrangling of the early days, many may have felt that it was not worth their while staying on. There was no opposition to make party discipline a necessity, and as the lines separating the various groupings were not clear-cut, voting was mostly a matter of personal whim. In previous *Cortes*, lobbying had always played a cardinal role in determining voting alignments, but as few deputies

---

[1] *La Igualdad*, 5 June 1873, 'El espíritu provincial'.
[2] *The Times*, 10 June 1873; *Diario*, 18 June 1873, Forasté's speech.
[3] González Sugrañes, op. cit., p. 242, App. K.

represented specific interests it was in the lobbies in this *Cortes*, too, that the real decisions were taken.[1] Attempts were made to form regional groupings but these did not crystallize into actual parties. The Catalan deputies alone tended to vote together and to act as a solid body. Their interest in finishing the Carlist war provided them with a binding link, lacked by the Andalusians, the other main regional group (with the possible exception of their desire for free trade).

The composition of the *Cortes* was patently unequal to the tasks facing it. These were summed up by *La Igualdad* under three heads: to finish the war, to solve the financial problem, and to institute social and economic reform.[2] Neither of the first two tasks differed in principle from those which had faced earlier *Cortes*. It was in the field of social reform that the Federals showed most originality, but even here there was nothing like agreement on the main lines of policy. The publication of a social programme in *La Igualdad* on the eve of the *Cortes* meeting reflected Pi's view that social reform was a vital prerequisite for stability by widening the basis of their support.[3] This concern of Pi and his supporters with the social question distinguished them from both the Castelarian Moderates and the Intransigents. The Moderates paid lip service to social reforms, but their main consideration was to ensure social order. The Intransigents, on the other hand, had put forward an extreme social policy at the end of 1872 in a bid for popular support, but these proposals were now dropped. In their published programmes little emphasis was laid on social reforms, the main stress being on political and administrative reform involving the concentration of political power in the hands of trusted revolutionaries. A grant of office had drawn off Córdoba y López, the Intransigents' 'social theorist', leaving the soured and violently anti-socialist Roque Barcia as the main Intransigent spokesman. The aim of his programme was simply to prevent any further concentration of power in the hands of the central Government by letting provinces elect their own civil governors and their own legislatures, which would then contribute men and money for the

[1] *The Times*, 11, 12 July 1873.   [2] *La Igualdad*, 2 June 1873.
[3] Ibid., 27 May, 1 June 1873, 'Ni individualismo puro ni colectivismo puro'.

Carlist war as each saw fit.[1] There was no mention of social or
economic reform and the refusal of the International to accept
the profferred hand of the Intransigents shows what little value
they placed on their former expressions of social extremism.

The programme outlined in *La Igualdad* went farther than the
majority of Federals would have wished. Most could agree on
basic reforms to ameliorate labour conditions by reducing working hours to nine hours a day, by guaranteeing a daily minimum
wage of six *reales*, and by prohibiting child labour and safeguarding women in industry. The limitation of the programme of the
Barcelona *sociedades obreras* to these aims confirms the moderate
nature of Federal working-class supporters.[2] The party were
genuinely agreed on the mixed-jury system to arbitrate on labour
troubles, but other reforms implying interference with property
distribution had far less support. The abolition of collateral inheritance, the leaving of only one-fifth to the beneficiary in direct
inheritance, death duties as high as one-fifth of the estate, expropriation without indemnity on grounds of public utility, and
expropriation of landed estates which had been left derelict for a
period of more than four years, brought a distinct socialist menace
which the Castelarian Moderates thought it was the purpose of
federalism to avoid. Pi's early views on the agrarian problem
were now being reflected in this programme. It was evident that
some Federals were at last beginning to take the agrarian situation
seriously. In May a commission had been set up (which included
Fermín Caballero as one of its members) to report on it and even
Orense, who had previously scorned the rural areas introduced
a project for agrarian reform in the *Cortes* in June.[3] *La Igualdad*
promised a revision of the sales of common land and of municipal property, the annulment of 'illegal sales', the establishment
of collective ownership of woods and pastures under the care

[1] *La Justicia federal*, 8 June 1873. Cf. ibid., 20 June, where Barcia's call for the replacement of all consuls by men of 'revolutionary tendencies' reflects both the Intransigents'
empleomanía and his own ambition.
[2] González Sugrañes, op. cit., p. 45, App. H. Carrera Pujal, op. cit., p. 231, cites an
example of a mixed jury in March under the Federal Roca y Gales to regulate wages and
hours of work.
[3] *Gaceta*, 10 May, 22 June 1873. Cf. Braulio Mañueco, *La Revolución en la propiedad por
los cotos redondos*, Madrid, 1873.

of the *Ayuntamiento*, and, where evidence of legal sale could not be proved, expropriation in the interests of society without indemnification. All this presaged a thorough overhaul of existing property rights based on earlier disentailing laws. The outlining of this socialistic programme in *La Igualdad* and the announcement by Cala and Díaz Quintero, two of the leaders of the Centre, that they were 'socialists' did not endear Pi, with whom the programme was most closely associated, to either the Moderates or Intransigents. This was made clear in the second week of June when the crisis over the first ministry exposed his lack of a following.

On the 7th, after a quiet week when *actas* were presented and officials appointed, the new *Cortes* was constituted. Its first act was to have a nominal vote on the form of government in which only two votes were cast against the Federal Republic.[1] Figueras then resigned his powers into the hands of the *Cortes*, which now had to appoint a new ministry. Two courses were open to it: either to grant a deputy the power to select his own ministers or, in the tradition of direct democracy, for the *Cortes* to elect each minister itself. In either case, the *Cortes* arrogated the right to determine the composition of the ministry, as even if a deputy selected his own ministers he then had to have them accepted by the *Cortes*. This issue, involving the claim of the *Cortes* to control each member of the executive, was posed when Cervera suggested that Pi, 'the most convincing, most inflexible and most honest Federal', should be granted powers to form a ministry. It was significant that at this moment Pi enjoyed the confidence of the Right rather than the Left or Centre, for the most bitter opposition to this proposal came from them, led, rather surprisingly, by Benot, who had been closely associated with Pi's policies in the past and who now protested that this would give the executive too much power. Benot argued that if the Executive were not completely dependent on the *Cortes* there could be an opening for a Spanish Napoleon III. Throughout June the Intransigents feared a military dictator even more than the Carlists.

This first attempt to reduce the Executive to a cipher was defeated by 143–79, but the second string to the Intransigent bow,

[1] *Diario*, 7 June 1873. The voting was 219–2. García Ruiz and Rios Rosas voted against.

riotous and vocal opposition, greeted the announcement of Pi's ministry on the evening of the 8th. This exposed the essential factiousness of the new *Cortes* as well as the bitter and irreconcilable antagonism between the republican leaders. Pi had been forced to select his new ministry from hardly known figures, as neither Figueras, Castelar, nor Salmerón were willing to serve under him. But Pi persisted in drawing his ministers from all factions except the Intransigents (Estévanez no longer enjoyed their confidence) and although heavily rejected on the Right it reflected the balance of forces in the *Cortes*.[1] The uproar which greeted the announcement of the comparatively unknown names and the placards in the streets asking 'who is Pedregal?' not only represented the cry of the discontented and soured politician who had failed to get office, but was also a comment on the failure of the Federal leaders to sink their differences. It showed, too, how little was the personal support on which Pi could rely. Out of sympathy with the Intransigents and the Moderates of the Right, he represented no one and no interest except his own conception of federalism.

A policy of conciliation which Pi enunciated on 8 June might have kept the various factions working together in opposition during the monarchy but was no longer practical politics once the Federals were in sole power. By June he could no longer rally republican opinion with the magic of his name. The Intransigents despised him for his lack of revolutionary zeal after 23 April and his refusal to be stampeded into a premature declaration of the Federal Republic made him the butt for the attacks of Roque Barcia. The Moderates feared him for his advanced social views and for his desire to widen the appeal of republicanism. Over all, there was his aloofness, his enigmatic silences, his strength of character; he lacked the panache of Castelar and all the rhetorical qualities which were the stock-in-trade of his contemporaries; his dogmatism and his fanatical belief in a federal revolution directed by himself gave to his politics a lack of flexibility and a *naïveté* which made him blind to the main motivating forces behind the Federal movement. His

[1] Pedregal, Palanca, Carvajal, Cervera were moderate and well-tried Federals; Oreiro had Radical sympathies. Sorní, Pi, and Estévanez were from the Centre.

conception of politics ruled out any attempt to rally sectional interests. Although the fact that 32 out of 49 civil governors were Catalans[1] led to the accusation that he favoured Catalan interests, he was out of sympathy with Catalan regionalism. He had quarrelled with Almirall, to whom he had become the symbol of the Madrid politician. Only after his fall from power did Pi come to recognize Almirall's importance.[2] It was Figueras rather than Pi who enjoyed a high prestige in Catalonia. By 9 June, when *El Estado catalán* closed down, and after Figueras had fled, Almirall had despaired of Madrid politics and returned disillusioned to Barcelona—'we have not lost faith in our principles but let us now be platonic lovers of federalism'.[3] The Andalusians, for their part, were under Intransigent influence, were uninterested in the Carlist war except when it started to have repercussions in the south, and had lost confidence in Pi. For support Pi had to look to those Federals who had been returned from traditionally non-Federal areas, but it was precisely from these areas that deputies tended not to take up their seats.[4] He therefore tried to continue a policy of conciliation and mediation in a political situation which demanded decisive leadership rather than the attempt to reconcile incompatible viewpoints.

The rejection of Pi's nominees on the 8th forced Figueras and the former Ministry to remain in office, and for two days the crisis continued unresolved. But this, the strongest possible combination, could not stay in office owing to the hostility of the *Cortes* to Tutau's finance proposals and to its own internal disagreements over the financial issue. In a secret session of the *Cortes* on the 9th Figueras, by dramatizing the mutiny which had broken out at Igualada, succeeded in obtaining powers to name his own ministry which had been refused to Pi on the previous day. Nevertheless, he failed to form a ministry; Pi refused to take part in it, piqued, it was thought, by the *Cortes*'s show of confidence in Figueras;

[1] Pugés, op. cit., p. 174, quoting *El Eco de España*.
[2] Carrera Pujal, op. cit., p. 232 n.
[3] *El Estado catalán*, 9 June 1873.
[4] It is difficult to talk of Intransigent voters coming from any particular region. From the fifty most frequently recurring Intransigent voters in June–July, only one came from Catalonia but thirteen from the Andalusian provinces, three from Valencia, and two from Murcia. The others were fairly evenly distributed, with Madrid and its environs providing four.

Castelar refused to form one and Salmerón was unable to do so.
During the 9th and 10th no member of the Government appeared
in the *Cortes* and Pi remained at the Ministry of the Interior and
did not even attend the meetings of the Council of Ministers. By
the afternoon of the 10th the deadlock was complete, with all the
Federal leaders unable or unwilling to form a ministry. The last
attempt to form a 'party of order' failed when Figueras, ill, rebuffed by Pi, and despairing of a solution, left secretly by train
for France on the evening of the 10th. His flight exposed the
bankruptcy of the official leadership.[1]

When Contreras and Pierrard learnt late in the night that
Figueras had fled they tried to stage a coup with the Madrid
garrison. The conditions seemed favourable. Figueras had taken
over the Ministry of War when Nouvilas had been forced to
return to the Carlist front, thus his flight enabled Pierrard, as
an Under-Secretary, to take over. What he did not realize was
that Salmerón and Castelar had already alerted Socias, the Captain-
General of Madrid, who had forewarned the garrison commanders of a possible Intransigent coup. As Socias had exceeded
his authority by giving orders to the Civil Guard, Estévanez, the
Civil Governor, had mobilized the militia against what he believed
to be a coup by Socias. In the confused situation Pierrard and
Contreras found themselves outmanœuvred. Estévanez was no
longer under their influence and Socias had anticipated their movements. The night's experience with Estévanez's prompt action
showed Castelar and Salmerón the danger in pursuing any policy
which had not the support of the Civil Governor. On the morning
of the 11th, therefore, they approached Pi, who had the confidence
of Estévanez, to see if he would form a new ministry.[2] He could
have succeeded this time in naming his own ministry, but the

---

[1] Figueras's full account of the crisis and of the coolness between him and Pi is printed
in Pi y Arsuaga, op. cit. v. 195–203. Figueras had wanted to resign after his wife's death,
but Pi persuaded him not to.

[2] Ibid., pp. 189 et seq.; Bermejo, op. cit. iii. 433–9; M. Morayta, *Las Constituyentes de la
República española*, Paris, 1909, pp. 70–72. Socias's account is in his speech in *Diario*, 17
June 1873. Cf. *The Times*, 18, 20 June, and F.O. 72/1340, 12 June 1873, Layard to Granville,
where Estévanez is reported to have tipped off Contreras and Pierrard that Salmerón and
Castelar were forming a party of order. Estévanez's behaviour before and after the coup
does not tally with this report that he was an accomplice.

refusal of either Salmerón or Castelar to accept office decided him to leave the nomination to the *Cortes*. The election of the new ministry was subject to ardent lobbying by the various factions and Pi was again left at the mercy of an inexperienced factious *Cortes* and of the nonentities they might happen to choose.

On 11 June the new ministry was elected with under half the deputies voting. This ministry, which was to last, like the first ministry of the Republic, for only thirteen days, reflected the division of power in the *Cortes*. Pi remained as Minister of the Interior. Muro and González, two hitherto unknown lawyers, were Ministers of State and Justice; Ladico, an obscure button merchant from Port Mahon, became Minister of Finance; Benot, in sympathy with Pi's social views, was Minister of Public Works; Anrich, a naval officer who later turned Carlist, was Minister of Marine; Sorní, the most closely associated with Pi, was Minister of Overseas, the least important post in the cabinet. Finally the most controversial, Estévanez, who a bare fortnight earlier had expressed a wish to Figueras never to be a minister, became Minister of War. Unpopular with officers because of his own shady military past, he had shown by his behaviour as Civil Governor of Madrid that he could be trusted once his ambition had been satisfied. This appointment was to bring the first crisis, illustrating once again the difficulty of the Federals' relations with the Army. It was a ministry of conciliation, even if Pi had not chosen it himself, but whatever its drawbacks, conciliation after the failure of any of the others to form a party of order seemed, on the morning of the 11th, to be the only possible policy.

On the 13th Pi presented his programme to the *Cortes* in his opening speech.[1] Now, at last, the *Cortes* was presented with a coherent statement of official Federal policy. 'For the first time', commented Layard,[2] 'we have in official shape what may be considered the real federal republican party as distinct from Castelar's milk and water faction and the Intransigents who want "everything for everybody down to the women".' Pi had never indulged in the platitudes of utopian republicanism and this speech was in

[1] Vera, op. cit. ii. 571–80.
[2] B.M. Add. MS. 39123, 14 June 1873, Layard to Granville.

character, a lucid and comprehensive review of the dangers facing the régime and of his intended policy. The first need was to finish the war. It was typical of his approach that he should see the Army problem mainly as a question of justice. To prevent it from becoming an instrument of party politics it must be justly treated. He promised to review the *hojas de servicio* and to ensure that promotion should be for military efficiency and not political services. To encourage efficiency in the field *tribunales de honor* should be set up to reward those who had served loyally for a year in face of the enemy. He promised that the 18,000 men due for release would be placed on the reserve which the Ministry was preparing.

From military reforms he passed to the state of finance; the cost of the war budget was continually rising, mainly because of the increases in pay which the Republic had been forced to grant. The main difficulty in finance was that a budget for 1873–4 could not be presented until the Constitution had been accepted as only then could the fiscal attributes of the federal states be fixed. In the meantime, all the Government could do was to try and reduce the floating debt and cut expenditure. He did not offer tax concessions and pointed out that 'necessity which is almost always superior to laws' would mean the adoption of unpopular measures. He satisfied the anticlericals by promising the separation of Church and State and the subjection of the Church to the laws of ordinary associations. Free and obligatory education was promised, but neither here nor elsewhere was the problem faced of how this was going to be achieved. Reforms were to apply to overseas territories; slavery in Cuba was to be abolished.

The controversial social question was left to the end, but the reforms outlined were mild compared to the programme of *La Igualdad*. Pi emphasized that all political revolutions entailed an economic revolution and stressed the role of the Federals in bringing the working class into political life, assuming that the workers did not want to overthrow the existing social structure but only wished to enjoy the fruits of owning property. Land reform would be introduced to widen the distribution of property.[1] He

---

[1] The International's reaction was to advise its members on 15 June to 'keep apart from farcical bourgeois politics' (Guillaume, op. cit. iii. 86).

again traced most of Spain's political troubles to the uncontrolled
disentailing policies of previous liberal legislation and announced
that in future any alienation of state property would be by gradual
sale so that the landless labourers could acquire land by paying
over a series of years. He deplored the wastefulness of the growing
number of strikes, and promised to introduce mixed juries to
arbitrate on labour disputes, but the limit of the State's intervention must be to 'sanction the work of social spontaneity'. Child
labour, however, must be controlled and an attempt made to
educate the workers. Finally, Pi ended by calling for the speedy
discussion and passing of a Constitution without which all reforms
would be useless.[1]

There was little in this speech to elicit enthusiastic response
from either the moderates or extremists. His anticlericalism and
promise of colonial reforms were applauded, but otherwise there
was little enthusiasm. Salmerón's speech, which followed on his
election to the presidency of the *Cortes*, was in complete contrast
and was very unfavourably received by the Left and Centre.
Where Pi had stressed class conflict and the necessity to widen the
basis of the Republic's support, Salmerón stressed that the Republic
must not be monopolized by Republicans; that if it was to survive
the conservative classes must be reassured. The attitude of *El
Imparcial*, the paper still with the widest circulation, was indicative
of a reaction against Pi which the majority in the *Cortes* were
beginning to share as well.[2] In spite of the mildness of Pi's references
to the wider distribution of property there were no illusions that
this would be a prelude to further socialistic measures. On the
14th Pi proposed that all *Ayuntamientos* should be renewed,
admitting that much of the disorder of the past month had been
due to the continuation of monarchists in local government. If he
thought that this would mollify Intransigent opinion he was mistaken, for they persisted in demanding the nomination of convinced Republicans to lessen the risks of a republican defeat from

[1] In his apologia (Pi y Arsuaga, v. 293) Pi complained how although he wanted a committee appointed on 13 June to draft a Constitution, one was not appointed until 20 June
and even then the draft was not presented for discussion in the *Cortes* until 17 July and not
till 18 August that debates on it began.
[2] *El Imparcial*, 14, 15 June 1873.

free elections. Araus, speaking for them, thought that the Executive should nominate new *Ayuntamientos* to take over office until federation. Pi refused to consider this proposal and the *Cortes* agreed that municipal elections should start on 12 July and provincial elections on 6 September.[1]

The weaknesses of the new Government were soon revealed during the debates in the *Cortes* between 17 and 20 June when it was clear that it was divided over the crucial question of how to solve the financial crisis. An increase in taxation was inadvisable politically, but whereas Catalan deputies called for extraordinary taxation to cover war expenditure, those from Andalusia wanted no more taxation without first getting political and administrative reforms. The success of any new loan was extremely doubtful in view of the régime's inability to inspire confidence. The possibility of an American loan in return for commercial concessions in Cuba, which had been broached at the end of 1872, does not seem to have been re-examined—perhaps for fear of antagonizing the Catalans. The Government was therefore left with the alienation of national assets for which precedent had already been set in the sale of the Rio Tinto mines to an English company in 1872. Ladico's solution was to farm out the State's tobacco rights in the Philippines.[2] This raised a storm of protest, but it was nothing when compared with the implications of Socias's attack on Estévanez for the part he had played during the night of 10–11 June. Pi defended his War Minister, but he could hardly afford to ignore the deeper implications of Army discontent at the appointment of an ex-captain who had deserted in Cuba and at Estévanez's interference with the *hojas de servicio* as part of his Army reforms.[3]

Socias's attack on Estévanez, the unpopularity of Ladico's finance schemes, and the continuing opposition of the Intransigents in the *Cortes* divided the Government so deeply that Pi had to admit on the 21st that it could no longer agree on a common policy. In resolving this ministerial crisis, Pi had to rely on Castelar's support. His proposal that Pi should be given power to solve the

[1] *Diario*, 19 June 1873.
[2] Ibid., 18 June 1873; Estévanez, op. cit., pp. 442–3; Bermejo, op. cit. iii. 444–8. For a review of Ladico's financial schemes see *The Times*, 27 June 1873, 'Spanish Finance'.
[3] Estévanez, op. cit., pp. 450–1.

crisis himself was carried in spite of the inevitable Intransigent opposition. Pi again tried to form a ministry which would represent all views in the *Cortes*—with the exception of the extreme Left. He offered posts to Cala and Díaz Quintero, but both refused, pleading the lame excuse of their own incompetence. Failing to get this support from the Centre, the new Ministry was drawn almost wholly from the moderates of the Right. Maisonnave, Gil Berges, Jose Carvajal, Ministers of State, Justice, and Finance, were Castelarian in sympathy; the two from the Centre, Suñer y Capdevila in the Ministry of Overseas, and Pérez Costales, a doctor from Coruña in the Ministry of Public Works, were the only two sympathetic towards Pi's policy of conciliation. Finally, because of distrust of Contreras and Pierrard and the seriousness of the Carlist situation which required Nouvilas's retention as commander of the Army of the North, Pi chose as Estévanez's successor González Iscar, whose crypto-Alphonsism was unknown to him.[1]

When the ministerial crisis was finally resolved by the announcement of the new Ministry on the 28th, its predominantly Castelarian composition and the fact that it had been ushered in with Castelar's support virtually killed any influence Pi had retained on the Centre and Left. When, two days later, he succeeded in obtaining from the *Cortes* extraordinary powers, his capitulation to the Moderates seemed complete and his verbal assurances to the Left that these powers were to be used against the Carlists and not against them could not disguise the fact that the policy of conciliation had broken down. His decision to ask for extraordinary powers was determined by developments during the previous ten days, when a number of factors had underlined the need to conduct the Carlist war more vigorously. There was the threat of a possible Carlist–Alphonsist *rapprochement* implied in the visit of Isabella to Rome and of increasing Alphonsist penetration in the Army of the North. Then, at the end of June, Serrano's influence seemed to be reviving. His name was being linked with a unitarian republic in some Madrid circles, and at Bayonne Layard, who saw him there, reported that he was in touch with Cabrera and the

[1] Vera, op. cit. ii. 591–2; Pi y Arsuaga, op. cit. v. 223–4.

constitutional Carlists.[1] The need to reach a conclusion in the
Carlist war before a Bourbon reconciliation had taken place, before
Alphonsist intrigues had undermined the Army, and before
Serrano had rallied the exiles at Bayonne was paramount.

Pi was threatened by a manifesto of the Catalan deputies on 28
June, urging a withdrawal to Catalonia and the declaration of an
independent canton unless the Government showed itself capable
of restoring order. The seriousness of the situation in Barcelona
had been demonstrated only too clearly nine days earlier when
the militia had had to break up a Committee of Public Safety set
up by Intransigents and Internationalists in the *Ayuntamiento*.[2]
Further graphic descriptions in the *Cortes* on the 30th of the
deteriorating situation in Navarre and in Catalonia by Zabala
and Antonio Orense emphasized the need for stronger government power. But once again it was a grave miscalculation to
think that extraordinary measures to defeat the Carlists would
be accepted by the Intransigents on the strength of mere verbal
assurances—these were no substitute for those political concessions for which they had been continually clamouring. The
Intransigents paid lip service to the idea of a full-scale Carlist
war, as had been shown in Luis Blanc's proposal of the 20th for
the *Cortes* to adjourn and for deputies to put themselves at the
head of the volunteers, but they were only interested in the war
in so far as it would enable them to squeeze concessions out of the
Government. Whereas the Catalans who were directly involved
called for a strengthening of the Government's powers, the
Intransigents could only put up factious opposition calls for a
Convention or suggest impractical schemes like Blanc's.

A deteriorating situation on the Carlist front was accompanied
by news of further disturbances in Andalucía in the last week of
June. At Carmona, San Fernando, and San Lúcar de Barrameda
the motives behind local riots seem to have been primarily social
and were symptomatic of an increase of Internationalist influence.[3]
But Seville was the main trouble centre, where it was felt that arms

---

[1] B.M. Add. MS. 39123, 24, 29 June 1873, Layard to Granville.

[2] F.O. 72/1340, no. 9, 30 June 1873, Macdonnell to Granville (Layard was on leave
until October); González Sugrañes, op. cit., pp. 314–19.

[3] Guichot, op. cit., p. 441.

were deliberately being withheld from the people. On 23 June, after unsuccessful demands for arms at the *Ayuntamiento*, extremist elements succeeded in obtaining them from the undermanned artillery barracks. A conflict threatened to develop between the armed extremists and the small military garrison, which the extremists wanted to disarm even though, as a gesture of good-will, the troops had been withdrawn outside the city.[1] As a con-ciliatory gesture Pi appointed La Rosa, a Sevillano deputy, as Civil Governor. He arrived on the 29th and was instructed by Pi on the 30th to impress on Sevillano Federals that legal action could only be taken through the *Cortes*. The situation had become menacing, because of the arrival from Málaga of Eduardo Carvajal and some thousand volunteers. Carvajal's purpose may have been to declare an Andalusian canton, but he seems to have been more interested in obtaining arms from Seville which would enable him to establish his own position in Málaga against that of his main rival, Solier. Early on the 30th the Málaga Federals, with the Sevillano extremists, attacked the *Ayuntamiento* and established a revolutionary junta—a 'Committee of Public Safety' under an Internationalist Mignorance. Where the threat from the presence of regular army units had united the Federals, the threat of social extremism divided them, and because the Moderates rallied to La Rosa, he was able to dissolve the junta, to foil the proclamation of the canton, and to compel Carvajal to return to Málaga, which he was only too willing to do after securing the arms and artillery which would enable him to dominate that city.[2]

In Madrid, Pi's proposal on 30 June to suspend the constitutional guarantees in view of the grave Carlist situation brought tension to a climax. The arrival of troops in the capital on the previous day emphasized the determination of the Government not to be over-awed by any Intransigent threats, while the rejection by 176–16 of an amendment, proposed by the Navarrese Intransigent Olave, that the suspension should be limited to the three provinces over-run by the Carlists, was also an indication that the Government

[1] Ibid., pp. 448–56; Bermejo, op. cit. iii. 458–61: F.O. 72/1340, nos. 3 and 9, 27 and 30 June 1873, Macdonnell to Granville, enclosures from Seville consul.
[2] F.O. 72/1340, nos. 33 and 38, 9 and 14 July 1873, enclosures from Málaga consul.

would have the support of the majority should it want to use these powers against the extremists.[1] Confirmation of Intransigent fears that Pi's emphasis on the Carlist menace was merely a mask to do this seemed to be supplied by the decree of Hidalgo, Estévanez's successor as Civil Governor of Madrid, published on the 30th, which declared a curfew in the event of public disorder and empowered government agents to enter private houses in the interests of public security. These measures reassured the Moderates but had a disastrous effect on the Intransigents. After a violent exchange on 1 July calling for the dismissal of Hidalgo, Orense announced the *retraimiento* of the Intransigent deputies.[2] It was the last effective political act of the 'patriarch' of Spanish republicanism; it was also the most effective blow which could have been given to the authority of the Republic. It came as the climax to a long period of Intransigent disillusion with Pi's policies since 23 April, but it seems that Pi himself shared the conviction of *La Igualdad* that this was not the prelude to armed revolt, for he tried to attract them back to the *Cortes*—a vital prerequisite for any discussion on the Constitution, which still remained the main object of his policy. Obsessed with the idea of a directed federal revolution and feeling that the absence of a Constitution was the main obstacle to public order, he continued to see himself as the only guarantee that the Federals' ideal would not be betrayed. But the significance of the *retraimiento* was that it was a vote of no confidence in Pi by those who now regarded themselves as the only genuine Federals and who had no scruples about resorting to physical force if they were unable to get their own way constitutionally in the *Cortes*. To think that he could regain the confidence of the Intransigents without satisfying their craving for office was political shortsightedness, but to believe that a policy of conciliation was still practicable was political suicide when the Centre, on whom he relied for most of his support, began to break up. Since the ministerial crisis of 21 June Pi had gradually been forfeiting the

---

[1] *The Times*, 10 July 1873. An occasional correspondent estimated that only a quarter of the 8,000 militia would support the Intransigents.

[2] *La Igualdad*, 3 July 1873; cf. *The Times*, 10 July 1873, 'The Madrid Government and the Intransigents'. Hidalgo, a friend of Rivero, was an unwise choice as Estévanez's successor.

support of the only section of the *Cortes* on which he could base a genuine policy of conciliation. Díaz Quintero's opposition to Castelar's proposal for Pi to be granted powers to solve the crisis on that occasion was followed by his and Cala's refusal to serve in a new ministry and by considerable support from the Centre for the Intransigent Armentia's proposal of the 27th for the *Cortes* to be turned into a National Convention and for the setting up of a Committee of Public Safety.[1] Among those, too, who signed an Intransigent manifesto of the 5th were many of the Centre, including Quintero and Cala.[2] It is true that two days later the Centre published its own manifesto pledging continued support for Pi,[3] but its tone and enthusiasm soon changed—first under the influence of the convincing attacks on the Government by the monarchists Robledo and Collantes, by García Ruiz, and by Castelar himself (on 8 July in a speech which Collantes described as the 'funeral oration of the Republic'), and secondly by the events of the second week of July which utterly destroyed the whole concept of conciliation.

On the 9th occurred a double disaster—the defeat of Cabrinetty's column by the Carlists at Alpens in Catalonia and the socialist outbreak at Alcoy. In Barcelona the news of Alpens had created an atmosphere of panic and when, on the 12th, the Civil Governor called for the mobilization of able-bodied men to go to the front, the local Internationalist leaders, playing on the workers' fears that they would lose their jobs, declared a general strike. Although the strike had a momentary success, the militia stood firm and the majority of workers refused to respond to the Internationalists' call for immediate social revolution. By the 15th the factories had reopened and on the 18th a *Junta de Salvación y Defensa* representing all the Catalan provinces had been set up to consider means of raising an armed force. Its resignation eight days later underlined that Catalonia had more to gain from co-operation with a strong central government than by any form of opposition.[4] Cabrinetty's defeat and its repercussions in Barcelona were significant because

[1] *Diario*, 27 June 1873—eighty-two supported this proposal.
[2] *La Igualdad*, 5 July 1873—fifty-seven deputies signed.
[3] Ibid., 7 July 1873.
[4] González Sugrañes, op. cit., pp. 363–4, 375 et seq., 384–6, Apps. C and D.

they meant that the Catalans, on whom Pi might have rested a policy of conciliation and used as a counterweight to the Intransigents and the Castelarians, were now forced to criticize his vacillating policy and to demand even stronger government in order to stave off the growing Carlist threat.

The events at Alcoy, however, were of more immediate importance as they enabled moderate and conservative elements to combine in calling for stronger government in the face of social disorder. A strike in the industrial paper-making town of Alcoy on the 7th had been exploited by the local branch of the International and the mayor, Albors, a Federal of long standing, had been the main victim in a number of killings which were immediately highlighted in a series of atrocity stories, in which *La Igualdad* rivalled the Right-wing press in recounting how heads had been carried round the town on pikes, women outraged, and victims soaked in paraffin and burnt.[1] It was particularly indignant that a Federal factory owner 'who treated his workers as companions' should have had his property razed. The whole of the Federal press, including *La Justicia federal*, was loud in its condemnation, but whereas *La Igualdad* and *La Discusión* used it to underline the need for stronger government, the Intransigents were only too willing to use the Government's embarrassment for their own purposes. Pi's reaction was to order Velarde at Valencia to march with all his available forces on Alcoy. At this moment, with the Government's attention diverted, the Intransigents staged their own successful coup at Cartagena.

After 23 April the Madrid Intransigents had gradually become aware that their power, although so effective in intimidating the Radicals, did not influence government decisions. Their energies, therefore, were switched to fomenting provincial resentment at the Government's putting off the declaration of a Federal Republic. The initiative for this seems to have come originally from Nicolas del Balzo, a member of the Intransigent *Junta del Centro*, who, after a visit to Cartagena, reported to Rispa y Perpiñá, the junta's

[1] *La Igualdad*, 13–16 July 1873; Lorenzo, op. cit., pp. 323–5; Bermejo, op. cit. iii. 470–6. The Internationalist leader was Severino Albarracín, a primary school teacher who had shortly before been active in a Federal club in Valencia. The most recent study is R. Coloma, *La Revolución Internacionalista Alcoyana de 1873*, Alicante, 1959.

president, that the fleet there would support any rising to declare an independent canton.[1] Unable to win over Rispa to the idea, del Balzo approached Barcia, who immediately sent Cárceles Sabater, a Madrid medical student, to Cartagena and Andalusia on a fact-finding mission. His enthusiastic report led Barcia to establish a Committee of Public Safety which included Contreras, Pierrard, and six Intransigent deputies. Rispa accepted the vice-presidency of this committee, but only, according to him, with the intention of forestalling the coup by persuading the committee to include members of the Centre group in the *Cortes* whom he thought would be able to restrain Barcia and Contreras. When this ruse failed he went to Pi advising him to buy off Barcia with an ambassadorial post and to take Contreras and Pierrard into custody. Pi, perhaps over-cautiously, refused to act on Rispa's information.

On 10 July *La Justicia federal* had printed a manifesto of the Madrid Committee of Public Safety calling for similar committees to be set up in the provinces. By a fortunate coincidence Alcoy distracted the Government at this critical moment. Plans had been drawn up for a general insurrection by the Committee at Madrid: the deputy Santamaría was to raise Valencia and Colonel Moreno de Cristo was to collaborate with Brigadier Guerrero, in command at Monjuich, in staging a coup at Barcelona; Fantoni, another deputy and a leader in the 1869 rising, was to raise Seville; Salvochea, in Cádiz, was in touch with Contreras; Aniano Gómez was to raise Bejar, which, like Alcoy, had a reputation for social discontent; the deputy Riesco was to raise Salamanca, and Poveda and Arce, also deputies, were to raise Murcia. Finally a Committee of War under Contreras was set up to co-ordinate activity. Pi, forewarned by the events at Seville and suspecting that Málaga might be the focus of a new rising, ordered Ripoll to concentrate all available forces on Córdoba, the key rail centre of Andalusia. This small force thrown together on 9 July numbered 2,000 men and arrived in Córdoba on the 10th. At the same time Pi ordered the Civil Guard into Málaga and the regiment of Iberia, stationed at Murcia, to proceed by sea to Málaga by way of Cartagena.

[1] The only inside account of the genesis of the cantonalist rising is Rispa y Perpiñá, op. cit., pp. 239–46. Unfortunately he gives no dates.

Whatever date had been fixed by the Madrid Committee for a rising the events at Cartagena forced its hand.

At a public meeting at Cartagena on 11 July there had been enthusiatic support for the Madrid Committee of Public Safety and for two of its agents present at the meeting, Gálvez Arce, a colourful Murciano, and Cárceles Sabater.[1] Whether these men had any precise intructions from Madrid for an actual date to declare a canton is impossible to say, but their decision to stage a coup seems to have been determined by purely local considerations and provides an example of how the Intransigents' central organization had no control over the initiative of local Federals. On 4 July the Government had rashly allowed the Federal militia in Cartegena to take over the garrison duties for a week in Fort Atalaya dominating the town. If a coup was to be made it must be before the military returned to this key position, before units of the fleet, in which the Federals had contacts, sailed, and before the municipal elections fixed for the 12th could confirm the Moderates in office. At dawn on the 12th Barcia replied to a telegram from Cárceles asking for instructions, telling him to wait, but at a meeting in Cartagena on the morning of the 12th it was decided to rise immediately. The *Ayuntamiento*, dominated by moderate Federals, tried to resist but was deposed and replaced by a revolutionary junta that same morning. Once this initial coup had taken place it was decided to fix Cartagena as the focal point of the Federal revolt, and with the possession of the strongest naval base in the country to force the Government's hand. On the evening of the 13th Contreras left Madrid and, although Pi tried to intercept him, he arrived safely at Cartagena on the 14th and took over military command. The advantages of Cartagena as a centre were obvious. Its federalism was unquestioned, the ring of forts made it almost impregnable from the land and difficult to approach from the sea—it had withstood a siege of forty days by

[1] Puig Campillo, *El Cantón murciano*, Cartagena, 1932, pp. 69 et seq. The *matrículas del mar* had been abolished by decree 23 Mar., and the sailors' discontent at not being released may have been worked on by the local branch of the International. But this is one of many unsolved problems of the Cartagena canton. See E. S. Jiménez, *Cartagena, recuerdos cantonales*, Barcelona, 1874, and Ramón Sender's vivid fictionalized account of the canton in *Mr. Witt among the Rebels*, London, 1937.

30,000 troops in 1844; the majority of the fleet was in port and the discontent of the sailors, which had been marked as early as May, guaranteed their support; the Arsenal was well stocked with ammunition thanks to Ferrer, an artillery officer, one of Pierrard's nominees in the War Office, and its geographical position would enable the Cantonalist fleet to cover the Federal-dominated coast-line from Cádiz to Barcelona.

Pi first heard of the coup by telegram from the *Ayuntamiento* on the morning of the 12th, but he waited for official notification from the Civil Governor of Murcia, Altadill, which did not arrive until the early hours of the 13th. This initial delay gave the Cantonalists a necessary breathing-space, but the key to the situation really lay with the availability of troops. Ripoll had to remain at Córdoba to watch Seville and Málaga. The two regiments of Iberia and Mendigorria, which arrived in Cartagena on the 14th to embark for Málaga, deserted *en masse* to the Cantonalists. The only trustworthy force available was Velarde's column, which had entered Alcoy on the morning of the 13th. What is difficult to explain is why Velarde was not immediately ordered to march on Cartagena. In fact he received no orders to move to Murcia until the 18th, which by then was too late. Pi attributed this delay, in his apologia, to deliberate sabotage by the Minister of War, González Iscar, but it was Pi who had to face the charge of incompetence by Prefumo, a deputy for Cartagena, and of complicity from one of own ministers, Maisonnave.[1] Assaulted from the Right, Pi was unable to appeal to the Left because hardly any were present in the *Cortes* on the 14th. On the 15th there were insufficient deputies to hold a session of the *Cortes* at all, but, at a private meeting of those present, Pi still clung to the belief that if a Constitution was voted in permanent session and a ministry formed from all three sections of the *Cortes* the crisis of a general revolt could be avoided. Inside the Ministry there were divisions with Maisonnave for a policy of resistance and Suñer y Capdevila and Pérez Costales for one of conciliation. When this issue was put to the vote with

[1] Pi y Arsuaga, op. cit. v. 309–10, who also prints some relevant telegrams, pp. 350–3; *Gaceta*, 14 July 1873, Prefumo's speech, in which he said that he warned Pi that Altadill was not to be trusted and that Pi had had ample warning of the revolt.

less than a third of the deputies present and Pi's suggestion for a ministry of conciliation defeated by 76–50, the crisis came to a head.

The final blow fell when, in deference to Pi's wishes, Castelar produced a draft Constitution on 17 July which he had drawn up in twenty-four hours. But the fact that Díaz Quintero, one of the eight dissenting members of the twenty-five on the Constitution committee, disapproved of it, presenting at the same time his own alternative, exposed as wishful thinking Pi's belief that a Constitution would solve the problem. It was precisely this question of the Constitution and the basic conflict over the boundaries of the proposed states which provided the main bone of contention. In Castelar's draft the divisions following Pi's idea were based on the historical provinces; in Quintero's draft they were based on the existing administrative divisions of 1834.[1] In both cases the divisions were arbitrary, conforming to no linguistic or geographical feature. The conflict between the two viewpoints was a political one, but if Quintero's showed greater realism in that smaller rather than larger units would be more acceptable to Andalusian opinion, even he did not carry political fragmentation to its logical conclusion as the Federals of Utrera, Torrevieja, Tarifa, and other small towns were to do a few days later by declaring their own independence. Although the two drafts were not discussed until 11 August, the initial division of opinion was an added reason for Pi's decision to resign on the 18th. The Intransigents meanwhile had returned under Orense and, forming with the rump of the Centre, were willing to give to Pi the vote of confidence which they had withheld earlier. This was insufficient, however, to save him and after the Intransigents failed to get the vote for a new President of the Executive Power postponed in order to send for their supporters in the provinces, Salmerón was voted in by 119 votes against Pi's 93.

Thus Pi's ministerial career came to an end. It was an end, too, of his position as mentor and leader of the Federals which he had enjoyed since 1869. For the rest of his life he would only be the leader of a faction, a minority even among Republicans. He made

[1] Pi y Arsuaga, op. cit. v. 261–76, 364–84.

unsuccessful bids to return to power during the remainder of the Republic's short life, but the events of July killed his policy of conciliation. Republican unity became a fiction as the Carlist threat, Alphonsist activity, the social extremism of Alcoy, and the Cantonalist revolt forced Federal sympathizers further to the Right or to the Left. Conciliation was only practical politics when both sides had enough in common to agree on fundamental principles. By July this common agreement no longer existed. It may be doubted whether it ever really had existed, but now conditions were such that no one, except Pi, believed that there could be anything in common between the Cantonalists and the Republicans of the Right.

'Pi's fall', commented *The Times* correspondent,[1] 'was a striking illumination of the rapidity with which a political reputation may be utterly ruined. When Figueras fled he came as the saviour of the situation. He finished by being accused of betraying both parties in order not to alienate either.'

For the rest of 1873 the conflict was waged between those who, still Federals in name, were willing to sacrifice federalism for a policy of order and those whose federalism was the bitter fruit of disillusion and frustrated ambition and who had nothing to lose from the ruthless exploitation of local fears and grievances.

[1] *The Times*, 28 July 1873.

10

Cantonalism and the Collapse of the Republic, 1873–4

WHEN Pi fell from power no one mourned his passing. The Federal press had turned against him and while it admired his honesty it deplored his policy. Others thought that now he had been freed from the embarrassments of conciliation he would put himself at the head of the extremists, where it was felt he really belonged. In the *Cortes*, the Right feared the social implications of his policy; the Left had done their best to make it impossible for him to govern at all and the spokesmen of the Centre, Cala and Díaz Quintero, had demolished his hopes of drawing up a Constitution quickly by presenting an alternative draft. Many of those in the Centre who had voted for him in preference to Salmerón only did so out of personal loyalty, not because of sympathy with his policy.[1] Once the cantonalist revolt had broadened, Salmerón was assured of their support although in drawing up his Ministry he had leaned almost exclusively on the Right. Maisonnave, Pi's bitterest critic in his Ministry, took over the Ministry of the Interior, Carvajal was retained in that of Finance, and González Iscar in that of War—in spite of his equivocal behaviour over the ordering of Velarde to march on Cartagena—Oreiro, an ex-Radical, took over the Ministry of Marine. The other Ministers, Soler y Pla, Fernández González, and Moreno Rodríguez, were all sympathetic to the Right. Only Palanca, Minister of Overseas, came from the Centre.

Within four days of Salmerón coming to power large and small towns from Castellón to Cádiz had declared themselves independent cantons. On 19 July Seville, Cádiz, Valencia, Almansa, and Torrevieja declared themselves independent cantons. On the 20th

[1] *La Igualdad*, 19, 22, 23 July; *La Discusión*, 21 July 1873.

Castellón and Granada. On the 22nd Salamanca, Bailén, Andújar, Tarifa, and Algeciras. Most of these were ephemeral, lasting only a few days before collapsing in the face of apathy and lack of support, but in the case of the main Federal centres of Seville, Cádiz, Cartagena, Málaga, and Valencia Salmerón had to face a formidable threat to the Government's authority which needed force to suppress. If cantonalism was the logical end of Pi's Federal theories the actual revolt was also a 'desperate protest of the country against the apathy of the government and the *Cortes*'.[1] The declaration of the Cartagena canton had been the main cause of Pi's downfall, but it was not the signal for similar outbreaks elsewhere. One of the features of the revolts was the inefficacy of the attempts of the Madrid Committee of Public Safety to control or co-ordinate the rising—none of its emissaries, neither Fantoni at Seville, Santamaría at Valencia, Moreno de Cristo at Barcelona, not even Pierrard at Seville, were responsible for initiating the revolts. In every canton except Castellón, Salamanca, and Cartagena the initiative lay with local, and in most cases entirely unknown, Federals. Pi believed that his own fall was the main cause in the spread of the revolts elsewhere. This was partially true and it was borne out to a certain extent by the Cádiz and Seville press.[2] Salmerón had never enjoyed the confidence of the provincial Federals and even less so since his speech as the new President of the *Cortes* on 13 June and the laudatory article in *El Imparcial* the next day; but Pi's own dilatoriness had been outspokenly condemned on the very day of his resignation by the leading paper of the Cádiz Federals:[3] 'The Assembly is achieving nothing. Pi passes the time in conference with these and those and resolves nothing. There must be immediate federalism otherwise the provinces will make it themselves.' If Pi's fall was the signal for the extension of the cantonal outbreak it was due to distrust of Salmerón rather than to confidence in Pi. Having previously ruined Pi's attempts

[1] Vera, op. cit. ii. 754; Estévanez, op. cit., p. 453.
[2] Pi y Arsuaga, op. cit. v. 315; *La Andalucía*, 22 July 1873, quoting the Cádiz press with approval.
[3] *La Federación andaluza*, 18 July 1873. Cf. *El Cantón murciano*, 24 July 1873, and Ávila Federals quoted in Puig Campillo, op. cit., pp. 115-17, 'We follow the same paths as under Isabella II, although a republic.'

at a policy of conciliation, the Intransigents, particularly those at Cartagena, began to hope for Pi's return to power as soon as it was apparent that the movement had collapsed in the rest of the country and that the only policy was to try and enter into negotiations with Madrid. After Salmerón and Castelar had come to power, determined to crush the revolt by force, Pi's return to office was the only hope left for a solution by negotiation. As the Centre turned increasingly to Salmerón for leadership, and in view of the continuing absence of deputies from the *Cortes*, Pi was forced to base any return to power on the extreme Left. After his resignation he temporarily retired from the *Cortes*, but when he returned on 6 September to dispute the new Presidency of the Executive Power with Castelar, he only gained 67 votes against Castelar's 133. This drop from the 93 he had gained against Salmerón on 18 July marked the extent to which he was losing the support of the Centre. From September onwards, therefore, his efforts were directed towards trying to establish contacts with the Cartagena rebels and to rally those deputies who were not present in the *Cortes*. But his role was a minor one and this policy showed little signs of being a threat to the Madrid Government. For the first time since 1869 Pi did not occupy the centre of the republican stage.

The last six months of 1873 fall into two parts, one dominated by Salmerón as President from 18 July until 6 September, the other dominated by Castelar from then until 3 January 1874. Salmerón had to deal with the subjugation of the outbreaks in Andalusia, whereas Castelar had the more difficult task of subduing Cartagena; both had to face the implications of a full-scale Carlist war. Salmerón's task was at first a comparatively easy one and by the middle of August only Málaga and Cartagena remained to be subdued. His policy, announced on 19 July, acclaimed by the monarchist *El Imparcial*, challenged the Cantonalists to a head-on struggle.[1] This was shown by the extremely unpopular decree declaring the Cantonalist fleet pirates, virtually inviting the inter-

[1] *El Imparcial*, 20 July 1873; *Gaceta*, 21 July 1873, decree of piracy. The movements of the fleet off shore at Cartagena may be studied in detail in F.O. 72/1399, 1400, Cartagena Insurgents. For Salmerón's other measures see Bermejo, op. cit. iii. 495 et seq.

vention of the German and British squadrons off shore. He also showed his determination by appointing Pavía to the command of the army of Andalusia (superseding Ripoll, who was a suspected Alphonsist sympathizer and whose force was in a state of disorganization) and by calling a conference of generals on the 20th, irrespective of their political affiliation, to ask their advice. As a result of this conference Salmerón started to prepare the ground for a reinstatement of the artillery officers. He promised to reestablish the military ordinances and courts martial. The first expression of the new spirit in the Army was to be seen in Pavía's expedition to Andalusia. With barely 2,000 men under his command he broke the back of the revolts there in a matter of weeks at the same time as Martínez Campos crushed the canton at Valencia.[1]

Córdoba, the key to Andalusia, was prevented from declaring its independence by the rapid and unexpected arrival of Pavía on 23 July. Seville was stormed on the 28th and after two days of fierce street fighting surrendered. Cádiz was entered two days later without a struggle, as the canton had already collapsed through internal divisions. On 12 August Granada was entered without a fight. At Valencia, on 8 August, Martínez Campos entered the city after a bombardment and street fighting. The other cantons which had been declared at Castellón, Almansa, Algeciras, Tarifa, Torrevieja, Andújar, Bailén, San Lucar de Barrameda, Ecija, Fuenteovejuna, and Salamanca all collapsed, even before force had been used. Only Málaga and Cartagena remained. Salmerón's power broke over his inability to subdue Málaga. He was unable to do so because of the blackmail of Palanca, Minister of Overseas and protector of Solier, Civil Governor of the province and the nominal head of the Málaga canton, who threatened to force a ministerial crisis should Salmerón order Pavía into the city. As Palanca's influence in the Centre was strong, he constituted the the main threat to Salmerón's policy of subjugation. When Pavía threatened to resign if not allowed to march on Málaga, Salmerón was placed in a dilemma which he could only solve by resigning, claiming, with some inconsistency in view of his promise to support Castelar, that he was doing so because he disapproved of

[1] M. Pavía y Rodríguez, *La Pacificación de Andalucía*, Madrid, 1878.

the renewed application of the death penalty which the generals wanted restored to maintain discipline.

By mid-September the revolts had been crushed everywhere except at Cartagena, where the Federals were entrenched in a natural stronghold. Salmerón had succeeded in stemming the most formidable Federal revolt since 1869; but then the rebels had ranged against them a united army and a government unhampered by a Carlist revolt; now the Government was distracted by a Carlist war, the Army was riddled with discontent, the vast majority of the officers were anti-republican, many men now refused to obey their officers and in some cases showed active sympathy with the Cantonalists, and, finally, the greater part of the fleet was in the hands of the Cartagena rebels. Why was it that Pavía's small force of 2,000 men and Martínez Campos's small task force could stamp out this revolt in a few weeks?

The collapse of the rising, like that of 1869, was due firstly to lack of leadership; Contreras, Gálvez Arce, and Barcia, the most important figures of the revolt, were men of negligible political capacity who still thought in outmoded terms of spontaneous revolution and who were completely out of touch with Federal opinion outside the walls of Cartagena. But lack of leadership alone is insufficient to explain a collapse which was due rather to the lack of anyone to be led. The truth was that, by the middle of 1873, the Federals had ceased to have any mass following except possibly in Barcelona, but even there the low returns at the elections in May suggested a falling off in enthusiasm. The refusal of Barcelona to join the revolt doomed it from the outset.[1] A Committee of Public Safety had been set up there on 18 July, but it was distinguished from the others by asking the Government's permission before enforcing its decrees. The aim of this Committee, which voluntarily dissolved itself on 26 July, was to organize resistance to the Carlists rather than to carry through any widespread social or political revolution.[2] The failure of the *somaten* in

---

[1] Engels rightly stressed this in his 'Bakuninists at Work' (*Revolution in Spain*, London, 1939, p. 227), although his assertion that their declaration of a general strike on 14 July prevented Barcelona's participation in the cantonal movement would seem to over-exaggerate both their importance and its effectiveness.

[2] Pi y Arsuaga, op. cit. v. 334; González Sugrañes, op. cit., pp. 357 et seq., p. 400, App. P.

May and Carlist attempts to isolate Barcelona from the rest of Spain, underlined the need to retain close contact with Madrid. The Barcelona Moderates' attitude to the revolt may be judged by their welcome to the news of the fall of the Valencia canton which released a competent general for the Catalan front.[1]

The revolts were the work of fanatical minorities who soon alienated what little support had not already been lost by tactless policies. At Cádiz, in the elections in 1869, 5,039 had voted republican; in July 1873 this had dropped to 2,917, and, more significantly, the outgoing mayor, Salvochea, was only third in popularity. Yet it was Salvochea who led and organized the Cádiz rising. This may have been his reaction to a decline in popularity which was a result of his policy as mayor when he had alienated potential supporters by levying forced loans and by shifting the burden of the *consumos* from the consumer to the retailer, and by his excessive anticlericalism in defiance of the Madrid Government. Salvochea lacked the support of public opinion beyond a faithful following among the Cádiz poor; the militia were opposed to the Cantonalists and when Pavía's army arrived from Seville the Moderates claimed that order had already been restored by their own efforts and lodged a violent protest against the indiscriminate disarming of all the militia.[2]

At Seville the division was not so pronounced because although Pavía's force was 'republican' the fact that it was mainly composed of Civil Guards and *carabineros* meant that it symbolized the centralized State, which helped to create a sense of unity among the Cantonalists, but the threat of social extremism which had been a factor in June, and the fact that the Internationalist Mignorance, president of the Committee of Public Safety then, was on the revolutionary junta set up on 19 July, predisposed the more moderate militiamen to give up the struggle rather than be associated too closely with the social extremists. At Valencia, too,

---

[1] Ibid., p. 410.
[2] *La Federación andaluza*, 17 July, 5, 6, 7, 10 Aug. 1873. The fullest account of the Cádiz canton is in F.O. 72/1352, nos. 59, 60, 62, dated 20, 26 July and 18 Aug. 1873, reports from Reade, the Cádiz consul, justifying his part in the consular commission which took over from Salvochea until the relieving army arrived. Reade was favourably impressed by Salvochea, but not by his followers.

there was a similar division although, as in 1869, all shades of opinion collaborated in the revolutionary junta. But the rumour that this junta was negotiating with Madrid led to its overthrow and replacement by a more radical one. Social extremism, underlined by the official support given to the canton by the local branch of the International, accounts for the fact that finally it was again the Moderate militia men who handed the city over to Martínez Campos. At Málaga, which had been virtually independent since March, the division was determined by the personal rivalry between the extremist Carvajal and the Moderate Solier, who had established his position there in Carvajal's absence at Seville and who had the advantage of Palanca's protection and the support of the Madrid Government.[1]

In all these cases the pattern of conflict was similar: Intransigent losses at the municipal elections held on 12 July stimulated a sense of grievance and the determination to use the first opportunity to overturn by force new councils duly elected by universal suffrage. In no case, except in Cartagena, did any of the revolutionary juntas justify their coups by an appeal to universal suffrage and it was only the pressure brought by the military which forced the junta at Cartagena to yield.[2] Most of the juntas were formed from only the 'active Federals'—those in the militia and in the clubs.[3] The majority of even those who sympathized with the idea of federation held aloof.

The example of Cartagena and the advent to power of Salmerón predisposed the extremists to revolt, but the main incentive came from the withdrawal of garrison troops from southern towns to reinforce the garrison at Madrid and more particularly to strengthen the Carlist front. At Málaga the troops had been disarmed as early as March and the city had refused to admit any replacements. On the basis of a bargain with Madrid that it would not become a focus of revolt, Málaga succeeded in remaining virtually

[1] Guichot, op. cit., pp. 473 et seq.; Vera, op. cit. ii. 749–51; *New York Herald*, 1 Sept. 1873; F.O. 72/1341, no. 39, 15 July 1873, Macdonnell to Granville, enclosure from Málaga consul.

[2] F.O. 72/1339, no. 521, 13 Nov. 1873, Layard to Granville, enclosure from Pauli, vice-consul at Cartagena.

[3] *La Igualdad*, 22 July 1873.

independent and enjoying 'boom conditions'.[1] At Seville the garrison consisted of only seventy Civil Guards and an equal number of *carabineros*—both of which corps were hostile to the Federals.[2] At Cádiz the small garrison of artillerymen joined the Cantonalists, but the refusal of the marines at Carraca to join the revolt condemned the rising to failure. At Valencia the outbreak at Alcoy and the appearance of Carlist bands in the Maestrazgo had left the city without a garrison, and the rising was made in the belief that any investing force would desert and join the rebels as the units at Cartagena had done.[3] It was, in fact, only at Cartagena that the military did obey the predictions of the Federals and join the revolt in any strength, but only, it seems, on the assumption that they would be immediately sent home to their families.[4] The disillusion of the men and the ambitions of their officers constituted the main division within the Cartagena canton, and the eventual capture of the fortress was due to its betrayal by the officers.

Although plans were made for a rising by the Committee of Public Safety at Madrid, the Madrid Intransigents seem to have played very little part in the initiation or the subsequent organization of the revolts, with the exception of Cartagena and where the rebels sought justification for revolt in the presence of seven deputies in Cartagena, five in Valencia, and the support of seventy more in the *Cortes*.[5] Contreras left for Cartagena on the 13th in order to ensure that the port would be the focus of a revolt which he believed the plans of the Madrid Committee would generalize. Barcia followed towards the end of July only after it had become

---

[1] F.O. 72/1353, nos. 8 and 10, 7 and 14 Mar. 1873, consul at Málaga to Granville. *P.P.* LXVII, 1874, p. 871, Málaga consul's report for 1873.

[2] Brandt, op. cit., p. 216. For Cádiz see N. Muiños y Muiños, *La Marina en San Fernando*, &c., Cádiz, 1873.

[3] *New York Herald*, 23, 30 Aug., 1 Sept. 1873. Both the *Herald* and the *Tribune* had correspondents in Valencia in the belief that, as in 1869, it would put up the most spirited resistance.

[4] *El Cantón murciano*, 23 July 1873. For the civil–military divisions see F.O. 72/1399, nos. 495, 503, 575, dated 3, 8, 23 Nov. 1873, Layard to Granville, enclosures from Pauli, and also F.O. 72/1400, nos. 65, 69, dated 16, 17 Jan. 1874.

[5] *El Cantón murciano*, 24 July 1873. Pi y Arsuaga, op. cit. v. 485–8, prints a manifesto of the Madrid Committee of Public Safety dated as late as 28 Oct. It was unsigned and there is nothing to suggest it was in any sense a directing body.

clear that the general rising had failed. The agents of the Committee had little success in initiating revolts. At Castellón, González Cherma, a local deputy, came from Madrid to put himself at the head of the canton, 'the logical consequence of the declaration of a federal republic' as he described it, but its refusal to cooperate with Valencia and complete lack of support condemned it from the outset. At Salamanca, Riesco, another deputy, declared a canton, but it petered out within hours. At Barcelona Brigadier Guerrero, in command at Montjuich, refused to follow Moreno de Cristo, the Committee's agent. Santamaría, sent to Valencia, got no farther than Albacete where he was stopped by the Government. Fantoni, sent to raise Seville, does not figure in the canton's organization. As deputy for Utrera he must soon have been disillusioned by the way in which it resisted the attempts of Seville to force it into the Seville canton.[1]

A distinction may be drawn between those cantons like Cartagena and Seville, which, having established themselves, began to try and expand outside their own immediate sphere of influence and those like Valencia, Málaga, and Cádiz where, either because of internal divisions or because of military resistance, they were preoccupied with internal affairs. One of the main features about the Seville and Cartagena cantons was the strong resistance they encountered from towns which did not want to exchange tutelage to Madrid for the tyranny of a new capital.[2] The attempt of Seville to incorporate Utrera into the Sevillano Canton cost it the loss of twenty Cantonalists killed, 200 wounded, and a humiliating rebuff.[3] Huelva, which Seville anticipated would join in, firmly announced its intention of remaining loyal to Madrid. The Cartagena Cantonalists immediately alienated surrounding towns by their attempts to raise money from them. Murcia, resenting Cartagena's lead, refused to contribute its full share. Lorca, made to pay a forced contribution on 16 July, sent to Madrid for pro-

---

[1] *El Porvenir* (Seville), 10 Aug. 1873, manifesto from the Utrera Federals resisting the demands of the Seville Federals to 'assist them against the Assembly'. Pierrard arrived in Seville after the declaration of the canton to take over command of its forces.

[2] *La Igualdad*, 24 July 1873. Cf. *El Imparcial*, 26 July 1873, 'El Movimiento cantonal', and *The Times*, 5 Aug. 1873, 'Report on the Condition of Spain'.

[3] *La Andalucía*, 24 July 1873, Guichot, op. cit., pp. 485 et seq.; *La Federación andaluza* (Huelva), 23 July 1873.

tection as soon as the Cantonalists had departed after lecturing the inhabitants on their lack of co-operation and on the Cantonalists' aims:[1] 'We wish to free the provinces from ruinous taxation. We want the free development of local wealth and to free our sons from the immorality of great centres which imitate French caesarism.' The bombardment of Almería and the threat to bombard Alicante by the Cartagena fleet, excused officially because of the 'refusal of the army to withdraw' from those towns, was, in fact, provoked by nothing more than their refusal to contribute the sum demanded as a war-tax. Only after the Cantonalists failed to compel surrounding towns to contribute to their expenses did they resort to coining their own money, selling state property in the Arsenal, and declaring that all debts incurred by the canton were to be charged to the Madrid Government. Desperately short of money, faced with widespread unemployment because of the dislocation of work, they were forced to compel surrounding towns to pay contributions.[2] Elsewhere, the pretensions of provincial capitals to establish themselves as cantonal capitals also provoked resistance. Loja, half-way between Granada and Málaga and disputed by both, refused to co-operate with either and called to Madrid for protection. The first act of the Castellón canton was to cut communications with Valencia and to refuse to co-operate with the larger city which it regarded as a potential rival. Jerez, between Cádiz and Seville and a Federal centre, refused to declare a canton or to submit to either city. Complete absence of co-ordination and bitter rivalry between the various centres of resistance doomed the revolts of 1873 as effectively as it had those of 1869.

But why did this rash of cantonalism start to break out at a time when the champion and leading protagonist of federalism was in power? An analysis of Cantonal decrees and of their programmes gives some clue to the motives of the rebels and exposes the frustration which had been built up by the Government's inactivity.[3]

---

[1] *El Cantón murciano*, 1 Aug. Cf. *La Igualdad*, 18 July 1873.
[2] *El Cantón murciano*, 5, 12, 26 Aug., 18 Sept. 1873; Puig Campillo, op. cit., pp. 267 et seq.
[3] The Cádiz decrees are in *La Federación andaluza*, 17, 22 July 1873; Cartagena's in *El Cantón murciano*, from 23 July; Málaga's in *Actas capitulares* from 8 July; and for Granada

Pi had resolutely refused to replace *empleados* in the administration other than those, like civil governors, responsible for public order. Where Federal zeal went unrewarded there was a fund of discontent which found its outlet at Seville and Cádiz, where the first decrees dismissed all *empleados*. Both Cádiz and Valencia were declared free ports; freedom of trade was regarded by Cádiz Federals as the prerequisite of a revived prosperity. Tobacco, which unlike salt was still a government monopoly, was demonopolized. Smuggling, which had thrived on high port tariffs and customs dues, now offered few prospects for the smugglers whom the Cantonalists released from prison as the 'victims of an unjust society'. At Cartagena some 1,500 convicts were also released for humanitarian reasons and with the more practical purpose of employing them as scavengers, although this did not ease the unemployment problem, which was already acute through the stoppage of the lead mines at La Unión.[1] Points in the Federals' official programme, which had not yet become law, were decreed at Seville and Cádiz. The right to work was recognized and working hours reduced to eight. All state property was taken over by *Ayuntamientos*. Anticlericalism was a prominent feature in the cantons' programmes; not only Church property and its wealth was to be used in the public interest but religious teaching was to be abolished and replaced by 'universal morality'. Anticlericalism was most extreme at Cádiz where it reflected Salvochea's fervid hostility to the Church.

Whenever unpopular taxes like the *consumos* were abolished financial decrees penalized the wealthy, as at Cádiz, Seville, and Granada where a direct tax on property was decreed to compensate for losses from the abolition of indirect taxes. At Málaga, where the social element tended to be less pronounced, the Cantonal authorities were compelled to levy forced loans, and at Cartagena, where the authorities were anxious to avoid socialistic implications, the abolition of the *consumos* led to the setting up of a jury to calculate what direct taxes should be paid, but there was to be no

---

see *La Revolución federal*, 31 July 1873. A cantonal government complete with a foreign minister was established at Cartagena.

[1] *El Cantón murciano*, 23 July, 17 Aug. 1873; *El Imparcial*, 16 July 1873.

question of penalizing the rich in order to win over the poor, as
at Granada, where the Committee of Public Safety decreed the
halving of urban and rural rents. At Cartagena, in fact, de la Calle,
a member of the junta, was replaced because of his socialist proclamations.[1] Although in Cádiz, Seville, and Granada Internationalist influence might account for some social extremism,
the Cantonalists' programmes were mainly political, and even in
these centres the roots of the revolt must be sought mainly in the
inability of the Government at Madrid to initiate the political
and administrative revolution for which the small minority of
frustrated office-seekers were clamouring. As the Cádiz junta put
it, in justifying the dismissal of the *empleados* in the *Diputación
Provincial*, the Government had 'not satisfied the revolutionary
hopes of the electors'; but, as those electors had already shown
what their wishes were, it is difficult to see that the revolts directed
against the new *Ayuntamientos* as much as against the Madrid
Government were anything more than the last despairing fling
of those Federal extremists who, seeing the failure of the Intransigents in Madrid to force a premature division of the country and
the Government's determination not to be intimidated, decided
to make a bid for power.

The collapse of Cantonalism outside Cartagena confirmed that
Federal Republicanism could no longer be described as a mass
movement even in the traditionally Federal areas. It exposed their
internal weaknesses and divisions and their violent hostility to the
Internationalists, who, it was claimed, had been responsible for
bringing discredit on them. When on 5 August *La Igualdad* wrote
that 'the insurrection has become internationalist, separatist and
anti-Spanish', critics were quick to point out how they were
laying the blame for their disenchantment on the International.[2]
The latter's official support for the Valencian canton and for the
'democratic federal republic with all its logical consequences'[3]
enabled the Government to raise the bogy of Alcoy to discredit

[1] Puig Campillo, op. cit., p. 360. A number of refugees from the Paris Commune were
in Cartagena but they do not seem to have exerted much influence.

[2] *El Imparcial*, 6 Aug. 1873.

[3] *El Mercantil valenciano*, 10 Aug. 1873, manifesto of Barrientos, president of the local
branch of the International.

the Cantonalists, the anti-Federals to point out the inevitable results of federalism in practice, and Federal apologists to make the
Internationalists the scapegoat for their own failures. Although
the correspondent of the *Bulletin jurasien* in Madrid admitted
that the risings were 'the work of military or political chiefs who
have tried to exploit for their own personal ambition the idea of
the autonomy of the canton', and though the risings had not been
made by the Internationalists except at Alcoy and San Lucar de
Barrameda, the few cases where Internationalists had co-operated,
very much in a minority, at Seville, Granada, and Valencia, were
exaggerated by the Right-wing press in order to discredit the
Federals.[1] How anxious the Federals were to dispel any idea that
they were social extremists is to be seen in the violence of their
attacks against the Internationalists.[2]

The most important result, however, was the way in which the
Cantonalist revolt, by splitting the Federals and by exposing the
threat of social extremism, stimulated the return of more conservative elements to political activity. The immediate result at both
Cádiz and Seville was for Conservatives and even Alphonsists to
be represented on the juntas which were established to restore
order. At Valencia the leading paper hoped that cantonalism
would finally convince the propertied classes to take an active
interest in local politics and join the local militia so as to prevent
it from being dominated by the 'people'.[3] In spite of the protests
of the moderate Federals, the political initiative, even in such
centre as Cádiz, Seville, and Valencia, passed out of their hands
altogether. Not only this, but cantonalism made it easier for those
like Castelar, whose federal faith was weakening, to carry out
fundamentally anti-Federal policies.

Salmerón's ability to suppress the Andalusian cantons was due
to his decision to trust generals like the anti-Federal Pavía and the
monarchist Martínez Campos. Once that decision had been taken

[1] Guillaume, op. cit. iii. 87–8.
[2] *La Andalucía*, 3 Aug., 'Guerra a la Internacional'; *La Igualdad*, 26 Aug. 1873, and the
attitudes of Vera, op. cit. ii. 750–1, and Puig Campillo, op. cit., ch. vii.
[3] *La Igualdad*, 15 Aug.; *El Mercantil valenciano*, 15 Aug. 1873, 'Reflexiones'. At Valencia
the conservative elements boycotted the militia, forming their own vigilante association
as at Madrid.

it was only a matter of time before the generals would make their support conditional on the restoration of the military ordinances and the death penalty. Salmerón's power was therefore not dependent so much on his following in the *Cortes* as on his relations with the Army. Constantly aware of the weakness in his own Government, due to Palanca's influence with the rump of the Centre, he hesitated to capitulate to the Army, but it was finally the contradictions between his need to reassure both the Centre and Pavía at the same time which forced his resignation on 6 September.

The arrival of Don Carlos in Spain in July, increasing Carlist activity, and Isabella's appointment of Cánovas as official leader of the Alphonsists on 23 August, presaging a more directed Alphonsist effort, argued for the strengthening of the Government and its release from the hampering criticisms of a factious *Cortes*. Salmerón himself had considered an adjournment after the debates on the Constitution during the second week of August when the gap between the two drafts seemed unbridgeable.[1] But both unsureness about his own support and reluctance to yield to the Army had prevented him from taking this extreme step. Castelar, however, had fewer doubts: he was not in need of Centre votes—in fact, Salmerón had remained in power only due to Castelar's benevolence. In face of these threats, therefore, Castelar did not balk at measures to mollify the Army and as there was the risk of opposition in the *Cortes*, through the return of Cantonalist sympathizers, he accepted the necessity of an adjournment. Always susceptible to foreign republican opinion, he was assured of Gambetta's support in pursuing a policy of order, 'the only hope for the survival of the republic in Spain'.[2] When Salmerón resigned on 6 September, Castelar's hand was strengthened by the attempt of the unrepentant Pi to stage a political comeback but, after Rios Rosas's brilliant attack on his past policies and Salmerón's unqualified support for Castelar, the latter's majority was assured and by 133 to 67 votes gained by Pi, Castelar was elected President

[1] F.O. 72/1341, no. 98, 16 Aug. 1873, Macdonnell to Granville, according to private information.
[2] Letter of Gambetta to Castelar, 29 Aug. 1873, Gambetta, *Lettres*, ed. D. Halévy and E. Pillias, Paris, 1938.

of the Executive Power with Salmerón as President of the *Cortes*. Only fourteen days after coming to power the *Cortes* was adjourned and for the next three and a half months, from 20 September until 2 January 1874, Castelar ruled by decree.[1]

The first batch of decrees on 21 September suspended the constitutional guarantees, created a press censorship, and reorganized the artillery corps, thus severing all links between the moderates and the rest of the party. Although many Federals regarded this as the great betrayal, Castelar still did not break with federalism. On 8 July he had said that he would 'never, never consent to a unitarian republic'; in his policy speech of 8 September he still called himself a Federal and Martos could refer to his policy as one 'attempting to save the Republic without any diminution of federalism'.[2] For the first time since he had come under his influence in exile, Castelar was freed from Pi's tutelage. On 16 September he admitted that Pi had been the main policy-maker in the early ministries of the Republic and that he himself had been in constant disagreement with him—it was only with the greatest reluctance that he had remained in the Ministry after 23 April when the policy of conciliation with the Radicals had broken down. Whereas at that time Pi's policy had been one of conciliation within the party Castelar's now was one of attempted conciliation between the Right-wing Federals and the Radicals and Conservatives. It is their response to Castelar's policy of order which constitutes the main thread in the political history of the last three months of 1873.

Biarritz had become the centre for Radical and Conservative exiles after 23 April. Here the Alphonsists hoped to establish a union of all three groups to overthrow the Republic. But Serrano's final break with Isabella in July and Castelar's advent to power in September with a policy of order encouraged Conservatives, Radicals, and even Alphonsist to return to Spain and intrigue in their own interests.[3] Cánovas's arrival in Madrid in September

---

[1] *Gaceta*, 20 Sept. 1873, 124 voted for adjournment, 62 against it.

[2] Letter of Martos to Grijalba dated 1873 in *El Sol*.

[3] Ibid. Letters of Grijalba to de Castro and his wife, 14 and 27 July 1873, describe Isabella's fury at Serrano's finally breaking off the friendship of twenty years. Lema, *De la Revolución a la Restauración*, Madrid, 1929, ii. 609 et seq., is the fullest account of Alphonsist activity.

gave a new impetus to Alphonsist organization and propaganda, which until then had been mainly centred on subverting army officers. This posed a dilemma for the Radicals and Conservatives, impelling them towards closer co-operation with the moderate Federals in order to avoid the greater evil of a Bourbon restoration.

Radicals and Conservatives now attempted to clarify their positions with respect to republicanism. On 6 October, at a meeting of some 300 Radicals under the presidency of Martos, the majority were in favour of a Unitarian Republic. For the first time García Ruiz saw the widespread acceptance of his programme. But this acceptance of unitarian republicanism on a predominantly anti-socialist programme did not command the assent of all Radicals, for on the 8th Gasset y Artime, influential because of his control of *El Imparcial*, announced that he was in favour of a monarchy—of the mysterious Rey X.[1] After this, it was not until 25 October that the Radicals, after failure to make an alliance with Serrano, were sufficiently agreed to publish a manifesto declaring their support for Castelar and announcing their intention to return to political life.[2] Serrano, as usual, had refused to be committed and at a meeting of his party opinion had been divided, with Sagasta attacking the idea of any alliance with the Radicals and arguing against Topete, who considered that a unitarian republic was at least preferable to a Bourbon restoration. Part of the unreliability of the Conservatives was that no one was sure who was under obligation to the Alphonsists—this was particularly true of their military wing. This led the Radicals to abandon the Conservatives when they saw an opportunity to return to the *Cortes* by making an agreement with Castelar to fill the eighty-six seats in the *Cortes* which had been declared vacant through forfeiture because of the implication of deputies in the cantonalist revolt and of appointments to public office. It seemed highly likely, in view of Castelar's need to ensure a majority in the *Cortes* on its meeting on 2 January, that he would 'work' these

---

[1] *El Imparcial*, 80 ct., *La Época*, 70 ct. 1873, for the Radicals' divisions. The Radical programme is printed in Pi y Arsuaga, op. cit. v. 593-9, App. I.
[2] *La Discusión*, 28 Oct. 1873.

Cantonalism and the

elections and the Radicals calculated that they would be more acceptable than unreliable Federals, especially as the Centre was now calling for 'genuine' Federals to be returned.[1]

Castelar's reaction to these new developments was cautious. It was clear that Serrano intended to remain at the centre of political intrigue when he refused the command of the Army of the North at the end of October and Castelar had no intention of alienating him by forming an alliance with the Radicals. The difficulties in reducing Cartagena and the intractable Carlist war made Serrano's adhesion, with what influence he still had in the Army, worth the support of all the Radicals. Furthermore, the diplomatic complications with the United States over the *Virginius* episode, which both highlighted the Republic's failure to solve the Cuban problem and threatened a diplomatic break and possible war with its only foreign sympathizer, emphasized the need not to add to his domestic difficulties by alienating either of his possible allies.[2] Appointments of Radicals and Conservatives to diplomatic posts in late November showed his awareness of trying to keep a balance between the two groups. At the end of October he optimistically told Layard that Cartagena would fall within fifteen days, but after Layard had arranged an interview between him and Turner, the retiring vice-consul there, who gave a graphic description of the strength of the defences and the enthusiasm of its defenders, Castelar was compelled to reconsider his policy towards it.[3] His first reaction was to try and suborn the officers of the garrison. This failed because of the vigilance of the junta. There was then no alternative, if Cartagena was to be reduced before the *Cortes*

---

[1] F.O. 72/1341, no. 462, 14 Oct. 1873, Layard to Granville; *El Federalista*, 29 Oct. 1873, manifesto signed by Orense, Cala, Benot, Quintero, and Roure. Layard believed that Sickles was the inspiration behind this paper.

[2] The *Virginius*, owned by the exiled Cuban junta at New York, was making fraudulent use of the U.S. flag when it was intercepted off Cuba by a Spanish patrol. Fifty-three suspected rebels, including some U.S. citizens, were captured and summarily shot in early November. There was little to distinguish between the hysterical reaction of the non-republican and republican Spanish press. Fortunately for Castelar, Fish did not share Sickles's bellicose attitude. The fullest account is in Nevins, op. cit., pp. 673 et seq.

[3] F.O. 72/1399, no. 503, 11 Nov. 1873, Layard to Granville. For the plot see no. 575, 27 Nov. 1873, enclosure from Pauli. The bombardment began on 26 Nov. and López Domínguez took command on 12 Dec.: see his *Cartagena—memoria y comentarios sobre el sitio de Cartagena*, Madrid, 1877.

met, but to start a bombardment, strengthening the Army's hand and, by appointing López Domínguez, Serrano's nephew, to the command of the besieging force, drawing closer to the Conservatives.

The main danger in the continued resistance of Cartagena lay in the way in which Pi, in Martos's words, was 'working with rare skill and perseverance' to stage a political comeback. He tried to do this by intriguing with the Cantonalists and by rallying the Centre, who were becoming increasingly restive under Castelar's repressive policies. Provided the Cartagena rebels held out until the meeting of the *Cortes*, he could then try and organize the discontented parliamentary Federals, win a majority, and so come to terms with the Cantonalists. It is difficult to determine the extent of Pi's actual contacts with the rebels, although Turner affirmed that they were in constant communication and Layard reported that Pi was in touch with both Sickles and the Cuban rebels.[1] Certainly Sickles's effusive admiration for Castelar in early September had been replaced by mid-November by his belief that he was a failure and his government done for.[2] But whatever Pi hoped to gain from Sickles's support, the key to any reversal of Castelar's policy lay with the *Cortes*. But the initiative in exploiting the discontent of the Centre did not come so much from Pi as from Salmerón, who, after supporting Castelar in September and October, began to break with him in late November.[3] Salmerón disapproved of the way in which Castelar was giving Maisonnave a free hand to 'work the elections', while his attempts to find a *modus vivendi* with the Papacy and to rally Catholic opinion roused all Salmerón's doctrinaire anticlerical bile. He disliked, too, the Government's increasing dependence on Radical and royalist generals in the key commands, like the Radical Pavía at Madrid, the Alphonsists Martínez Campos and Jovellar in Catalonia and

---

[1] B.M. Add. MS. 39124, 22 Nov., 9 Dec. 1873, Layard to Granville. Cf. letter from Martos to Grijalba, op. cit., undated. In early December, in a speech at the *Casino Ateneo Federal*, he argued that immediate federalization was now the only solution (Pi y Arsuaga, op. cit. v. 564).

[2] Letter of Sickles to Fish quoted in Nevins, op. cit., p. 692.

[3] Pi y Arsuaga, op. cit. v. 562–3, manifesto of 18 Nov., signed by twenty-two deputies of the Left and Centre. See also p. 570.

Cuba, and the Conservative López Domínguez at Cartagena. These disagreements led Salmerón to draw closer to Pi and to Figueras, who had returned from his self-imposed exile in the middle of September. Castelar recognized the dangers of a new republican front drawing its main support from the wavering Centre and the parliamentary extremists.

He was left with no illusions about military opinion after an interview with Pavía on 24 December, when the Captain-General of Madrid stressed the unlikelihood of Castelar securing a majority on 2 January and suggested that the *Cortes*'s reunion should be indefinitely postponed. Pavía reflected the widespread fear of the Army and of the artillery officers in particular, that a return to power of either Salmerón or Pi would mean the reversal of Castelar's favourable policy towards them. The failure of López Domínguez to take Cartagena quickly, and the news that Pi, Figueras, and Salmerón were meeting to co-ordinate policy for 2 January, led Castelar to try and effect a reconciliation with Salmerón, but this fell through, perhaps because, as Layard suggested, the two men were rivals for the first Presidency of the Republic, but Salmerón now believed that only specifically Federal policies could prevent the return to power of anti-Federal parties. Salmerón demanded a complete reversal of Castelar's policy; a reorganization of the Ministry so as to include the Centre and the dismissal of the royalist generals. Although the ministers concerned were willing to resign, Castelar thought they should all stand together. But underneath he was in a hopeless state of indecision as Layard described on the 27th. 'Castelar is unable to make up his mind between the Federals and the Conservatives. When he came here he cried like a child.'[1] With the *Cortes* in recess and many Federal papers suppressed it was impossible to gauge the party's opinion accurately, but he eventually decided to risk the possibility of a coup by Pavía in the belief that, in the divided state of republican opinion he would be able to rally the waverers with the magic of his rhetoric. But even taking into account the inability of Pi and Salmerón to agree, the chances of doing this with Cartagena still resisting were remote.

[1] B.M. Add. MS. 39124, 27 Dec. 1873, Layard to Granville.

Meanwhile meetings were held by the opposition parties, but no firm agreement had been reached. Serrano agreed to support Castelar if he would declare against federalism. Martos was in touch with Serrano staking a claim to direct a government under the nominal presidency of Serrano, but he was an embarrassment as the artillery officers did not trust him. After Pavía had failed to convince Castelar on the 24th, he consulted the commanders of the Armies of the North, Centre, and Catalonia to sound them on their support for a coup should Castelar fail to obtain a vote of confidence, and in another fruitless interview with Castelar on 1 January warned him that the Army would break up if the Government were defeated. However, there was little unanimity of plan as distrust between Radicals and Conservatives precluded any definite agreement being reached and the artillery officers refused to take part in any coup which would put Martos into power. It was only after Sagasta had reassured Pavía on 1 January that a coup would have the support of both parties that he persisted with his plan. His object was to anticipate any attempt at an Intransigent come-back either in the *Cortes*, should Castelar fail to get his vote of confidence, or by a coup in the capital. If Castelar were defeated, Pavía planned to overturn the *Cortes* and to set up a national government of conciliation to include all elements of opinion except the extreme Federals.[1]

After Castelar had defended his policy in the opening session of the *Cortes* on the 2nd, a vote of confidence was taken in the early hours of the 3rd, but the old Castelarian magic had lost its spell and the combined votes of the Left and Centre defeated the Government by 120 votes to 100. Even this vital issue had failed to stir little more than half the deputies to attend. On his resignation, the Centre and Left were about to elect Palanca the new President of the Executive Power, a compromise as neither Salmerón nor Pi enjoyed the confidence of both, when Pavía struck, and, marching troops into the *Cortes*, drove out the deputies. Helpless in face of armed aggression inside the *Cortes* building, the Federals were equally helpless outside in the city where their militia, numbering some 6,000 men, allowed itself to be meekly

[1] F.O. 72/1365, no. 14, 4 Jan. 1874, confidential, Layard to Granville.

dissolved. Only in Zaragoza and Barcelona and a few Catalan towns unaffected by cantonalism and where Federals were still dominant was there any flicker of resistance.[1] The coup dissipated all hopes of a negotiated settlement for the Cartagena Cantonalists and on 10 January Fort Atalaya, key to the land defences, was betrayed to López Domínguez. Three days later government troops entered the town. Although the Republic lingered on in name until the coup of Martínez Campos on 28 December it was a Unitarian Republic dominated by monarchists—'Spanish Mac-Mahonism' in Cánovas's depreciatory phrase. The Duke's Republic had succeeded the Republic of the Intellectuals.

After the *Cortes* had been cleared of protesting deputies in the early hours of 3 January, Pavía called a meeting of Radicals, Conservatives, Alphonsists, and García Ruiz, the one genuine Unitarian Republican, for the purpose of selecting a national government of conciliation under the presidency of Serrano, but Castelar's refusal on that same morning to accept the offer of a ministry signified a complete break in continuity, and the refusal of Cánovas to commit the Alphonsists to participation in the Government meant that, instead of being 'National' as Pavía had proposed, it would merely be an alliance of Conservatives, Radicals, and one Unitarian Republican.[2] The new Ministry reflected an alliance of political parties which had lost their significance—Serrano and Topete representing the old Unionists, Sagasta (who, by siding with Cánovas in favour of a provisional neutral government, showed his independence of Serrano) and Balaguer from the old Progressives, Echegaray, Mosquera, and Martos from the old Democrats, and finally García Ruiz, the lonely Unitarian Republican. The 3rd of January was the moment for which he had waited and worked for fourteen years, but although the new Government's manifesto of 8 January reflected his ideas and although he was given the important Ministry of the Interior, he was of little consequence as he had influence with neither party nor a following in the country; like Pi, he had to pay the price for

---

[1] Vera, op. cit. ii. 876–9; Rispa y Perpiña, op. cit., pp. 253–7.

[2] For 1874 see A. Houghton, *Les Origines de la restauration des Bourbons en Espagne*, Paris, 1890; Fernández Almagro, *Cánovas*, and his *Historia política de la España contemporánea*.

political consistency. His failure to ingratiate himself with Sal-merón, who refused his offer to sit on a parliamentary committee, emphasized his isolation from the Federals. Even his attempt to give expression to his hatred of federalism by trying to exile Pi and others was frustrated by the rest of the Government and he had to be content with exiling to the Marianas the unknown Cantonalists of Cartagena. In fact, his position as Minister of the Interior had been merely a compromise solution to by-pass the rivalry of Martos and Sagasta for the post.

The personal rivalry between these two men constituted the main danger to the stability of the new régime. Already before the end of January, Pavía was beginning to realize that his coup, made, as he assured Layard, 'in the interests of the country and not in those of a political party', had only served to bring out the latent rivalry between the two groups. There was inevitably the eternal quarrel over the distribution of offices for the vacant civil governorships and for replacements in the *Ayuntamientos*, and the traditional Radical distrust of Sagasta was a continual irritant. But these differences, important in preventing unanimous action within the Government, were insignificant beside army opinion, the cardinal factor in Serrano's Republic of 1874, as in that of its predecessor. After Castelar's reorganization of the Army, the officers were once again becoming a coherent political force. The fall of Cartagena had brought the new Government badly needed prestige, but the use made of its strengthened position in closing down Alphonsist clubs alienated officers, among them Martínez Campos, who resigned from the command of the Army of Cata-lonia on 23 January. Furthermore, the generals distrusted the Radicals—they could hardly forget that it was they who had abolished the artillery corps and had acquiesced in the anti-military policies of February and March 1873. When Pavía called for conciliation he was tacitly admitting the Radicals' lack of influence in the Army. But in the struggle against the Carlists, Serrano, like Castelar, was forced to appoint officers for their military efficiency and not for their political opinions. Such, for example, was the appointment of Concha to the command of the Army of the North. This reliance on royalist generals had political repercussions

in May when Radical agitation forced Serrano to remodel the
Ministry so as to exclude them altogether. When Zorrilla returned
to Spain in August with a profession of republican faith their
alienation from Serrano's régime was complete. Serrano, however,
was in no position to dispense with Radical support, for since his
break with Isabella in the previous July his own influence in the
Army had seriously diminished.

If Layard's information was correct it seems that even as late
as November Serrano might have responded to renewed ap-
proaches from Isabella and become the Alphonsist leader, but
neither his 'dignity nor his honour' would permit him to go over
to Alphonso.[1] But by this time, with his political survival at stake,
he was scarcely in a position to put his honour first. Although he
might have overestimated the divisions and rivalries between the
civil and military supporters of Alphonso and between reactionaries
like the Marqués de Molins and Liberals like Cánovas, it could only
be a matter of time before impatient Alphonsist generals—the
fierce reactionary ex-Governor of Cuba Valmaseda, Jovellar, the
young ambitious Martínez Campos, and political opportunists
like Primo de Rivera—joined forces in overthrowing a Government which was too unpopular to risk an appeal to the country
and which had broken with its only allies. When Serrano, after
long vacillation, at last left for the Carlist front on 9 December
the opening had been made for which the generals had waited.
At the same time as Primo de Rivera at Madrid was assuring
the Government of Martínez Campos's loyalty to the régime,
the latter was travelling to Sagunto near Valencia, where, on
29 December, he pronounced for Alphonso with a brigade of
infantry. Primo, at Madrid, seconded the movement. The fate of
the Republic rested with Serrano, but, hesitant to the end, he was
unwilling to appeal to force, doubting his own following in the
Army. The militia had been disbanded and the Federals could not
be expected to defend a régime which had persecuted them. When
the Republic collapsed on the night of 30 December and when,

---

[1] B.M. Add. MS. 39124, 7 Oct. 1874, Layard to Derby, where he reports that the banker
Salamanca's niece had been deputed by Isabella to offer Serrano the leadership of the
Alphonsists. See also 25 Nov. where he reports that Isabella was even proposing the
marriage of Alphonso to Serrano's daughter!

the next day, Cánovas announced the first Ministry of a restored Bourbon Monarchy, the six-year revolutionary period came to an end. The Restoration, like the expulsion of Isabella and in spite of Cánovas's efforts, had been engineered by generals. It was now his turn to curb the Army's power.

II

Conclusion

AFTER Pavía's coup republicanism ceased to be an effective political force for more than two generations. Rumours of a republican revival in April 1874 and January 1875 could be discounted by the Government in view of the mutual recriminations and divisions of the Federal leaders and the apathy or exile of their supporters. Salmerón's break with Castelar, Castelar's virtual repudiation of his past in a speech at Granada on 26 May in which he also declared his benevolence towards Serrano's régime, Pi's disagreements with Salmerón and Figueras in a policy meeting in the latter's house early in 1874, and, finally, the reappearance of Zorrilla with a profession of republicanism in August 1874 set the tone for the remaining years of the century. In spite of attempted reconciliations, republican divisions tended to increase rather than diminish.[1] As a republican wit put it: 'the republican party breakfasted with Ruiz Zorrilla, lunched with Figueras and Pi, had afternoon tea with Salmerón and dined with Castelar'.

Pi led the rump of the old Federal party who continued to cling to the doctrine of the past. The Federals could still be assured of a following among the provincial professional and lower-middle class although in the 1880's the emergence of specifically Catalan parties began to draw off some of their supporters, at the same time as the reviving Anarchist movement and the new Socialist party drained off potential working-class support. Salmerón and Figueras remained nominal Federals although firmly anti-pactist. Salmerón graduated from an abstract theorist to an intriguer and a political realist who became a leading figure in the formation of the *Solidaridad catalana* in the early years of the twentieth century, using it to try and get rid of Lerroux and Sol y Ortega, who repre-

[1] Rodríguez-Solís, op. cit. ii. 741 et seq.; Vera, op. cit., pp. 947 et seq.

sented the Zorrillian legacy in republicanism which he had always
hated.[1] Castelar was the most isolated of the republican leaders
after the Restoration, refusing to associate with any group with
either federalist or socialistic tendencies and condemning the very
utopianism he had been instrumental in encouraging.[2] He led the
small group of Possibilists, but his benevolence to the Restored
Monarchy was regarded as a betrayal, and in Pi's case the bitterness
between the two men only ended with Castelar's death in 1899.
Finally, and in many ways the most significant of the republican
factions, were the new Progressive Republicans consisting of ex-
Progressives and ex-Radicals led by Zorrilla. Their programme
was the 1869 Constitution under a republican form of government. For the first time there was a body of republicans led by
a professional politician and entirely divorced from the control
of intellectual theorists. Zorrilla's persistent conspiratorial activity
during the 1870's and 1880's, which forced him to spend many
years in exile, recall to mind Prim's activities of the 1860's rather
than those of other republican leaders. Zorrilla's political realism
enabled him to see that Federal failure had been mainly due to
their alienation of the Army, hence his efforts were directed towards
trying to stage a republican comeback by working on officer discontent, which, with the system of political promotion, was still
a grievance. The foundation of the *Asociación republicano militar*
in 1883, with its strength among the lower officers, and the re-
publican-inspired *pronunciamientos* between 1883 and 1886, was
evidence of this new phenomenon of military republicanism.[3]

Zorrilla and Salmerón often worked in close co-operation, but
they never succeeded in fusing their two parties. In 1893, largely
on Salmerón's initiative, the three main republican groups met to
create the *Unión republicana*, but this was merely a nominal union
for electoral purposes in which each party retained its individual
identity. The tendency of Republicans to split rather than coalesce
was exemplified two years later when Zorrilla died and his party

---

[1] Pabón, *Cambó*, pp. 270–1.
[2] Letter of Castelar to Zorrilla, 25 Aug. 1876, in Chaix, op. cit., pp. 104–5. For Castelar's
views during the Restoration see *Correspondencia de Emilio Castelar, 1868–98*, Madrid, 1908,
and García Escudero, *De Cánovas a la República*, Madrid, 1951, ch. i.
[3] Chaix, op. cit., pp. 134 et seq.

divided into a right-wing under Sol y Ortega and a left-wing under Lerroux.[1] This was the beginning of Lerroux's tumultuous political career. His rise under the aegis of Zorrilla's opportunism marks the release of republicanism from the artificial web of federal theory in which it had become ensnared after 1868. Although Lerroux called himself a Federal at the beginning of his career his voluble rabble-raising hastened the process begun by Zorrilla by which republicanism became a movement of professional opportunist politicians, divorced from ideological considerations. The First Republic had exposed the weakness of intellectuals in politics. By 1898 most intellectuals regarded politics with scepticism and, unlike those of 1868, they did not see political action, let alone republicanism, as a channel through which the country might be regenerated. Political developments, particularly the foundation of a Socialist party in 1879, the growing hold of Anarchism on large sections of the working class in Barcelona and in Andalusia, and the emergence of Catalan nationalism further whittled away potential republican support and exposed the inability of republican politicians to come to terms with changing conditions. It was only in the 1920's when academic freedom was threatened, as in the 1860's, that intellectuals returned to the political arena fanning the embers of a smouldering republican tradition. Under the Second Republic this tradition with its anticlericalism, antimilitarism, and support for regional autonomy was revived. In the Republican *Cortes* there was even a Federal party with seventeen deputies, among whom sat Pi y Arsuaga, Pi's son, providing a tenuous link with its ill-fated predecessor.

What was the significance of the nineteenth-century Federal movement and what position must be assigned to Pi y Margall in modern Spanish history? He was responsible for making nineteenth-century Spanish republicanism synonomous with federalism; by his theorizing he gave coherence to the popular desire for greater independence from centralized government, giving doctrinal form to a tendency which had been a marked feature of Spanish life since the collapse of the centralized State during the War of Independence. Yet what success was achieved by the

[1] Pabón, op. cit., pp. 219 et seq.

movement which he initiated was not due solely to the intellectual force of his arguments or the moral fervour of a handful of enthusiasts working under his inspiration. His idea found an echo because it helped to canalize the frustrated hopes and ambitions of the hitherto politically inarticulate. Its main popularity undoubtedly came from its frontal assault on the power of the Army, which had assumed such proportions that an attack on it and on the centralized State had become synonomous. It was in their anti-*quinta* campaigns and in their assault on high taxation embodied in a burdensome system of indirect taxes which enabled the Federals to claim they were a mass movement.

One of the Federal movement's main features and one of its weaknesses was that it appealed to two conflicting impulses—on one side that of isolated communities which resented the disturbance of a traditional way of life by the agents of a centralized power, exemplified most vividly in the popular reaction to the sale of the common lands during the 1850's, and on the other that of industrial and commercial interests which resented the domination of landowners in government and the sacrifice of economic interests in order to pay the patronage bills for a handful of political adventurers at Madrid. But federalism succeeded in canalizing neither of these impulses—the industrialists and merchants were frightened off by the social implications of federal anarchy and the Federals were at first uninterested, and later unable to mobilize rural discontent.

The Federals' posturing as a regenerating movement was a symptom of their doctrinaire origin. Claiming to be a Spanish solution to a Spanish problem, it was as imitative, in theoretical terms, as the liberal ideologies imported from France which it was trying to replace. The ambivalent attitude of the Federal revolutionaries towards the French republicans of the 1790's— wanting to emulate their successes but to avoid their mistakes— reveals the difficulties of making a revolution without having any clear-cut precedents. There was truth, too, in Valera's assertion that[1] 'without Proudhon and Pi's boundless enthusiasm for him no one would ever have thought in Spain of federal republicanism'.

[1] Quoted in Juretschke, op. cit., p. 58.

In the 1850's and 1860's a reading of Proudhon had seemed to substantiate Pi's earlier ideas and yet, suitable though Proudhon's ideas may have been under French conditions, where an independent peasantry and small-scale co-operative enterprises might constitute a barrier to the expansion of monopoly capitalism, they were at that time unsuited to Spanish conditions, where the agrarian revolution had still to be made. In the few rural areas touched by the Federals the labourers were illiterate, desperate men who equated federalism with the break-up of the centralized State from which they expected a redistribution of land. Where there was already a prosperous satisfied peasantry, as in the Basque Provinces and Navarre, there was also an ideology to hand in Carlism. 'In the Basque Provinces', wrote *La Igualdad* hopefully,[1] 'there are only two political forces, Carlism and Federalism.' But the feeble record there of the Federals in elections showed that the Federals had nothing to teach the Carlists. The Carlists and not the Federals could tap the reserve of Spanish tradition in opposition to the centralizing policies of the Liberals. Although Pi recognized the vital importance of the agrarian problem he was unable to interest the party in it until it was too late.

In fact, the Federal movement began and ended as an urban movement, centring on the struggle for the control of local government and the patronage dependent on it. It also remained a minority movement, clearly shown after the dogma of universal suffrage had been discredited in 1869. This republican idea had already been laid low in France in 1849 when a monarchist majority had been returned in the elections. In Spain universal suffrage produced a similar result—not, as in France, because a conservative independent peasantry, fearing the political radicalism of the capital, equated their interests with a monarchy, but because the power of the *caciques* over a depressed rural population remained unbroken. Without breaking the power of the landlords the Federals would remain a minority and like Ledru-Rollin in 1849 they could only cover their confusion by appeals to armed force—a sign not of their strength but of their weakness. Even though the myth of universal suffrage was exposed in 1869, the

[1] *La Igualdad*, 8 Aug. 1872.

Federals were reluctant to try and base their support on sectional interests. They claimed (like the Falangists later with whom they have some superficial resemblance) to be a national regenerating movement and not a party representing 'sordid' personal interests.[1] Hence their vague professions of faith instead of specific policies and their deliberate refusal to commit themselves too deeply on any issue save that of political federalism and army reduction for fear of alienating potential supporters. But the discontents of the Right tended to be drawn to the romanticized Carlist utopia of the past and those of the Left to the International's utopia of the future, leaving the Federals as the party of the middle- and lower-middle-class discontents; those people whose main resentment was against a political system which denied them the fruits of office because they had no influence at Madrid. Although attacking the evils of *empleocracia* the Federals were indirectly encouraging it. Claiming to cure the disease of Spanish society, they were caught in the paradox that the dominant motive of their active supporters was the prospect of attaining office under a Federal system where gifts would be in the hands of numberless small centres of government rather than concentrated in the capital. So far from destroying *empleocracia* federalism held the bright promise of perpetuating and extending it.

Federal republicanism, therefore, did not break with the past but developed within the orbit of traditional Spanish politics. But because it lacked any firm basis in a social class, the reformers were unable to break the monotonous pattern and were condemned to the sterility of factional conflict and personal rivalries. As Engels observed at the time, Pi was the only one of the Republican leaders who recognized the need for basing the Republic on the support of the workers, but Engels argued from the experience of industrialized countries and what appeared a clear-cut issue to

[1] Both were minority movements led by idealists and followed by unscrupulous adventurers. Both found support in universities, appealing to youthful idealism reacting against political clichés. Both thrived on the frustrations and resentments of the lower-middle class and small professional man. Both thought in terms of class harmony, anti-clericalism, Iberian union, the return of Gibraltar, and saw themselves in the vanguard of a new movement of international as well as national regeneration. Both shared a tradition of direct action. Obviously such parallels should not be pressed too far, but the Federal movement was not only a precursor of twentieth-century republicanism.

him was complicated by the backwardness and isolation of Spanish society. Political action in terms of an area wider than the limits of family or kinship relationships is a comparatively sophisticated concept and presupposes a different sort of political maturity than could be found among Spanish workers at that time. It is important to remember that it was only the Carlists, working within a scale of traditional values, not against them, who became the only effective mass movement in nineteenth-century Spain. Paradoxically, too, the granting of reforms urged by Federals worked against them. Universal suffrage lowered the quality of their support and made it easier to tilt at abuses which gained them a few cheap votes rather than to work out the deeper implications of their theories. Liberty of the press after 1868 became another barrier. The Federals' press now had to provide for a proletariat of needy journalists who were forced to perpetuate sterile disputes in order to justify the continued existence of their papers. The quality of radical journalism was never higher than during the period when Nocedal's press laws were operative in the 1860's.

Yet even though its political history was one of failure the Federal movement was something more than the mere squabble for office and the clash of personal rivalries. Federalism was the first political movement in Spain to try and generalize politics, to educate public opinion, and to mobilize it to overthrow a political system which had encouraged the abuse of power. Their aim was to turn the *pronunciamiento* of 1868 into a genuine revolution. To do this meant a frontal assault on the Army. That this was political suicide should not obscure its significance. Their policy towards the Army was, in fact, too successful; they succeeded in sapping its power by sowing distrust between officers and men, but the collapse of the Army came too late—at a time when the Federals themselves needed it to defend the Republic from the attacks of counter-revolutionaries. They had lost the confidence of the officers without gaining that of the men. The men who might have become Federal revolutionaries only did so at Cartagena; elsewhere they became a disorganized rabble anxious only for loot and drink before being demobilized and returning to more conventional society. How far the Federals could have won them over by the promise of substantial economic and social reform is a moot point. The fact that they never tried to do so was a comment on the unreality of their policy. When, during the cantonalist revolt, the Government was forced to rely on Civil Guards and *carabineros* to suppress the Andalusian cantons, the wheel had turned full circle, for now the Republic was equated with the protectors of the *caciques* and the agents of unpopular taxes, those officials of centralized power which it had been the purpose of federalism to destroy. Estévanez's abolition of the *cuerpos francos* followed by Castelar's reorganization of the Army in September 1873 was recognition that Federal policy towards it had failed. Castelar's own scruples and the Army's distrust of Federal intentions precluded any firm alliance between the two forces. But although republican hostility towards the Army was to be modified later, anti-militarism remained an integral part of the Spanish republican tradition.

The Federals were also the first party to make a frontal assault on the privileged position of the Church by demanding separation of Church and State. Although largely a formulation of dogmatic rationalists and commanding little support in the country, it was a reaction as much against the Liberals' hypocritical use of the Church as against the Church itself. Divesting the Church of its landed property and attempting to control its movable wealth, the Liberals were unwilling to push their anticlericalism to its logical conclusion by separating Church and State and continued, in the graphic words of *La Igualdad*, to see 'God as a member of the Civil Guard protecting the sanctity of property'.[1] Whatever the wisdom or otherwise of attacking the Church and catholicism in a traditional and culturally atavistic society, the Federals were the first to formulate that particular rationalist brand of anti-clericalism which was to become another thread in the republican tradition.

Once the Federals were in power, civil war and their own divisions prevented an extensive programme of reforms, but in their decrees abolishing nobility, making the judiciary independent, abolishing slavery in Puerto Rico, in their proposed factory

[1] *La Igualdad*, 9 Apr. 1873.

legislation, and in their attempts to make women play a constructive part in political activity, they embodied progressive attitudes
which became stock features of later Spanish republicanism.

In addition to the formulation of a republican tradition the
Federal movement was important for its influence on two other
movements which played a central part in subsequent Spanish
politics—Catalan political regionalism and Anarchism. Although
Catalanism dates from the 1830's it was the 1868 Revolution which
enabled it to find an effective political expression among the strong
and comparatively homogeneous Catalan Federals. Almirall,
whose book *Lo Catalanisme* was the most important justification
of Catalan particularism, had been the leader of the Barcelona
Federals, but from 1869 he was determined not to play a subor-
dinate role to Madrid.[1] Symbolic of his independence was his
refusal to become a deputy until 1873 and hence inevitably, so he
argued, to become like Pi, a Madrid politician. In March 1873 he
had moved with his paper, *El Estado catalán*, to Madrid, but, irritated
by Pi's lack of sympathy with Catalan aspirations and despairing
of republican politics when Figueras fled, he returned disillusioned
to Barcelona. Still nominally a Federal, he began to build up a
purely Catalan movement, founding in 1879 the *Diari català*,
convening the *Congreso catalanista* in 1880, and setting up the
Centre català in 1882, which marked his final break away from
the Federals and foreshadowed the setting up of a Catalan party
uncompromised by links with any Madrid group. The *Bases
de Manresa* of 1892, supported by both Right- and Left-wing
Catalan parties, marked a culminating point in the movement of
Catalan political particularism. The energies of many Catalan
intellectuals, following Almirall's lead, were now canalized into
justifying Catalan nationalism. The 'Generation of 1898' revealed
the dichotomy between those intellectuals concerned with 'Spanish'
problems and rejecting political solutions and the Catalans taking
an active part in political organizations aiming at autonomy.

Pi, however, refused to see any basic difference between the
aims of the Federals and the Catalanists and although he came to

---

[1] *Lo Catalanisme*, Barcelona, 1886. See also his *Obras completas*, Barcelona, 1902, 2 vols.
A. Plana, *Les Idées politiques d'en Valentí Almirall*, Barcelona, 1905; Pabón, op. cit.,
pp. 119 et seq.

sympathize with Catalan regionalism—a sympathy which earned him the high honour of being President of the *Jochs Florals* in 1901 (for which he had to learn Catalan for his address)—he never really appreciated the emotional driving force behind it.[1] As Rovira i Virgili, a leading Catalan propagandist, put it:[2]

> Pi y Margall was a Federal. Almirall a Catalanist. In the first there was more dogma, more doctrinal truth. In the second, more life, more real truth.

Marti i Julia, a Catalan Federal pointed out this discrepancy to Pi in 1881, but his attitude was paternalistic: 'You are very young. . . . with age you will see reality better, you will leave these exaggerations and will become good Federals.' But in the 1880's he was the patriarch who found that his acolytes were turning to new gods. Catalanism was a nationalist phenomenon and the main springs of nationalism had little place in Pi's severely rationalist approach to political activity. The farthest he was willing to go in his credo, *Las Nacionalidades*, was to stress the historical factors which made federalism so applicable to Spanish conditions, but this historical emphasis was used merely to give added conviction to arguments which had already been developed.

Federalism presupposed giving equal weight to each of the federal units, but the greater wealth, political maturity, and national consciousness of the Catalans turned their politics into a force which paid little heed to the other regions in Pi's scheme. There was a grain of truth in Almirall's assertion that federalism had been a retrograde step for Catalan regionalism but, on the other hand, it was through the Federal party that Catalans experienced the exercise of political power unhampered by control from Madrid.

Federal ideas may be traced as well in the development of

---

[1] Pi i Margall, *Articles, proleg den Gabriel Alomar*, Barcelona, 1908, pp. 62–63, 68–69, 92–93. Cf. Trinchant y Fornés, *Pi y Margall ante el regionalismo, el federalismo y la unidad de la patria*, Madrid, 1900.

[2] Rovira i Virgili, *La Questio de Catalunya*, Barcelona, 1913, p. vii. Rovira was a prominent example of the new theorist of Catalan nationalism. Admiring Pi's qualities, he claimed to be a 'true Catalan'. The excessive abstraction of Pi's thought he explained by the fact that Pi had cut himself off from his real roots in Catalonia. See also Rovira's articles in the *Revista de Catalunya*, 1926–34.

Spanish Anarchism. The myth of spontaneous revolution, reliance on mass enthusiasm, a moralism which rails against the corruption of the capital foreshadows later anarchist mentality. The myths of federal revolutionaries were those of anarchist enthusiasts—the main contrast being in the social compositions of the two movements with the Anarchist emphasizing economic rather than political federation. Both showed instinctive distrust of centralized control and continually struggled to keep the initiative in local federations. On a less exalted plane a comparison between the two reveals the shared dilemma of ardent visionaries who find that the weakness of their movement compels them to resort to the tactics and methods of the underworld. The elusive figure of Salvochea, a Spanish Blanqui, the leader of the 1868 Cádiz rising and the 1873 canton, who spent twelve years in prison, and was a legendary figure among Andalusian Anarchists, provides a link between the Federal visionaries of 1868 and the utopian Anarchist of 1900. But the most significant link between federalism and anarchism is to be found in the ideas and personality of Pi himself. When he died in 1901 he was described in the leading anarchist review as 'the master of all Anarchists who are over forty'.[1] In explaining this we come to the real significance of Pi's career, his anticipation of anarchist ideas and the myth of his character.

In 1900 the anarchist writer Urales published an interview with Pi in which the latter had expressed his ignorance of anarchist ideas but told how he was giving the subject serious thought.[2] Yet later in the 1930's *La Reacción y la Revolución* was frequently reprinted by the anarchist press. Pi was hailed as their forerunner and coupled with Cervantes as the two great men produced by Spain.[3] This fulsome praise was not due solely to Pi's anticipation of later anarchism in the idea of the autonomy of the individual but also to the fascination of his character. It was this as much as, if not more than, his ideas which compelled their admiration. Estévanez, who had cause to be grateful to him, wrote of him:[4] 'For politicians who struggle for power, for the crowd who only appreciates material results, Pi was a failure. For those who admire

[1] *La Revista blanca*, 7 Dec. 1901.   [2] Ibid., 10 Nov. 1900.
[3] *La Reacción y la Revolución*, p. 8.   [4] Quoted in Albornoz, op. cit., p. 86.

all the grandeur of moral triumphs, Pi y Margall was the conqueror of the nineteenth century.' It was a sentiment already stressed by the anarchist writer of his obituary:[1] '. . . integrity in a corrupting society has a value which only those can appreciate who have wanted and succeeded in maintaining their public and private life untarnished'. When Rivero's intemperance was recalled or when it was remembered that in 1874 members of the Government had attended the funeral of Sagasta's mistress whose husband was at the Carlist front, the austerity of Pi's own private life took on an almost mythical significance.

The contrast between Pi's influence during his years of power and later is curious and yet explicable. During his active political career up to 1873 he was the grey eminence of Federal Republicanism. His name rarely appears in the press or in pamphlets. Foreign observers, including Layard, who are continually mentioning Castelar, scarcely ever mention his name. Although he was the brain and the power behind the movement he was a mystery even to his own followers, but his personal qualities were appreciated even at this time: 'In an age when modesty is the rarest gift', wrote a non-Federal Valencian paper in 1873,[2] 'and where din and ostentation, self-praise and cunning are the necessary conditions of success—Pi is the contrast, with the probity of a Cato and his almost exaggerated modesty.' Cañamaque, writing in the late 1870's, could echo this judgement although still puzzled by his aloofness:[1] 'He is an enigma, a mystery, a tremendous unresolved X. But he has been, and will always be, one of the most worthy, most modest, purest characters of Spain.'

Pi was enigmatic because he chose the reality rather than the trappings of power. During the Republic by far the greatest part of his time was spent in the Ministry of the Interior and not in lobby intrigues or on the floor of the *Cortes*. He could dispense with popularity because of his ability to dominate with the force of his personality the few able men who were the hard core of the Federal leadership.

[1] *La Revista blanca*, 12 Dec. 1901. Cf. Roci Roca, *Pi, esbós biografic*, Barcelona, 1923, pp. 74 et seq.
[2] *El Mercantil valenciano*, 22 Feb. 1873.
[3] F. Cañamaque, *Los Oradores de 1869*, Madrid, 1879, pp. 171–3.

All this was changed in the 1880's and 1890's. The revolutionary impetus of the immediate post-1868 period had enabled him to work behind the scenes guiding the enthusiasm generated by the federal ideal. Political failure had tarnished this and had broken the uneasy co-operation which only his will had prevented from breaking up earlier. From the late 1870's Pi was only the leader of a minority faction, so for the first time he began to do what Castelar had been doing since the 1860's—touring the country making political speeches and bidding for support against the other republican factions. It was only in the Federal revival of the 1880's that he became more than a name to the Federals in the provinces.[1] Previously he had been only the man who had prevented the immediate declaration of the Federal Republic, but helped by the eulogistic biography of Vera y González and by the success of his own tours the myth began to crystallize. Where some, like Castelar, had changed their political colours, and others, like Zorrilla, had become Republicans for opportunistic reasons, Pi became the symbol of adherence to rigid principle, admired for his unswerving loyalty to an idea. Rigidity and lack of flexibility, inability to adapt theory to changing conditions, all of which could be counted as political vices, now became virtues.

The bitter experience of political failure did not lead him to modify his theory. There is no real development in Pi's thought, only a change in emphasis necessitated by altering political circumstances. Thus the economic arguments of the 1860's for widening the social base of the Democrats were quietly shelved and increasing prominence was given to the purely political aspect of federalism. After 1873 early arguments were not abandoned; they were merely bolstered by additional historical arguments. It is true that disillusion is the dominant note of his apologia of 1874, but disillusion with his colleagues and with his own shortcomings—the theory on which his policies had been based could not be wrong. Although the Left had attacked him as savagely as the Right, it was significant that he should seek to defend himself from the attacks

---

[1] V. Suárez Casañ, *Apuntes para la historia del renacimiento federal en España. Viaje de Francisco Pi y Margall a Valencia*, Madrid, 1883. In 1881, just before Almirall broke with Pi, the two men made a propaganda tour of Catalonia.

of the former and not from those of the latter. If he criticized himself it was because he did not trust the people enough, not that he trusted them too much. Here were the ingredients of the myth which helped to establish him in the Anarchist hagiography: devotion to an ideal, loyalty to an idea put above personal considerations, and implicit trust in the wisdom of the 'people'.

During the last twelve years of his life the Pi myth began to crystallize as, increasingly isolated by the developments of new parties representing sectional interests, he waged a lone campaign on behalf of unpopular causes. Foremost was his campaign in his own paper *El Nuevo Régimen*, from its foundation in 1891, on behalf of Cuban independence and his condemnation of Spanish colonial policy. This required considerable courage at a time when the violently jingoistic Spanish press universally condemned any talk of dismembering Spain's remaining colonial possessions. During the war fever of 1898 his plea for sanity was drowned in the hysterical demands of frustrated national feeling for war with the United States. In Cuba, nevertheless, his name is still remembered, streets are named after him and articles continue to be written about him. At home, Pi's attempts to put the Anarchist outrages of the closing years of the century into proper perspective and to protest against the barbarities of the police and arbitrary imprisonment were construed as implying approval of violence and terror, as earlier he had been accused of encouraging the excesses of Alcoy.

In the final analysis it is the figure of the austere, modest, disinterested thinker—such as Azorín described and admired—the incorruptible in a corrupt society, the fearless defender of lost causes, which struck the imagination of Federals and Anarchists alike. The man whose life had been devoted to ideas was remembered not for those ideas so much as for his personal qualities. This was what was admired by the Peruvian radical González Prada, an inspirer of the *Aprista* movement, what Cubans have recognized, and what can still be savoured in conversations with the diminished but persisting Federal *coreligionarios* who, despite years in the political wilderness, still cling to their vision of Pi y Margall, 'honest, sincere, a man of the people'.

APPENDIX

The Political Ideas of Pi y Margall

THE kernel of Pi's ideas are to be found in *La Reacción y la Revolución* (1854) and in *Las Nacionalidades* (1876). Whereas the first was little more than an expanded political pamphlet, deliberately polemical and having a practical end in view, the latter work was better arranged, more cogently argued, and uncluttered by superficial learning. Nevertheless, there are few new ideas in the latter work, which is mainly an amplification of views which had been expressed but not developed in 1854. Then, Pi had been trying to put forward a theory to combat the idea of the 'sovreignty of the people' by which power was distributed qualitatively and to show how the laws of historical development made revolution inevitable and continuous; in 1876 he is concerned to show how precedents for federal organization may be traced throughout Spanish history. If federalism failed in Spain, he implies, it was not because it was misconceived but because these precedents were not fully known or appreciated. Although in the latter work he still saw the aim of political organization as the safeguarding of individual liberty, the emphasis has moved to the *pueblo* and the *municipio* as the basic social and political unit. The highly individualist and anarchist position he adopted in 1854 was not developed and was only revived by the Anarchists seeking a justification for their own action in the last years of the century.

In *La Reacción y la Revolución* Pi had two main aims in view—to popularize the idea of historical progress obeying rigid laws and to establish the principle of the sovereignty of the individual as a justification for universal suffrage and as the starting-point for a Democrat political theory. Pi sees two main principles at work in society—Liberty and what he calls 'Social Fatality'. Humanity is opposed to Man, both being subject to different laws. When we talk of Progress, he writes, we refer to institutions or the progress of Humanity, or the human race.[1] The development of Humanity is subject to an historical law. This law he calls 'Social Fatality'. It has been explained in the Hegelian view of historical development. Fatality is the dramatic name Pi gives to Progress achieved through the working out of the Hegelian dialectic. He

[1] *La Reacción y la Revolución*, p. 21.

considered the views of the leading social thinkers from Vico onwards on Progress. Vico, though, admitted a limit to human progress; for him humanity was imprisoned within an inflexible circular development. Pi rejected this in favour of unlimited progress, a conception, he says, which he owed to Herder, whilst it is Hegel who has explained how this Progress is achieved.[1]

'Progress', however, does not occur in the same way in Man's development because his distinguishing feature is his liberty, which is derived from and rooted in his consciousness. Pi defines Liberty as the independence of the will from all external motive, the determination of our acts by the intelligence.[2] This liberty is absolute but for the limitations of our physical nature, the resistance of the sensible world, and the finite character of our intelligence. Intelligence is the distinguishing feature of human liberty, but as our intelligence is finite it is continually erring, mistaking the accidental for the absolute; thus anyone claiming that his belief is the Absolute Truth is mistaking the true nature of ideas.[3]

Once Pi has explained the Hegelian triad he thinks that the law of Progress has been sufficiently demonstrated. Once he accepts it, the corollary must be that only its uninterrupted fulfilment can put an end to our revolutions and miseries.[4] The main obstacle to its fulfilment is *nuestra libertad mal educada* and he therefore sees the problem as one of education—by means of a free press, free discussion, universal suffrage, liberty of association, all the things, in fact, for which he and the Democrats were agitating; but whereas the Democrats did not base this programme on any firm principle beyond a belief in the natural harmony of interests, Pi roots it in the necessity to recognize the existence of inexorable laws of historical development. Education must enlighten people on the nature of these laws, people must be shown the rational principle behind historical development and be made aware that revolution is a continuous process. 'Revolutions are the result of bad laws,' he comments, 'men all love order, only in desperation do we appeal to disorder.'[5] Bad laws, for their part, come from ignorance of the laws underlying historical development.

None of this was original; it was the stock political application of Hegelianism, but although at this stage Hegel dominated Pi's thinking, Pi thought that in Proudhon's theory of antinomies an explanation of Progress was also to be found.[6] This idea, however, is not developed

[1] Ibid., pp. 36–37.   [2] Ibid., p. 237.   [3] Ibid., pp. 25–29.
[4] Ibid., p. 46.   [5] Ibid., p. 290.   [6] Ibid., pp. 39–42.

and one wonders if in fact P recognized the basic difference between the two thinkers. Nevertheless, although he accepts Hegel's account of historical development he is reluctant to accept Hegel's sacrifice of the individual to the State. Where, therefore, Pi is willing to accept Hegelian explanations for the development of *hombre humanidad*, he is unwilling to accept the implications of Hegelianism for *hombre individuo*.[1] He anticipates Proudhon in his insistence on the need for federalism and the breaking down of power by decentralization in order to safeguard this freedom, but in 1854 as an Hegelian, he was so obsessed by the need to find a 'synthesis' that he developed a pantheism which he thought would reconcile the two contradictions of *hombre humanidad* and *hombre individuo*.[2] This pantheism served two purposes—it saved him from the implacable conclusions of the Hegelian dialectic and also exalted the inalienable sovereignty of the individual. 'God lives in me and I in God, we are almost confounded in the sea of existence.' His attempt to strike a synthesis is only important for the way it reveals his mode of thought at this time. This he claimed was 'scientific' and his violent attack on religion and on sentimentalist thinkers like Lamennais or Pierre Leroux and on many of his Democrat colleagues are based on their lack of scientific precision.[3] Yet is is difficult to see what was scientific either in his acceptance of the Hegelian metaphysic or in his profession of pantheism. It has been suggested that two important influences on Pi's book were Herbert Spencer and Stephen Pearl Andrews, but there is little reflection of either in Pi's mode of thought. Pi did not follow Spencer's close analogy with the physical sciences and although it might be argued that the phrase 'unity in variety' which was to recur frequently in later writings might bear an analogy with the biological sciences, it was, in fact, derived from Hegel.[4] Andrews, for his part, showed an acute preception of the value in the elucidation of social processes of the 'rigid methods of scientific induction from observed facts'[5] which is far removed from Pi's own use of a metaphysical system to provide the basis of a political ideology. For all its claims to be scientific, Pi's thought in 1854 was firmly rooted in a metaphysical tradition shared by other contemporaries who also regarded historicism as a science.

Pi also examined the nature of 'Reaction'—'that state of mind and

---

[1] *La Reacción y la Revolución*, pp. 228–30. [2] Ibid., ch. ix.
[3] Ibid., pp. 45, 176, 188. [4] Ibid., pp. 44, 231; cf. *Las Nacionalidades*, p. 87.
[5] S. P. Andrews, *The Science of Society*, New York, 1951, p. 17. The suggestion of the influence of Andrews and Spencer is made by Brenan, *Spanish Labyrinth*, p. 358.

Appendix

261

thought fundamentally opposed to Progress and Revolution'. Reaction in its widest sense was the slave of historical tradition, the arm of power, and the sword of Property, Monarchy, and the Church. These last two depended for their efficacy on a sense of mystery, their appeal and their sanction were based on hallowed associations stretching back into the beginning of recorded history. This, Pi considered, was nonsense and old-fashioned, for the predominating factor in the nineteenth century was doubt. Doubt was general, for faith could no longer withstand the examination of reason.[1] Mystery lies at the core of religion, but now there can be no mystery: Pi claims to have cross-examined many so-called believers and to have found nothing but scepticism and hypocrisy. This strong insistence on doubt cannot be understood unless the fanatical moral undercurrent of Pi's thought is appreciated. Doubt and hypocrisy must be the prevailing moods, he argues, in an age when Liberals, still nominally Catholic, have plundered the Church and when religion has been used as a pretext for going to war in the Crimea.[2] But scepticism need no longer be the refuge for the doubters for the relations between Man, God, Humanity, and the World can be explained by Philosophy, which he defined elsewhere as 'the science or the reasoned and systematic knowledge of what is, of the absolute'.[3] Doubt is the antithesis to Faith, Philosophy the synthesis. Religion must be demolished because religions are unscientific. Religions rarely, if ever, use the language of science. He made no distinction between a religious or a scientific truth, the only criterion for the truth of a belief is if it is scientific or not. Religions, he concludes 'are really no more than a starting point for the reason of man'.[4] Most of the ideas on religion merely repeated what he had already written in his condemned *Historia de la Pintura* of 1851.

But the main interest and importance of the work lies more in his attempts to define his concept of 'Revolution'. Five main points emerge from his argument.

The Revolution will be the embodiment of Justice.[5] But this idea, which was fundamental to Proudhon's concept of Revolution, is not developed. Proudhon had written in his *Idée générale de la Révolution* that 'a revolution is, in order of moral facts, an act of sovereign justice proceeding from the necessity of things which consequently carries its own justification and which it is a crime for statesmen to resist'.[6]

---

[1] *La Reacción y la Revolución*, pp. 78 et seq.   [2] Ibid., pp. 50–51.
[3] Ibid., p. 154; *Estudios sobre la Edad Media*, Madrid, 1872, p. 50.
[4] *Estudios sobre la Edad Media*, p. 55.   [5] Ibid., p. 175.   [6] A. Berthold ed., p. 123.

But it was not until 1858 and his *De la Justice* that Proudhon's idea was more fully developed.

The Revolution will mean the destruction of power. 'Power', he wrote, 'like religion and property does not stem from anyone's will, it exists by itself and it works constantly, obeying the fatal conditions of its own life.'[1] He sees power as a kind of disembodied will which, he asserts, can only be limited and finally destroyed by extreme decentralization, leaving to the central power no more than the attributes of attending to matters of 'general interest'. This destruction of power, he insists, must be the dogma of the Democrat party.

The Revolution will give expression to 'unity in variety', the 'law of the world'. The Revolution wants unity but it rejects the absurd unity of the centralized State. Pi therefore argues for a federal republic, pointing out the contradictions in the idea of a centralized republic by examining the failures of French republicanism. Federalism will give greater spontaneity to municipal life, destroy dynasticism which he still thinks is a major cause of war, and will lead to the achievement of Iberian Union and will remove Cuba's discontents.[2]

The Revolution will embody the idea of contract. This will replace authority as the basis of the new society. As man is sovereign and as sovereignty is, by his definition, absolute and indivisible, man is the fount of all law and any power which seeks to impose itself in defiance of the individual is a negation of sovereignty.[3] As man has to live in society and as his sovereignty cannot be alienated the only method for two sovereigns to unite is by mutual contract. 'Society is or is not a society by virtue of my consent.'[4] This consent must be personal. Like Proudhon in *Du principe fédératif*, Pi shows unqualified hostility to legal fictions.

The Revolution will be social as well as political.[5] As a result of the 'contract', economic forces would be harmonized: how this will happen is not explained as a discussion on it was postponed to the third part of the book, which was not allowed to be published. With this economic harmony, social problems would be resolved, but there would be no immediate revolution for the 'Revolution' was essentially evolutionary. In one place, where he refers to his preference for federalism by social categories rather than by provinces, there is a hint of later Anarchist federalism, but like so many other points it is left undeveloped.[6]

The second part of the book is less interesting from the standpoint

---

[1] *La Reacción*, p. 181. [2] Ibid., pp. 206–8, 216 et seq. [3] Ibid., pp. 177–8.
[4] Ibid., p. 180. [5] Ibid., p. 213. [6] Ibid., p. 181.

of Pi's thought, as it is devoted to specific criticisms of contemporary administration. Here he outlined sweeping reforms, the abolition of civil and military governors, the reconstitutions of the old historic provinces. He attacked Rome and the position of the Church, arguing that there could be no compromise between Rome and the Revolution. He criticized Spanish colonial policy, deplored the decline of commerce, and called for a drastic overhaul of the Army.[1] But because he never published the third part of the book many of his economic ideas remained undeveloped until his journalistic activity of 1857–8.

It was not until *Las Nacionalidades* in 1876 that he returned to a full-scale consideration of the Federal idea which he had outlined in 1854. Since that date he had come increasingly under the influence of Proudhon and in doing so had abandoned the Hegelian premisses of 1854. In 1876 he admitted that his method had changed and that instead of arguing from hypothesis he had paid close attention to observed facts.[2] Reason, he even admitted, could be deceptive if it conflicted with experience. His purpose now was twofold—to examine what constituted true as opposed to false nationality and to justify his federal ideas by appeals to past Spanish history. It is evident that he was disturbed by the emergence of new national States like Germany and Italy, disliking larger and larger concentrations of power. 'Liberty only finds a refuge in small divided countries' he comments.[3] But he disliked even more the appeals to race, language, natural frontiers, and even history which were used to justify the new nationalism. The only basis, in his opinion, for the creation of new nations was if the autonomy of the newly absorbed units was preserved with only a surrender to the central power of control over matters of defence and common interest.[4]

Spain provided an example of what happened if local autonomies were sacrificed to the interests of the centralized State. One of the main purposes of Pi's book was to argue that national unity in Spain had only been achieved through the granting of *fueros* to towns which were only then willing to support the policy of unification.[5] Once any attempt was made to whittle down these *fueros* the sanction for the continued existence of the national State vanished. From the Pérez affair onwards, Pi argued, this process had gathered momentum until it reached a climax in the arbitrary division of the country into forty-nine provinces for the administrative convenience of the Moderates in 1833.

[1] Ibid., pp. 265–8, 275–7, 283, 290.
[2] *Las Nacionalidades*, Introduction, pp. vii–viii. [3] Ibid., p. 15.
[4] Ibid., pp. 23–27, 82. [5] Ibid., pp. 219 et seq.

Pi used historical examples to confirm his view that the *pueblo* or *municipio* was the 'natural' unit of society. 'The city', he writes, 'is the first and most natural of political groups.' Or again, 'There is no doubt that other political groups are real but none is as real as the city in the eyes of all people. It is one, indivisible, definite, concrete. The idea of the State as well as that of the *"patria"* must be mere abstraction in the city', and again, 'It is futile to claim for the nation greater substantiveness than the city'.[1] He found the main proof for this thesis in the vitality of local life generalizing from the experience of the War of Independence and the junta tradition stemming from it. When the centralized State collapsed it was local juntas which took over the resistance against Napoleon.[2] 'It is in spontaneous acts that the characteristics of nations as well as of individuals are best revealed.'[3] To substantiate this view he cited the example of the Basque Provinces, relating their resilience to their *fueros*, allowing them to develop according to their own traditions. Their *fueros* provided a practical example of a relationship with the central power which ought to be extended to the other hisorical provinces.[4] The attempt of the Liberals to abrogate these *fueros* had been yet another example of the perversion of the principles of government. Pi's continual appeal to the historical provinces was based on the way in which differences in civil legislation and varying conditions of land tenure tended to follow the old divisions. By showing these differences and by appeals to local custom Pi could emphasize his point that problems which were peculiar to particular parts of the country could only find solution within the framework of a Federal State.[5]

The basic premiss of his Federal theory was that the *pueblo* was the natural unit of society.[6] Its origin was to be found in the satisfaction of the economic needs of families. The family itself was not a society because, Pi argued, it was formed by necessity and not by liberty. The basis of any society was reciprocity of rights but in marriage these did not exist because of the obvious inferiority of women. This rather unconvincing argument was designed to prevent the logical application of Pi's idea of freedom of contract to the affairs of the family—a deduction which would have admitted women to equality with men. Once families had contracted to form a *pueblo*, these *pueblos* contracted

---

[1] *Las Nacionalidades*, pp. 116–18, 126, 292–3. The words *ciudad, pueblo*, and *municipio* seem to be synonymous in this work.
[2] Ibid., pp. 236 et seq.
[3] Ibid., p. 242.   [4] Ibid., pp. 259 et seq.   [5] Ibid., pp. 266–74.
[6] See the interesting discussion on the *pueblo* in J. A. Pitt-Rivers, *People of the Sierra*, London, 1957.

together to form a province and finally the provinces contracted together to form States.[1] In all these contracts the pact, freely entered into, by equal parties, was the cardinal link which could be broken if the contract was abused.

The idea of the pact which Pi still retained in 1876, and which continued to be the distinguishing feature of the Federals, had been outlined in 1854 and finally clinched by Proudhon's arguments in *Du principe fédératif*. This provided Pi with a theory for organizing the State *abajo-arriba*. Abstract and impracticable, it was nevertheless a theory which found a response by attempting to counter the prevailing tendencies of Spanish nineteenth-century government.

[1] Pi y Margall, *La Federación*, ed. Correa y Zafrilla, Madrid, 1880, pp. 184 et seq.

GLOSSARY

Abajo–arriba. The two words mean 'under and 'above', hence the use of this form to refer to a federation created from below with provinces taking the initiative in declaring a federal republic. The opposite *arriba–abajo* refers to the creation of a federal republic by a constituent *Cortes* which itself determines the federal units.

Acta. Certificate of election presented by all deputies before taking their seats in the *Cortes*. A deputy could either be accepted *sin protestas* or, if there had been electoral irregularities, *con protestas*, with a debate to decide the validity of the election.

Alcalde. Mayor. Under the *Ley Municipal* civil governors were empowered to replace a mayor by a representative of the Government should there be complaints against him. This power was often abused and used as an excuse for government intervention, particularly at election time.

Ateneo. 'Athenaeum'—*The Ateneo* always refers to the Madrid *Ateneo*, founded in 1835.

Ayuntamiento. Local council, or it may refer to the building in which it meets. Presided over by an *alcalde* assisted by *concejales*.

Benévolos. 'Benevolents': those Federals who were prepared to form tactical alliances in the *Cortes* with monarchist parties, especially the Radicals. Cf. *Intransigentes*.

Cabotaje. Coasting-trade.

Caciquismo. The domination of a rural area by a *cacique* who might be either a landowner or a landowner's bailiff, who 'managed' the elections. Particularly prevalent in Andalusia.

Calamares. 'Squids.' The nickname given to Sagasta's followers in 1872, because they stuck to office under all circumstances.

Camarilla. The coterie of private advisers round the monarch—in particular the clerical neo-Catholics in the 1860's.

Cantón. 'Canton.' The Spanish use of the word has no specific juridical meaning. It was used in 1873 to refer to any area which declared its independence of Madrid.

Carabinero. Soldiers used specifically against smugglers; customs and excise police.

Carbonario. The Spanish equivalent of the Italian *carbonaro*. They flourished as late as the early 1860's.

Caudillismo. From *caudillo*, a leader; hence rule by a strong man, and particularly by a soldier.

Centralistas. The name given in Catalonia after Espartero's fall in 1843 to those wanting a *Junta central* established, on which all the provinces would be represented. They objected to Madrid taking the initiative in establishing a new government.

Cesante. A retired or suspended bureaucrat: someone who loses his office as a result of a change of government. *Cesantía* was the pension received by a retired official. There is a vivid picture of the *cesante* in Pérez Galdós's novel *Miaou*.

Consumos. The French *octroi*: the excise tax levied by local authorities on essential foodstuffs which had to pass barriers set up at the entrances of towns manned by *consumeros*.

Cortes. The Spanish Parliament. It refers to both Houses—the *Senado* and *Congreso*, but it is more generally used to refer to the Lower House. In 1873 when the two Houses were fused the new body was sometimes referred to as the *Asamblea*.

Cuerpos Francos. 'Free-corps.' The republican volunteer army established after conscription was abolished in February 1873. It was itself abolished in July.

Diputación provincial. The governing council of a province elected by the *Ayuntamientos*.

Empleado. Employee, an office-holder.

Empleocracia. A term used in the nineteenth century to describe a society dominated by a spoils system which creates an overgrown bureaucracy.

Empleomanía. The 'rage for office' which characterizes such a society.

Fronterizo. The popular name for Serrano's followers in 1872 who wanted an understanding with Sagasta.

Fuero. Privilege or exemption granted to a province, group of provinces, or town. Particularly important in the nineteenth century were the Basque and Catalan *fueros* threatened by the Liberal centralized State. Among the most valued were the right to compound for certain taxes, exemption from conscription, and the use of a different penal and commercial code.

Generalidad (Catalan **Generalitat**). The body in 1873 in which the four Catalan provinces Barcelona, Gerona, Tarragona, and Lérida were represented. Their representatives were elected by the separate *Diputaciones*.

Gobernador Civil. Civil Governor. After the centralizing decree of 1833 the centrally appointed representative of the Government; one in each of the forty-nine provinces.

Gobernador Militar. Military Governor. The military equivalent of the Civil Governor, whom he could supersede if the constitutional guarantees were suspended. Their immediate superiors, the captain-generals, were in military command of provinces grouped by regions.

Guardia Civil. Civil Guard. The armed rural police established in 1843 to suppress banditry. Subject to army discipline and under the control of the captains-general. They were put temporarily under civil control in March 1873.

Intransigentes. 'Intransigents': those Federals who repudiated any sort of understanding with monarchist parties.

Jefe político. 'Political chief' or the urban agent of the Government party.

Jornalero. A day-labourer, hired on a daily basis. Also a *bracero*.

Junta. This word can be used in almost any context to mean a 'board' or 'council'. In the nineteenth century it had a more precise political meaning as a revolutionary committee. A junta in this sense is an *ad hoc* body and does not necessarily imply that its members have been elected to it. The 'junta tradition' refers to the practice of setting up local juntas whenever the central government has been overthrown by force.

Masovería. A Catalan tenure system similar to the French *métayage*, by which the tenant pays to the owner a proportion of the produce as rent.

Matrículas del mar. 'Sailors' register': hence naval conscription.

Mitin. The Spanish form of 'meeting', used to refer to a public political meeting.

Motín. A street demonstration, riot. There is a Spanish saying 'El mitin se convierte en un motín'—the meeting turns into a riot.

Pairalisme (or *aristocracia de alpargatas*) refers to the patriarchal-type society in the Catalan interior where the peasant holder of most land in a village is socially dominant.

Partido de la porra. Literally 'party of the cudgel'—used to refer to any armed group, employed by *caciques* or political parties, to intimidate political opponents.

Peninsulares. The name given in Cuba to recent arrivals from Spain or to Spaniards not born in Cuba. Used in contrast to *Criollo*, creole.

Personalismo. Use disparagingly to refer to anyone who put personal interests before principle. Perhaps also as 'personality cult'.

Pretendiente. An office-hunter.

Pronunciamiento. An insurrection by soldiers.

Pueblo. 'People': used in the nineteenth-century sense of 'the people'. Cf. *le peuple*, *il populo*. A small town or village.

Quinta. Conscript. Originally every fifth man drawn by lot for military service, by the nineteenth century it had become a general term for conscription although lots were still drawn if the number required was small.

Rabassaire. The name given to a Catalan tenant who rents land on the *rabassa morte* system in which the land reverts to the owner when three-quarters of the vines planted on it have died.

Real. One hundred *reales* equalled approximately £1.

Retraimiento. Withdrawal from the *Cortes* by an individual or a party, sometimes, but not necessarily, the prelude to armed revolt.

Tertulia. 'Social gathering.' The meeting-place of political parties, cf. the Federals' *casino* or *club*, words very rarely used by other parties.

Trabajos. From *trabajar*, to work. Refers to the sounding of opinion before a coup is made.

Vecinos honrados. The name given to vigilante organizations set up by non-republicans during the First Republic. More precisely, the inhabitants of a certain district who have no criminal record—hence the contrast of the popularly recruited *voluntarios de la libertad* (q.v.).

Voluntarios de la libertad. 'Volunteers of Liberty': a popular militia organization set up spontaneously in Sept.–Oct. 1868, but immediately disbanded by the Provisional Government. Re-established by decree in Feb. 1873, they became the official republican militia.

BIBLIOGRAPHY

A. (1) BIBLIOGRAPHIES

BURGO, J. DEL. *Fuentes de la Historia de Espana: Bibliografía de las luchas políticas y Guerras Carlistas en el siglo XIX*, 3 vols., Pampluna, 1953–5.

SÁNCHEZ ALONSO, B. *Fuentes de la Historia Española e Hispano-Americana*, Vol. III, 3rd edition, Madrid, 1952.

LAMBERET, R. *Mouvements ouvriers et socialistes: chronologie et bibliographie. L'Espagne, 1750–1936*, Paris, 1953.

VARIOUS. *Índice Histórico Español*, Barcelona, 1953–61.

(2) REFERENCE WORKS

VARIOUS. *Enciclopedia Universal Ilustrada Europea-Americana*, Espasa Calpe, 1926–61.

FERNÁNDEZ DE LOS RIOS, A. (editor). *La Asamblea Constituyente de 1869: biografías de todos los representantes de la nación*, Madrid, 1869.

VARIOUS. *Los diputados pintados por sus hechos. Colección de estudios biográficos sobre los eligidos por el sufragio universal en las Constituyentes de 1869*, 3 vols., Madrid, 1869–70.

MOLINS, E. DE, *Diccionario biográfico de escritores y artistas catalanes del siglo XIX*, 2 vols., Barcelona, 1889.

HARTZENBUSCH, E. *Apuntes para un catálogo de periódicos madrileños, 1661–1860*, Madrid, 1894.

CHAVES, M. *La prensa sevillana: historia y bibliografía*, Seville, 1896.

OSSORIO Y BERNARD, A. *Diccionario de periodistas*, Madrid, 1903.

B. UNPUBLISHED SOURCES

(1) *Layard Papers (British Museum)*

Layard's reports provide an invaluable source for this period because of his close personal friendship with Prim and Serrano.

(i) B.M. Add. MSS. 38932–3. Volumes II and III of Sir Austen Henry Layard's Memoirs entitled 'The Story of my Mission to Spain'.

(ii) B.M. Add. MSS. 38997–39006. Ten volumes of private correspondence, 1869–74.

(iii) B.M. Add. MSS. 39121–4. Four volumes of letter-books of semi-official correspondence with occasional dispatches from A. H. Layard to Lord Granville.

B.M. Add. MSS. 39121. 21 Nov. 1869–15 Nov. 1870.

,,　　,,　　,,　39122. 17 Nov. 1870–6 June 1872.

,,　　,,　　,,　39123. 10 June 1872–6 Oct. 1873.

,,　　,,　　,,　39124. 14 Oct. 1873–12 Mar. 1877.

(2) *Foreign Office Records (Public Record Office)*

Series F.O. 72.	1866. Vol. nos.		1125	Sir John Crampton dispatches
(Spain)	1868.	,, ,,	1186	,, ,, ,, ,,
	,,	,, ,,	1191	Consuls' reports
	,,	,, ,,	1192	,, ,,
	1869.	,, ,,	1207–11	Crampton, Ffrench, Layard dispatches.
		,, ,,	1218–20	Consuls' reports
	1870.	,, ,,	1232–7	Layard's dispatches
		,, ,,	1246–7	Consuls' reports

Series F.O. 72.	1871.	Vol.	nos.	1274–6	Layard's and Ffrench's dispatches
(Spain)		„	„	1280–2	Consuls' reports
(*cont.*)	1872.	„	„	1309–13	Layard's dispatches
		„	„	1320–1	Consuls' reports
	1873.	„	„	1336–44	Layard's and Macdonnell's dispatches
		„	„	1350–3	Consuls' reports
		„	„	1399–1400	Cartagena Insurgents
	1874.	„	„	1365	Layard's dispatches
Series F.O. 63.	1870.	„	„	969–70	Sir Charles Murray's dispatches
(Portugal)					

C. PUBLISHED SOURCES

(1) *Cortes debates and government decrees*

References to debates have been made in most cases to the *Gaceta de Madrid*. It is more convenient to use and print debates as well as government decrees. When a fuller record is required, such as composition of committees, draft legislation, voting lists, &c., the *Diario de sesiones* must be used.

Diario de sesiones de la Asamblea Constituyente, Madrid, 1869–70.
Diario de sesiones de las Cortes, Madrid, 1870–3.
Diario de la Asamblea Nacional, Madrid, 1873.
Diario de las Cortes Constituyentes de la República Española, Madrid, 1873–4.
Gaceta de Madrid, Madrid, 1868–74.

(2) *Printed documents and reports*

(i) *Documents diplomatiques francais*, 1re série, tome 1, Paris, 1929.
(ii) G. BONNIN (ed.). *Bismarck and the Hohenzollern Candidature for the Spanish Throne: the documents in the German diplomatic archives*, London, 1957.
(iii) *Parliamentary Papers* (British Museum).

In the absence of reliable Spanish figures for the state of trade and industry the consuls' reports on commerce in these papers provide a useful source, although as the consuls themselves admitted their figures were often gleaned from private and not official sources.

P.P. Vol. 1857, XXXVIII	P.P. Vol. 1870, LXIV, LXX
„ „ 1857–8, LV	„ „ 1871, LXV, LXVI
„ „ 1859, XXX	„ „ 1872, LVII, LVIII
„ „ 1862, LVIII, LIX	„ „ 1873, LXIV, LXV
„ „ 1867–8, LXVIII	„ „ 1874, LXVI, LXVII
„ „ 1868–9, LXVIII, LIX, LX	„ „ 1875, LXXV, LXXVI, LXXVII

(3) The Spanish Press

The history of Federal Republicanism is very largely contained in its press. Here changes of policy may be followed, the reactions of public opinion gauged, besides providing a mine of republican ideology and the only source for party directives and manifestoes. Although there are complete files of the most important, *La Igualdad* (of which the British Museum newspaper library at Colindale has files from 2 Jan. 1872 to 30 Dec. 1874), there are serious gaps in the files of other papers. Except in isolated cases it is not possible to follow reactions in the provincial press. The two provincial Federal papers with the most complete files are *El Estado catalán* and *La Andalucía*. Municipal archives are on the whole disappointing, in their press collections. Both Cádiz and Barcelona are useful for 1868, but only at the latter is a detailed study of the press possible over any period longer than a few months. Málaga archives are almost useless for press sources as hardly anything has survived except a book of press cuttings. The Hemeroteca at Madrid has odd copies of a few provincial papers, but apart from *El Cantón murciano* has no consecutive files of provincial papers. The following are those consulted:

(a) Dailies and weeklies

Unless otherwise stated all papers are Federal in complexion. Some copies of rare journals can be found as enclosures in F.O. dispatches.

(i) Madrid (Biblioteca Nacional and Hemeroteca)

La Discusión, 1857–66, 1869–74.
La Democracia, 1860–6.
El Pueblo (Unitarian), 1860–6, 1869–74.
La Igualdad, 1869–74.
La Bandera Roja, 1869, August–September.
El Combate, 1870 (Nov.–Dec.) and 1872 (2nd period), 27 Jan.–29 July.
El Estado catalán, 1873 (Mar.–June).
La Justicia federal, 1873 (May–July, irregular).
La España federal, 1873 (Mar.–Apr.).
La Democracia republicana, one copy only, 4 Mar. 1869.
La Anarquía, one copy only, 2 Apr. 1869.
El Galimatias, one copy only, 1 Oct. 1869.
El Federalista, one copy only, 29 Oct. 1873.

Non-republican papers

La Iberia (Progressive), 1857.
El Imparcial (Democrat–Radical), 1868–74.
La Época (Conservative–Alphonsist), 1870–3.
El Pensamiento español (Carlist, ex-neo-Catholic), 1860, 1868–73.
La Regeneración (Carlist), 1869.
La Esperanza (Carlist), 1869.

El *Correo militar* (Military), 1869.
La *Emancipación* (Internationalist), 1871–3.
El *Condenado* (Internationalist), 1872 (1st volume missing).
Los *Descamisados* (satirical), 1873 (Mar.–May).
La *Guardia-Cantón* (satirical), 1873 (Aug–Sept.).

(ii) *Provincial Press*
Unless otherwise stated these have been consulted in the municipal archives of the towns concerned.

Barcelona
  Republican:
  El *Federalista*, 1868 (Oct.)–1869(Mar.).
  El *Cohete*, 1868 (only four copies, Oct.).
  La *Vanguardia*, 1868 (Oct.)–1869 (Jan.).
  La *Alianza de los Pueblos*, 1868 (Nov.)–1869 (Apr.).
  El *Estado catalán*, 1869–72.
  El *Pacto federal*, 1869 (Aug–Sept.).
  La *Redención social*, one copy only, 9 Apr. 1871.

  Non-republican:
  El *Diario* (Conservative), 1868–73.
  Boletín Oficial Revolucionario de la Provincia de Barcelona, 1868 (Oct.) (organ of the Junta).
  El *Protector del Pueblo* (organ of the *Fomento de la producción nacional*), 1869 (Mar.–Sept.).
  La *Federación* (organ of the Federal centre of workers' societies), 1869–73.

Cádiz
  La *Soberanía nacional*, 1868 (Sept.–Dec.).
  El *Amigo de los pobres*, 1868.
  El *Progreso democrático*, 1868 (Oct.).
  La *República federal*, 1868–9 (Nov.–Mar.).
  El *Pacto federal*, 1869 (July–Sept.).
  La *República federal Universal*, 1870 (Oct.).
  La *Federación andaluza*, 1873 (May)–1874 (Jan.).

Cartagena (Hemeroteca, Madrid)
  El *Cantón Murciano* (the official journal of the Cartagena canton reprinted in 1891), 1873 (22 July–4 Nov).

Granada (Hemeroteca, Madrid)
  La *Revolución federal*, 1873, one copy only, 31 July 1873.

Málaga

El Diario mercantil (non-political), 1867–9.
El Eco revolucionario (Federal), 1868 (only four copies, Oct.).
El Papel verde (Extremist), two copies only (15 Dec. 1867 and 25 June 1869).
La Aurora boreal (non-political), 1871 (four copies only).
La Revista de Andalucía, 1874.
(For press cuttings see Escobar y Serrano, *Efimérides históricas malagueñas*, Madrid, 1915.)

Seville

La Andalucía, 1868–73 (files for 1870 missing).
El Porvenir, 1868.

Valencia

El Diario mercantil, 1868–9.
El Mercantil valenciano, 1873.

(b) Reviews

Republican

La Federación española, 1870–1.
La Ilustración republicano Federal, 1871–2.
La Justicia social, 1869–71.

Non-republican

La Revista ibérica (Krausist-inspired), 1861–3.
La Revista del movimiento intelectual en Europa (informative), 1865.
La Revista de España (liberal), 1869–74.
La Revista blanca (Anarchist), 1898–1901.

(4) Foreign Press (British Museum Newspaper Library, Colindale)

British

The Times, 1868–74.
The *Eastern Post* (London), 1871 (Apr.)–1872 (Sept.) (for reports of the International's correspondent in Spain).

France (Bibliothèque Nationale)

La Revue politique et littéraire, 1868 (Nov.)–1869 (Jan.).

United States

New York Herald, 1869 and 1873 } reports of Valencia correspondent.
New York Tribune, 1869 and 1873

(5) Pamphlets

The pamphlet literature of these years was enormous. Those consulted, which are listed here, mainly concern federal republican ideology, although some illustrative of other points of view have been included. Some are to be found bound in five volumes entitled 'Guerra Civil, folletos' in the British Museum, but the majority are in the pamphlet section of the *Biblioteca Nacional*.

ALMIRALL, V. *El Renacimiento catalán, las leyes forales y el Carlismo*, Barcelona, 1868.

—— *Idea exacta de la Federación; la República Federal Española*, Madrid, 1873.

ALTADILL, A. *La Monarquía sin Monarca*, Barcelona, 1869.

ANON. *España federal; consideraciones sobre la Revolución de Septiembre. El federalismo única solución de los problemas planteadas por la Revolución. Meditaciones de un pobre*, Madrid, 1868.

ANON. *¿Quién es el Rey?*, Madrid, 1869.

ANON. *¡La Revolución! ¡Abajo la ignorancia!, ¡Abajo la miseria! ¡Viva la República!*, Paris, 1868.

ANON. *Historia de un idea —- España y Portugal*, Madrid, 1869.

ANON. *Candidatura de Don Fernando de Portugal*, Madrid, n.d.

ANON. *Narváez y Castelar*, Madrid, 1864.

ANON. *Las Insurrectos de España y los de Cuba*, La Habana, n.d.

ANON. *L'Espagne en république*, Paris, 1868.

APARISI Y GUIJARRO, A. *El Rey de España*, Madrid, 1869.

—— *La Cuestión dinástica*, Madrid, 1869.

ARCOS, S. *A los electores de diputados*, Madrid, 1868.

ARENAL, C. *A los vencedores y a los vencidos*, Madrid, 1869.

—— *El reo y el verdugo*, Madrid, 1867.

ASCANDONI, J. M. *Guerra a la demagogía*, Madrid, 1872.

AYLLÓN ALTOLAGUIRRE, M. *Proyecto de constitución democrático-federal de la República Española*, Madrid, 1873.

BARCIA, R. *El Evangelio del pueblo*, Madrid, 1869.

—— *La Revolución de la iglesia en España*, Madrid, 1869.

—— (prologue). *La Constitución de la Nación Española y la Constitución de 1812*, Madrid, 1869 (notes by Rodríguez-Solís).

—— *Conversaciones con el pueblo español*, Madrid, 1869.

—— *Cartilla política. El Papado ante Jesus Cristo*, Madrid, 1870.

—— *La Revolución por dentro, o sea la república federal explicada por ella misma*, Madrid, 1870.

—— *¿Quieres oir pueblo? O la cabeza de barba azul*, Madrid, 1872.

BRAULIO MAÑUECO, F. *La Revolución en la propiedad por los cotos redondos*, Madrid, 1873.

CALAVIA, M. *Reflexiones acerca la gloriosa Revolución de Setiembre*, Madrid, 1868.

CANCIO, M. J. *El pasado y el presente de la política española*, Madrid, 1865.

Cariño, P. *Sucesos de la Bisbal*, n.d.

Castelar, E. *La Fórmula del Progreso*, Madrid, 1857. *El socialismo: ¿es un signo de decaimiento de la sociedad o sea sistema de progreso?*, Madrid, 1859.

—— *La Redención del esclavo*, Madrid, 1859.

—— *Cartas a un obispo sobre la libertad de la Iglesia*, Madrid, 1864.

—— *Cartas de Emilio Castelar a los republicanos*, Madrid, 1868.

—— *Discurso pronunciado en la inauguración del comité republicano*, Madrid, 1868.

—— *Defensa de la Fórmula del Progreso*, Madrid, 1870.

Córdoba y López, F. *Cuatro palabras acerca de la pena de muerte*, Madrid, 1864.

—— *Verdad, conveniencia y justicia. Carta a doctores del distrito de Alcázar de San Juan*, Madrid, 1865.

—— *La Conspiración republicana — proclamas de los meses de junio, julio y agosto*, Madrid, 1868.

—— *La Salvación del pueblo o la república democrática federal*, Madrid, 1871.

—— *La Verdadera Revolución; artículos publicados en El Combate*, Madrid, 1871.

—— *Una Fecha fratricida; diez y seis de noviembre de 1870*, Madrid, 1871.

Degollada, R. *El Pacificador de España. Don Baldomero Espartero para rey de los españoles*, Barcelona, 1869.

Domenech, I. *Idea práctica de la federación española*, Madrid, 1870.

Fernández de Córdoba, F. *Memoria sobre los sucesos políticos ocurridos en Madrid en los dias 17, 18, y 19 de julio de 1854*, Madrid, 1855.

Fernández Herrero, M. *El Federalismo. Organización, resoluciones y conducta del partido*, Madrid, 1870.

García Ruiz, E. *La Democracia, el socialismo y el comunismo, según la filosofía y la historia*, Madrid, 1861.

—— *La Intolerancia religiosa*, Madrid, 1862.

—— *Los Neos*, Madrid, 1864.

—— *La Revolución de España, con la historia de los movimientos de enero y junio de 1866 y la del mes de agosto de 1867*, Paris, 1867.

—— *¿Que debe hacer el pais?*, Paris, 1868.

—— *La República democrática unitaria*, Madrid, June 1869.

—— *Desde mi campo neutral*, Madrid, 1870.

—— *Los siete artículos capitales — o sea la democracia gobernada*, Madrid, 1872.

—— *Historia de la Internacional y del federalismo en España*, Madrid, 1872.

García Tejero, A. *La Fe de los partidos*, Madrid, 1860.

Garrido, F. *Propaganda democrática: instrucción del pueblo*, Madrid, 1850.

—— *El Pueblo y el trono*, Madrid, 1854.

—— *Espartero y la Revolución*, Madrid, 1854.

—— *La República Democrática Federal*. (Prologue by Castelar, Madrid, 2nd edition 1856, 8th edition 1869, 17th edition 1881.)

—— *La Democracia y sus adversarios*. (Prologue by Orense, Barcelona, 1860.)

—— *Biografía de Sixto Cámara*, Barcelona, 1860.

—— *El socialismo y la democracia ante sus adversarios*. (Prologue by Mazzini, London, 1862.)

278 *Bibliography*

GARRIDO, F. *La Rebelión carlista, la religión católica y la República federal en España*, Lisbon, 1874.

—— *La Cooperación*, Madrid, 1879.

GRIMALDI, A. *Emilio Castelar: semblanza moral*, Cádiz, 1868.

GÜELL Y FERRER, J. *Rebelión cubana*, Barcelona, 1871.

HERRERO, S. *La Revolución y los partidos liberales*, Valladolid, 1868.

IVARS Y ROS, G. *Necesidad de que se unan los partidos avanzados, siquiera sea para que el progresista entre en el poder*, Madrid, 1864.

JIMENO Y CABAÑAS, A. *El Partido republicano de Valencia ante la Historia. Memoria de los sucesos de octobre de 1869*, Valencia, 1870.

JOARIZTI, A. *Los Progresistas, los demócratas y los individualistas*, Madrid, 1861.

LABRA, R. *La Abolición y la Sociedad Abolicionista Español*, Madrid, 1874.

LAFUENTE, R. *Málaga y sus opresores*, Oran, 13 enero 1869.

LEMONNIER, C. *La Ligue Internationale de la paix et de la liberté*, Paris, 1869.

—— *Les États-Unis d'Europe*, Paris, 1872.

LLAUDER, L. M. *El Desenlace de la Revolución Española*, Barcelona, 1869.

MAÑE Y FLAQUER, J. *La República Federativa*, Barcelona, n.d.

MANTEROLA, V. DE. *El Espíritu carlista*, Madrid, 1871.

—— *Don Carlos o el petroleo*, Madrid, 1871.

MARTÍ, J. *La República española ante la Revolución Cubana*, Madrid, 1873.

MAS, S. DE. *La Iberia. Memoria sobre la conveniencia de la unión pacífica y legal de Portugal y España*, 4th edition, Madrid, 1856.

MIRAFLORES, MARQUÉS DE. *Candidatura del duque de Aosta para rey de España*, Madrid, 1856.

MUIÑOS Y MUIÑOS, N. *La Marina en San Fernando. Reseña histórica de los sucesos ocurridos en el departamento de Cádiz y defensa del arsenal de la Carraca*, &c., Cádiz, 1873.

OCON, J. D. *Los Heroes de Valencia*, Marsella, 1869.

ORENSE, J. M. (MARQUÉS DE ALBAIDA). *¿Que hará en el poder el partido progresista?*, Madrid, 1847.

—— *Lo que hará en el poder el partido democrático y lo que hará en el poder el partido progresista*, Madrid, n.d.

—— *Los Fueros*, Madrid, 1859.

—— *La Democracia tal cual es*, 2nd edition, Madrid, 1862.

—— *Treinta años de gobierno representativo en España*, Madrid, 1863.

—— *Ventajas de la República federal*, Madrid, 1869.

—— *La Empleocracia*, Madrid, 1872.

PAUL Y ANGULO, J. *Memorias de un pronunciamiento*, Madrid, 1869.

—— *Verdades revolucionarias*, Madrid, 1872.

PAVÍA, A. *Solución práctica a la cuestión social. Una conferencia popular a San Isidro*, Madrid, 1871.

PAZ, A. DE. *España y Portugal*, Madrid, 1861.

QUENTAL, A. DE. *Portugal perante a revolução de Hespanha*, Lisboa, 1868.

REVILLA, M. DE LA. *Historia y defensa de la Declaración de la Prensa Republicana*, Madrid, 1870.

RIBOT Y FONTSERÉ, A. *Autonomía de los partidos*, Madrid, 1856.

RIERA, J. *El Catolicismo y la República federal*, Madrid, 1873.

ROMANI Y PUIGDENGOLAS, F. *El Federalismo en España*, Barcelona, 1869.

—— *A los demócratas federales de Igualada*, Barcelona, 1868.

RUBIO, C. *Progresistas y demócratas. Como y para qué se han unido. ¿Pueden constituir una sola comunión en lo futuro?*, Madrid, 1865.

RUIZ Y CAMPOS, J. *Baldomero I; rey de España*, Madrid, 1868.

RUIZ ZORRILLA, M. *A sus amigos y a sus adversarios*, Madrid, 1882.

SAGRA, R. DE LA. *Remedios contra los efectos funestos de las crises políticas y de las paralizaciones comerciales*, Madrid, 1855.

SALMERÓN, N. *La forma de gobierno*, Madrid, 1868.

—— and CHAO, E. *Proyecto de bases de la constitución republicana federal de España presentado a la Asamblea Federal de 1872*, Madrid, 1872.

—— and others. *La Legalidad de la Internacional*, Madrid, 1871.

SERRACLARA, G. *La Nueva Inquisición*, Barcelona, 1870.

SUÑER Y CAPDEVILA, F. *Dios*, Barcelona, 1869.

TRESSERA, C. *¿Los Anarquistas, los socialistas y los comunistas son demócratas?*, Barcelona, 1861.

—— *Catecismo democrático-republicano*, Madrid, 1868.

—— *Cuadro sinóptico del derecho democrático*, Barcelona, 1869.

TUBINO, F. M. *Esto matará a aquello*, Seville, 1864.

—— *Patria y federalismo*, Seville, 1873.

VALCARCEL, A. *Sistema del gobierno republicano democrático-federal*, Madrid, 1869.

VASALLO. *Un Capítulo para la historia del alzamiento de Sevilla*, Madrid, 1869.

VARIOUS. *Almanaque democrático. Por varios socios del Ateneo catalán*, Barcelona, 1864–5.

(6) Memoirs and letters

ALVÁREZ VILLAMIL and R. LLOPIS (ed.). *Cartas de conspiradores*, Madrid, 1929.

BERNHARDI, T. VON. *Aus dem Leben Theodor von Bernhardis*, vol. ix (in *Spanien und Portugal: Tagebuch Blätter aus den Jahren 1869–71*), Leipzig, 1906.

CASTELAR, E. *Correpondencia, 1868–98*, Madrid, 1908.

ECHEGARAY, J. *Recuerdos*, 3 vols., Madrid, 1917.

ESTÉVANEZ, N. *Fragmentos de mis memorias*, Madrid, 1903.

FERNÁNDEZ DE CÓRDOBA, F. *Mis memorias íntimas*, 3 vols., Madrid, 1886–9.

FLÓRES GARCÍA, F. *Recuerdos de la Revolución*, Madrid, 1913.

GAMBETTA, L. *Lettres*, ed. D. Halévy and E. Pillias, Paris, 1938.

GAMERO GUTIERREZ. M. *Mis primera ochento años*, Madrid, n.d.

GRIJALBA, MARQUÉS DE. *Páginas secretas de la Restauración* (letters printed in *El Sol*, March 1924).

GÜELL Y MERCADÉR, J. *Cosas de Reus*, Reus, 1900.

HUGO, V. *Actes et Paroles*, Paris, 1938.

JIMÉNEZ ENRICH, S. *Cartagena, Recuerdos cantonales*, Barcelona, 1874.

LAFARGUE, P. *Correspondance*, Paris, 1955.

LEIVA Y MUÑOZ, F. *La Batalla de Alcolea o memorias políticos y militares de la Revolución Española de septiembre de 1868*, 3 vols. Córdoba, 1879.

LEÓN Y CASTILLO, F. DE. *Mis memorias*, Madrid, 1921.

LORENZO, A. *El proletariado militante*, Mexico, 1945.

MAZZINI, G. *Scritti*, vols. 45, 47, 50, 52, 53, 73, 74, 87, 88. Edizione Nazionale, Imola, 1906–43.

RÉCLUS, E. *Correspondance*, vol. i, Paris, 1911.

RÉGNAULT, H. *Correpondance*, Paris, 1904.

RISPA Y PERPIÑA, F. *Cincuenta años de conspirador: memorias político-revolucionarios, 1853–1903*, Barcelona, 1932.

ROURE, C. *Recuerdos de mi larga vida*, Barcelona, 3 vols., 1927.

SALDANHA, DUKE OF. *Memoirs*, ed. J. Smith, Count of Carnota, 2 vols., London, 1880.

SANROMA, J. M. *Mis memorias*, 2 vols., Madrid, 1887.

THIERS, L. A. *Notes et souvenirs, 1870–3*, Paris, 1901.

—— *Thiers au pouvoir: texte de ses lettres*, ed. G. Bouniols, Paris, 1921.

(7) *Works by Republicans*

(a) *General histories*

GARRIDO, F. *Historia del reinado del último Borbón de España*, 3 vols., Barcelona, 1869.

PI Y ARSUAGA, F., and PI Y MARGALL, F. *Historia de España en el siglo XIX*, 5 vols., Barcelona, 1902.

RODRÍGUEZ-SOLÍS, E. *Historia del partido republicano español*, 2 vols., Madrid, 1892–3.

VERA Y GONZÁLEZ, E. *Pi y Margall y la política contemporánea*, 2 vols., Barcelona, 1886.

(b) *Other works*

ALMIRALL, V. *Obras completas*, 2 vols., Castilian edition, Barcelona, 1902.

—— *Lo Catalanisme*, Barcelona, 1886.

ALTADILL, A. *Los Misterios de Barcelona*, 2 vols., Barcelona, 1862.

BARCIA, R. *El Dos de Mayo*, Madrid, 1846.

—— *Filosofía del alma humana, o sea teoría de los actos externos y internos del hombre*, Madrid, 1857.

—— *Teoria del Infierno o la Ley de la Vida*, Madrid, 1868.

—— *Historia del Sitio de Cartagena*, Madrid, 1874.

CALA, R. DE. *Los Comuneros de Paris*, 2 vols., Madrid, 1871.

CÁMARA, S. *Espíritu moderna o sea carácter del movimiento contemporánea*, Madrid, 1848.

CASTELAR, E. *Historia del movimiento republicano en Europa*, 9 vols., Madrid, 1874.

DÍAZ QUINTERO, F. (ed.). *Enciclopedia Republicano Federal Social*, Madrid, 1872.

FERNÁNDEZ HERRERO, M. *Historia de las Germanías de Valencia*, Madrid, 1870.

GARCÍA RUIZ, E. *Dios y el Hombre*, Madrid, 1863.

—— *Historias*, 2 vols., Madrid, 1876.

GARRIDO, F. *L'Espagne contemporaine*, Bruxelles, 1862.

—— *La España contemporánea*, 2 vols., Barcelona, 1865 (expanded version of the above).

—— *Historia de las clases trabajadores en Europa*, Madrid, 1870. (Prologue by E. Castelar.)

MORAYTA, M. *La Comuna de Paris*, Madrid, 1872.

OLIAS, M. DE. *La Influencia de la religión católica en la España contemporánea*, Madrid, 1876.

PAUL Y ANGULO, J. *Les Assassins du Général Prim et la politique en Espagne*, Paris, 1886.

PI Y MARGALL, F. *Historia de la pintura en España*, Madrid, 1851.

—— *La Reacción y la Revolución*, Madrid, 1854 (reprinted by *Revista blanca*, Barcelona, n.d.).

—— (Introduction). *Obras completas de Mariana*, Madrid, 1864.

—— *Estudios sobre la Edad Media*, Madrid, 1873.

—— *La República de 1873: apuntes para escribir su historia*, Madrid, 1874.

—— *Las Nacionalidades*, Madrid, 1876.

—— *La Federación* (Introduction by Corea y Zafrilla), Madrid, 1880.

—— *Articles. Proleg den Gabriel Alomar*, Barcelona, 1908.

—— *Cartas íntimas*, Madrid, 1911.

—— *Opúsculos: Amadeo de Savoya*. Madrid, 1914.

—— *Las Clases jornaleras*, Madrid, 1915.

—— *Lecciones del Federalismo*. Edited by Sánchez Pérez, Madrid, 1917.

PUJOLA Y VALLES, F. *Pi y Margall*, Barcelona, 1902.

ROBERT, R. *Prisiones de Europa*, Barcelona, 1862.

RODRÍGUEZ-SOLÍS, E. *Los Guerrilleros de 1808; historia popular de la guerra de la Independencia*, 2 vols., Madrid, 1877.

—— *La Mujer, defendida por la historia, la ciencia y la moral*, 3rd edition, Madrid, 1878.

SALMERÓN, N. *Obras completas*, Introduction by G. Azcárate, Madrid.

SUÁREZ CASAÑ, V. *Apuntes para la historia del renacimiento federal en España. Viaje de D. Francisco Pi y Margall a Valencia*, Madrid, 1883.

TRINCHANT Y FORNÉS, J. *Pi y Margall ante el regionalismo, la federalismo y la unidad de la patria*, Madrid, 1900.

TUBINO, F. M. *Estudios contemporáneos*, Seville, 1865.

—— *Historia del renacimiento literario contemporáneo en Cataluña, Baleares y Valencia*, Madrid, 1880.

(8) *Published works by contemporaries*

(a) General histories

BERMEJO, I. A. *Historia de la Interinidad y Guerra Civil de España desde 1868*, 3 vols, Madrid, 1875–7.

BURGOS, J. DE. *Anales del reinado de Isabella II*, 6 vols., Madrid, 1851.

HUBBARD, G. *Histoire contemporaine de l'Espagne*, 6 vols., Paris, 1869–83.

LAUSER, W. *Geschichte Spaniens von dem Sturz Isabella's bis zur Thronbesteigung Alfonzo's*, 2 vols., Leipzig, 1877.

PIRALA, A. *Historia de la Guerra Civil y de los partidos liberales y carlistas*, 5 vols., Madrid, 1853.

—— *Historia contemporánea*, 5 vols., Madrid, 1876.

RUBIO, C. *Historia filosófica de la Revolución Española de 1868*, 2 vols., Madrid, 1869.

VILARRASA, E. M., and GATELL, J. *Historia de la Revolución de Septiembre*, 2 vols., Barcelona, 1874.

(b) Other works

ANTERQUERA, J. M. *La Desamortización eclesiástica*, Madrid, 1885.

BORREGO, A. *La Revolución de Julio de 1854*, Madrid, 1855.

—— *De la Organización de los partidos en España*, Madrid, 1855.

—— *España y la Revolución*, Madrid, 1856.

BRAGA, T. *Soluçãos positivas da politica portuguesa*, vol. iii, *Historia das ideias republicanas em Portugal*, Lisboa, 1880.

—— *As ideias modernas na Literatura portuguesa*, Vol. I. Porto, 1892.

CABALLERO, F. *Fomento de la población rural*, Madrid, 1863.

—— *Reseña Geográfica-Estadística de España*, 2nd edition, Madrid, 1868.

CÁNOVAS DEL CASTILLO, A. *Problemas Contemporáneos*, vol. ii, Madrid, 1884.

CHERBULIEZ, V. *L'Espagne politique, 1868–1873*, Paris, 1874.

COSTA, J. *El Colectivismo agrario*, Madrid, 1898.

—— *Oligarquía y Cacicquismo*, Madrid, 1902.

CURROS, E. *Eduardo Chao*, Madrid, 1893.

FERNÁNDEZ DE LOS RÍOS, A. *Mi misión en Portugal*, Paris, 1877.

FUENTE V. DE LA. *Historia de las sociedades secretas antiguas y modernas en España*, Vol. I, Lugo, 1870–1.

GONZÁLEZ SUGRAÑES, M. *La República en Barcelona*, 2nd edition, Barcelona, 1903.

GUICHOT, J. *Historia de la ciudad de Sevilla y los pueblos importantes de su provincia*, Seville, 1885.

GUILLÉN ROBLES, F. *Historia de Málaga y su provincia*, Málaga, 1873.

HANNAY, D. *Emilio Castelar*, London, 1896.

HAY, J. *Castilian Days*, London, 1897.

HOUGHTON, A. *Les Origines de la restauration des Bourbons en Espagne*, Paris, 1890.

KLAPP, M. *Revolutionsbilder aus Spanien*, Hannover, 1869.

LABRA, R. *La República y las libertades de Ultramar*, Madrid, 1897.

—— *La Política colonial y la Revolución Española de 1868*, Madrid, 1916.

LAUSER, W. *Aus Spaniens Gegenwart; Kulturskizzen*, Leipzig, 1872.

LÓPEZ DOMÍNGUEZ, J. *Cartagena; Memoria y comentarios sobre el sitio de Cartagena*, Madrid, 1877.

MAGALHÃES LIMA. *O Socialismo na Europa*, Lisboa, 1892.

MAÑÉ Y FLAQUER, J. (ed.). *La Revolución de 1868 juzgada por sus autores*, 2 vols., Barcelona, 1876.

MARTOS, C. *La Revolución de Julio en 1854*, Madrid, 1855.

MARX, K., and ENGELS, F. *Revolution in Spain*. Reprint of articles, London, 1939.

MAZADE, C. DE. *L'Espagne moderne*, Paris, 1855.

—— *Les Révolutions de l'Espagne contemporaine, 1854–1868*, Paris, 1868.

MOLINA, C. *Los Cantones suizos*, Madrid, 1869.

MUÑIZ, R. *Apuntes históricos sobre la Revolución de 1868*, 2 vols., Madrid, 1884–6.

PASTOR, L. M. (ed.). *Conferencias Libre Cambistas*, Madrid, 1864.

PAVÍA Y RODRÍGUEZ, M. *La Pacificación de Andalucía*, Madrid, 1878.

—— *El Ejército del Centro*, Madrid, 1878.

PÉREZ GALDÓS, B. *O'Donnell*, Madrid, 1920.

—— *La Primera República*, Madrid, 1944.

—— *Amadeo I*, Madrid, 1953.

PÉREZ PUJOL, E. *La Cuestión social en Valencia*, Valencia, 1872.

PIRALA, A. *El Rey en Madrid y en las Provincias*, Madrid, 1871.

PROUDHON, P.-J. *L'Idée générale de la Révolution au XIXᵉ siècle*, Paris, 1851.

—— *De la Justice dans la Révolution et dans l'Église*, 3 vols., Paris, 1858.

—— *La Guerre et la Paix*, Paris, 1861.

—— *La Fédération et l'Unité en Italie*, Paris, 1863.

—— *Du principe fédératif*, Paris, 1863.

—— (translation). PI Y MARGALL: *El Principio federativo*, Madrid, 1868, 2nd edition 1870.

—— *La Filosofía del Progreso*, Madrid, 1868.

—— *De la capacidad política de las clases populares*, Madrid, 1870.

—— *El sistema de las contradicciones económicas, o la filosoffía de la miseria*, Madrid, 1870.

—— (other translations). ROBERTO ROBERT: *Teoría de la contribución*, Madrid, 1862.

—— *Polémica sobre la cratitud del crédito y legitimidad del interés entre Bastiat y Proudhon*, Madrid, 1869.

—— *La Revolución en el siglo XIX*, 2nd edition, Barcelona, 1869.

'STRADA'. *L'Europe sauvée et le Fédéralisme*, Paris, 1868.

TESTE, L. *Viaje por España (1872)*, Valencia, 1959.

VALERA, J. *Obras completas*, vols. 34, 35, Madrid.

ZUGASTI, J. DE. *El Bandolerismo. Estudio social y memorias históricas*, 10 vols., Madrid, 1876–9.

D. MODERN PUBLISHED WORKS

(1) *Books*

ALBORNOZ, A. DE. *El Partido republicano*, Madrid, n.d.

AZORÍN. *Lecturas españolas*, Nelson ed., n.d.

—— *De Granada a Castelar*, Austral, 1944.

BERKOWITZ, H. C. *Pérez Galdós*, Madison, 1948.

BLASCO IJAZO, J. *Historia de la prensa zaragoziana*, Zaragoza, 1947.

BOLÓS Y SADERRA, J. *El Carlismo en Cataluña. Conspiraciones en los años 1869-70-71*, Barcelona, 1930.

BONNER, H. B. *Charles Bradlaugh, his Life and his Work*, vol. i, London, 1894.

BOULIGNY, J. DE. *Los Sucesos de Cádiz en la Revolución de Septiembre 1868*, Madrid, 1918.

BRANDT, J. A. *Toward the New Spain*, Chicago, 1933.

BRENAN, G. *Spanish Labyrinth*, 2nd edition, Cambridge, 1950.

BREY MARIÑO, M. *Viaje a España del pintor Henri Régnault, 1868-70*, Valencia, 1949.

BURY, J. P. T. *Gambetta and the National Defence*, London, 1936.

BUTLER CLARKE, H. *Modern Spain*, Cambridge, 1906.

CABALLÉ Y CLOS, J. *Clavé y su tiempo*, Barcelona, 1949.

CARAVACA, F. *Pi y Margall*, Barcelona, 1935.

CARREIRO, B. *Antero de Quental*, 2 vols., Lisbon, 1948.

CARRERA PUJAL, J. *Historia política de Cataluña en el siglo XIX*, vols. iv and v, Barcelona, 1958.

CARRO MARTÍNEZ, A. *La Constitución española de 1869*, Madrid, 1952.

CHADWICK, F. E. *The Relations of the United States and Spain*, 2 vols., London, 1911.

CHAIX, G. *Ruiz Zorrilla*, Madrid, 1934.

DÍAZ DEL MORAL, J. *Historia de las agitaciones campesinos: Córdoba*, Madrid, 1929.

DIEZ DEL CORRAL, L. *El Liberalismo doctrinario*, Madrid, 1945.

DOLLÉANS, E. *Proudhon*, Paris, 1948.

DUTARD, A. *L'Octroi en Espagne*, Toulouse, 1910.

ETTINGER, A. A. *The Mission to Spain of Pierre Soulé, 1853-5*. New Haven, 1932.

FERNÁNDEZ ALMAGRO, M. *Cánovas, su vida y su política*, Madrid, 1951.

—— *Historia política de la España contemporánea*, Madrid, 1956.

GARCÍA DE CASTRO. *Los Intelectuales y la Iglesia*, Madrid, 1934.

GARCÍA ESCUDERO, J. M. *De Cánovas a la República*, Madrid, 1951.

GARCÍA VENERO, M. *El Nacionalismo catalán*, Madrid, 1944.

GENER, POMPEYO. *Cosas de España*, Barcelona, 1903.

GONZÁLEZ POSADA, A. *Estudios sobre el régimen parlamentario en España*, Madrid, 1891.

—— *Evolución legislativa del régimen local en España*, Madrid, 1910.

GONZÁLEZ PRADA, M. *Anarquía*, Santiago de Chile, 1936.

GONZÁLEZ SERRANO, V. *Nicholas Salmerón*, Madrid, 1903.

GRAELL, G. *Mañé y Flaquer*, Barcelona, 1903.
—— *Historia del Fomento del Trabajo Nacional*, Barcelona, 1911.
GUERRA Y SÁNCHEZ, R. *Guerra de los diez años, 1868-78*, La Habana, 1950.
—— *Historia de la nación cubana*, vol. iv, La Habana, 1952,
GUILLAUME, J. *L'Internationale: Documents et souvenirs*, Paris, 1909, 4 vols.
HOWARD, M. (ed.). *Soldiers and Governments* (R. Carr, 'Spain: Rule by generals'), London, 1957.
HUGHEY, J. D. *Religious Freedom in Spain*, London, 1955.
JARNÉS, B. *Castelar, el hombre de Sinai*, Madrid, 1935.
JIMÉNEZ, A. *Juan Valera y la Generación de 1868*, Oxford, 1956.
JOBIT, P. *Les Éducateurs de l'Espagne moderne*, 2 vols., Paris, 1936.
JOVER, J. M. *Conciencia obrera y conciencia burguesa en la España contemporánea*, Madrid, 1952.
JURETSCHKE, H. *España ante Francia*, Madrid, 1940.
LEMA, MARQUÉS DE. *De la Revolución a la Restauración*, 2 vols., Madrid, 1927.
LLOPIS Y PÉREZ, A. *Historia política y parlamentaria de D. Nicholas Salmerón y Alonso*, Madrid, 1915.
LÓPEZ MORILLAS, J. *El Krausismo español*, Mexico, 1956.
LUZ, P. DE. *Los Españoles en busca de un Rey*, Barcelona, 1948.
MARTÍ, C. *Orígenes del anarquismo en Barcelona*, Barcelona, 1958.
MARVAUD, A. *L'Espagne au XIXᵉ siècle*, Paris, 1915.
MASRIERA, A. C. *Los buenos Barceloneses*, Barcelona, c. 1924.
—— *Barcelona isabelina y revolucionaria*, Barcelona, 1930.
MÉNDEZ BEJARANO, M. *Idealismo jurídico-político y historia interna de la Revolución de Septiembre de 1868*, Madrid, 1919.
MENÉNDEZ Y PELAYO, M. *Historia de los Heterodoxos españoles*, vol. vi (vol. xl of the *Edición Nacional* of the *Obras completas*), Madrid, 1948.
MONTALVOR, L. DE (ed.). *Historia do regimen republicano em Portugal*, Lisbon, 1932, 2 vols.
MONTI, A. *L'Idea federalistica nel Risorgimento italiano*, Roma, 1922.
MONTOLIU, M. DE. *Aribau i la Catalunya de seu temps*, Barcelona, 1936.
MORATO, J. J. *Historia de la Sección Española de la Internacional, 1868-1874*, Madrid, 1930.
—— *Historia de la Asociación del Arte de Imprimir*, Madrid, 1925.
MORAYTA, M. *Las Constituyentes de la República Española*, Paris, 1909.
—— *La Masonería española*, Madrid, 1915.
NETTLAU, M. *Miguel Bakunin, la Internacional y la Alianza en España, 1868-73*, Buenos Aires, 1925.
NEVINS, A. *Hamilton Fish; the Internal History of the Grant Administration*, New York, 1936.
OLIVAR BERTRAND, R. *El caballero Prim*, 2 vols., Barcelona, 1952.
—— *Asi cayó Isabella II*, Barcelona, 1956.
OLIVESI, A. *La Commune de 1871 á Marseille*, Paris, 1950.

OLLIVIER, E. *L'Empire liberal*, vol. xi, Paris, 1895–1918.

OYARZÚN, R. *Historia del Carlismo*, Madrid, 1939.

PABÓN, J. *La Revolución portuguesa*, vol. i, Madrid, 1941.

—— *Cambó*, Barcelona, 1952.

PITT-RIVERS, J. A. *People of the Sierra*, London, 1957.

PLANA, A. *Les Idées politiques d'en Valentí Almirall*, Barcelona, 1905.

PUGÉS, M. *Como triunfó el proteccionismo en España*, Barcelona, 1931.

PUIG CAMPILLO, A. *El Cantón murciano*, Cartagena, 1932.

RAMOS OLIVIERA, A. *Politics, Economics and Men of Modern Spain*, Gollancz, 1946.

RAUCH, B. *American Interests in Cuba, 1848–55*, New York, 1948.

RENOUVIN, P. *L'Idée de Fédération européenne dans la pensée politique du XIXe siècle*, Oxford, 1949.

REPIDE, P. DE. *Isabella II*, Madrid, 1932.

REVENTÓS, M. *Els moviments socials a Barcelona durant el segle XIX*, Barcelona, 1925.

RIVAS, N. *Anecdotario histórico contemporáneo*, 3 vols., Madrid, 1944–5.

—— *Políticos gobernantes*, 2 vols., Madrid, 1946.

ROCA I ROCA, J. *Pi i Margall. Esbós biografic*, Barcelona, 1921.

RODEZNO, CONDE DE. *Carlos VII, Duque de Madrid*, Madrid, 1944.

ROMANONES, CONDE DE. *Los cuatro Presidentes de la Primera República Española*, San Sebastián, 1939.

—— *Sagasta o el Político*, Madrid, 1930.

ROMERO FLÓRES, H. R. *Reflexiones sobre el Alma y el Cuerpo de la España actual, 1900–1932*, Madrid, 1933.

ROVIRA I VIRGILI, A. *La Questio de Catalunya*, Barcelona, 1913.

SAIZ, C. *La Revolución de 1868 y la cultura femenina*, Madrid, n.d.

SARDA, J. *La Política monetaria y las fluctuaciones de la economía Española en el siglo XIX*, Madrid, 1948.

SARRAILH, J. *Martínez de la Rosa*, Paris, 1930.

SENDER, R. *Mr. Witt among the Rebels*, London, 1937.

SERRA HUNTER, J. *Les tendéncies filosofiques a Catalunya durant el segle XIX*, Barcelona, 1925.

TASSARA GONZÁLEZ, J. *Apuntes para la Historia de la Revolución de 1868 en Sevilla*, Sevilla, 1919.

TENCAJOLI, O. F. *La Nascita del Duca degli Abruzzi e l'abdicazione del Re Amadeo*, Roma, 1934.

TIRADO Y ROJAS, M. *La Masonería en España*, 2 vols., Madrid, n.d.

TREND, J. B. *Origins of Modern Spain*, Cambridge, 1934.

VICENS VIVES, J. *Historia social y económica de España y América*, vol. iv, part ii, Barcelona, 1959.

—— *Biografies catalanes*, vol. xi. *Els Catalans en el segle XIX*, Barcelona, 1959.

VILLAURRUTIA, MARQUÉS DE. *Serrano, el Duque de la Torre*, Madrid, 1929.

Viñas Mey, C. *La Reforma agraria en España en el siglo XIX*, Santiago, 1933.
Woodcock, G. *Pierre-Joseph Proudhon*, London, 1956.

(2) *Articles*

American Historical Review, 1950, vol. lv, Willard A. Smith, 'The Background of the Spanish Revolution of 1868'.

Annuari dels Catalans, 1924–5, C. Capdevila, 'Pi i Margall a Barcelona'.

Caribbean Historical Review, 1954, Dec., T. Mathews, 'Confederation of the Greater Antilles'.

Cuba contemporánea, 1921, vol. xxvii, Conangla Fontanilles, 'Pi y Margall y la Independencia Cubana'.

Economic History Review, 1955, Aug., M. W. Flinn, 'Spanish Ore Supplies'.

El Sol, 1930, 17 Dec., Rovira y Virgili, 'La juventud de Pi y Margall'; 'Pi y Margall, joven. Los origines de su heterodoxia'.

—— 1933, 3 Dec., Azorín, 'El Pacto'.

—— 1933, 17 Feb., Fernáadez Almagro, 'Setenta años después'.

Fortnightly Review, 1872, Mar., E. Castelar, 'Figueras'.

—— 1878, June, E. Grant Duff, 'Emilio Castelar'.

Hispanic American Historical Review, 1939, vol. xix, C. W. Clark, 'Marshal Prim and the question of the cession of Gibraltar to Spain'.

—— 1957, vol. xxxvii, C. J. Bartlett, 'British reactions to the Cuban insurrection, 1868–78'.

Journal of Modern History, 1953, Sept., Willard A. Smith, 'Napoleon III and the Spanish Revolution of 1868'.

La España moderna, 1903, vol. clxxvi, J. Pérez de Guzman, 'Como se formó el último Ministerio Radical'.

—— 1894, vol. lxiv, A. Pirala, 'El secreto de un Consejo de Ministros 1870'.

—— 1894, vol. lxiv, A. Pirala, 'La Venta de Cuba'.

—— 1903, vol. clxxvi, J. Pérez de Guzman, 'Las Cortes y los Gobiernos del reinado de Isabella II'.

La Revue Socialiste, 1889, May, B. Malon, 'Le Socialisme en Espagne'.

Movimento Operaio. Rivista di storia e bibliografía, 1956, July–Aug., A. Saitta, 'L'idea d'Europa dal 1815 al 1870'.

—— 1956, Jan.–June, F. della Peruta, 'Il socialismo risorgimentale di Ferrari, Pisacane e Montanelli'.

Occidente, vol. xii, No, 2, R. Colapietra, 'Profilo di Alberto Mario'.

—— vol. xi, No. 2, C. A. M. Hennessy, 'Intellectuals and Politics in Spain'.

Publications of the Modern Languages Association of America, 1953, Sept., R. Mead, 'González Prada; Peruvian judge of Spain'.

Quarterly Journal of Economics, 1947, Nov., vol. 62, Sarda, 'Spanish prices in the nineteenth century'.

Revista bimestre cubana, 1918, vol. xiii, 'Wilson y Pi y Margall' (reprint of a letter written by Pi to Wilson).

Revista bimestre cubana, 1924, vol. xxxiv, R. Lendrian, 'En el centenario de Pi y Margall'.

—— 1933, Jan., Dihigo y Mestre, 'El profundo humanitarismo de Pi y Margall' .

——1947, vol. lix, J. Conangla Fontanilles, 'Pi y Margall'.

Revista de Catalunya, 1924, (vol. i) July–Dec., C. Capdevila, 'J. A. Clavé'.

—— 1926, (iv) Jan.–July, M. Font, 'El club dels Federalistes'.

—— 1926, (iv) J. Xirau i Palan, 'La ideología de Pi y Margall'.

—— 1928, (viii) Jan., Rovira i Virgili, 'La psicología de Pi i Margall'.

—— 1928, (ix) July, Rovira i Virgili, 'La gloria de Pi' and 'Polémica sobre Pi i Margall'.

—— 1929, (xi) July, Rovira i Virgili, 'Estudis sobre Valentí Almirall'.

—— 1934, (xxi) July, Rovira i Virgili, 'La davallada del Federalisme Regionalista'.

Revista de Estudios Políticos, 1944, vol. viii, Suárez Verdaguer, 'La Internacional en las Cortes de 1871'.

—— 1956, no. 90, R. Olivar Bertrand, 'Puntualizacions al torno del '73'.

Revista de la Facultad de Letras y Ciencias, 1924, vol. xxxiv, J. Conangla Fontanilles, 'Pi y Margall ante la historia y la gratitud de Cuba'.

Revue de Catalogne, 1929, Mar., Apr., Jean Camp, 'Frédéric Mistral et les Catalans'.

Revue des Deux Mondes, 1865, Sept., C. de Mazade, 'Les Crises du Libéralisme en Espagne'.

—— 1867, Sept., C. de Mazade, 'La Révolution et la réaction en Espagne'.

—— 1870, Sept., E. Renan, 'La France et l'Allemagne'.

Revue Hispanique, 1924, Apr., M. Nuñez de Arenas, 'D. Ramón de la Sagra, reformador social'.

INDEX

Abolicionista, El, 85 n.
Acosta, J., General (1819–87), 179 and note, 188, 190.
agrarian problem, 21–22, 29, 106, 107, 200, 206, 247, 248; *see also* Church and common lands.
Albarracín, S., 214 n.
Albors, A., 214.
Alcázar San Juan, 119.
Alcolea, battle of (1868), 47.
Alcoy, social disturbances at, 213–14; *also* 166, 215, 217, 219, 227, 231, 232, 257.
Alerini, 155 n.
Algeciras, 223.
Alicante, 46 n., 53, 229.
Alliance of Social Democracy, 158, 176; *see also* International.
Almansa, 220, 223.
Almeria, 229.
Almirall, V. (1840–1904), leader of Barcelona Federals, 68–69, 70, 72; views on clubs, 95; and *El Estado catalán*, 99, 114, 184; withdraws to Barcelona, 203; and Catalan nationalism, 252–3; *also* 101, 111, 183, 256 n.
Alora, 61.
Alpens, Carlist victory at (1873), 213.
Alphonsism, -ists, leadership of, 145, 233; returns at elections, 148 n., 163 n., 191 n.; and Army, 168, 209–10, 237, 241; their intrigues, 234, 235; *also* 68, 143, 180, 193, 219, 223, 232, 240.
Alphonso XII de Bourbon (1857–85), 136, 139 n., 242.
Alsina, P. (1830–?), Federal deputy, 66, 68, 88, 96.
Altadill, A. (1828–80), novelist and Federal journalist, 67, 83 n., 98 n., 217 and note.
Amadeo I, King of Spain, Duke of Aosta (1845–90), as candidate for throne, 137; elected king, 139 and note; attitude of political parties to, 143–5; and Hidalgo crisis, 167–9; abdication, 169, 170; *also* 138, 140, 141, 142, 151, 162.
Amigo del Pueblo, El, 98.
Ampurdan, 65, 116.
Anarchists, -ism, xv, 10, 244, 246, 252, 254, 257, 262.
Andalucía, La, 55, 99, 112, 133.
Andalusia, and September Revolution, 36; Federals and, 53 et seq., 104, 107, 160; revolts in, 21, 119, 210–11; *also* 16, 66, 194, 208, 215, 222, 223, 246. *See also* Andalusians.

Andalusians, 55–56, 199, 203.
Andrews, S. P., 260.
Andújar, 223.
Anrich, 205.
Antequera, 53, 57.
Anton Marín, Plaza, 43, 94, 166, 191.
Aragón, 36, 42, 101, 111.
Aranda, Conde de, 22.
Araus, A., 208
Arcos de la Frontera, 53.
Arenal, C., 85.
Armentia, 213.
Army, the, and politics, 3–4, 5, 167, 168, 210; reform proposals, 10, 206; and Prim, 37, 44 and note, 127 n.; and Serrano, 143, 160, 172, 236, 242; and Federals, 176–81, 205, 233, 238, 239, 241, 247, 250–1; *also* 13, 20, 42, 56 n., 80, 106 n., 162, 163 n., 209, 223, 224, 237, 245, 263. *See also* artillery officers, militia, *quintas*.
Artillery officers, 27, 167, 180, 181, 238, 239, 241.
Asociación de la Juventud republicana, La, 94.
Asociación librepensadora, La, 94.
Asociación republicano militar, La, 245.
Assembly, first Federal (1870), 125, 128, 129, 131, 134; second Federal (1871), 149; third Federal (1872), 158, 159, 160; fourth Federal (1872), 162, 164, 165, 172.
Assembly, National (1873), Federal position in, 171–2; *also* 178, 182, 183; Permanent Commission of, conflict between Federal and Radicals, 185–7, 190.
association, freedom of, 17, 66, 82.
Ateneo, Catalan, 67; Catalan Workers', 66, 67, 95; Madrid, 18, 24, 90, 93, 131; republican, 94; women's, 86.
Azorín, 33, 257.

Babeuf, G., 156.
Baeza, 54, 166.
Bailén, 223.
Bakunin, M., 96.
Bakuninism, -ists, xv, xvi, 67, 82, 157.
Balaguer, V. (1824–1901), Progressive politician, 52 n., 64, 75, 108.
Balearic Islands, 111.
Balzo, N. del, 215, 216.
Barbastro, 161.
Barberá, V., 129.
Barcelona, Pi and, 7, 11, 135, 189; Federals in, 64–72, 95, 104, 224; press at, 68, 114; revolt of 1869 at, 86, 115–16, 118, 121;

U

PRINTED IN GREAT BRITAIN
AT THE UNIVERSITY PRESS, OXFORD
BY VIVIAN RIDLER
PRINTER TO THE UNIVERSITY